TEAM-BASED HEALTH CARE ORGANIZATIONS
Blueprint for Success

Jo Manion, MA
Manion and Associates
Altamonte Springs, Florida

William Lorimer, PhD
William Lorimer and Associates
Rockville, Maryland

William J. Leander, MBA
Co-founder and Director
PFCA, Inc.
Atlanta, Georgia

AN ASPEN PUBLICATION®
Aspen Publishers, Inc.
Gaithersburg, Maryland
1996

Library of Congress Cataloging-in-Publication Data

Manion, Jo.
Team-based health care organizations: blueprint for success / Jo
Manion, William Lorimer, William J. Leander.
p. cm.
Includes bibliographical references and index.
ISBN 0-8342-0782-6
1. Health care teams. 2. Health services administration.
3. Organizational change. I. Lorimer, William. II. Leander,
William J. III. Title.
R729.5.H4M36 1996
610'.68—dc20
96-19770
CIP

Aspen Publishers, Inc., grants permission for photocopying for limited personal or
internal use. This consent does not extend to other kinds of copying, such as
copying for general distribution, for advertising or promotional purposes, for
creating new collective works, or for resale. For information, address
Aspen Publishers, Inc., Permissions Department, 200 Orchard Ridge Drive,
Suite 200, Gaithersburg, Maryland 20878.

Orders: (800) 638-8437
Customer Service: (800) 234-1660

About Aspen Publishers ▪ For more than 35 years, Aspen has been a leading professional
publisher in a variety of disciplines. Aspen's vast information resources are available in
both print and electronic formats. We are committed to providing the highest quality
information available in the most appropriate format for our customers. Visit Aspen's
Internet site for more information resources, directories, articles, and a searchable
version of Aspen's full catalog, including the most recent publications:
http://www.aspenpub.com
Aspen Publishers, Inc. ▪ The hallmark of quality in publishing
Members of the worldwide Wolters Kluwer group.

Editorial Resources: Ruth Bloom
Library of Congress Catalog Card Number: 96-19770
ISBN: 0-8342-0782-6

Printed in the United States of America

1 2 3 4 5

With loving appreciation,
To my father,
who taught me how to dream,
and
To my husband,
who has always encouraged my heart to follow its dreams.

—Jo Manion

To B.E. Lorimer,
for setting the standard in health care leadership.

—Bill Lorimer

To Moo,
for a lifetime of love and inspiration.

—Bill Leander

Table of Contents

Foreword

The magnitude of the changes in health care necessitates that management seriously look at new styles of management if they are going to engage the employees, particularly professionals, in changing how the work of patient care is accomplished. The public is demanding change and wants a different response to their personal health needs. The payer wants a cost-effective delivery system, and the employers want their employees on the job. Everyone wants a timely—if not immediate—response and this demand alone requires management to rethink how to engage the various stakeholders in designing a new system of delivery. It will not be acceptable to reshuffle work, and it is not acceptable to reduce the workforce without changing how the work is accomplished.

These three authors have correctly identified the key to reshaping the health care system through the use of teams of people within the organization. Every employee, sometime or another, has expressed the desire to influence management and to be part of the decision making within the organization. With the declining number of management positions, employees now have the opportunity to make the impact they have been seeking. To do so means they must engage in a continuing learning process. To be successful, management must be willing to share the accountability, evidence trust that the employees can do the job, provide the opportunities to learn—both from the successes and the failures, and recognize that successes are not overnight phenomena. The benefits of team leadership in an organization will be evidenced in increased productivity, improved levels of satisfaction from all the stakeholders and, eventually, in an improved bottom line for the organization, which may be the key to surviving in these chaotic times.

My experience in management over the past 25 years and the insights I gained while serving as the Director of "Strengthening Hospital Nursing: A

Program to Improve Patient Care" (a Robert Wood Johnson and Pew Charitable Trusts national program) serve as the basis for me to give my wholehearted support to the concept of team-based organization. It will require continuous learning on everyone's part to establish a new and valuable relationship between management, employees, and the consumer. The authors have successfully laid out the steps, the potential pitfalls, and the challenges in a logical fashion, thus providing the reader with knowledge they will need to make the transition to a successful team-based organization.

My congratulations are extended to Jo Manion, Bill Lorimer, and Bill Leander for clearly setting forth the concepts of team-based organization. Theirs is a very timely piece of work and if professionals in the field will take seriously the wisdom so thoughtfully presented in this book, they will find themselves well positioned for the future. The authors have done their part. Now it's up to the readers to put it into practice. Good luck—the future is yours to create!

Barbara A. Donaho, RN, BSN, MA, FAAN
Former President and Chief Executive Officer
St. Anthony's Hospital
St. Petersburg, Florida

Preface

What is this "team" thing everyone is talking about? Is it only the latest buzzword, accompanied by the usual hype enticing the unsuspecting to jump on yet another bandwagon? Or is it a substantial change in the way we organize and provide services in health care? If it is a real trend toward a different organizational health care model, what's new about it? Haven't we always worked in teams? What's the big deal? This book not only will answer these questions, but it will focus on the challenges peculiar to health care organizations planning to replace or supplement traditional hierarchical structures with semiautonomous teams in order to flatten management, revitalize employees, and enhance productivity.

American business and industry have been experimenting with and converting to team-based structures for more than 20 years. Using teams is not a new concept for health care organizations accustomed to highly effective operating and emergency room teams or interdisciplinary rehabilitation teams.

Yet, despite the significant and well-publicized successes of self-directed work teams in other industries, extensions of formal team structures to encompass all health care functions and operations are only now attracting broad interest in the health care industry. Momentum toward these flatter, more flexible, and more responsive team-based organizations is building rapidly, as providers feel rising pressure to improve their cost-effectiveness and their patient outcomes in the midst of the ongoing nationwide debate about health care.

This book goes beyond the buzzwords and offers a practical, real-life approach to the implementation of teams in health care. It draws on the collective experience of the authors who, as consultants, have worked with organizations making the journey toward team-based structures and cultures.

Case studies reflecting factual approaches show how pioneering organizations are successfully transforming their cultures and work forces using self-directed work team structures. This book also provides readers with tips, tools, and techniques drawn from the authors' actual experiences helping members of the health care community make these major transformations. Whether you are an executive considering implementing teams throughout your organization or a manager who is interested in developing teams in your department or on your shift, you will find this book required reading as you undertake the journey.

Team-based organizations are a new model for health care and offer possibilities for organizational improvements and increased satisfaction for employees and employers alike. Although not easy to implement, effective teams enable organizations to respond better to the demands of our rapidly changing health care environment. Teams are a remarkable way to forge a partnership between leaders and employees, producing an undreamed-of synergy as they build on the strengths of everyone in the organization. Teams thrive on the challenges of the future and give us the best chance for capitalizing on the scarcely tapped energy of human potential.

Acknowledgments

No one could possibly write a book about teams without first recognizing the achievements of the pioneering individuals and organizations around the world who have previously built, studied, experimented with, learned from, and—thankfully—written about teams. We are proud to be identified with this great community.

This is a book about and for teams, written by a team. As authors, we owe many debts of gratitude. To our colleagues and families who supported us through towers of notes, writer's block, and final deadlines. To our publisher, Aspen Publishers, Inc., and their fine staff of professionals, including: Jane Garwood, Mary Anne Langdon, Ruth Bloom, Neal Pomea, Laureece Woodson, and our project coordinator, Cathy Frye.

But, most of all, we must thank the many teams of dedicated health care associates who have taught us vastly more than we will ever be able to teach them. It is to their persistence, courage, and grace under immense pressures that our work is dedicated.

Introduction

This book is divided into three major sections. The first section, "Imperatives for Success," establishes a sturdy foundation including the rationale for teams, a structural design approach, a cultural design philosophy and process, and a step-by-step methodology for implementing teams. Chapter 1 examines the justification for teams in health care, particularly in light of skepticism generated by their current trendiness in other industries. In addition, teams are defined, categorized, and distinguished from other entities that might appear to be teams, but aren't. Chapter 2 focuses on the structural side of establishing highly effective teams. It offers a step-by-step methodology for designing teams that are most well suited to efficiently and effectively performing the work at hand. Chapter 3 presents a complete discipline for initiating and building an effective, competent team and identifies useful indicators leaders can apply to assess a team's growth and progress. Finally, Chapter 4 lays out the critical steps to be followed in implementing teams organization-wide or just within individual departments.

The second section, "Challenges for Leadership," examines what can go wrong and what leaders must assure goes right during such major organizational transformations. Chapter 5 details typical problems encountered by the three major types of teams found in most health care organizations. Real world examples and case studies are used to illustrate classic team pitfalls and dilemmas. After this close look at the likely perils, Chapter 6 focuses on six key leadership elements necessary to successfully deal with problems and offers suggestions for analyzing and strengthening these crucial leadership areas. Chapter 7 goes further to describe and explore several new leadership roles and responsibilities necessitated by team-based organizational structures and cultures. Chapter 8 raises the issues of managing change and dealing effectively with ensuing psychological and emotional transitions. A case study follows one hospital's actual experience moving through the five phases of change. This chapter also offers helpful tips for the transition process, so leaders can learn to identify each stage and better assist themselves and others to achieve healthy outcomes. The final chapter in this section places all these leadership issues in historical perspective. Through an overview of lessons researchers and practitioners have learned from a half-century of experiences and experiments with teams across a broad spectrum of industries, Chapter 9 explores the genesis of modern team theories and strategies.

The third section, "Special Issues for Health Care," zeros in on issues that are particularly problematic for our industry. Chapter 10 explores the extraordinary opportunities and challenges of multidisciplinary teams and provides a three-stage plan, case studies, and strategies for establishing and working effectively with these professionally complex organizations. Chapter 11 overviews a multi-level approach to meet the transforming organization's education needs, details necessary support systems, and reveals the key lessons learned from training teams. Chapter 12 illustrates and explains common organizational barriers that can prevent successful conversions to teams. This chapter provides practical methods and techniques that leaders and teams can use to eliminate these obstacles and assure smoother and more successful structural and cultural transformations.

Finally, a Bibliography containing suggested readings is included for those readers interested in further pursuing team theory and practice.

PART I

Imperatives for Success

CHAPTER 1

Why Teams? Why Now?
Moving to a
Team-Based Organization

WHY TEAMS? WHY NOW?

Amidst the chaos and confusion of this final decade of the millennium, the challenges confronting health care leaders are unsurpassed by any faced in the past. The entire health care industry is beset by economic forces compelling change. Mergers and closures of hospitals, increasing percentages of services under managed care contracts, decreasing reimbursement, increasing specialization, restructuring and reengineering of our organizations, unbridled consumer expectations, payer demands for value, spiraling costs, and increasing competition all are causing health care leaders to think in new ways and consider options undreamt of in years past. The magnitude and complexity of these challenges are such that no individuals, no leaders, can meet them successfully without the full involvement and commitment of their employees. Teams are a way to tap into the potential of our employees—the potential to contribute in significant ways, to accept increasingly higher levels of responsibility, and to reap the benefits when employees feel the commitment that ownership of their work brings.

Coincidentally, we are also experiencing significant societal changes, not the least of which is the evolution of our work force. Health care workers today are more knowledgeable than ever before, relying not just on formal education but on the availability of information through the print and electronic media and computer networks. Older, more experienced, and more mature workers predominate in many of our organizations. These are workers who want to contribute at a higher level, who have the capabilities to move into managerial roles that no longer exist. In our organizations, we have created a high level of expectations for employee involvement with the implementation of staff action committees, quality teams, shared governance models, primary nursing, and by teaching and encouraging managers to empower their employees.

All of these forces are causing us to reexamine our current management practices and structures and create new alternatives that better enable us to meet the demands of the future. Today's health care leaders must have a work force that is knowledgeable, willing, and able to participate fully in decision making for the organization. Developing a team-based structure is an attractive alternative for ensuring employee participation. Moving into teams is much more than creating a feeling of camaraderie and "teamwork." Teams are a radically different way of driving decision making in the organization.

Today's work force is smart, capable, and well informed. Teams are a way to capitalize on the possibilities offered by this pool of talent and to release potential for improved productivity, better decisions, and process innovation that has been previously untapped. The essence of a successful team-based organizational structure entails two things. First is a move to a new collaborative relationship between managers and employees. Cooperation, communication, and coordination have always been elements in successful manager–employee relationships. Collaboration involves these three elements but goes even further to include mutual problem solving and decision making where managers and employees together work out problems, find solutions, and make decisions. This doesn't mean that teams run the organization. Management still determines what needs to be done, but teams figure out how to do it. With teams, it is possible to flatten the management hierarchy.

Second, in the team-based organization there is a transfer of real power to the team. This is a far more fundamental change than shifting people on the organizational chart. The team has clearly defined responsibilities and higher levels of authority for carrying out these responsibilities. The manager doesn't just give the team permission to make a decision; certain decisions become the team's responsibility. Teams must have substantive work and real responsibility, not just tasks the manager no longer wants to do or responsibilities that are minimal or superficial.

Organizations that successfully evolve to a team-based structure discover that what seems at first to be a fairly straightforward structural change has actually changed the essence of their organization. It is this essential shift increasing employee involvement that results in a synergy and resilience, enabling the organization to respond more rapidly and innovatively to changes in its environment. One of our clients has called this shift "lessons in real-time change." A common error or stumbling block occurs when an organization implements teams without recognizing the importance of both designing the structure of the team and altering the way people work together.

Teams are an exciting possibility for the future of our organizations. The flexibility and responsiveness of well-designed teams hold potential solutions to many of the problems existing in today's health care organizations. Most futuristic organizational structural designs being promoted involve teams in their scheme of things. Models of the "adhocracy," "networked organizations," flattened or eliminated hierarchy, or "clustered" organizations are based on the belief that teams will surpass individuals as the primary performance unit in organizations of the future (Katzenbach and Smith 1993, 19). Health care leaders must avoid the temptation to use teams as a quick-fix approach to the problems they face and, instead, carefully consider the far-reaching ramifications of this cultural change and their fundamental willingness to embark on this journey of transformation. Those with the courage to do so will find their success increasingly dependent upon their ability to understand teams and teamwork.

WHAT IS A TEAM?

Not since the term "hip" in the 1960s has a single, seemingly simple word meant so many things to so many people. The word "team" carries many connotations, most involving people who join together to accomplish a result. Most of us are familiar with sports teams. In the work world, however, we broadly and vaguely apply the word when we refer to the organization or entire department as a "team." Leaders who talk about the great "team effort" expended by their employees truly believe they understand what a good team is. What they are actually referring to is the *way* people work together. A team is more than teamwork. It is a specific structural unit in the organization. Teamwork—the ways people work together cooperatively and effectively—may be a value held within the community of the organization. Using the terms "team" and "teamwork" synonymously in an organization implementing the structural units of designed work teams leads to significant confusion.

Teams have been defined in a variety of ways. Larson and LaFasto (1989) suggest that a team has two or more people and a specific performance objective or recognizable goal to be attained. Coordination of activity among the team members is required for the attainment of the team goal or objective. Jon Katzenbach and Douglas Smith, in *The Wisdom of Teams,* define a team as "a small number of people with complementary skills who are committed to a common purpose, performance goals, and approach for which they hold themselves mutually accountable" (1993, 45). This definition goes beyond teamwork and focuses on the structural elements required to create an effective team. For this reason, we have found this definition to be the most helpful in understanding a process for building teams. Our adaptation of this definition for the health care field is:

A team is a small number of consistent people committed to a relevant shared purpose, with common performance goals, complementary and overlapping skills, and a common approach to their work. Team members hold themselves mutually accountable for the team's results or outcomes.

Most of the research on team effectiveness comes from the social sciences and organizational development sources and has been focused predominantly on psychological factors. Katzenbach and Smith (1993) have identified, through their research, the characteristics of highly effective teams. These include: a common purpose, agreed-upon performance goals, a common approach for the work, complementary skills, and mutual accountability. Larson and LaFasto (1989) identify similar key characteristics: a clear, elevating goal, a results-driven structure, competent members, unified commitment, a collaborative climate, standards of excellence, external support and recognition, and principled leadership. With a focus on the structural elements of effective teams, these authors provide concrete, practical direction for developing teams. Their research contributes to our working knowledge of teams.

Working Groups versus Real Teams

As a result of their extensive research and conversations with people and teams in organizations around the United States, Katzenbach and Smith (1993) distinguish among working groups, pseudo-teams, and real teams. Although their research was conducted primarily in business and industry, their findings apply equally to the health care environment. Working groups differ from teams in their areas of responsibility, levels of authority, approach to the work, and accountability (Table 1–1).

Basically, working groups are collections of individuals who come together for a joint effort, but whose outcomes rely primarily on the individual contributions of its members. On the other hand, a team has members who work collectively in a way that magnifies the group's impact, above and beyond that generated only from individual efforts. This is the effect of synergy. The team's collective effort is greater than the sum of its individual efforts.

In an effective working group, individuals come together to communicate, coordinate, and cooperate so that each is better able to do his or her job. But the focus is on individual roles, tasks, and responsibilities. An example of this in health care is the interdisciplinary rehabilitation "team." At a "team" conference, the physical therapist presents the findings of his or her assessment and shares the plan of care subsequently developed. The social worker dis-

Table 1-1 Comparison of Working Groups and Teams

Working Group	*Team*
Relies on individual contributions	Relies on collective contributions
Comes together to share information, solve problems, etc. to help individuals do their jobs better	Comes together to solve problems and make decisions to improve the team's work and group performance
Members do NOT take responsibility for results other than their own	Members share a common purpose and goals and hold themselves mutually accountable for results

cusses his or her findings and communicates about the discharge plan. A nursing assessment and plan of care is shared. All the professionals involved in caring for the client follow this same pattern. The work of these professionals is communicated and coordinated and everyone cooperates with each other. As a result, their individual professional performance is improved and the client benefits.

If, however, these interdisciplinary rehabilitation professionals formed a real team, as defined here, their purpose for convening would be expanded. Instead of coming together simply to coordinate, communicate, and cooperate, they would also collaborate. Each professional would still share the results of his or her specific assessment, based on discipline-specific skills and observations. Once the assessments were shared, however, the members *as a team* would discuss and determine the goals, consider various alternatives and methods of reaching the goals, and jointly develop an action plan. The client and family would also be involved closely as part of the process. The result is an improved collective effort, a higher degree of shared accountability, and a greater benefit for the client. The synergy of the team's effort results in more creative solutions and alternatives than in the previous example.

Another example of a group that often fits the description of a working group rather than a true team is at the executive level in the organization. Individual executives often represent specialized knowledge and they come together to coordinate and communicate their efforts. They may work together collaboratively to create a vision for the organization and to develop a strategic plan. Most of their work, however, may be as individuals. For example, the human resource executive plans for policy changes in his/her area of responsibility and informs fellow executives of the actions to be taken. Or perhaps the human resources executive has made decisions after discussion with the chief executive officer (CEO). The entire team, however, is involved in the discussion only after the decision is made.

The most significant distinction between a working group and a team is in the area of accountability. Members of a working group are not accountable for the actions of the group. They are only held accountable for their individual efforts or actions. Team members hold themselves accountable as individuals but they are also mutually accountable for the team's outcomes. They have established performance goals and expected outcomes that are continually evaluated and measured. Each team member is held equally accountable for the team's outcomes. This distinction is significant. In the previous example of the interdisciplinary rehabilitation team, the physical therapist is a highly skilled and competent practitioner, but unless other team members carry out the agreed-upon plan for physical rehabilitation, the desired outcomes may not be attained.

Consider the example of the traditional maintenance department in a hospital. One member of the department, an electrician or plumber, may have very high individual standards for work performance. When this individual is asked to make a repair, the work is done right the first time and the department rarely, if ever, receives a complaint about work that was completed. In the whole department, however, there are an extraordinarily high number of call-backs to redo or correct work performed by others in the department. The high-performing individual goes home at night and feels satisfied about a job well done and a contribution to the organization as a whole but pays little attention to performance quality in the rest of the department.

When this department is reorganized into teams, reducing the number of call-backs to a reasonable, low level becomes part of the team's standards. Individual members are accountable for the quality of their work, but they must also become involved in problem solving if the outcomes of the team fall short of expected standards. All members of the team feel ownership and responsibility when standards are not met, and they feel the accomplishment of work well done when quality standards *are* met. In other words, the high-performing plumber or electrician is no longer satisfied only with performing well but now begins accepting responsibility for coaching fellow team members and improving the performance of the entire team.

Not all work benefits from team effort. The key characteristics of work benefiting from a team are delineated in Figure 1–1. Some work is highly specialized or individualized and would not benefit from the collective efforts of a team. In some instances, work may benefit from collective effort, but a good working group can accomplish the task. Working groups involve less risk. They spend little time doing the work of becoming a team, such as establishing their purpose and goals, because in most cases, a leader sets this direction. Meetings are organized by agendas and are efficient in getting the information communicated and decisions made. Each member of the working

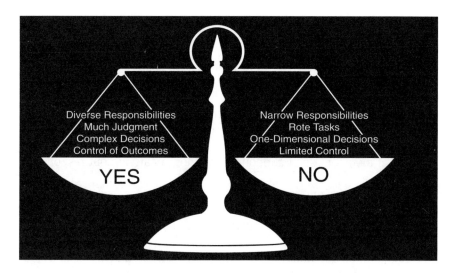

Figure 1–1 Key Characteristics of Work Benefiting from a Team

group has an individual assignment or responsibility to meet. If the work does not require a team to do it, it is foolish to expend the time to develop a team.

The Danger of Pseudo-Teams

Pseudo-teams are entities in the organization that think they are teams (Katzenbach and Smith 1993). The danger is that they don't realize they are stuck in behavior that often results in ineffective outcomes. Results are disappointing and neither members nor the organization realize it is because they haven't done the work of becoming a real team. Common behaviors seen in pseudo-teams include lack of a common purpose, a purpose with which members cannot identify, inability to focus on a goal, poor relationships among members, interpersonal attacks, members whose personal ambition overshadows the common goal, inability or unwillingness to evaluate outcomes, lack of clear responsibility, and unknown or inappropriate levels of authority.

In health care, we frequently use "team" language when in fact what we are describing are working groups and pseudo-teams. A survey (Dubnicki and Limburg 1991) of health care executives asking about teams in their organizations revealed startling results. Up to 69 percent of respondents reported the following descriptions of so-called team behaviors in their organizations:

- Individual responsibilities and performance expectations are unclear.
- Team members do not consistently follow through on commitments.
- Decision making is slow.
- Individual members aren't committed to the team.
- Team members interact ineffectively with others outside the team.
- Team meetings are not effective.
- Team members don't support each other in carrying out responsibilities.
- Individuals are unclear about team goals.
- Calculated risk-taking is not encouraged.
- There are too many unnecessary procedures and policies and too much formality.
- Recognition and praise do NOT outweigh threats and criticisms.
- Team members don't feel free to experiment with new ideas.

Health care organizations considering the implementation of teams can learn from these lessons. They can learn what makes a real team and apply a discipline to the design and building of teams. A team-based structure is an effective way of ensuring employee participation in the workplace. Leaders in the hierarchy can use a team-based structure to develop a shared vision and commitment to the organization's strategic plan. Teams and hierarchy are not a contradiction but complementary structures that can result in more creative outcomes for the organization's clients.

TYPES OF TEAMS

A common mistake made by leaders who are interested in implementing teams is failing to recognize the differences among types of teams. There are at least three types of teams: primary work teams, executive or management leadership teams, and ad hoc teams. Each has specific design issues and characteristics to consider, which will be explored more fully in Chapter 5.

Examples of primary work teams include patient care teams, a specialty team in the operating room, or trauma team in the emergency department. Examples of leadership or management teams include the executive team or the department leadership team. These teams exist to lead others or to manage specific functions or processes. Ad hoc teams are teams that have shorter life spans and may be either problem-solving teams, such as quality teams, or creative teams such as a design or project team.

Any team has the capability of becoming a self-directed work team, meaning that it accepts increasingly higher levels of authority for its responsibilities. Wellins, Byham, and Wilson (1991, 3) say a "self-directed work team is an intact group of employees who are responsible for a 'whole' work process or segment that delivers a product or service to an internal or external customer." Orsburn and his colleagues (1990, 8) offer the following definition: "A self-directed work team is a highly trained group of employees, from 6–18, on average, fully responsible for turning out a well-defined segment of finished work."

Our definition of a self-directed work team is a team that contains all the essential capabilities, responsibilities, and authority necessary to do a whole piece of work. Thus, the type of team will determine its direction. For instance, the executive team provides executive leadership for the organization. A design or project team has the capability, defined responsibility, and authority necessary to design or manage the project which they have assumed. In fact, the lack of transfer of authority has been the problem with many quality teams. Their responsibility may have been well defined, but the team may have had neither the resources nor the authority to carry out its recommended actions and instead has had to make recommendations to a higher authority.

In our experience, a primary work team, such as a patient care team, a business office team, or a team of environmental service workers, will require redesign of work processes before it can fit this description of a self-directed work team. Work has become so fragmented and specialized that health care employees often have responsibility only for small pieces of the "whole piece of work." This concept will be discussed more fully in Chapter 2.

A primary work team can become self-directed regarding its direct technical work as well as department operational issues. For example, in one patient care department there may be 60 employees organized into five teams. Membership on the team is consistent, it doesn't vary from day to day. The team has a consistent patient caseload. Again, design of these teams is a critical factor in their success. The tendency is simply to assign certain caregivers on the first shift to one team, caregivers on a second shift to another team, and night shift staff to a third team. These teams may be responsible for all of or the majority of the patient's care required during their work shift, but they can't cover all of the care required by the patient. These teams don't fit the definition of a self-directed work team. The "whole piece of work" is the entire scope of services required by the patient including elements such as environmental needs, food service, laboratory tests, and surgical procedures.

Team design is based first on customer requirements. If the team is a patient care team, it will be designed around the needs of the patient care population. Caregiver teams are specifically designed in composition and specially cross-trained and multiskilled to meet as many patient needs as possible.

Instead of shift-specific teams, the caregiver team crosses shifts for most patient populations. As an example, two to three caregivers on the day shift care for a consistent patient caseload. They report to the two or three members of their team who work evenings, who, in turn, report to the team member who works nights. The team thus includes the caregivers on all shifts caring for the same group of patients. (See Figure 1–2.) With a similar design, these patient care teams can be responsible for as much as 85 percent of all services needed by their patients. In a complex organization such as today's hospital, it is virtually impossible for one team to provide all services. For example, when a surgical patient is in the operating room undergoing surgery, that patient cannot be the responsibility of the caregiver team.

In addition to providing patient care in a self-directed work setting, a primary work team is an ideal mechanism through which traditional managerial responsibilities can be shared. For instance, the team reviews its own financial performance reports and investigates budget variances, it determines supply and capital expenditure needs for the future, and orders its own supplies and equipment. Although a self-directed work team does not have to take on managerial responsibilities and become a self-managing team, many organizations are now defining the work of the team broadly to include these responsibilities. Throughout the rest of this book, we assume a self-directed team includes responsibility for at least some managerial tasks.

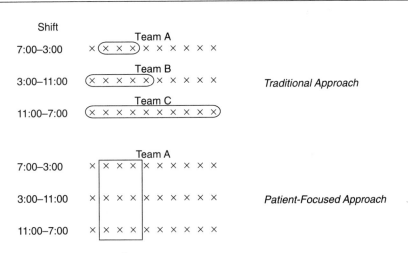

Note: X represents a patient.

Figure 1–2 A Cross-Shift Team Approach. *Source:* Reprinted with permission from *Reengineering Nursing and Health Care*, S.S. Blancett and D.L. Flarey, p. 249, Copyright © 1995, Aspen Publishers, Inc.

WHAT TEAMS ARE NOT

Teams are not models of shared governance. Both are structural entities designed to increase the involvement of employees in decisions relating to their work. But shared governance structures bring members of a specific discipline together to deal with the issues of the discipline, such as professional standards and credentialing. Teams are structures designed to accomplish specific day-to-day operations.

A common misconception in health care is that moving to a team-based organizational structure means reverting to a patient care delivery model of "team" nursing. Nothing could be further from the truth. In team nursing, team membership included whomever was scheduled to work on a given day. Membership changed daily and by shift. There was an attempt to provide consistency in patient assignments, but this was seldom achieved, to the frustration of many nurses.

Teams are not a panacea for all the ills of the organization. They solve problems but they also create new ones. They require a tremendous commitment in terms of education and energy to become a reality. The specific steps for a successful implementation of teams will be discussed in Chapter 4. They are not a quick fix. A team-based structure may be designed and established, but changing the way people actually work together and changing an organization's culture to focus on teams can take years to realize.

ADVANTAGES OF TEAMS

Teams are well worth the effort, and bring many advantages to the organization willing to commit to them. Exhibit 1–1 lists common advantages that a team-based work structure would bring to individual employees, to managers, and to the organization as a whole. These areas were identified by a group of 50 employees of a rural community hospital who were asked during an educational session activity to identify the potential advantages of teams.

Improves Performance Outcomes

Improved performance outcomes are the most important reason to implement teams. When the work to be accomplished requires a collective effort (i.e., more than one person to do it), the best outcomes occur when there is synergistic teamwork, with each team member contributing to the effort and each team member's quality of contribution being improved or enhanced as a result of ideas and stimulus others bring to the process. Organizations undergoing major reengineering or restructuring efforts have found that teams of employees who carry collective responsibility for project outcomes have very successfully produced the needed changes.

Exhibit 1–1 Advantages of Teams As Identified by Employees

Individual Advantages

Increased self-esteem, self-actualization
Opportunity to learn new skills
Greater ability to affect decisions
Greater job satisfaction
Increased autonomy
Sharing of knowledge
Increased peer respect
Increased creativity
Pride
Not working at cross purposes
Increased sense of belonging
Increased feeling of control
Improved flexibility
Increased confidence
Increased appreciation of others' efforts
Moved from I/me concept
Better utilization of skills

Managerial Advantages

More flexibility to do own job
Can concentrate on "managing"
Can draw from a variety of perspectives
Greater buy-in from staff
Problems solved at "local" level
A way to share the load, the
  responsibility
Able to focus at a higher level
No longer wasting time firefighting
Increased time for coaching/mentoring
Wealth of experience broadened
Less confusion
Increased productivity
Unity of purpose
Increased continuity
Less blaming, we/they behavior
Increased learning opportunities
Increased creativity

Gave a new perspective
Moved from being a director to a
  facilitator
Freedom to concentrate on other
  things
Able to do more, look better
Off the "hot seat"

Organizational Advantages

Less affected by staff turnover
Efficiency through improved
  organizational structure
Increased productivity
Better ideas/decisions due to work group
  synergy
More buy-in to institution's mission
Increased accountability
Input broader perspective, diversity,
  multidimensional
More goal consistency
Less expense, cost reductions
Improved value
Ownership, shared responsibility and
  accountability, collective problem
  solving
More synergy
Increased creativity
Increased commitment
Morale improved
More heads better than one
Improved quality
Increased customer satisfaction
A good marketing strategy
Decisions better, well-thought-out
Cohesive work units
Uniformity
More dedication
Less turnover

"Teams outperform individuals acting alone or in larger organizational groupings, especially when performance requires multiple skills, judgments, and experiences" (Katzenbach and Smith 1993, 9). Work has become increasingly complex during recent decades. Larson and LaFasto (1989) note that the problems we are facing are growing increasingly complex. Growth in complexity becomes magnified when the coordination is not only within but between organizations. The complexity of services that many of our clients require demands extensive coordination both within the organization and between health care agencies. Many hospitals are forming or joining integrated health networks or regional consortia. The need for collaboration is now an irrefutable fact of life.

In *Tales of a New America*, Robert Reich (1987, 126) says, "Rarely do even big ideas emerge any longer from the solitary labors of genius. Modern science and technology is too complicated for one brain. It requires groups of astronomers, physicists, and computer programmers to discover new dimensions of the universe; teams of microbiologists, oncologists, and chemists to unravel the mysteries of cancer. With ever more frequency, Nobel prizes are awarded to collections of people. Scientific papers are authored by small platoons of researchers." In short, our contributions will increasingly result from our ability to work in teams and to understand teamwork.

This is true in health care. Teams fit the nature of our work. The family physician of earlier times who saw patients any time of day or night, performed needed laboratory tests and treatments, and taught the family about the care needed, just doesn't exist any more. The complexity of health care today has resulted in increasing specialization and compartmentalization of services. It is virtually impossible for any one health care professional to provide all services needed by the patient. Instead, many individuals work together to provide them. They work together more effectively if structured in well-designed teams and if they understand the true nature of teamwork.

Synergy is a common result of teamwork. Synergy is best described as combined outcome. In effective groups you get more than the sum of the individuals' best efforts. The ideas, skills, and knowledge of each member complement the others and spark creativity in a way that just doesn't happen when individuals work alone.

Increases Employee's Acceptance of Responsibility

With downsizing, right-sizing, and decreasing ratios of hours of care per patient day, it is imperative that all employees contribute their utmost to the organization. New expectations for performance are being set. It is no longer acceptable for employees simply to come to work, put in their hours, and go home. Employees who are fully engaged in their work and participating at higher levels of responsibility are those who will be employed in the future.

During the past decade, many health care organizations have undertaken extensive work to empower employees. Empowerment is possible when responsibility is clearly identified and when the employee is capable of accepting the responsibility, has the appropriate level of authority to carry it out, and is held accountable for performance. If any of these four elements is absent, empowerment does not occur. In the direct patient care arena, primary nursing was instrumental in establishing a new model of responsibility and accountability for nurses. Primary nursing is a delivery system, not an all-RN staffing model as many people assume (Manthey 1989). The essence of primary nursing involves the establishment of responsibility, authority, and accountability of the nurse for an identified caseload of patients.

Effective patient care teams rely on these same principles. They must be capable, have clearly identified responsibility and appropriate levels of authority, and must hold themselves mutually accountable for their outcomes. In fact, patient care teams could be considered a natural evolution of the primary nursing delivery system. Consistency is a key factor for the teams as it is for the assignment of the primary nurse.

Teams have the capability of increasing employees' level of responsibility acceptance for several reasons. When real responsibility and authority is transferred to the team, members feel more ownership. This actually can be frightening at first. In the past, when managers made decisions it was easy enough for employees to disregard them or implement them half-heartedly. This is no longer true when the team has made the decision, especially if it used consensus.

Likewise, one employee in a group of 30 will find it easier to remain detached and uninvolved at the monthly staff meetings. Contrast this situation to being one of a 10- to 12-member team in the process of making a decision. Apathy and nonparticipation are obvious and more likely to be addressed, especially if team members have established participation as a shared expectation.

Empowers Teams at Higher Levels

Accountability and responsibility acceptance increases in a team-based organization. Leaders who have shared responsibility with employees in the past will find they can transfer more responsibility to a team. For instance, it is unlikely that a manager of a traditionally organized department would turn over responsibility for developing the annual budget to any one individual in the department. A team of employees, however, can more easily assume this responsibility. For example, a team of biomedical engineers in one organization were given the responsibility and clearly defined parameters for hiring additional team members. Well-trained and educated teams of employees can assume many of the traditional responsibilities held by managers and supervisors.

Frees Managers for Other Functions

What will managers and supervisors do if the teams assume their long-held responsibilities? This is a frightening thought for many managers and supervisors in today's organizations. Yet, most of these same individuals would admit that the majority of their time is currently spent in dealing with day-to-day operational crises, supervising workers who could be far more responsible, and dealing with relationship issues between employees. If teams take over these responsibilities, managers can focus on long ne-glected aspects of their jobs such as coaching, mentoring and teaching employees, or developing long-term plans for their work area. As long as managers remain bogged down in day-to-day crises, their involvement in creating the new organization will be limited. Their leadership potential will be throttled. During the current era of great change, organizations need leadership. The department benefits as well. When the people who are clos-est to the work are making the decisions, the decisions made tend to be better.

Supported by Societal Trends

In the early 1980s, John Naisbett (1982) reported a major societal trend when he noted that we are in the midst of evolving from an industrial society to an information society. Peter Drucker (1989, 180) identified the impact of this societal evolution when he said, "In their field, they (knowledge workers) are superior to their employer no matter how low their standing in the organ-izational hierarchy. The knowledge worker is thus a colleague and an associ-ate rather than a subordinate. He has to be managed as such." Teams are a way to organize knowledge workers in partnership models as opposed to superior–subordinate relationships.

The demographic trends and the aging of America also support the move to team-based organizations. The baby boomers, Americans born between the years 1946 and 1964, account for fully one-third of our population and the majority of our work force. The first of the boomers are now in their fifth dec-ade. Ken Dychtwald (1990), author of *The Age Wave*, points out that the is-sues of this age group are the predominant issues of American society. As this group further matures, it seeks ways to make real contributions in organ-izations and to make a difference. In previous decades, the route for this was through entering the management ranks. In this decade, with the flattening of the hierarchy, this is no longer an option. Teams are a way to capitalize on this employee potential.

Creates Higher Employee Satisfaction

When teams have real responsibility and authority, the decisions they make are theirs. The feeling of increased ownership and control within their work life leads to higher levels of employee satisfaction. Two sociologists, Peter and Patricia Adler (Larson and LaFasto 1989, 113) found increased intense loyalty in organizations with teams. Their research revealed two significant findings: (1) intense loyalty is greater in organizations where productivity is based on group performance, and (2) intense loyalty is increased when individuals depend on the success of the group for their own success.

At Lakeland Regional Medical Center in Lakeland, Florida, staff satisfaction levels rose following their move into teams (Leander, Shortridge, and Watson 1996). Data were gathered on three measures: intent to stay, autonomy, and stress. Employees in teams on restructured units showed a 5 percent improvement in their intent to stay. In fact, the turnover is lower in the team environment than in the rest of the organization. Anecdotally, individual staff members have expressed concerns about leaving the organization in the future, asking "Where will I find something like this anywhere else?" and "Who else is doing teams?" Employees in the team environment also perceived themselves to have greater autonomy at a 10 percent higher rate than those in the unstructured, traditional departments. They also perceived their work environment to be less stressful than that of their colleagues in a traditional patient care unit.

CONCLUSION

In summary, teams are far more than the latest management fad to sweep across the country. In health care, they represent a way to create flexibility and resilience within a bureaucratic structure. Teams increase the involvement of employees in organizational work and decision making. Teams reengage the interest and commitment of employees who may have long since "psychologically terminated" from the organization. Teams produce outcomes in a competitive environment increasingly dominated by a managed care market. Teams are essential for any health care organization committed to empowering employees and increasing the level of innovation in the organization. Teams are not without problems or difficulties. Dumaine (1994, 92) sums it up nicely: "Yes teams have troubles. They consume gallons of sweat and discouragement before yielding a penny of benefit. Companies make the investment only because they've realized that in a fast-moving, brutally competitive economy, the one thing sure to be harder than operating with teams is operating without them."

CHAPTER 2

Designing Highly Effective Teams: Striking a Cultural and Structural Balance

In the first chapter, the transformation to a team-based organization was described as the challenge of the decade for health care providers. The starting point for meeting this challenge is a thorough understanding of the true nature of teams. Knowing "what teams are and what they aren't" helps an organization avoid common pitfalls in establishing highly effective teams. It's just that, however—a starting point. The journey to teams has other potential hazards, as the following, all-too-familiar scenario reveals:

> After much consideration, the executive council of a 400-bed tertiary care institution in the Midwest launched a program to bring teams to its organization. A catchy name was pasted onto the program—"Teams 2000." Behind this program was the promise of a better tomorrow through improved performance. Part of these expected improvements was enhanced job satisfaction from a more empowered and intrinsically rewarding working environment. In addition, the program was touted as a means to position the institution strategically for the future by delivering higher service levels at substantially lower cost. The sources of these savings were to be primarily the reduced hierarchy of a flattened organization, plus the productivity increases achieved through the synergy of teams.
>
> In the ensuing months, this program for establishing teams sat atop everyone's strategic agenda and out-of-pocket investments mounted. Various books and videos were distributed. Outside support was hired to conduct widespread team-building workshops and facilitation training. People all over the organization spent a significant amount of time planning for teams and taking part in a series of educational sessions. Staff within many units

and departments were regrouped from their individual jobs into teams.

A year or so later, after what seemed like a continual stream of investments, a true team-based organization still had not emerged. Sure, the organization had picked up the "team thing" well enough. Everyone talked teams and used many of the right buzzwords. Lots of people were working together and spending time in team meetings. There had been some initial increases in job satisfaction. Yet despite these superficial changes, the reality of teams had not lived up to its promise. Not even close.

It seemed that teams were just not gelling and no team was any greater than the sum of its individual members. In other words, the teams continued to be collections of individuals that could not seem to break through to new levels of productivity or decision making. As a result, the expected performance improvements in service and costs simply did not materialize. The momentum behind the program gradually faded. Investment dried up. Other actions on the executive group's strategic agenda overshadowed the organization's transformation to teams. Frustrated managers reacted to economic pressures by breaking up newly formed teams and reverting to the old way of doing things. The pursuit of teams at this institution gradually died without any fanfare or announcement.

A CRUCIAL BALANCE

What went wrong? The culprit in this unfortunate scenario—and in countless others just like it—is not what was done. It's what *wasn't* done. The pursuit of teams at this institution was dreadfully out of balance. The organization concentrated exclusively on changing the cultural side without addressing the structural side. Not enough attention was paid to defining the best designs for the teams to help them succeed over the long haul. The lesson learned? Teams simply cannot succeed without striking the crucial balance between their cultural and structural requirements—no matter how many team-building workshops they attend or videos they watch.

Case Study: "The Crumbling Cardiac Care Teams"

The managers of a recently redesigned cardiac care unit in a 500-bed academic medical center were more than concerned about the development of their care teams. They fully expected to hit some bumps in the road in the first few months as teammates struggled to work together as a fully functional team. Many months later, however, the road remained as bumpy as ever and the unit's performance measures showed it.

One incident typified the problems plaguing the teams. Lucy, a member of one of the teams, had reached her breaking point one busy morning on the unit. Obviously angry and frustrated, she cornered her manager and asked to leave the team. "This team stuff is for the birds! I give up. I want to go back to my old job where I at least knew how things worked!"

After calming her down a bit, the manager asked her to explain what had gone wrong. "The usual. We're full up with patients. Since I am the only team member who performs respiratory treatments, I always become the bottleneck when we're busy. It happens every single time we're full!" She went on to explain that her teammates get upset with her because they often have to wait for her to perform those treatments (or work around her when they are all competing for the patient) before they can tackle their own duties. Lucy finished with, "Hey, there's only one of me to go around! I try to talk to them about the problem, but they don't want to hear it."

Incidents like this one were happening more frequently on the unit. The managers were very concerned. It was apparent to everyone on the unit, including the medical staff, that the cardiac care teams were crumbling.

In the above case study, what is the underlying problem? Is the problem between Lucy and her teammates cultural (e.g., inability to negotiate priorities, poor conflict resolution skills, a need for more coaching in acceptable behaviors) or structural (e.g., work flows break down during busy periods, bad team design makes one member a regular bottleneck)? Yes and yes. The truth is that all of these factors are in play here. Clearly, the cultural side of the team needs work. But all of that work will be for naught if the structural side is repeatedly allowed to introduce stresses and obstacles beyond the team's control.

Why is the structural side of teams so important? The essence of the transformation to teams is behavior. Transforming from traditionally individualistic jobs to highly effective teams can only be accomplished through significant changes in staff and manager behaviors. It is easy to see how the cultural side (e.g., education and coaching) of teams is directly related to behaviors. The structural side of teams, however, has just as great an impact on changing behaviors. The structure of many internal "systems" encourages certain behaviors while suppressing others. For example, how performance is defined, measured, and reported and how work flows are laid out and operationalized both directly influence how staff and managers think and act by telling them what is most important for success. As a result, addressing either the cultural or structural side of teams without a balanced emphasis on the other introduces terrible friction into the organization because it puts one side out of sync with the other.

This chapter explores a key element of the structure of highly effective health care teams—their design—the often forgotten element that can doom the development of teams to mediocrity or even failure. The evidence is overwhelming: Proper team design leads to better performance results by providing a fertile ground in which the organization's cultural investments can take root. The importance of striking a balance between the cultural and structural sides of teams holds true regardless of their type—clinical teams or support teams, teams within a single department or across the entire organization. Without a sound design, the pursuit of teams is likely to end up like the ill-fated cardiac care teams scenario—just another change program that consumes scarce resources but never lives up to its promise. A time-proven approach to designing highly effective teams is explored along the following outline:

- A further definition of primary work teams
- An overview of a four-step design methodology
- A detailed description of each of these steps

PRIMARY WORK TEAMS

Special Characteristics

There is a very real difference among various types of teams: leadership teams, ad hoc teams, and primary work teams. Leadership teams typically are not designed per se. Instead, membership is determined by the organizational chart—those in specific management positions are on the team. Ad hoc teams are characterized by their relatively short existence because they are disbanded when the work is completed. Therefore, the benefits of investing in a rigorous design methodology are not as great as for primary work teams. Primary work teams, on the other hand, are indeed ongoing entities. The team stays together over time and, consequently, its success depends on whether members work together efficiently and effectively. Consequently, a sound design is crucial to primary work teams given their special characteristics.

Any type of team shares a common purpose and mission but may not have overlapping or shared responsibilities among its members. Primary work teams must have shared responsibilities in that multiple members are multiskilled in a "core" set of skills that complement the individual expertise of each member (Zazzara 1994). Unlike many other teams, primary work teams are ongoing organizational entities. The team stays together over time with a consistent set of members to serve largely the same customers. As such, the success of a primary work team depends upon how efficiently and effectively its members can work together to reach new performance heights not achievable by individuals working independently. The ultimate measure of success for a team is the extent to which the performance of the whole is greater than the sum of its parts.

Important Lessons

The design methodology outlined here focuses on primary work teams that bring together a mix of shared responsibilities and individual expertise through a consistent membership. Let's begin with a few hard-earned lessons. A primary work team will fail if:

- its size or structure (i.e., the supply) is not well tailored to meet the specific needs of its customers and the work these customers represent (i.e., the demand).
- it has the wrong mix of members.
- the right combination of shared responsibilities and individual expertise does not exist within the team.
- it cannot fluidly shift activities and priorities among its members to adapt itself quickly to unexpected changes in workload, priorities, and customers' needs.

In conclusion, the primary work team will fail if it behaves like a collection of individuals in narrowly defined jobs—in other words, in the traditional approach taken by health care organizations. In light of these risks and the significant investments required to establish teams, taking the time to design the team *right* is a small price to pay for long-term success. The kiss of death for most efforts to establish teams is to slam together existing jobs without the benefit of a sound design.

Extended Teams

The work or service required by customers of a health care organization often spans more than one work shift. Consequently, many organizations have discovered that primary work teams perform best when they extend across shifts rather than just within shifts. For example, Team A may have two members on day shift, two members on evening shift, and one member on night duty. These five people are still part of one cohesive team. They almost always work with each other day-in and day-out. This type of extended team enables greater levels of ownership because the team has more complete control over meeting customers' needs and, therefore, over producing the desired outcomes. Greater autonomy means greater self-direction and vice versa (provided the team's decision-making boundaries are clearly laid out).

The bad news is that customers' needs often vary from shift to shift. For example, the clinical needs of many patients vary in terms of "how much of what is done" from shift to shift. Similarly, the tasks that can be performed by a business office team also vary between shifts (with little, if any, work at night since no patient would endure a nighttime question about a payment issue). Therefore, the design of all extended primary work teams must be done on a shift-by-shift basis if the teams are to be tailored fully to the needs of their customers. Each shift may need to have a slightly different design (Figure 2-1).

Take, as an example, a pediatric care unit and a neonatal intensive care unit. In pediatrics, most scheduled admissions arrive during the day. The majority of procedures also are performed then. Play activities are under way during both the day and evening hours. At night, however, most pediatric patients are asleep. Therefore, the number of caregivers on the night shift is fewer than that on days. In the neonatal intensive care unit, however, the care requirements for patients are much the same around the clock. As a result, the number of caregivers is relatively constant across shifts.

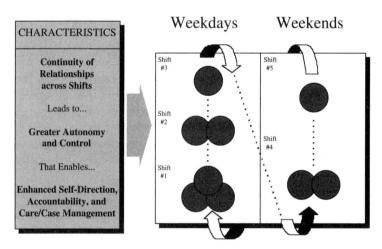

Note: This schematic shows a sample configuration for an extended primary work team. The important point is cross-shift continuity of relationships. The number of members on each shift varies across departments and organizations.

Figure 2-1 Extended Teams

The good news is that the design methodology is broadly applicable to virtually any type of primary work team across any shift. It works with clinical teams providing direct patient care. It works with technical teams performing diagnostics or therapeutic services within central departments. It even works with support and administrative teams, whether these are on patient care units or within centralized departments. Designing extended primary work teams in a shift-by-shift manner is a key to their success regardless of the customers they serve or the work they perform.

OVERVIEW OF DESIGN

Four Key Steps

The design of highly effective health care teams is a four-step methodology. (See Figure 2–2.) Together, the following steps systematically whittle away at all of the possible designs until only the best of the best remains:

1. Define the total pool of work for the team.
2. Differentiate the responsibilities within this pool.
3. Narrow the field to attractive alternative designs.
4. Identify the single best design to implement.

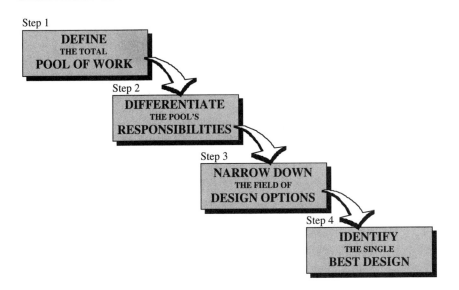

Figure 2–2 Overview of Design Methodology

The first step is to define the team by determining the total pool of work to be performed. This pool of work represents all team responsibilities: clinical, technical, support, and administrative. Those responsibilities include duties as well as any and all required interactions (e.g., meetings, discussions with physicians) and decisions.

The second step in design is to differentiate each responsibility in the team's pool of work across a few key characteristics and constraints. This differentiation sorts those responsibilities according to how long they take, how often they are required, and who can perform them. This is a key step in determining the skill mix and span of the team.

The effect of the second step is to break up the total pool of work into smaller "buckets" of responsibilities—each bucket containing a set of responsibilities that differ from the rest. During the third step, these buckets of work are used to narrow down the field of possible team designs. All possible designs are evaluated vis-à-vis a pair of important criteria: (1) how well the team will work together as a team rather than as a collection of individuals (cultural), and (2) how much additional cost or savings is associated with running the team (structural). These criteria and the evaluation highlight the handful of desirable designs.

The fourth and final step in team design is the selection of the one best design to be implemented. Up to this point, the design methodology has been fact-based and analytical. The payback for this discipline is a handful of desirable alternatives, all of which would lead to good cultural and structural benefits. Selecting the best-of-the-best design is often a judgment call. Here, common sense and consideration of less tangible factors, particularly political sensitivities, come into play.

Common Pitfalls

Each step in this design methodology has its own pitfalls to be avoided. These pitfalls will be discussed below as part of a more detailed exploration of each design step. There are also a couple of general problems that plague any team design process. Recognizing and sidestepping these traps keep the process valid and thereby ensure the resulting design will yield the results needed and expected by the institution.

The first pitfall ties back to the sequence of steps: It is allowing the design process to get bogged down in a premature quagmire of politics. Note that the intangible considerations, especially political sensitivities, are introduced only after the factual considerations have narrowed the field of possible designs to a handful of attractive options. Facts first, politics second. This simple rule maintains the validity of the design process and ultimately the outcomes of the teams. Any dramatic change process, such as the transformation to teams, is sure to entail perceptual and political battles. Count on it. Prepare for it. Politics are a vital aspect of life in a health care organization. For good or for bad, change cannot succeed without reckoning with the politics.

The key to success, however, is to concentrate that impact at the back end of the design process rather than upfront. Why is doing this so important? For one thing, by the time politics enters the equation, a handful of attractive design options has already been discovered. Any one of these designs will lead to positive results. Letting politics sway the selection of one of these options versus another is not a big deal. In fact, allowing this to happen can be a valuable means of reaching consensus and political "win–wins."

Another reason why "later is better than earlier" for political compromises is that many anticipated political battles become moot during the design process. For example, one organization's announcement of plans to establish multidisciplinary teams in an area for acute medical patients touched off some heated protests. These patients required a lot of respiratory care. Accordingly, the plan called for many respiratory-related duties to be included in the team's pool of work. A battle ensued over multiskilling other team members to perform these duties. In retrospect, it was fortunate that the battle raged on for a few weeks. During that time, the group designing the teams kept its head down and completed the process. As a result, the best team design did not call for any respiratory multiskilling. The demand was so consistently high and the duties so complex that respiratory therapists and technicians were instead integrated into a few teams—producing a far less volatile staffing issue.

Change and politics go hand in hand. The fourth step in the design methodology recognizes and formalizes this reality. That is where politics belongs to the greatest extent possible. This is not to say that a group designing teams should delude itself into assuming that anything goes. There very well may be sacred cows that should be excluded from the design process. To include such legacies wastes time and could jeopardize the value of any resulting designs. Having said this, the leaders of the transformation to teams should gauge their own effectiveness by the number of these sacred cows allowed to wander freely in the pastures, as well as by how consistently political battles are held to the end of the design process. Fewer and later are better.

The second general pitfall in designing highly effective teams is the blind pursuit of precision. Health care workers are trained to be precise. They are rewarded for it. In clinical interventions and technical activities, decimal places count. They don't in team design. General ranges are close enough, for example, when it comes to quantifying how long it takes to complete a responsibility. In team design, it pays to be more concerned with reasonable ranges and relative differences than with absolute precision. In other words, worry about accuracy—not precision.

What is wrong with precision? Nothing, if more is better. But more isn't always better. For example, the design of teams in one organization's outpatient clinic seemed to go on forever. One camp in the group doing the design had extensively analyzed the volume for a certain responsibility. After slicing and dicing the data every which way, they concluded the volume to be handled by the team was 11.6 per shift. Another camp thought that was wrong and criticized the data collection and analysis. They thought the volume had to be more like 15. After several iterations of "going back to the drawing board" without breaking this stalemate, the group designed the team under both camps' best assumptions. Those designs were identical. It turned out that this particular design was the best as long as the volume in question was between 9 and 18. Think about the wasted resources.

More precision is not always better. Many health care professionals (and consultants), however, have trouble with this truth. Their natural tendency is always to dig deeper, to gather more data, to reanalyze. In team design, this tendency is too time-consuming and costly for any marginal benefits that normally are realized. It pays to use good reliable information at a reasonable level of detail but only to dive down into precision when absolutely necessary—such as when a limited number of responsibilities dominates a team's pool of work and, therefore, small differences in the estimated "time spent per" can lead to major swings in the team members' skill mix or span (the number of customers or patients handled by the team).

Summary

Determining the pool of work, differentiating this pool through characteristics and constraints, narrowing down the field of possible designs using specific criteria, and selecting the best design to implement is a four-step methodology that leads to sound designs. Design is a key element of the structural side of teams. The methodology is intuitive and the analyses are not very complex. The real challenge is staying true to the methodology and avoiding the general pitfalls—premature politics and undue precision—as well as those lurking behind each step in the design of highly effective health care teams. Each of these steps will now be explored in detail.

STEP ONE: DEFINE THE POOL OF WORK

The first step in design is to define the total pool of work to be performed by the team. Accomplishing this step takes much more than copying a list of tasks from existing job descriptions. The following process will shed light on what it takes to accomplish this first step successfully:

- Gathering the facts related to team responsibilities
- Defining a diverse pool of work
- Facing common pitfalls in this design step

Gathering the Facts on Responsibilities

The transformation to a team-based organization is a major change for any traditional health care organization, but change is nothing new at most institutions. Change efforts like continuous quality improvement/total quality management (CQI/TQM), patient-focused care, restructuring, and reengineering are under way everywhere. While these efforts have their differences, they all share one very important trait: The basis for significant and sustainable results is a close and rigorous review of the work to be performed.

This work encompasses all responsibilities of the team as a whole (not necessarily of any particular members—that comes later). These responsibilities can span clinical, technical, support, and administrative duties. They should include all expected and needed interactions between the team and others (e.g., making rounds with physicians). They should also include all time-consuming decisions that cannot be made while performing other duties. In general, the pool of work reflects all processes, functions, and tasks necessary to add value to the customer. (See Exhibit 2–1.)

Nothing collapses as quickly or with such damaging consequences as a change effort that relies on perceptions and gut instincts rather than on fact-based decision making for its direction. Existing perceptions and instincts are, by definition, products of the old way of doing things, that fading world that is being replaced by a new order. Since what worked in the past may not work in the future, all ground rules are changing. As a general rule, meaningful change depends upon shifts in mental paradigms and conventional approaches that can only be brought about through the force of facts. The transformation to a team-based organization is certainly no exception to this general rule. The transformation from a traditional, individualistic organization to one made up of teams is tough enough without disregarding the need for reliable facts.

The first major step in designing highly effective teams is to answer the question, "What pool of work will be performed by the team?" The response must piece together a complete picture of the work represented by all the team's customers. These customers may be patients, physicians, other staff, and even external constituencies. Regardless of the type of customer, the picture of the work must quantify the full spectrum of each team's responsibilities, including any decision making.

Exhibit 2–1 Sample Pool of Work

Typical Responsibilities of a Nursery-Based Team

Review care plan, adjust as needed
Provide care for umbilical cord
Set up and administer TPN and lipids
Take and record weight
Change diaper as needed
Etc.

Note: This schematic shows a partial list of typical responsibilities performed by primary work teams within a nursery setting. The exact responsibilities vary across organizations.

Defining Diverse Work

The phrase *full spectrum* is worth repeating. Chapters 3 and 9 will explain more fully the importance of giving a team the "whole piece of work." The performance benefits of teams are greatest when their work is broadly defined to include entire processes or functions. This finding means that a team's work should include the responsibilities and activities needed to give the team total ownership of an entire process or function and not just of a small piece. To accomplish this, each team must perform a diverse set of responsibilities that typically goes beyond the confines of any traditional job, perhaps beyond any one existing department.

There are several good reasons why giving teams broadly defined, diverse work allows them to achieve their fullest performance potential. Reason number one is increased job satisfaction. Continually relying on someone outside the team (for permission, oversight, a service, etc.) is damaging to people's morale, motivation, and work ethic. Studies have shown that one of the greatest sources of staff stress and dissatisfaction with today's narrowly defined health care jobs is lack of autonomy and control. This stress can be seen in the eyes of a collections clerk having trouble collecting an account because someone in the admitting office did not gather all of the pertinent information from the patient. It can be heard in the voice of an RN hurriedly talking on the telephone with a technician in radiology about a missing chest x-ray while the physician is impatiently pressing for immediate answers. Without doubt, giving teams greater control over entire processes or functions increases job satisfaction.

Reason number two is better outcomes and results. As team-based organizations have shown, accountability for entire processes dramatically improves efficiency and decision making by reducing handoffs, false starts, delays, breakdowns, and redundant activities. These improvements, in turn, lead directly to better outcomes and results. In other words, there is a relationship between external reliance and red tape: More reliance on others leads to more red tape. This relationship hits institutions right in their bank account. The primary economic benefits of teams—reduced hierarchy and increased productivity—are derived from the improved efficiency and decision making unleashed through greater autonomy and accountability. Less autonomy and accountability mean less savings. In addition, many of the expected service level improvements arise from overhauled, streamlined processes that can only evolve when a single entity (e.g., a team) has ownership of the big picture.

The issue of sole ownership of a function requires the organization to think beyond traditional barriers. For example, when this principle of team design is discussed, the first reaction of nursing caregivers often is, "We're already responsible for all of the nursing care the patient needs on this shift." This reaction reflects a lack of consideration of the patient's needs from the patient's perspective. The patient does not live in shifts. The patient's needs go beyond nursing, including many diagnostic, therapeutic, and support services. Thus the definition of the work needed by the patient is much broader than traditionally considered.

Reason number three is full utilization of staff on a more consistent basis. Ensuring each team has a diverse pool of work enables its consistent and full utilization. Let's assume for the moment that all work is either "on demand" or "deferrable." On-demand work should be done right away, like a bank teller waiting on the next customer in line on a Friday afternoon, or a patient requiring a pain medication. Deferrable work, such as filing reports or ordering supplies, can be done later at a more convenient time as long as it gets done within the appropriate window (e.g., that shift). In health care organizations, the amount of on-demand work usually has highs and lows across the day. For example, in a patient care setting there is usually a flurry of on-demand work in the early morning followed by an early afternoon spike. It then tapers off throughout the rest of the day. By giving teams a diverse pool of work, they can be busy in the morning with on-demand responsibilities and stay equally busy in the late afternoon with their deferrable work. As such, a diverse pool of work is a must for keeping a lid on the costs of running teams.

Many of the desirable benefits of the transformation to teams may depend upon how their pool of work is defined. This hard-earned lesson applies to clinical teams as well as to support teams and to all primary work teams in between. The tangible benefits of a diverse pool of work are both cultural and structural.

Facing the Common Pitfalls

What are some of the most common pitfalls in defining a team's work? Not surprisingly, the single most common pitfall is an overly narrow pool of work. A classic example of this trap was the organization in which medical record coders were replaced with so-called teams. A lot of team education was invested but their day-to-day duties remained virtually unchanged—doing the same pool of work they performed in their original, narrowly defined jobs. They still concentrated on coding records and chasing down missing information, documents, charges, and signatures (i.e., work beyond their control). These teams existed in name only, more akin to a new paint job than to a rebuilt engine. Needless to say, they failed to meet expectations.

This pitfall is at least part of the reason why "team nursing" differs from our current concept of team. In traditional team nursing, the members of the team for the day were responsible for a relatively narrow pool of work and they usually divided the tasks amongst themselves (rather than sharing responsibilities for all of the work). For example, two nurses caring for a total of eight patients would each handle four. Divvying up is not sharing.

Another way in which a team's pool of work can be defined too narrowly is to concentrate only on the team's clinical or technical responsibilities. The traditional managerial responsibilities assumed by the team must also be incorporated into the pool of work. If the team is going to become more self-directed or self-managed by assuming some of these responsibilities—such as staff scheduling, negotiating priorities, monitoring supplies and costs, and even interviewing potential new team members—these transfers of authority should be planned and conducted in a systematic manner. Each transfer should be reflected in the team's pool of work for design purposes. In addition, the pool of work should also include all work required for a group of individuals to behave as a team. This particular work—participating in team meetings, educational sessions, and continuous improvement forums—takes time. While the increased efficiency and effectiveness of teams will more than make up for this work over time, it must be considered early in a team's development and design.

Another common pitfall is throwing many diverse but unrelated responsibilities into the pool. There is such a thing as too much diversity. The work performed by each team needs to be cohesive—responsibilities should interrelate toward accomplishing a common goal. Cohesive work is ideal for teams because it allows some multitasking (i.e., performing two tasks at the same time, such as assessing or educating a patient while giving him or her a bath). At the same time, having an interrelated set of responsibilities further helps the team to reduce its reliance on others. For example, if the patient care team is responsible for transporting the patient to a central service, the team and the patient are not kept waiting until a central transporter arrives. Furthermore, the team can use the transport as a forum for education and even assessment—turning this task into a higher-value activity.

In general, defining a pool of work around entire processes or functions is the best way to ensure it is both diverse and cohesive. That's the upside. The downside is that this can be easier said than done, given the long tradition of narrowly defined jobs and isolated departmental turfs in health care organizations. Crossing those lines is a common challenge in establishing effective teams; current jobs are usually too narrowly defined to represent a diverse enough pool of work.

The greatest challenge in defining the pool of work lies in the move to multidisciplinary solutions—primary work teams whose members come from different professions. The responsibilities of multidisciplinary care teams, for example, can include work traditionally performed by RNs, LPNs, patient care associates/nursing assistants (PCAs/NAs), respiratory therapists, physical therapists, EKG technicians, phlebotomists, housekeepers, and admitting personnel. Bringing this tremendously diverse pool of work under the control of a single team can be a monumental task given organizational resistance and inertia. Chapter 10 delves deeper into the special challenges of multidisciplinary teams.

This is just one example of the diversity of work that could be considered when designing this particular type of clinical primary work team. Obviously, the definition of work for a support team would be very different. The point is that all of these responsibilities are in one way or another tied to key outcomes related to the customer. Diverse yet cohesive.

A fourth trap relates back to the general pitfall of the blind pursuit of precision. Groups often are tempted to do a full-blown time-and-motion study across existing jobs to identify each detail of the pool of work. Like good industrial engineers, they come to the table with lists of responsibilities such as "go get chart" and "put gloves on." They also tend to propose too many "just in case" duties that may occasionally arise just to be sure some time will be allotted for these. Smells like precision.

As a rule of thumb, nothing should become a responsibility in the pool of work unless it takes at least 5 to 10 minutes to complete. Anything smaller should be included in a higher-level responsibility. For example, "change wound dressing" is actually comprised of many little tasks. The only time small tasks should not be rolled up is when the skill set or licensure constraints dictate that the same person could do them all. To keep sanity in the design process, monitor the level of detail of the responsibilities in the team's pool of work.

A final common pitfall in determining the pool of work is assuming that each responsibility is handled in a purely sequential, one-at-a-time manner. Surely, many team responsibilities (especially when they are comprised of many little tasks) will be handled that way. The best workers got to be the best, however, because they learned to do two things at one time, often called multitasking or parallel processing. For example, experienced nurses don't just ambulate a patient. While they are helping the patient down the hall, they are also assessing and teaching.

Keep an eye on multitasking as the pool of work takes shape. Combine responsibilities if they are typically performed together today, or could be if the narrow definitions of existing jobs did not preclude it. Multitasking is not "gaming" team design if introduced appropriately. It makes the pool of work reflect how things really get done.

Summary

The basis for any successful change effort is a fact-based definition of the total pool of work to be performed by the team. (See Figure 2–3.) The more diverse yet cohesive this pool of work, the greater will be the cultural and structural benefits to teams—higher morale and motivation, better outcomes and results, greater staff utilization, lower costs. Defining the right pool of work and avoiding the many pitfalls threatening an otherwise straightforward step are key ingredients in the recipe for team success.

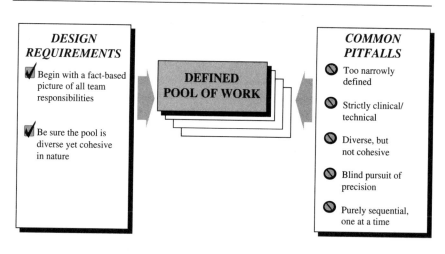

Figure 2–3 Defining the Pool of Work

STEP TWO: DIFFERENTIATE THE RESPONSIBILITIES

In the previous section, a simplistic example was used showing only two types of responsibilities: on demand and deferrable. In reality, work is much more complicated than any either/or description. The second step in the design methodology is to differentiate each responsibility in the team's pool of work across a few key characteristics and constraints. Step one's pool of work establishes the "what." It is also important to know the "how" and "by whom" introduced in step two (Exhibit 2–2). Although it takes time, piecing together the characteristics and constraints of work will pay huge dividends later in highlighting the best team design. Like educational sessions, it's an investment in the teams' success that should not be taken lightly. Considering the following information protects this investment by properly differentiating teams' responsibilities:

- The time required to perform the responsibility
- The expected frequency with which each is performed
- Any competency restrictions to be considered
- Common pitfalls faced in this design step

Time Required

The first characteristic and constraint is the estimated time required to perform each responsibility once (i.e., how long). Since a team's work may include dozens of responsibilities, it is important to arrive quickly at reliable estimates for each. One helpful hint is to limit the options. For example, allow the group designing the team to estimate the time required to perform a responsibility at 10, 20, 30, 45, or 60 minutes. The group must choose the closest option for each responsibility. Remember, no 12.5-minute estimates allowed.

As long as there is general consensus, the chosen option for each responsibility can be taken as final. The majority of responsibilities can be handled this way when the group consists of people experienced in that work. A more in-depth (and time-consuming) investigation is needed only in those few cases when the "experts" can't agree. In this way, much time is saved compared to doing in-depth research on each responsibility.

There are several helpful hints for choosing the best option for each responsibility. As silly as it sounds, it helps to remind people just how long a minute really is. People tend to overestimate how long a task takes to perform. This may be if worst case situations (i.e., the exceptions) rather than the norm (i.e., the rule) stand out in memory, or if people know these time

Exhibit 2–2 Characteristics and Constraints

| | Per Shift Estimates | | |
Typical Responsibilities	Time Required	Expected Frequency	Competency Restrictions
Review care plan, adjust as needed	5	1	RN Only
Provide care for umbilical cord	15	1	"Any Licensed"
Set up and administer TPN and lipids	20	.5	"Any Licensed"
Take and record weight	5	1	None
Change diaper as needed	5	4	None

Note: This schematic shows a partial list of typical responsibilities performed by primary care teams within a nursery setting. The exact responsibilities varies across organizations.

estimates will eventually determine how much work each team member will have to perform.

The danger to avoid here is establishing unnecessarily expensive teams that would result from inflated time estimates. One easy method to help the group make better time estimates is to ask everyone to sit silently and make note of the passing of a specified time period. People will be amazed at how long five minutes really is once they sit quietly through this exercise. As an alternative, identify one or two things everyone does at home (e.g., wash dishes, make the bed) that fall within each time option. The group can then ask, "Well, is it more like walking the dog or putting out the trash?"

Another helpful hint is to choose the estimating process carefully. One method is to have people make their estimates individually in writing. Those with no experience in a responsibility should opt out of submitting that estimate. The value of this approach is that the group can readily see how much consensus exists for each responsibility. Usually one or two people dominate the discussion when estimates are only made verbally in a group forum. The written format—perhaps using a simple check-the-box form—can even help the group define what it means by agreement (e.g., majority rules or two-thirds vote). When agreement is not reached, the group gives itself a fixed amount of time to do so through open discussion. Failing that, the matter is resolved through direct observation of experienced workers actually performing that responsibility.

When it comes to estimating the amount of time required to perform the managerial responsibilities, the team might consult with the manager as the best source of reliable information. The manager's estimates may reflect years of experience performing those responsibilities as an individual. The actual time estimate reflected in the team's pool of work may be longer. The team may be slower at first as they acquire the requisite new skills. At the same time, carrying out those responsibilities as a team may take longer than for an individual.

Expected Frequency

Another key characteristic and constraint of work is the expected frequency with which the team will perform each responsibility (i.e., how often). Expected frequency is the number of times during its shift that the team is likely to perform that responsibility for each of its customers. For example, a frequency of 2.0 means that during the course of any given shift a team can expect to perform two EKGs for each patient in their care. Traditional managerial responsibilities may range in frequency from daily (e.g., finding coverage for staff on time off) to rarely (e.g., interviewing candidates for team positions). It pays to keep a few hints in mind because, as with the time required, the tendency is to assume higher frequencies than really exist.

From the start, frequency and the entire team design should be defined in terms of what should be and not necessarily what is. While these cardiac inpatients today may receive two EKGs per shift, a better practice may be to perform only one. By defining frequency in this way, we can promote best practices in the new design. New clinical guidelines, protocols, and pathways are essential vehicles for determining what should be. National best-practice and benchmarking data also exist.

Another helpful hint for gauging expected frequency is to use the rule of "80 percent right" for all of a team's customers. Granted, teams may have to perform the same responsibility numerous times for different customers. In the above example, most patients needed two EKGs per shift. Some patients, however, actually needed only one while others needed three. Going with two EKGs as the expected frequency is usually a safe bet as long as the ones and threes are the clear minority (e.g., 20 percent of the time) and the twos are the clear majority (e.g., 80 percent of the time). This bet is even safer if the ones and threes are roughly split since "for every one there is a three" means that, on average, a frequency of two EKGs is about right.

What happens if there is no clear majority? If the above example were skewed such that half of the patients needed one EKG and the other half needed five, the rule of "80 percent right" doesn't apply. In this situation, the group designing this team has two choices. One choice again is to use the average of three EKGs. Another choice is to stop the presses. Such a large difference in expected frequency (or in time required for the same responsibility, too) may be a flag that separate team designs are needed to handle what appear to be two different customer types. If this same situation exists with other mainstream responsibilities, consideration should be given to any team's ability to handle both customers capably at the same time. Perhaps different teams need to handle these different types of patients.

Competency Restrictions

The third key characteristic and constraint are competency restrictions (i.e., by whom). The pool of work includes the full range of responsibilities a team as a whole will perform for its customers, or for itself in terms of managerial responsibilities, and the work required to function as a team. This definition in no way means that all team members can or should perform every responsibility. There are often limitations regarding which member(s) can perform certain responsibilities. Highly effective teams combine shared responsibilities among members with the individual expertise of each member.

For example, a 200-bed acute care hospital on the West Coast established financially oriented access-management teams within a central department. The team's work included patient registration, record coding and abstraction, transcription, and billing. Given its steep learning curve, record coding was removed from the list of shared responsibilities. Not every team member would have been skilled enough at coding all records. Initial competency could not be reached by all members. Coding also had a relatively low expected frequency and the rule book repeatedly changed. Even if all members could be trained in coding they probably could not maintain their skills over time. Ongoing competency, therefore, could not be maintained across the entire team. These restrictions suggested that only one member of each team should code records. The team as a whole, however, still maintains responsibility for this activity.

The other major source of competency restrictions is applicable licensure regulations. Many states have regulations governing the allied health care professions that dictate which functions can be performed by health care workers. In some states, for example, only an RN can start an IV, not an LPN or respiratory therapist. Licensure varies by state so it pays to research.

A helpful hint is to recognize that disagreement about competency restrictions may be a symptom that tasks were inappropriately rolled up into higher-level responsibilities. One part of the team design group may agree that only an RN can assume a certain responsibility while others think any licensed professional can do it. Both may be right. For example, combining the tasks of complex patient assessment with taking vital signs (because these tasks traditionally have been done together, not because they must be) leads to a situation in which one part of the responsibility (the complex assessment) may be licensure constrained while the other (the vital signs) is not. Before the disagreement is attributed to perceptions and politics, be sure the responsibility does not include tasks that do indeed have competency restrictions. If so, separate the tasks accordingly.

On the other hand, competency restrictions are often subjective. It is difficult to say how many times a team member must perform a task to stay skilled. Do they have to do it as often as the specialists in the central department or on the patient care unit? Probably not, since that level of volume usually exceeds what's needed to keep competent. So the answer is somewhere between zero and that level. It often helps to review the literature and consult with other organizations regarding their experiences facing this challenge. If worse comes to worst, make an educated guess but hedge the risk by thoroughly testing competencies in a live setting before training is complete, then monitor the performance of that responsibility for awhile after the team is implemented.

Common Pitfalls

Every step in the design methodology has its pitfalls. Falling into one of these traps in this second step can lead to teams with a larger staff than what is needed. Teams will have a richer skill mix and/or smaller span than necessary.

One common pitfall in differentiating responsibilities by their characteristics and constraints is the "flaw of small numbers." This flaw is revealed when the sum of individual decisions doesn't add up to projected totals. How can this flaw be detected early? A stubby pencil and a few calculations do the trick. Use the time required to complete a task and expected frequencies of the responsibilities to arrive at a rough approximation of the number of full-time equivalents (FTEs) needed in the teams. Now approximate the number of FTEs performing those same responsibilities today.

Compare the two numbers. Teams are more productive than individuals. If the number of FTEs in the teams is greater than today's number, the flaw of small numbers may be at work. If so, ensure that all reasonable assumptions about multitasking were indeed made. Return to the time required and expected frequency assumptions and revisit them from top (i.e., the responsibilities with the biggest result when their time required is multiplied by expected frequency) to bottom. To avoid looping back to repeat design steps, check for the flaw of small numbers periodically throughout the process.

Another common pitfall is falling victim to internally imposed restrictions. Health care organizations have worked for many years within the confines of narrowly defined jobs. Given this long tradition, it is easy for these organizations to believe incorrectly that the tight constraints on who can do what tasks are imposed from the outside rather than perpetuated from the inside. People often confuse traditional practices with legal and regulatory mandates. This problem arises, for example, in designing teams for an intensive care (or emergency services) setting. Caregivers there traditionally have consisted of RNs. Not surprisingly, the first pass at determining who can perform each responsibility in the future team's pool of work leads to most tasks being constrained to RNs. The group designing the team gradually realizes that many responsibilities do not fall into this bucket. Other professionals can complement and support the RNs as part of the teams.

Another problematic challenge is determining how to apportion managerial responsibilities. Most team design processes have found that these responsibilities are almost uniformly spread among team members. Early in design (and in some cases in implementation), however, one team member may be tagged for this role. This imbalance in power, while seemingly harmless, can be detrimental to the team if left unchecked. It leads to hierarchy within the team that inevitably results in team-destructive behaviors. This is not to say that informal leaders within teams are necessarily a bad thing. One team member may carry a bit more of the leadership role for a time, in the best interests of the team. But the transformation to teams is undermined when the imbalance in power leads to the emergence of a pseudo-supervisory role within the team.

The telltale symptom of this pitfall is a pool of work with very little work to share across team members. Most of the responsibilities are either divvied up among members or concentrated in one member, usually the most credentialed. Both are the product of traditional thinking. Both leave very little shared work in the middle. These teams will perform as a collection of individuals, not as a true team.

This common pitfall is most dangerous during the design of multidisciplinary teams. As discussed in Chapter 10, crossing traditional jobs, departments, and turfs adds a new level of subjectivity and emotion to the identification of competency restrictions.

Summary

Time required, expected frequency, and competency restrictions represent key characteristics and constraints that differentiate the responsibilities in a team's pool of work (Figure 2–4). They also dictate the cost-effectiveness of the team by directly affecting skill mix and span. A powerful pair of common pitfalls—the flaw of small numbers and falling for internally imposed restrictions—turn an otherwise straightforward step into a challenging one. Meeting that challenge is of paramount importance to the teams' long-term success.

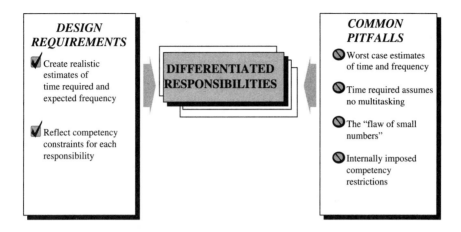

Figure 2–4 Differentiating Responsibilities

STEP THREE: NARROW DOWN THE ALTERNATIVES

The stage is now set for the design of highly effective teams. The "what, how, and by whom" of each responsibility in the team's pool of work is established in the first two design steps. Step three uses these findings to narrow down the field of all possible team designs to a handful of attractive alternatives. To do so, this step considers the following:

- The distinct "buckets of work" in the pool
- Adequacy of skills as a screening criteria
- The team dynamics of each possible design
- Cost-effectiveness of team personnel
- The source of savings through teams
- Common pitfalls faced in this design step

Buckets of Work

Once a team's work is differentiated across the key characteristics and constraints, the picture that emerges can perhaps best be described as "buckets of work." The number of buckets is determined by the degree to which competency restrictions are in force with one distinct bucket for each applicable restriction. For example, a nursing team could have three buckets of work: "RN Only" for those responsibilities that only an RN can perform, "Competent Licensed" responsibilities that can be performed by any prepared licensed person, and "Competent Unlicensed" for the rest of the work that can be performed by any properly trained caregiver. For multidisciplinary teams, other buckets might exist, such as "RRT Only" for those responsibilities that only a respiratory therapist can perform. The relative sizes of these buckets are determined by the amount of work each contains. The more work in the bucket—based upon the estimated times and expected frequencies of responsibilities—the larger the bucket. For a nursing team, the three buckets described above typically represent 25 percent, 30 percent, and 45 percent of the total pool of work, respectively. The number of distinct buckets of work and their sizes vary with the types of patients and the associated team responsibilities (Exhibit 2–3).

As this section explains, the healthiest team designs have only a few buckets with a significant percentage of the work being in the "Any Competent Member" one. Too many buckets or too small an "Any Competent Member" bucket shows that the design process fell victim to one or more pitfalls—either defining too narrow a pool of work and/or imposing internal restrictions.

Whether formally or informally, most groups designing teams think and talk in terms of these buckets (although the term may vary). A helpful hint to keep these buckets from becoming obstacles is to avoid reading too much into them. In the above example, the fact that the "RN Only" bucket was 25 percent of a team's total workload does not mean that only one in four team members will be RNs. Think of the buckets as minimum thresholds. No fewer than 25 percent of a team's productive hours can come from RNs but the best design may have much more.

The next step in the methodology is to identify all possible team designs based on the buckets of work. The group designing the teams should brain-

Exhibit 2–3 Sample Buckets of Work

Patient Type	Percent of Workload by Competency Restriction			
	RN Only	Any Licensed	RRT Only	Any Competent
Surgical Cardiac	15%	30%	5%	50%
General Medical	10%	25%	10%	55%
Intensive Care	40%	20%	15%	25%
Pediatrics	10%	25%	5%	60%

Note: This schematic shows a list of typical buckets of work for various patient types. The exact buckets and associated percentages vary across organizations. These buckets do not represent desired skill mix of care teams.

storm without judging at this point whether one design is better than another. Political sensitivities also come in later. A design cannot be found to be the best if it was never considered. Once done, the next challenge is finding the handful of attractive designs in this wide array of possibilities. Objective criteria are needed to evaluate and rate each design. To be meaningful, these criteria must relate to the factors that most directly affect the performance of a primary work team. Can the team do the work at hand? Will the members work well together as a team? Will the team operate cost-effectively? The answers to these three fundamental questions form the criteria needed to distinguish a good team design from a bad one. Each of these criteria will eliminate a few options from further consideration until what remains is the best of all possible designs.

Adequacy of Skills

Can the team do the work? Only if the skill mix of the possible design meets the minimum thresholds represented by the buckets. The adequacy of skills criterion screens out any design options that simply do not represent the skills needed to deliver and maintain quality. In the above example, any design option that has fewer than 25 percent and 30 percent of its productive hours coming from RN and any "Competent Licensed" team members (respectively) cannot meet this threshold and would not pass this screen. A team of one RN and one other licensed member would pass this screen while one RN and one unlicensed member would not. In the earlier example of access management teams, any design options that do not include an experienced coder would be eliminated for the same reason.

The number of design options screened out based on adequacy of skills depends upon the number of distinct buckets. A greater number of options are eliminated early on when the work is carved up by many competency restrictions (e.g., many distinct buckets). This is another reason to ensure that competency restrictions are minimized to include only those legally mandated. Artificially imposed restrictions eliminate a large number of design options from further consideration—options that otherwise might have been among the best. A more homogeneous pool of work with few constraints (e.g., few distinct buckets) will generally allow the vast majority of options to pass straight through the adequacy of skills screen.

Team Dynamics

Those options that have adequate skills must then demonstrate that they have healthy team dynamics. Will members work well together as a team?

This screen is a culturally oriented measure of the ongoing structural working relationships among the team's members. Many teams start out fine (while the excitement of being part of something new still exists) only to slip back gradually to traditional individualistic behaviors and practices, like dividing up the work among members without any shared responsibilities. More often than not, however, the root cause of this regression in performance is poor team dynamics imposed by a bad design.

Three important factors separate teams with healthy dynamics from those without. The first is the degree to which the work is well balanced across members of the team. A primary work team performs best when the workload is spread evenly among all of its members. This dynamic promotes a feeling that "we're all in this together . . . each of us is pulling our weight." Otherwise, the culture side of the team collapses as resentment builds among the team members.

The balance in workload must hold true in peak periods as well as in slow ones. When it doesn't, the team suffers the fate of Lucy and her teammates in the earlier case study. The structural side of the team also begins to break down as members with disproportionately heavy workloads become bottlenecks or eventually are forced to cut corners and take half measures in order to keep up with the rest of the team. Quality and service take a nose dive.

The second factor contributing to healthy team dynamics is a significant amount of shared responsibilities among members. Structurally, shared responsibilities allow teammates to shift priorities as the work at hand changes unexpectedly. Shared responsibilities act as a buffer so that the team can respond quickly when greater than expected help is needed in one area rather than another. When one team member is tied up, another can step in to keep things moving.

Like balance, shared work has cultural implications as well. It reinforces the values of broadly defined roles. Shared work is the key to ensuring that each team member continually works with the others. Teammates together assess the status of the work at hand and reprioritize accordingly. They talk, negotiate, and reach consensus on the best course of action. This interaction strengthens the team's bonds and enables synergy among team members. The combination of balanced and shared responsibilities ensures the team works together as an integrated resource.

The third key factor in determining team dynamics is the extent to which each team member is individually challenged to practice and hone his or her unique skills. It is not enough to achieve a balanced and shared team design. Team members also must be able to use their individual expertise frequently. For example, a respiratory therapist on the team should spend significant time performing respiratory assessments and complex treatments, and coaching other members in their delivery of routine treatments. A respiratory therapist fully occupied with bathing patients and passing meal trays will be less than challenged—and less than happy.

Balanced, shared, and challenged are the three key factors in design that most influence the team's dynamics, with powerful cultural and structural implications (Exhibit 2–4). How can the most likely team dynamics of each design option be evaluated? Here's where the hard work in differentiating the pool of work by characteristics and constraints pays dividends. Using the resulting buckets of work, an index is calculated for each factor across all remaining design possibilities that passed the initial adequacy of skills screen. For example, for any one team design, the amount of shared work is calculated based upon the size of the buckets that are not restricted to only one member. These three indices are summed up for each possible design. Next, these sums are compared across designs. Those design options with the above average summary indices pass through this team dynamics screen—the rest are eliminated from further consideration. Once again, time taken up front to define fully all the team's work and to differentiate each responsibility is pivotal in designing highly effective teams.

Personnel Cost-Effectiveness

Only a few of the original, brainstormed possibilities for team design will meet the adequacy of skills and team dynamics criteria. These options then will encounter the third and final evaluation criterion—personnel cost. So far in the design methodology, the economic impact of implementing teams has been ensured only indirectly, by taking the time to structure a team for success avoiding common pitfalls in this process. The personnel cost criterion evaluates each option on its relative wages/salaries per customer (or other appropriate unit of work). The personnel cost criterion ensures that the institution receives a payback for its investment in the implementation of teams.

There are several ways to nail down the economic impact of teams. The most reliable method is to do cost accounting of personnel costs. In its basic

---

Exhibit 2–4 Factors in Intrateam Dynamics

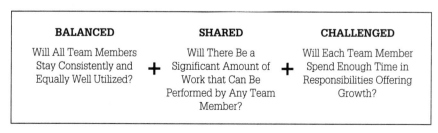

BALANCED		SHARED		CHALLENGED
Will All Team Members Stay Consistently and Equally Well Utilized?	**+**	Will There Be a Significant Amount of Work that Can Be Performed by Any Team Member?	**+**	Will Each Team Member Spend Enough Time in Responsibilities Offering Growth?

form, cost accounting associates a cost with each chunk of work by reviewing who is doing the work and how much they cost. A simplified example—designing teams to handle general surgery patients—will illustrate how this approach helps to quantify and compare costs across options.

The first part of cost accounting is to estimate the personnel cost incurred today to perform each responsibility in the team's pool of work. Assume that the team's only responsibility is to perform routine respiratory treatments. Today, those treatments are delivered by respiratory therapists within the respiratory care department. The annual wage cost for those therapists is $500,000. The particular treatments to be performed by the team represent 50 percent of the total workload of the respiratory therapists. General surgery patients (the customers handled by the new teams) account for 20 percent of all demand for those treatments. Using this information, the present personnel cost of delivering those treatments is at least $50,000—20 percent of 50 percent of $500,000 (overhead from the central department should also be included). If 1,000 of these treatments are delivered each year, the average personnel cost per treatment is $50.

The next step is to estimate what it would cost if the team delivers those treatments. For each design option, the annualized personnel cost is calculated based on the mix of members (using average wage rates for each job classification represented in the team). Then, based on the pool of work and resulting buckets, an expected span is determined. This span establishes how many total teams will be needed for each design. Note that each design option may have a unique skill mix of members and span. There may well be a different number of teams needed for each option. Multiplying the number of teams by the annualized cost for each option reveals the projected cost of performing those respiratory treatments (assuming that supply costs remain constant). This annualized cost is divided by the 1,000 treatments per year.

Thanks to cost accounting, the chore of evaluating the cost-effectiveness of each design option becomes easier. Design options costing more than $50 per customer or unit of work are economic losers. The institution would lose money on every treatment performed. These options would only be considered if they offered unique quality or service advantages not otherwise achievable. Design options costing less than $50 are economic winners. The organization would save money using these teams. The least costly design options recover investment costs and begin yielding economic paybacks the fastest.

That was a simplified example but the approach and logic are the same whether the team has one responsibility or dozens. The present personnel cost of performing all responsibilities in a team's pool of work will be the sum across many existing jobs and perhaps even departments. There are some subtleties of cost accounting that the organization's accounting or financial planning department can handle, but the underlying logic and approach is the same.

In evaluating the remaining options only those designs that are economic winners will pass the personnel cost criterion. Those remaining design options, therefore, are all attractive. Their team's members have adequate skills to get the job done. Their solid team dynamics ensure they are set up to function well as teams, and the designs are less expensive to run than the existing organizational model.

Sources of Savings

How do teams yield savings? The cultural and structural balance of teams combine to give the organization its savings. Culturally, highly effective teams allow reduced overhead—particularly hierarchy and those positions needed to support hierarchy. As teams assume greater accountability and increased decision making, the need for management control over their actions fades. Self-directed teams need little supervision; what they do need is coaching and facilitation.

Structurally, the economic gains of teams are rooted in a sound design. Good designs bring a diverse pool of work to the team. This work is normally handled through informal, verbal communications. No forms. No telephones. No computers. Just people. There is reduced infrastructure. In an individualistic organization, there are many job classifications whose only purpose is to bridge the gaps between other jobs and departments. This infrastructure coordinates, schedules, documents, transports, and so on—all activities that add no direct value to the customer. A team-based organization needs less infrastructure to keep it humming.

Furthermore, shared responsibilities allow the team to stay better utilized and more productive than is possible within many traditional jobs. There is often some built-in down time in narrowly defined jobs either because the work is sporadic (e.g., a transporter waiting for the next call to transport) or the work depends on someone else to complete. This dependency imposes a "hurry up and wait" environment as one job holds up another. Such down time is neither the product of laziness nor of poor work ethic. It is the product of compartmentalized jobs—the result of bad structure, not bad people.

Common Pitfalls

There are a few common pitfalls that threaten this third step in the design methodology. The first pitfall is relying strictly on subjectivity to rank possible designs according to their team dynamics. Groups designing teams are tempted to judge how well teams will work together based on their past experiences. Unfortunately, these experiences are usually limited in terms of bringing together people from different backgrounds. Their best guess regarding probable dynamics may be way off. For example, groups often predict that a team of two RNs would function well. Some organizations, however, have found that this design does not work because the members split the patients between them rather than working as a team. Avoid this pitfall by using quantitative indices to gauge and compare the degree to which work is balanced and shared and members are challenged.

Another common pitfall is the tendency to regard smaller teams as less costly simply because the annual personnel costs per team are lower. Let's use a simplified example to describe this fallacy. Assume only two options remain for the design of a care team. One design option has a total of five members, two members each on day and evening shifts plus a single member on nights. Another option has one more member on each shift, for a total of eight members. The annual wages and benefits of these two options are $200,000 and $320,000, respectively.

At first glance, the smaller design appears to be the least costly. But this assumption could be a terrible mistake. Given the specifics of the workload per patient, the number of patient days handled by a team under these two design options are 1,100 and 2,000, respectively. The personnel cost per patient day for the five-member team design option is about $180 compared to $160 under the eight-member option. The larger team, able to handle disproportionately more patients than the smaller team, is the most cost-effective. It is important to translate all costs—present jobs and future teams—into a cost per customer or other appropriate unit of workload.

The cost accounting approach described above helps avoid this trap. It can also be used to avoid the flaw of small numbers when the current cost (i.e., pre-teams) to perform responsibilities is determined during the second step in the design methodology (characteristics and constraints). Cost accounting, however, poses the danger of trying to be unnecessarily precise. Whether the percentage of workload represented by a particular responsibility is 21 percent or 23 percent of the central department is not likely to sway the design process toward or away from an otherwise attractive design. It simply doesn't matter. Get these percentages close, say plus or minus 5 percent, and proceed with the design methodology. As noted, the blind pursuit of precision will bring things to a grinding halt.

Summary

Adequacy of skills, team dynamics, and personnel cost-effectiveness are three key criteria for evaluating all possible designs for a team (Figure 2–5). Lots of possibilities are considered. Only a handful of alternatives are se-

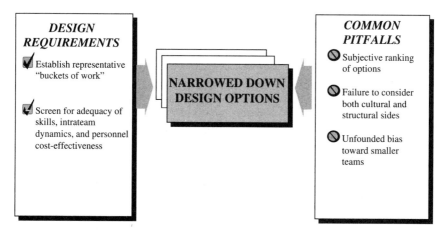

Figure 2–5 Narrowing Down the Design Options

lected. Thanks to objective criteria, however, this handful can do the job. Their members will work well together. The institution will save money. All that remains is to choose the one best design to implement.

STEP FOUR: IDENTIFY THE BEST OF THE BEST

The last major step in designing highly effective teams is to choose the one design for implementation. This design should be the best of the best. Step four of the design methodology entails the following four aspects:

- A matrix to isolate the most attractive design(s)
- Matching designs to strategic priorities
- Other political and less tangible considerations
- Common pitfalls faced in this design step

Attractiveness Matrix

The first aspect of the final selection is to clarify the relative advantages and disadvantages of the remaining design alternatives. All options are attractive but some are stronger in dynamics. Some are stronger in cost. The rest are good, but not great, across both criteria.

A useful tool for selecting the best design uses information already available for each of the remaining options. It is a two-by-two attractiveness matrix (Figure 2–6). The matrix's vertical axis separates options based on their relative team dynamics. The sum of the indices (balanced, shared, and challenged) is used to plot each option. The further up in the matrix, the stronger

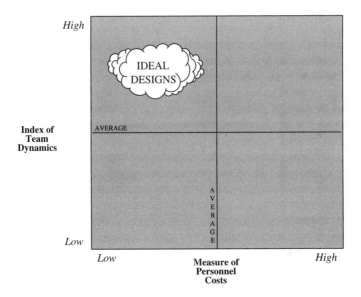

Figure 2–6 Attractiveness Matrix. *Source:* Reprinted with permission from PFCA, © 1995.

the dynamics. The center line dividing the top and bottom half of the matrix is the average across all remaining options. The horizontal axis plots the relative personnel cost of the options. This cost is expressed in annual wages per customer (or unit of workload). The further right, the higher the cost and, therefore, the less attractive the option. The center line dividing the left and right halves of the matrix is the average cost.

By plotting each option on this matrix, their relative advantages become apparent. Options in the top-left part of the matrix have it all: superior dynamics and low cost. Options in the bottom-right quadrant have good dynamics and cost (or else they would not have passed the evaluation of the prior step) but other options may be better in one or both. The attractiveness matrix points out the specific trade-offs between options. For example, moving from the top-right to bottom-left gains better cost-effectiveness but sacrifices some team dynamics.

Strategic Priorities

The important point to keep in mind during this selection process is that all of the remaining options are solid. The institution can't go wrong with any of them. The dynamics will be good and the personnel cost will be less than it is today, whichever option is selected. Therefore, the selection of the best is a matter of picking the one that is most in line with the institution's strategic priorities for the transformation to teams. Those priorities first must be articulated clearly and ranked. This should have been done early on—as input to the group designing the teams.

For example, an institution placing top priority on economic savings might restrict itself to an option in the left side of the matrix (low personnel cost). Of course, this selection may require some added investment in the cultural aspects of nurturing good dynamics—paying for this investment with the added savings. On the other hand, institutions prioritizing dynamics would opt for options in the top half of the matrix even if it means giving up some savings. Knowing how each option matches the institution's strategic priorities is an integral part of selecting the best design.

Less Tangible Considerations

Up to now, the process has focused on fact-based design. This discipline has been rewarded with a handful of attractive design options, any one of which would set the teams up for lasting performance improvements. Before the final selection is made, however, it is time to factor in other considerations likely to affect the success of the transformation to teams.

The first such consideration is the political sensitivity of implementing each option. As mentioned earlier, politics are a force to be reckoned with in any change effort. Are there factions of the organization or medical staff that would strongly oppose or support one option over the others? Are some of the departments directly affected already hotbeds of unrest because of prior change efforts? Are there one or more sponsors in the organization who would be inclined to use their credibility and political power to champion a particular option? It may be useful to list the political pluses and minuses for each option before making the selection.

There are other considerations worth discussing as well. Does the organization have enough people with the necessary background/education to fill all of the member slots on these teams? If not, is it possible to start the teams with a skill mix other than the ideal and then gradually use attrition, hiring, and selective posting to achieve the right mix on each team? If this course is chosen, what is the economic impact vis-à-vis the expected savings? Are there existing change initiatives—cultural or structural—that could benefit from a particular design or be hurt by one? Are there departments, units, or jobs whose current situation suggests the time is right for a change? Would involving a department or unit now keep them from having to undergo another dramatic change in the future (i.e., change once, not twice)? Each institution pursuing teams will come up with its own set of important considerations to include in selecting the final team design for implementation.

Common Pitfalls

Reviewing the four–step methodology, it becomes apparent how much team design hinges on the various parameters and considerations, on factors such as time required and estimated frequencies of responsibilities in the pool of work, or current strategic priorities and political issues. In this way, the design of a team fits the working environment like a glove. That is as it should be. This fit is what ultimately allows teams to deliver remarkable results.

The longer-term pitfall, however, is not keeping that fit snug. An outdated team design can gradually, almost covertly, take back the performance benefits of teams. Nothing stays still inside health care organizations. External forces and continuous internal improvement and innovation constantly mold and reshape processes, services, functions, and activities. Consequently, the specific responsibilities of the team must evolve over time in order to maintain a diverse yet cohesive pool of work. This evolution allows the team to control its outcomes. For many responsibilities, time required and expected frequencies will shift as technologies, physician's practices, and clinical guidelines are refined. Regulatory measures and automation affect competency restrictions. Strategic priorities and political sensitivities change over time, too.

As these pivotal parameters and considerations change, so must the team's design in order to maintain an adequate fit with the current environment. Team designs must be revisited periodically. Once a year, leaders in team-based organizations should review all recent changes. They need to revisit work done in the original design and critique the applicability of each factor. As needed, they can revise the design. If past is prologue, a team's design will change every few years. When it does, the current design is shifted to the new over a period of months through careful work force management. It is a transitional period with some inevitable pains and new learning curves. But the teams do not go back to zero. Their members have learned to work in teams. So while there is a readjustment, making the transition over time keeps the railroad running and the results coming.

Case Study: "An Ad Hoc Team for Redesign"

As stated at the beginning of this chapter, sound design is a pivotal aspect of establishing highly effective primary work teams. In our experience with health care organizations nationwide, the methodology described here has proven to meet this challenge. It can also help set up effective ad hoc teams. Let's briefly examine how it applies to these temporary teams:

A 600-bed nonprofit hospital in the Northeast is engaged in major work redesign. It has identified a need for a temporary redesign team to collect relevant data, analyze that data, and recommend process and role changes to improve performance results.

In the interest of costs, it was assumed that membership in the redesign team could be a part-time responsibility. Some members could continue to perform their existing duties while serving on the redesign team. On the other hand, other members—depending on their skills and the stage of the redesign effort—could be full-time members. The tough decisions to make were how many redesign team members were needed and which would be full time.

Before making these decisions, the organization first prepared a complete overview of the workload for the redesign team. It defined the team's various responsibilities (pool of work), determined how often it would meet, how much time would be needed to collect data, etc., and what particular clinical, technical, and analytical expertise must be represented on the team (characteristics and constraints). Given these answers, the organization decided how many people with certain levels of expertise were needed on the team and which would have a part-time team assignment (criteria and evaluation). Finally, it determined the implications of possible redesign team structures on team dynamics and personnel costs (best of the best).

This organization used an abbreviated version of the four-step design methodology to establish a successful (from a cultural and structural perspective) ad hoc entity. In a matter of hours, it considered critical issues and made informed decisions with significant impact on the likely success of their work redesign effort as well as on their operating budgets.

Summary

Attractiveness matrix, strategic priorities, and other select considerations help an organization complete the final step in the methodology—selecting the best of the best designs for the team (Figure 2–7). Here, facts are supplemented with common sense, experience, and judgment—the group designing the team steps back and plans implementation.

CONCLUSION

The transformation to a team-based organization is the challenge of the decade for health care organizations. Striking a crucial balance between the cultural and structural side of teams is the key to meeting that challenge.

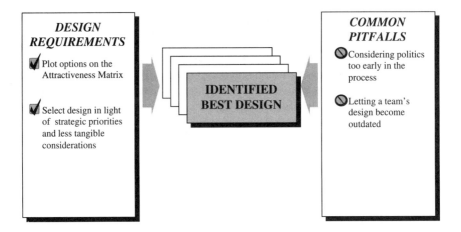

Figure 2–7 Identifying the Best Design

This balance unlocks the performance of teams—especially in terms of enhanced quality, better service, and reduced cost. A sound design is the foundation for this structural side.

A four-step design methodology, requiring just a few weeks of time, can help teams reach their fullest performance potential. Despite its importance, the methodology is rather straightforward. It begins with defining the team's pool of work. What is the team going to do? Next, each responsibility is differentiated based on a few key characteristics and constraints. What does it take to get that work done? Then objective criteria are used to evaluate possible designs and narrow down the field to a handful of attractive choices. Which possible designs have what it takes? Will the members work well as a true team? Will the institution save money through teams? Finally, strategic priorities and other considerations come into play as the best of the best designs is selected for implementation. Which design is best?

The real challenge is staying true to this methodology while avoiding the common pitfalls that can take a straightforward process and twist it and tie it in knots. Organizations with the discipline and fortitude to see the process through will reap the tremendous rewards of teams. Those that don't, won't. It's that simple—and that complex.

CHAPTER 3

Building New Teams: A Discipline

Whether you are converting to a team-based organization or simply trying to establish one effective team, the principles in this chapter will be critical to your success. Once you have designed your teams, establishing a specific approach to team development is important for attaining rapid results and improving your chances of success. Applying a discipline implies rigor and continuous learning, both of which are essential when establishing teams. We have found that building a discipline around the key elements suggested in Chapter 1 by Katzenbach and Smith (1993) has been very effective for the teams with which we have worked.

A DISCIPLINE FOR BUILDING A TEAM

A frustrating experience for many organizations is assigning personnel and resources to teams, but failing to achieve real team development. They never reap the benefits of true team synergy and continuous improvement. The previous chapter pointed out that specific design of a team is critical for future success. This chapter goes further and proposes that the finest team design will not produce an effective team if the team doesn't have the essential elements it needs to function well. Those essential elements, as described in Chapter 1, include:

- Meaningful purpose
- Consistent membership
- Specific performance goals
- Commitment to a common approach
- Complementary and overlapping skills
- Mutual accountability for outcomes

These various components are interdependent and together provide a discipline for building teams. If these elements are in place and the group of individuals is faced with routine work or a significant performance challenge (often called a crisis!), this group is likely to become a team as it does its work. Establishing these aspects of the team in a systematic, disciplined approach ensures rapid results. Each of these elements will be examined in detail. Examples from real teams will be shared.

Meaningful Purpose

Establishing clarity of purpose is an important initial step in building an effective team. A collective, meaningful purpose provides direction and sets the tone and aspirations for the team. Emotional commitment results when a team works to develop and clarify its unique personalized mission and purpose for existence. Staying focused on this purpose creates momentum for action. Author Stephen Covey (1989) says highly effective people "begin with the end in mind." In other words, they understand their purpose by understanding their goal. This is also true of teams. Members must be able to say, "As a team, we exist for the purpose of . . . . This is the work we do. It is the reason we are here."

Larson and LaFasto (1989) studied teams widely. They discovered a pattern in the ineffective teams they observed. Virtually all had a problem with purpose—it had become unfocused or politicized or the team had lost its sense of urgency. In some instances, the team's efforts had become diluted by too many competing goals and members were confused about their true purpose.

An example of this confusion occurred with a project team in a hospital undergoing major restructuring. The team had access to organizational databases, a high level of data analysis skills, and a history of rapid response and turnaround time on requests. The team's primary purpose was to lead and support the restructuring effort in the organization. Periodically, however, the team, or individual members, would be requested to handle other projects unrelated to their purpose because they worked faster than the hospital information systems department. The extent of this practice became clear when a crisis occurred involving bed placement issues during times of peak census. Physicians were demanding immediate solutions to the problem and the team was pulled off its regular assignments to respond. Several hundred man-hours were spent on this unrelated project; as a result team members felt discouraged, frustrated, and confused about their real purpose. Open discussion with the executive leading the team resulted in halting this practice and refocusing on the team's true purpose.

A good team spends time determining its specific purpose. Even when the team's purpose is self-evident (e.g., a patient care team), the team develops ownership when it, and not an external force, determines its purpose. In cases involving leadership teams, it can be more difficult to differentiate clearly the purpose of the team. Many times the purpose of a leadership team is confused with the individual roles that members play. For example, a leadership team of managers might believe its team purpose is to manage and lead the departments to which the members are assigned. This confuses the team purpose with the role of the individual manager. Instead, the real purpose for creating a leadership team of these managers may well be to create a shared vision for the division, to establish the necessary systems and structures to support this vision, and to provide consistency in leadership approaches to bring this vision to reality. This larger second purpose requires their collective effort and team synergy. The first purpose could be accomplished by a working group rather than a real team.

For members to commit themselves to the team the purpose must be relevant to each one of them. Effective teams don't just happen, they take time to develop. Through this development process they experience conflict and many difficulties. Commitment and full engagement of all team members is essential for the team to evolve to higher levels of self-direction. If the team's purpose is not meaningful to individual members, the resulting level of commitment will not be strong enough to endure difficult times. We've seen several examples of this:

Example One: A team of employees in the business office was established to reorganize the way services were being delivered to customers of their department. Several team members privately, but vehemently, believed that the current system was running just fine the way it was and that the team's purpose was a foolish exercise simply to make them feel more involved.

Example Two: A multidisciplinary team of health care professionals was established in an emergency department for the primary purpose of reducing costs. These individuals faced many quality and ethical patient care issues every day when they came to work. Although they clearly understood the ramifications of not controlling or reducing costs, they believed the administration's focus on cost reduction to the exclusion of other serious patient care issues was seriously unbalanced.

Example Three: One member of a leadership team didn't believe that a shared vision and consistent leadership were of much value and continued to manage his department in his own style, disregarding decisions and agreements made by the team. When the leadership team decided that all employees would be asked to accept increased responsibility and authority—to be empowered—all members of the leadership team were expected to act accordingly. The manager who preferred not to relinquish control and who did not empower the employees in his area created great dissonance in the organization when employees from other departments or divisions tried to work with his still-dependent employees.

The process of arriving at a purpose, which we call "purposing," results in each team having a written purpose statement that members participate in developing. It's tempting for the team's external leadership to want to develop the team's purpose and present it to the team, but this fails to establish team ownership. The team may need more time to come up with its own purpose and may encounter many difficulties sorting this through, but the resulting commitment to the eventual purpose will be worth the effort. The best teams invest a tremendous amount of time and effort exploring, shaping, and agreeing on a purpose that belongs to them, both collectively and individually (Katzenbach and Smith 1993).

Although the process for developing a purpose statement appears deceptively simple, it is not necessarily an easy task. Basically, the team meets and discusses its purpose in great depth. Many teams benefit from a facilitator or coach who can assist them in moving through the process. It begins with each team member reflecting on the following questions and then discussing their answers and ideas (Scott, Jaffe, and Tobe 1993):

1. Why do we exist as a team?
2. What do we do as a team?
3. Who are our direct and immediate customers?
4. How do we add value for our customers?
5. How is our team different and unique from other teams in the organization?

Once these questions are thoroughly discussed and everyone's answers are clearly understood, the team writes its initial purpose statement. It should be written as if it is changeless and timeless. This doesn't preclude future additions and modifications, but basically the core purpose of the team is enduring. It doesn't change overnight on a personal whim. The statement also includes both the ends the team is attempting to reach and the means to achieve them (Covey 1989). Expect this process to raise some tough issues needing resolution, such as further definition of the boundaries between teams.

This process does not occur in isolation—effective teams collaborate with their leadership to develop their purpose. It is an exceptional (and possibly an unwise) team that writes its own purpose with no external direction from organizational leadership. The team's direction may need guidance from professional standards or regulatory agencies. Teams composed of staff-level employees who have never engaged in this kind of activity will require a leader's active coaching and guidance. Besides providing support and coaching, the leader also facilitates the process by ensuring the team has the resources it needs to do its work at this early developmental stage. The primary resources are skilled coaching and sufficient time. Many groups never fully develop because they simply do not have the time to do the necessary work of becoming a team.

Once written, the purpose or mission statement can be evaluated using several key criteria. Is it consistent with the organization's mission? Does it support the overall mission? Is it congruent with the ideas and direction given by whomever established the team? Is the statement brief and to the point? Is it something a team member can easily repeat and share with others? How clear is the statement? Is it easy to understand and free of jargon? Can other people in the organization readily understand it?

Two other evaluation criteria that at first glance seem to be contradictory include specificity and generality. Is the statement specific enough to reflect the unique character and flavor of this team? If someone picked up this mission statement in a hallway, would they know to whom it belongs? On the other hand, is it broad enough to encompass future growth and expansion of the team's services and customer base? For example, an operating room team may define its purpose as "providing support, care, and technical expertise for patients during their surgical procedures," which is very specific but limiting. To allow for growth and expansion, the purpose statement could instead read "to provide support, care, and technical expertise for patients during their perioperative period . . . ." The second statement includes the possibility of pre- and postoperative visits and assessments as well as follow-up with the patient postdischarge. Last, is it a purpose statement that team members are proud of? Would they hang it on the wall in their work area? Tell others about it? Show it to physicians, families, or patients? Do team members feel good about it?

The first component of the mission statement is the team's purpose while the second is a statement of the team's values. Identifying and agreeing on important values fleshes out the mission statement and gives the team more specific guidance for its day-to-day work. Exhibit 3–1 is an actual mission statement of an executive team and its identified values. Exhibit 3–2 includes mission statements of two primary work teams in a medical patient care department. The mission statements in Exhibit 3–3 are from three leadership teams whose purposes were slightly different. Finally, a mission statement from a sterile processing and distribution department team (SPD team) is found in Exhibit 3–4.

Real teams never stop this purposing activity, but continually seek to further clarify their purpose throughout the life of the team. In some instances, the team changes its purpose or modifies it slightly. For example, a development team was formed in one hospital for the purpose of designing and driving the restructuring project. Their team's original purpose was to "support

Exhibit 3–1 Sample: Executive Team Mission Statement

As an executive leadership team, we exist to provide consistent leadership for the organization during the transformational period of converting to a team-based organization.

As a team we believe in the values of

Teamwork:	The ability to work synergistically together and cooperatively, working with others toward a common goal
Competence:	Being good at what we do; being capable and effective
Integrity and Honesty:	Acting in line with our beliefs, "walking our talk," and being sincere and truthful with ourselves and others
Communication:	Open dialogue and the exchange of views, communications that are open and honest in our dealings with each other and those we come in contact with
Creativity:	Finding new ways to do things, finding innovative solutions to issues and problems

Exhibit 3–2 Two Samples: Primary Work Team Mission Statements

Team 1

We exist to provide quality, consistent, and personalized care for our patients to enable them to achieve their highest functional level. We do this by:

- implementing an individualized, current plan of care
- using available resources in collaboration with other health care professionals
- working together as a team
- open, direct, and ongoing communication
- continually increasing our skills; learning from and teaching each other
- being timely and working in a cost-effective manner

Team 2

As a team we exist to provide quality, holistic care to our patients, their families, and caregivers through continuity, compassion, knowledge, and high expectations of ourselves and in collaboration with other health care professionals.

the organization's restructuring efforts by leading the design effort and facilitating implementation of teams." Two years later, the team's purpose changed slightly because its role changed. It then read: "We exist to support the organization's restructuring efforts by functioning as internal consultants to organizational leadership in the areas of team design and imple-

Exhibit 3–3 Three Samples: Leadership Team Mission Statements

---

Team 1

This leadership team exists to provide consistent leadership in the delivery of quality and cost-effective acute, rehabilitative, and preventive care for trauma, cardiovascular, and thoracic patients. We do this by collectively and collaboratively facilitating the empowerment and development of self-directed work teams.

Team 2

This leadership group exists to provide peer support, a problem-solving forum, enhanced communication, and coordination of joint efforts in order to improve patient care and to foster divisional cohesiveness.

Team 3

This leadership team exists to provide direction, guidance, and support to assist staff in the delivery of quality care to the surgical patients and their families. Decision making will be based on the patient-focused principles to achieve desired outcomes for patients, staff, and physicians.

Exhibit 3–4 Sample: SPD Team Mission Statement

We exist to provide quality service to meet our customers' needs by dispensing error-free supplies and equipment in a timely and efficient manner, which ensures infection control.

---

mentation." This may seem like a change in mere semantics, but in fact it signaled significant shifts in assignment of responsibility within the organization for the restructuring effort. Sometimes teams may disband when their purpose either no longer exists or has been met.

Consistent Membership

Consistent membership is a key element for a successful health care team. It is impossible to create the same levels of trust and effective working relationships if team membership changes from day to day or week to week. This concept is especially important in health care teams because of past experience with team nursing or other loose, imprecise applications of the word *team*. In team nursing, staff members scheduled to work during a shift were divided into so-called teams. The membership of the teams changed from day to day, although attempts were made to provide consistency.

Consistent membership is especially critical when unlicensed assistive personnel are members of a patient care team. Team members who are permanently assigned to the same team and who work together for months and years not only become comfortable with and knowledgeable about each other's skill levels, but also become more committed to sharing their knowledge and skills to develop fellow team members. This can prevent serious problems that could occur with unlicensed assistive personnel providing care for complex and critical patients.

Selection of team members is based on the type of team being formed. A leadership team may be composed of the managers within a specific division. An ad hoc team organized for creating a specific project, such as a design or project team, may require membership from all levels and many different areas of the organization. Depending on the scope of the project, assignment to the team may be a primary, full-time work assignment or an assignment completed in addition to or as a part of the employee's primary work assignment. For example, a staff member in the medical records department spends 20 percent of his or her time working on a project team responsible for redeploying the medical records function to the patient care units. Membership needs flow from the work to be accomplished, as will be discussed in Chapter 4.

Consistency does not mean that all team members will necessarily have a full-time assignment to the team. A part-time employee may be a consistent member of a primary work team. An executive may be a member of the executive leadership team in the organization and also a member of a divisional leadership team. The same executive also may serve on a quality team or special problem-solving team in the organization. In contrast, a direct caregiver member of a patient care team is more likely to be assigned on a full-time basis to this team. And, most of its work is done within the team assignment so it would be difficult for the staff member to be on multiple primary work teams. This employee, however, may also serve on an ad hoc team.

Specific Performance Goals

Closely related to the team's purpose are its performance goals. Larson and LaFasto (1989) found, without exception, that when an effectively functioning team was examined, it had a clear understanding of its purpose and clearly identified performance objectives and goals. These objectives and goals also serve as a measurement of the team's outcomes, giving the team the capability to hold itself accountable.

Two issues are important in this area. First, goals established by the team must be team goals rather than organizational goals. Teams take broad objectives or directives from the organization's management and shape them into specific, measurable goals for the team. Specific goals are clearly stated in concrete terms so that it is unequivocally possible to tell whether or not they have been met.

The second issue relates to the ability of team members to set goals. When team members have not been involved in this activity prior to their team membership, learning to write and establish solid goals must be part of the team's educational process. For individuals already skilled at setting goals, the process may appear simple. Just teach the team how to write a goal. But, establishing goals is a much higher-level skill than the basic mechanical process of writing the goal. It also entails the team's ability to envision a desired future for itself, to generate ideas of activities that will assist in reaching its desired outcome, to prioritize these activities, and to develop action plans for attaining the desired outcomes.

The mechanics of writing goals and objectives is relatively straightforward. A goal can be defined as "How much of what, by when?" To be useful, goals must have the following characteristics:

- reflect the core purpose of the team
- be feasible
- be measurable
- benefit others
- challenge the team

These criteria provide a way to measure the usefulness of the goal. Examples of team goals are included in Exhibit 3–5.

The best goals provide for "small wins" along the way and these small victories serve to remotivate and keep the team directed along the chosen path. The "stretch" component of the team's goals is critical for producing momentum, growth, and commitment within the team. If the goals are not ambitious, the team is not stretched and the highest level of team functioning often does not occur. Teams that face a significant challenge, or that develop their own ambitious goals have a greater sense of urgency that forces them to focus their efforts in a unified direction. This creates a sense of synergy within the team. The true strength of a team is realized when it faces and overcomes seemingly unbreachable obstacles to attain a worthy goal.

Commitment to a Common Approach

A common approach means that team members discuss, delineate, and agree on ways they are going to work together to accomplish their purpose. Common refers to the collective effort that is required, not an approach that

Exhibit 3–5 Examples of Team Goals

Primary Work Team Goals

1. Establish an effective, formal communication mechanism within the team by October 1.
   a. At the August 24 team meeting
      - Decide alternative times to have team meetings.
      - Establish a rotation schedule for team meetings through December.
      - Agree on purpose of team meetings.
   b. By September 30, develop a mechanism for communication on daily operational issues and problems. (Susan will lead ad hoc committee to make recommendation to team.)
   c. By September 30, establish expectations related to team meetings (including expectations for team members and team leader).
2. Identify the education needs of the team by December 1.
   a. Draft a needs assessment tool by September 15. (T. Evans)
   b. All team members complete the tool by October 10.
   c. T. Evans tabulates results and discusses at November 2 team meeting.
   d. Identify the top two priorities and develop action plans by December 1.

Executive Leadership Team Goal

1. Establish all elements of our team by April 15.
   a. At the January retreat day
      - Develop a purpose statement.
      - Identify team values.
      - Identify needed team roles and expectations for these roles.
      - Agree on team member expectations.
   b. At the February retreat day
      - Identify the common work of our team.
      - Establish a problem-solving process.
      - Agree on decision-making responsibilities.
   c. At the March retreat day
      - Develop a vision of team two years from now.
      - Establish action plans and structures for attaining vision.
      - Establish goals for the next year.
      - Establish outcome measures.
   d. At the April retreat day
      - Review progress.
      - Celebrate.

---

is ordinary or average. There is nothing common nor ordinary about a highly effective team. Agreement on a common approach can refer to a requirement as simple as team meetings. Where and when will they be held? Who will attend? Will an agenda be developed and who will do so? How and when will team members add to the agenda? Who leads these meetings? Will minutes be recorded and distributed? Agreement on a common approach is needed in these areas:

- working methods and team processes
- roles and responsibilities
- behavioral expectations
- the environment of the team

Let's examine each of these areas.

Working Methods and Team Processes

Working methods and team processes are often the most obvious of these four areas. Team members will discuss and agree to use common approaches where they will improve team effectiveness. An example of agreement on a common approach in health care organizations is the documentation system. If everyone documented on the patient record wherever, whenever, and however they pleased instead of following established guidelines, it would be very difficult to retrieve needed information and patient care would suffer.

Agreement on approach also includes issues such as the boundaries of the team, when team decisions need to be made, and when a decision is the responsibility of an individual. What is the work we do together and what is our individual work? What method will be used for problem solving? These distinctions can often be difficult to make. Are there specific idiosyncratic working methods I have been using as an individual that must be modified to be consistent within the team? These issues must be discussed openly when the team first forms and throughout the life of the team as new issues periodically surface.

Giving up their own ways of doing things can be difficult for individual team members. A group of recruiters in the human resource department decided they would become a team. They found it difficult to provide their individual services in an increasingly restructured team-based hospital. They became a team to improve service to the departments who were their immediate customers. The team included three recruiters and several clerical workers. Previously each recruiter had a specified functional area of responsibility, one each for nursing, professional staff (such as physical therapists, medical technologists, and respiratory therapists), and nonprofessional hospital staff (such as environmental service or food service employees). They had discovered in the past just how difficult it was to cover for each other's absences despite their willingness to do so. If one recruiter was away on business the other recruiters were unable to locate the absent recruiter's files or to understand that person's notes or method of collecting information. They became aware that as a team, they would need to discuss and agree upon a common approach to doing their work. As one of them asked, "Does this mean I can't do things in my own way anymore?" It may mean exactly that.

Roles and Responsibilities

Roles and responsibilities must be clarified for all involved. What is the difference between team and job roles? How will work of the team and job responsibilities be shared and/or separated? What functions are the team's responsibility and who will do what? What is the role of the manager in relation to the team? Let's examine each of these issues.

Team versus Job Roles. During early team formation, members often confuse team roles with job roles. On patient care teams, for example, a team member may assume the role of in-team leader and be a respiratory therapist by discipline. These are two separate and distinct roles. A patient care technician may assume the role of process observer during team meetings. Team members must be clear about their job roles, their responsibilities, and how they fit into the team's provision of service to their customers. Are there licensure constraints, regulatory requirements, or specialized knowledge that dictate which responsibilities the individual team member must provide for the team? Examples of these include the registered nurse who completes a thorough patient assessment or the coder on the medical records or business associate team whose skills are required for thorough and accurate medical record coding.

The more clarity within the team about professional/technical roles, the fewer the conflicts. Early team discussions must be held to resolve conflict when an internal expert's opinion (the registered nurse, the coder, or the human resource executive) is not accepted by the team. Does the team automatically defer to the expert's opinion or is there opportunity for discussion? Are there any situations in which the team can override the expert's opinion?

Performance standards and parameters are established for job or professional roles. These enable the team to measure the contributions of its members. These may be established by the team itself, but they are more likely developed by a shared governance structure within the organization (as discussed in Chapter 10) or by a team member's clinical discipline or profession.

Team roles differ from job or professional roles in that they are based on the unique needs of this particular team. With the help of a skilled facilitator, the team determines what it needs in order to function effectively. Is there a need for an internal team leader or facilitator? What responsibilities and authority does this include? Does this team member facilitate team meetings? Call team meetings? Develop an agenda? Complete performance appraisals? Represent the team on the department's leadership team? What exactly does the team need from someone in this role? A list of possible roles is generated and discussed. Common team roles include:

- in-team leader
- process observer
- education coordinator
- quality process data collector
- minutes recorder
- celebration or recognition person

Defining specific necessary roles is a responsibility of the team, although often, a role may be partially determined externally. Many organizations may wish to define the team role of in-team leader with specific role responsibilities and functions. Others leave it up to the team to decide.

Once the necessary roles are specified, the team shares its expectations of the individual in this role and the team member accepting the role in turn shares his or her expectations of fellow teammates. Although it takes time to clarify these roles and expectations, doing so helps prevent conflict over unmet expectations. A leadership team identified the need for a process person during team meetings. They identified the responsibilities of this role as:

- moving the team along by observing and sharing barriers to effective process
- monitoring the processing time and keeping team members to the project at hand
- sharing observations completely and honestly during evaluation sessions of the team's effectiveness

Defining the Team's Work. Boundaries between the team and its external manager must also be examined. If the team is responsible for its own work processes, the manager doesn't interfere unless there is a problem. In that case the manager's role is to coach the team in solving the problem, not to take responsibility for solving the problem. Distinguishing between the work of the team and the work of the external team leader is a critical step. Without it, there can be significant early problems in team formation. In a maintenance department team this became an issue that almost destroyed the team. Initially, the team had determined the work each member would perform and set specific outcome standards to measure performance. Later, the manager was dissatisfied with the quantity of work being accomplished by one team member, whom he believed wasn't carrying his share of the work.

He sent the team member a memo demanding more work. This encroached on the team's responsibility and was an unwise approach by this manager. The team was accomplishing its expected outcomes and believed the team member in question was doing important work (he was closely monitoring the computer to detect problems in the heating, ventilation, and medical gas systems). The team had determined the work to be done and the best ways to accomplish it. If there is a perceived problem with workload early in the team's formation, good coaching from the manager prevents the team from making inappropriate decisions about their work. As long as the team is meeting standards agreed upon by their external leader, how the work gets accomplished is strictly the team's responsibility.

Behavioral Expectations

The team builds a foundation for trust among members by establishing behavioral expectations. This process is usually most effective when it is facilitated for a group inexperienced as a team. Team members are asked to write down their expectations of teammates. These expectations are shared, recorded, and discussed until there is a mutual understanding and agreement about them. This agreement is often referred to as an operating agreement. These expectations must be real in the sense that they are important to all team members. Failure to meet them will be immediately addressed by other team members. Examples of actual team expectations are included in Exhibit 3–6.

Identifying and articulating behavioral expectations are key steps in early team formation for several reasons. They not only lay the foundation for trust, but they help prevent unnecessary conflicts. If problems occur, it is a powerful learning experience to return to the original expectations to determine what went awry. A recently formed leadership team provides a good example of this. The team developed and shared expectations with each other (Exhibit 3–7). These were discussed fully and both team and facilitator believed there was shared understanding. Within two months, the team was not doing well—there were missed communications, significant instances of noncooperative behavior, and growing mistrust within the team. Worse, the customers of the team began noticing the problems.

A pattern began to emerge. One of the team members was the source of the difficulties. This team member was directly sabotaging team efforts. The team met to discuss these issues. The original facilitator who helped the team develop its expectations was asked to return and helped the team talk through its unmet expectations. Although painful, addressing the unmet expectations was easier because they had been openly and collaboratively es-

Exhibit 3–6 Team Behavioral Expectations

1. To work toward the goals of the team and support the success of the team first, individuals second
2. To stay focused on the goal and complete tasks and projects within agreed-upon time frames (communicate any delays to all team members as soon as possible)
3. To value the diverse contributions of all team members as evidenced by a willingness to hear new ideas, confront issues that arise, and consider situations from a new or different perspective
4. To communicate openly, honestly, and directly with me, especially if I don't meet your expectations
5. To voice disagreement with a decision or approach and be willing to participate in finding an alternative
6. To give me constructive, helpful, and private feedback regarding my performance
7. To discuss our expectations of each other when we team up for a particular project
8. To respond actively to requests for help and be willing to renegotiate priorities
9. To offer help when able
10. To be on time for meetings and evidence an attentive attitude, open participation, and openness to all ideas and the work of all team members
11. To share the responsibility for group environmental and hospitality details (i.e., emptying and refilling ice cube trays, keeping bathrooms neat, clearing paper jams, etc.)
12. To keep team members up-to-date on whereabouts (i.e., through communication board, accessibility of calendars, etc.) including planned personal time off

tablished in the beginning. As a result of these follow-up sessions, several expectations were modified to be more specific. For example, one originally read: "To work toward win–win solutions on problems." It was discovered that the team member in question would raise issues and problems, initially trying to problem solve. When she became frustrated with the process she would withdraw, go out, and do things her way. This created significant problems between departments. The revised expectation became to "persist and work with me on difficult issues until we reach a mutually agreeable resolution." (See Exhibit 3–7, expectation number five.)

Clarifying expectations will not have the same results if the teams simply adopt the work of another team or group. Through the process of thinking, discussing, and agreeing, these expectations become real to the team. There is a stronger degree of commitment if the work is actually accomplished by each individual team. Although it takes time, expectations must be clarified not only between team members, but also between the external team leader who has expectations of the team (Exhibit 3–8) and the team's expectations of the external team leader (Exhibit 3–9). This technique applies for any people or teams that work together.

Exhibit 3–7 Executive Team Behavioral Expectations

As your team member, I expect you to:

1. Communicate in an open, honest, and direct manner with me.
2. Proactively keep team members alerted to issues that might affect them.
3. Give me feedback when my behavior creates a difficult or uncomfortable situation for you and be willing to work with me until we reach a win–win resolution.
4. Relate to me in a nonaccusing, nonblaming manner as evidenced by your open and honest communication, your willingness to accept responsibility for your own feelings, and your ability not to take feedback personally.
5. Persist and work with me on difficult issues until we reach a mutually agreeable resolution.
6. Have patience with my shortfalls, forgive me my mistakes as evidenced by your letting go of (not bringing them up in conversation, not referring to them as if they are current) past issues *once we agree they have been resolved.*
7. Take a learning attitude toward our work and especially our mistakes as evidenced by each of us first seeking to understand *our* own ownership and responsibility in the situation and by continually seeking to improve our performance.
8. Demonstrate your sense of humor.
9. Value my strengths—as evidenced by asking for my help, listening to my ideas and opinions, and treating them as valid.
10. Be responsible for assignments accepted to help the team meet its accountabilities.
11. Pitch in gladly, provide help when asked, and look for ways to help.
12. Ask for what you need and stay balanced as an individual.
13. Help the team and me be successful by offering your expertise, insight, ideas, and constructive suggestions.
14. Demonstrate confidence in each other by being a cheerleader (provide encouragement, focus on the positive, praise and stand up for each other), a constructive critic, and by assuming the best of me.
15. Respect each other's time by being punctual, not overusing "drop in" meetings, scheduling time when necessary, and coming prepared to meetings.
16. Be fully engaged and committed to the work of the team.
17. Identify those issues on which consensus is important (when decisions affect more than one center) and persist in working with me until consensus is achieved. Consensus occurs when each member can honestly say to other members:
    a. "I believe you understood my point of view"
    b. "I believe I understood your point of view"
    c. "I believe our decision was reached in a fair and equitable manner and I am willing to support the decision whether or not it was my first choice."
18. Share ownership of issues that cross center lines and work actively with me to solve them.
19. Participate fully in solving problems facing the team as evidenced by your win–win solutions.
20. Respect confidences and not share information we discuss with others without my knowledge and/or my permission.

Exhibit 3–7 continued

21. Be trustworthy as evidenced by honoring and meeting commitments made, being loyal to absent team members, and by presenting me in the best light to others.
22. Represent the team in a positive manner that presents us in a professional executive manner (i.e., as credible professionals) by modeling the culture and presenting a united front.

Exhibit 3–8 External Team Leader (Senior Executive) Expectations of Executive Team

1. To be responsible for assuring that the leaders/managers have the skills and resources to meet the needs of their units.
2. To develop the potential of all leadership team members and maximize (stretch) their contributions.
3. To be accountable for responsibilities identified (i.e., to ask, "Did I get the result I expected or needed as a result of my action or decision?") and to take corrective action if needed. To ask continually, "What can I do better?"
4. To make decisions and manage the center based on patient-focused tenets and principles.
5. To recognize when others need to be involved in decisions (i.e, it is also their "sandbox") and to include them in the decision making.
6. To be open and direct in your communications.
7. To ask for what you need.
8. To prevent surprises (i.e., keep me informed about situations that might escalate or create a problem).
9. To make mistakes and not avoid them.
10. To come up with solutions to problems or motivate the group to develop solutions.
11. To use all resources available.
12. To meet the organizational expectations for its leaders/managers (for example, presence at employee recognition functions, participation at management meetings, etc.).
13. To take care of yourself, balance your life, and stay healthy.
14. To continue to learn, grow, improve (feel good about yourself, but *never* settled, finished).
15. To think and solve problems at the structural level.
16. To see the big picture and help others see it.
17. Take responsibility and don't make excuses.
18. To extend patient-focused thinking, analytics, resources, etc.

The Team Environment

Highly effective teams also develop a common approach concerning their environment. Specifically, they work to create a collaborative environment, which means people work well together, communicate openly, and cooper-

Exhibit 3–9 Executive Leadership Team's Expectations of External Team Leader (Senior Executive)

---

1. To be open and receptive, to allow and encourage us to question and even challenge the status quo, the sacred cows, and each other's paradigms.
2. To clarify the nonnegotiables and work with me to prioritize.
3. To allow me to express my opinions and feelings without fear of punitive consequences.
4. To show confidence in my abilities as evidenced by your "assuming the best" in situations where you don't know all of the facts and your willingness to support my decisions and opinions even when they differ from your preference.
5. To tell us when your opinion differs and be sensitive about the impact (both positive and negative) of your positional authority.
6. To share learning opportunities and create access to additional learning so we can develop further.
7. To provide forward-thinking leadership.
8. To help us clarify shifting roles and responsibilities and specific levels of authority and operating parameters.

---

ate and coordinate their work. They also envision a preferred future, plan, do the work of the team, and work together to solve their mutual problems. Working together well refers both to the structural elements of the team and to the climate within the team.

Structural features include a clear definition of roles and responsibilities, establishment of clear lines of communication, and direct lines of accountability. Climate often refers to the relationships among team members and between the team and its leadership, both internal and external. Trust is a key characteristic of a highly collaborative climate. If team members don't trust each other, they have little hope of realizing the team's full potential. Stephen Covey (1994) believes trust is the essential foundation for teams or empowerment to work.

Trust results from a climate that includes at least these five elements: (1) honesty, (2) openness, (3) consistency, (4) competence, and (5) respect (Larson and LaFasto 1989; Bennis 1990). Let's examine each of these:

Honesty   Honesty means truth telling, integrity, and no exaggerations among team members.

Openness   Openness is a willingness to share opinions, ideas, and feelings, even when it is uncomfortable to do so. It is receptivity to new information and to the perceptions and ideas of others.

Consistency   Consistency refers to predictable behavior and responses. It means being there for fellow team mem-
bers, regardless of whether you are having a bad
day or not. It also means congruence between what
you say and what you do.

Competence   Competence means you can do the job for which
you were hired. You are capable of doing what is
expected of you.

Respect   Respect means unconditionally treating people
with dignity and fairness. In other words, my respect for you is based not on your educational de-
grees, or who your family is, or how much you own,
but rather because you are a human being deserv-
ing of respect.

In their research and examination of teams that communicate effectively,
Larson and LaFasto (1989) identified three themes that explain why a climate
of trust fosters teamwork. These are:

1. Trust allows team members to remain problem-focused. If trust doesn't
   exist, the concentration and energy of a team are diverted from its performance objectives and onto other issues. Information is not shared
   openly, communication is guarded, and people are not comfortable
   with each other. They can no longer focus clearly on the team's purpose.
   Effective team problem solving requires the open exchange of information and communication that a climate of trust brings. If team members
   enter problem solving with a hidden agenda or the idea of withholding
   key information, or just not participating fully, it will severely affect the
   quality of the solutions found and any decisions made.
2. Trust promotes more efficient communication and coordination, the
   very essence of collaboration. It reduces game playing and posturing
   and the need to position oneself carefully. If people are open and honest with each other, things are accomplished faster. Otherwise, much
   time is wasted trying to figure out what your teammate really meant,
   or being concerned that what you say may be misinterpreted. The
   team's ability to evaluate and improve its own performance is contin-
   gent upon team members' ability to be honest with themselves and
   each other. If team members cannot talk honestly about what went
   wrong and what went right, without feeling defensive or being accu-

satory, the team will not be able to self-correct and improve its performance.

3. Trust improves the team's outcomes. When there is trust, members are willing to share information with each other, even if it is negative. Team leaders who are good listeners will listen to negative information to avoid making big mistakes. If team members think they cannot make mistakes without incurring punishment, they won't take risks and will instead do what they can to avoid failure. Charles F. Knight, chief executive officer of Emerson Electric, talks about a climate in which people are likely to make good decisions:

> The person who is trying to create this environment must permit people to fail. You must find a way to permit failure because without that you're not going to get innovation or change. You are not going to get a rethinking process that is so vital. You are going to have to let some people try some things that you are not too certain about. Hopefully, this is controlled because when it is uncontrolled, you get yourself into deep trouble. But the challenge is to let people reach out, let people make mistakes in a controlled fashion and get the job done (Larson and LaFasto, 1989, 91).

It is important to define what behaviors make a good team player. The team member who brings out negative information, who points out when the team violates its own standards, who questions what seem to be incongruencies between stated values and behaviors, or who continues to push for clarity when other team members don't seem to have a problem, may be perceived as not being a team player. But when you examine these behaviors carefully, this individual may be highly committed to the success of the team effort and in fact, may be instrumental in keeping the team on track. On the other hand, the team member who is withdrawn, apathetic, and who doesn't participate fully but agrees with everything the team decides, may not be living up to his or her commitment as a team member.

Trust comes about when team members are involved and committed to each other and to the team's purpose. When team members work together and know their performance depends on the performance of the team as a whole, trust develops.

Complementary and Overlapping Skills

Specific skills needed within the team are defined by the work of the team and the needs of its customers. What is the right mix of skills the team needs to do its work? There are at least four categories of skills:

- technical or functional expertise
- interpersonal skills
- team process skills
- supervisory or management skills

The first step in creating an effective team is to understand its work and determine what specific skills are needed. Determining the right balance of these skills is the second step. The team must follow both steps for each category of skills.

Technical or functional expertise is the easiest example to use to demonstrate these concepts. The members of a caregiver team on an orthopedic patient care unit will represent a different set of disciplines than those on a caregiver team in the emergency department or surgical suite. Does every caregiver team on the orthopedic patient care unit need a full-time physical therapist? Probably not. The technical skills required in a medical records team will differ greatly from the skills in a team of educators. Determining this balance or adequacy of skills was explored in Chapter 2 on designing effective teams.

The concept of overlapping skills is also important when building a team. It is difficult, if not impossible, to have a team work collectively if none of the skills overlap and if each team member is so highly specialized that they are compartmentalized. This results in individual assignments and independent responsibility and is more characteristic of a working group than a team. This does not mean, however, that every team member must be completely cross-trained and multiskilled. Everyone on the team need not be indistinguishable from one another. For example, a surgical patient caregiver team consists of RNs, respiratory therapists, radiological technicians, LPNs, and perhaps patient care assistants. There is enough multiskilling so most team members can be versatile in providing for patient care needs, however, the unique contributions of members from each discipline are what gives the team its strength. To create a team where all members are completely interchangeable would negate this tremendous benefit and potentially introduce significant weakness.

In some teams the overlapping skills will occur in the interpersonal and team dynamic categories. Individuals may be on the team because of their highly specialized functional contributions (i.e., a data analyst and a social worker), but they share interpersonal skills and problem solving abilities with other team members. Some teams find it important to minimize differences in the technical expertise level among team members in order to optimize team flexibility. An unequal balance of responsibility may lead to conflicts and ongoing difficulties within the team.

Three common features of competent team members, as described by Larson and LaFasto (1989) are: (1) they have the essential skills and abilities needed by the team, (2) they have a strong desire to contribute, and (3) they have the capability of collaborating effectively. If an individual team member doesn't connect his or her contributions to the overall success of the team, synergy is not likely to result. One of the strongest and most persistent messages that emerged from the teams studied by these authors was the necessity of removing people from teams who were incapable of collaborating effectively with others. One such person can destroy a team.

Few teams have all the required skills at the outset. In fact, it is a mistake to focus too narrowly during the selection process on existing skills. More important is the capability of team members to acquire additional skills. Katzenbach and Smith (1993), in their extensive analysis of effective teams, found that virtually no team had all the needed skills in its early days, but all teams that reached a high level of performance had developed needed skills. A critical part of the team's work is to continue to learn and develop the skills needed to do its work.

Mutual Accountability

Accountability means that there is a review process for the accepted responsibilities. It also means holding yourself accountable for your outcomes and results. It is the process of retrospectively reviewing results to determine whether you met established standards and obtained the outcomes needed. If not, you then determine what you could have done differently and how you can correct the current situation. It is the essence of being a continual learner, of learning from our experiences.

It is important to distinguish between the internal accountability of an individual who is continually learning from experience and the external accountability commonly found within our work environment. Often there are only generalized formal methods by which we account for, or report, our results to others in the organization. These methods include reporting progress on goals, objectives, and attainment of financial targets, followed by annual, subjective performance appraisals. More instructive is the continual self-introspection of the individual or team that continues seeking ways to improve performance. This is the internalized philosophy of total quality improvement—always looking to make things better. How can I improve this? What could I or we do differently next time?

Mutual accountability differentiates a real team from a working group. In both teams and working groups, individuals hold themselves accountable for the outcomes of their assignments. A team, however, takes the next step—members hold themselves mutually accountable for the team's outcomes or results. They continuously measure themselves against their established goals and objectives. The team commits to and practices performance review, asking whether team results met expectations and taking corrective action when necessary. All team members are equally accountable for the team results. They don't wait for their external leader or the organization to hold them accountable. It is an ongoing practice within the team.

Establishing key team outcomes is an important first step for any team building accountability. What evaluation criteria will be measured? Criteria related to the performance of the technical/professional work of the team are often easier to establish for most beginning teams. These are standards that often have been measured in the past, such as accounts receivable days, patient satisfaction rates, and rate of critical incidences such as nosocomial infections or patient falls. More subtle are the outcomes expected of the team itself in becoming a team and accepting greater responsibility. Exhibit 3–10 illustrates the team outcomes established in one organization.

When the team's membership is consistent, it is possible to hold teams accountable for specific outcome measures. For example, a patient care team with consistent assignment of patients and consistent team members could be held directly accountable for the length of stay of a patient. Appropriate and acceptable reasons for variances must be identified and teams must not suffer punitive consequences for occurrences they cannot control. Now, however, it becomes possible to hold teams to account for negatively affected lengths of stay and to reward them appropriately for their positive impact on patient lengths of stay.

ESSENTIAL ELEMENTS IN OPERATION

Using this discipline for building effective teams has many possible applications within an organization. For example, these key elements can form the basis for starting new committees of the board of trustees. Most of the elements have direct application that, if used, could improve the effectiveness of committees in the organization. How much more effective would some long-standing committees be if they expired at the end of each year and had to prove effectiveness before being reestablished or continued for another year? They could be required to have a meaningful purpose, establish clear roles, establish responsibilities, clarify expectations, delineate goals, and measure accomplishments. Ineffective structures would be eliminated if they did not meet these criteria.

Exhibit 3–10 Team Outcomes Measures

	STAGE 1	STAGE 2	STAGE 3	STAGE 4	STAGE 5
ESSENTIAL FUNCTIONS					
I. The primary and essential work of the team	All team members are competent to perform the essential work of the team.	Team members are capable of functioning independently (including making decisions about how work is to be done).	Team members are responsible for maintaining their competency, establishing learning plans when needed, and meeting institutional requirements for competency validation.	Team members work interdependently and work flow is smooth and meets customer needs.	Team members are responsible for final decisions about their work and the quality of the outcomes, continually improving work processes.
II. Scheduling work and work flow	The in-team leader completes the work schedule on a timely basis.	Team members are responsible for arranging coverage for sick or absent team members.	Team members schedule their own vacations and arrange for coverage.	Team members cooperate and coordinate with other teams in the department to ensure adequate staffing.	The team works interdependently with other teams throughout the organization to ensure proper staffing in all departments.
INTRATEAM DYNAMICS					
III. Communications	Team meetings are held on a monthly basis,	Team members communicate openly, honestly,	The team is skilled at win-win negotiations and	The team assumes responsibility for resolving conflicts,	The team coordinates, communicates, and collaborates effectively

IV. Roles and Responsibilities	with at least 80% of team members attending and meeting minutes recorded.	and directly with each other and their customers (patients, family, physicians, internal customers) in an effective manner.	uses a problem-solving method to resolve issues and concerns effectively.	re: their primary and essential work with other teams in the department.	with other teams throughout the organization to solve problems and address issues or service improvement related to their primary and essential work.
	Roles and responsibilities for all team members are assigned and clarified with performance expectations.	Team members share the responsibility of hospital representation on committees and special events.	The team is responsible for identifying needed modifications in existing roles or additional roles.	Team members are responsible for ensuring the smooth rotation of role responsibilities.	All team members fluidly cross between the various team roles.
LEADERSHIP/ MANAGEMENT FUNCTIONS					
V. Human Resource Management					
a. Performance Improvement	In-team leader completes 100% of team member performance appraisals on time.	The team establishes objective performance standards.	The team measures individual team member performance and gives feedback on a quarterly basis.	The team measures team performance and evaluates results on a quarterly basis and takes necessary corrective action.	Team members coach each other on performance, sharing feedback and ideas on a consistent basis.

continues

Exhibit 3–10 continued

b. Interviewing and Selection	The team has identified the characteristics and skills needed by new team members.	Team members are trained in interviewing and selection process including all applicable regulations and necessary skills.	Team members participate in interviews of potential new members and make recommendations on selection.	The team interviews and selects new members according to established standards.	The team is responsible for contacting human resources to initiate the recruitment process and manages the entire selection process according to established standards.
VI. Planning	The team has established benchmarks in their ongoing performance improvement program.	The team monitors its actual performance against benchmarks and takes necessary corrective action.	The team has established short- and long-term goals that are used to measure team progress and effectiveness.	The team provides appropriate and timely input into the departmental and organizational planning process.	The team has a vision for their future that is aligned with the department and organization vision and that provides guidance for daily activities.
VII. Financial Management	The team carries out its work in a cost-conscious and cost-effective manner.	The team provides input and data analysis as justification for annual capital budget needs for the department.	The team monitors variances from expense and personnel budget and makes recommendations for corrective action.	The team develops its annual operating expenses and personnel budget for the team.	The team is responsible for financial projections and management of its expenditures, initiating action to remain within acceptable parameters.

Source: Copyright © 1995, Jo Manion and Joan Rodriguez.

STAGES OF TEAM GROWTH AND DEVELOPMENT

Understanding the design process and discipline inherent in creating an effective team is essential for success. It also helps, however, to appreciate the expected developmental cycle teams experience. Much has been written about the common stages of team development and an intellectual understanding of this theoretical concept is not what creates dilemmas for leaders. Instead, our experience has shown that having faith, courage, and optimism during the developmental process is often what is lacking. It's easy to talk about stages of team development but much more difficult to live through them with people. A key leadership intervention is to establish and understand the process (i.e., the discipline of the key elements) and then to respect the process and let it unfold at its own pace. Too many leaders are anxious for results and simply lack the patience for the team to develop its own wisdom and ways of working together.

The commonly cited stages of team development include forming, storming, norming, and performing (Tuckman 1965; Zenger et al. 1994). We've added an additional stage called transforming (Figure 3–1). Characteristics and descriptions of these stages follow.

Forming

This is the earliest stage of development and is often called the start-up or orientation period. The team does the work of defining tasks and responsi-

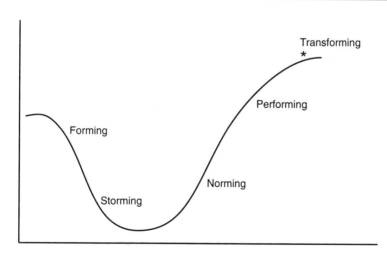

Figure 3–1 Stages of Team Development

bilities and how to accomplish them. Methods of dealing with problems are addressed and acceptable behaviors determined. Although some time is spent discussing concepts and issues, team members may be impatient to finish this and dig in to the real work. There may much discussion of irrelevant issues and problems and actual difficulty in identifying truly relevant problems.

Testing of the members in different roles often occurs during this early stage. This behavior is usually observed among team members and with the in-team and external team leader roles. Mixed messages from management are common, especially regarding transfer of responsibility and empowering the team with sufficient authority to carry out responsibility. Progress on team goals may be limited and frustrated by the fact that the team wants to be told what to do rather than take the initiative. Fear and excitement are common emotions.

Storming

This second stage is often the most challenging and most dangerous. Often called the stage of conflict, it is a necessary part of developmental progress. As the team develops common expectations, frustration and disagreement can set in. Team members often argue, even when they basically agree on issues. Defensiveness and competition appear and interpersonal disputes increase. "I told you this would never work" negativism may occur and almost everyone begins to question the wisdom of the journey. Actual sabotage may occur which, if unchecked, can create significant trust issues that must be resolved before any further progress can be made.

These negative interpersonal conflicts may be minimal if the team members have worked together before or if they genuinely like each other and will overlook minor frustrations. In these teams, negativism simply may focus on the work itself. The team may think it never has enough information, that it's out of the loop. Often concerns arise about excessive work or ability to assume new responsibilities. There may be frustration about the extra time it takes to accomplish its work and decreasing productivity. Impatience with lack of progress is common at this stage.

Norming

This stage is much more pleasant than the previous stage and is sometimes called the teamwork phase. There is a more systematic approach to problem solving and the team uses an agreed-upon approach for decision making. Functional relationships among members are negotiated and strong bonds begin to form. Relationships with external team leaders and other teams improve, but there may still be an overreliance on the internal team leader.

The team may find satisfaction and a sense of security in making new rules and establishing guidelines, but this can be overdone with too many rules and rigid expectations. There is, however, more acceptance of individual team member's strengths and weaknesses at this stage. As the norms for the team become clear, the team often shows a stronger attitude of learning. This stage feels good to everyone involved.

Performing

Often called achievement, this stage focuses on performance and results. Productivity and continued team development are the primary issues and consume a great deal of team attention. Members work together naturally in constructive ways to achieve common goals. If conflicts arise, they are addressed and resolved according to agreed-upon ground rules.

The team's spirit is high at this point with respect and trust for each other evident. Team identity and pride are intense, sometimes leading the team to become too autonomous. Sometimes, the team will protect a weak member rather than deal with nonperformance. Informal team "huddles" prevail, which help the team accomplish its work. The prevailing emotion is excitement over the team's accomplishments.

Transforming

This is often called the stage of change and it is added here to reflect the truly synergistic results of a highly performing team. Open communication is the norm and functions are now more loosely defined with team members moving freely among these responsibilities. The team owns problems that occur and works effectively to resolve them, considering various options and alternatives. When problems or conflicts occur, the team focuses on what went wrong rather than on who is at fault. Rewards are based predominantly on team performance rather than on individual contributions. Continuous improvement is a priority and part of the everyday work of the team.

There may be changes, such as losing a team member or redefining the team's mission, which force members to readdress previous work. The team has more experience now and weathers these challenges much easier as a result. The team has virtually total responsibility for its work. Detailed planning occurs. Performance appraisal is based on peer ratings rather than on the manager's observations. The team obtains its necessary outcomes in an exemplary manner.

Understanding these stages and allowing teams the freedom to experience them is important. If the leader doesn't expect teams to go through these stages, inappropriate action or coaching may occur. A classic example was a manager who served as the external leader for a team experiencing the second stage—conflict, or storming. Her initial reaction was to come down hard on the team to keep the conflict under control. She interpreted the conflict as a direct attack on her abilities as a manager and leader rather than as a normal stage of development.

Like the fly on a television screen who can only see the pinpoint directly ahead, one's perspective of the team's development is often skewed the closer one is to the team. By withdrawing a distance, by understanding the experiences of many teams, it is easier to interpret the team's stage of development.

CONCLUSION

These six elements—(1) meaningful purpose, (2) consistent membership, (3) specific performance goals, (4) complementary and overlapping skills, (5) commitment to a common approach, and (6) mutual accountability—play an instrumental role in the process of developing teams. Having the key elements in place does not guarantee an evolution to a high-performing team, yet no team reaches this level without these elements. When the team works together to develop each element, it embarks on the path to effectiveness. What it learns from this work helps the team fulfill its purpose and develops "teamness" at the same time. The wisdom of the team comes from its own experiences of working together (Katzenbach and Smith 1993).

Implementing teams in the organization or department is a rewarding, challenging, and growth-oriented process. Using the key principles outlined in this chapter can help smooth this process and increase the likelihood of achieving significant outcomes. Managing this process is a key leadership competency for the future of our organizations, and demands of leaders the ability not only to establish an effective process but to exercise patience and respect this process.

CHAPTER 4

Implementing Teams: Seven Steps for Success

Whether you implement a single team or convert the entire organization to a team-based structure, the same principles are at work. The scope of your project determines the extent to which the following steps apply. This chapter examines the process for converting a department or an entire organization to a team-based structure. The first section addresses the process that is most effective at the executive level when considering organization-wide implementation of teams. The second section focuses on departmental implementation of teams.

In some health care organizations that have implemented teams, a conscious decision to convert to a team-based structure never actually occurred. Instead, the organization undertook a process of reengineering or work redesign only to discover the logical structure that emerged was based on teams. For such organizations, several of the following steps would be superfluous.

ORGANIZATION-WIDE IMPLEMENTATION OF TEAMS

As the potency of synergistic teams becomes more widely recognized, either through their results in business and industry or through our experiences with teams in health care settings, more senior health care executives are contemplating converting their organizations to team-based structures. The conversion process is a major commitment for the organization and requires extensive leadership support and guidance. It requires a significant financial investment and entails major cultural changes by employees and leaders alike. The steps delineated in Figure 4–1 have been used successfully to implement teams.

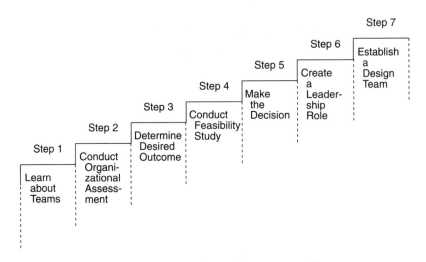

Figure 4–1 Steps for Organization-wide Implementation of Teams

Step One: Learn about Teams

Prior to making a decision to implement self-directed work teams in the organization, health care executives investigate and learn as much as possible about teams. Too often a decision to implement lacks true understanding of teams or is based on faulty information about the essential changes needed to become a team-based organization. Health care executives are under tremendous pressure today to find ways to reduce costs, improve efficiencies, and provide the highest possible quality of service. Teams are neither a quick fix nor a panacea for health care. The commitment to implement teams will endure if the decision is driven by knowledge rather than fear.

Learning about teams can occur in various ways. Reviewing the current literature and attending programs or seminars on self-directed work teams are obvious avenues for new learning. Direct communication and dialogue with other health care executives who are in the process of or who have already implemented self-directed work teams is another source of information. A note of caution to this second approach should be heeded: Many people think they have teams in place yet they have neither redesigned the work nor transferred any true responsibility to the team. In other words, some executives believe they have a team-based organization and self-directed work teams, when actual decision making and employee involvement in the organization are the same as there were in the traditional hierarchy. Careful questioning can alert you to the true situation. Ask, What are teams doing differently? What managerial responsibilities (hiring, budget preparation and monitoring, performance reviews) have been transferred to the teams? What increased responsibilities (decision making, scheduling, workload control) have the teams assumed?

Contacting businesses and organizations in other industries that have successfully implemented teams is another avenue for learning. Most lessons are transferable from one business to another. Creative approaches and ideas often arise from studying what works in other sectors of the economy. Site visits to businesses that have successful teams are helpful for directly observing the power of teams in action and for gaining insights applicable to health care settings.

Another source of learning at the executive level is to implement leadership teams, using the discipline identified in Chapter 3. Executives and leaders who have experience becoming a team possess insight and knowledge needed to make informed decisions about teams in the organization.

Step Two: Conduct an Organizational Assessment

The second major step in implementing teams is to complete an internal assessment of the organization's culture. What are the values and norms of the organization? (Not just the stated values, but the real values that people work by.) What behaviors are rewarded, either formally or informally? Are there elements of the culture that will inhibit the organization's ability to implement teams? Do established norms and rewards need to be changed? How resilient is the organization? The more accurate your assessment of the true culture and climate in your organization, the more likely you will identify potential implementation issues you will face. This assessment yields clues on how to implement teams, not whether or not you should do so.

For example, if you have been discussing employee empowerment for years and yet still have a hierarchical structure in which managers make decisions for employees and quality teams have only limited authority to implement their recommended solutions, you are at a twofold disadvantage. First, many of your employees may not have the skills or inclination to accept additional responsibilities. After all, they've done without them for years and still received their merit increases and salary adjustments. And, it is very probable that some of your best employees, those who sought more responsibility and true empowerment, have left and moved on to organizations that were more serious about empowerment. Second, talking about empowerment without actually doing anything about it creates significant dissonance in the organization. You are teaching your employees not to believe what you say. Trust will be a major issue. So, you may be starting this change initiative

with employees who are cynical and expect this to be the program "du jour." If they are patient, they can outwait this, your latest management whim.
What is the current level of employee involvement in your organization? Do managers routinely involve employees in decision making about aspects of work life that affect them? Or is there an attitude of benevolent paternalism? To what extent and frequency are employees involved in solving their own problems? Jack Orsburn and his colleagues (1990) have identified eight levels of employee involvement. (See Table 4–1.) Each level represents different managerial actions and at each level the employee is progressively more involved. Primary outcomes in the organization are identified for each level although these outcomes are not guaranteed. For example, at the lowest level in which managers make decisions and inform employees, the best outcome you will attain is conformance. Not all employees will conform, however, just because they have been told what action to take. Levels 3 through 6 address the degree to which the employee is involved in problem solving and can be compared to the quality improvement movement in the U.S. Level 7, as identified by Orsburn, is the first level in which employee involvement is actually built into the organization's structure. At this level, teams

Table 4–1 Levels of Employment Involvement

Level	Action	Primary Outcome
1. Information sharing	Managers decide, then inform employees	Conformance
2. Dialogue	Managers get employee input, then decide	Acceptance
3. Special problem solving	Managers assign a one-time problem to selected employees	Contribution
4. Intragroup problem solving	Intact group meets weekly to solve local problems	Commitment
5. Intergroup problem solving	Cross-functional group meets to solve mutual problems	Cooperation
6. Focused problem solving	Intact group deepens daily involvement in a specific issue	Concentration
7. Limited self-direction	Teams at selected sites function full time with minimal supervision	Accountability
8. Total self-direction	Executives facilitate self-management in an all-team company	Ownership

Source: Reprinted with permission from *Self-Directed Work Teams: The New American Challenge* by J.D. Orsburn, L. Moran, E. Musselwhite, and J. Zenger, Business One Irwin, © 1990.

are in place and form the basic organizational structure; accountability is the primary outcome.

Using these levels of employee involvement as an assessment tool has several ramifications. You can use them as a yardstick throughout the organization and to determine the levels of employee participation in various departments. They also serve as an indicator of how far you have to go to attain higher levels of involvement. If employees in most areas in the organization are only involved at Levels 2 or 3, you will have much work to do prior to implementing effective teams. Employees cannot progress from Level 1 to Level 8 without a great deal of staff and managerial development.

Using these levels of involvement as a self-assessment tool yielded significant insights for one organization with a five-year history of quality initiatives. Although they had instituted extensive employee quality education and had many fine examples of the process working well, the executive leaders reached several startling conclusions when they evaluated departments against these eight levels of employee involvement. First, the involvement of employees on quality teams was not as widespread as they thought. It was limited to several departments whose managers believed in employee involvement in decision making. Second, in many centralized departments, such as accounting, administration, medical records, linen services, environmental services, and plant operations, employees were involved only at Level 2. They realized they had been using team terminology much too loosely. Employees thought they already were teams because they had been involved at one time on a quality team.

The executive group concluded that it had much more work to do to implement effective teams. They realized they could use advanced teams in the organization as models and examples, and they redefined their team terminology so only real teams were defined as such.

There are many specific organizational assessment instruments available that can offer perspectives on organizational culture. These include measurement of key organizational attributes, such as flexibility, rate of innovation, the risk-taking climate, and levels of trust and confidence in management and administration, as well as morale and belief in the organization. Chapter 12 discusses in greater detail ways to identify and lower cultural barriers to implementing teams.

Step Three: Determine Desired Outcomes

Determining desired outcomes is the next step in implementing teams. What do you want to attain with the creation of teams? For example, do you want to increase the organization's responsiveness to market changes?

What level of employee involvement do you want to achieve? Do you want fully participating employees who take initiative and produce high-quality, superior work with little or no supervision? What is your vision for the organization? This step requires frank and open discussion and honest self-examination by executives. If you are not truly committed to changing the way decision making occurs in your organization, don't attempt to institute teams. Everyone will be disappointed with the results. Employees will be discouraged and the organization will squander resources that could have been put to better use. Those who are simply seeking ways to reduce costs and save money may be alarmed at the initial expenditures required to create effective teams.

Make a conscious decision about the level of employee involvement you are seeking. Be as specific as possible about what outcomes you expect from implementing teams. Will service improve and by how much? Will you reduce the number of management positions? What decisions will employees be making?

Understand that moving employees to higher levels of involvement takes a great deal of effort, attention, and commitment on the part of the organization's leadership. Employees cannot move to Level 6 overnight if they are currently functioning at Level 1 or 2. Once desired outcomes are identified, however, managers and leaders can prepare employees for teams by gradually and systematically increasing employee involvement in decision making and problem solving as it relates to their department's work. It can take years to build this strength within the organization, but it is worth the effort.

For further review of this step in team implementation, see the discussions of the team-based performance measures based on desired outcomes in Chapter 10 and outcome-based performance measures in Chapter 12.

Step Four: Conduct a Feasibility Study

Once you have identified desired outcomes, the next step is to conduct a feasibility study. While the assessment of your organization's culture will show you how to progress to teams, the feasibility study will answer the question, "Is it possible to develop teams here, right now?" Any organization can establish highly effective teams. Some organizations, however, may first need to invest in laying down new cultural foundations to allow the change to teams to take root.

The feasibility study can answer several pivotal questions. Given your culture and current level of employee involvement, what is the feasibility of successfully implementing teams? What are the benefits of a gradual departmental or area-by-area implementation versus a housewide or systemwide implementation? What are potential negative consequences and how can these be reduced or prevented? Are there any serious negative consequences that cannot be overcome? What will it cost for design work, education, and building renovation to support the work of teams? Are some of these costs expenditures that need to be made even in the absence of a team initiative? Are there departments where conversion to teams would be a simple process? Can you start with a pilot team or department? Can a pilot survive in your current culture and structure? How much time will conversion require?

Who are the key stakeholders and how do they feel about teams? What do they know about teams? Focus groups of employees can be used to determine employee reactions to possible team implementation. These groups can also identify cultural barriers that you may not have suspected.

Stakeholder analysis is critical for another reason—a major change initiative will fail in the face of strong opposition from key stakeholders who have the power to halt or sabotage this effort. If, for instance, the board of directors is close to withdrawing support for the organization's CEO and the CEO considers this a last ditch effort to save his or her job. Or perhaps union relationships within this organization have always been strained and bitter and unions have put management on notice that they will not tolerate a change in organization structure at this time.

Step Five: Make the Decision

Based on your assessment and results of the feasibility study, it becomes possible to make the implementation decision. The decision may be to go ahead, to delay, or not to implement teams. Teams may not be right for your organization or your community. With resources increasingly scarce in today's health care environment, deciding what NOT to do is at least as important as deciding what TO DO. Plunging the organization into a full-fledged implementation of self-directed work teams may require resources that are either unavailable or needed for more critical purposes. If major stakeholders, such as the board of directors, key members of the medical staff, or executive management, are nonsupportive, your implementation is unlikely to succeed.

Step Six: Create a Leadership Structure

If at this point, the decision is made to implement teams, the next step is to create a structure that assists in achieving your desired outcomes. In most organizations, this means selecting a steering committee and a design team. The steering committee consists of individuals, usually at the executive level, who will establish overall guidelines for implementation, manage the organizational process, and approve recommendations from the design team. The steering committee provides executive leadership for the effort including establishing a project purpose or mission statement, clarifying parameters and level of authority for the design team, and determining the scope of the project and initial implementation sites.

Step Seven: Establish a Design Team

The design team has the operational responsibility and knowledge to develop a full-scale implementation plan for the organization. This team intensively studies self-directed work teams and learns from the experiences of other organizations. It develops a vision of a future organization-wide team structure and designs the actual implementation process. The design team's specific process responsibilities include the following:

1. Assist with the design of self-directed work teams throughout the organization.
2. Develop specific expectations of managers/leaders related to the implementation of self-directed work teams.
3. Serve as a resource to internal managers and leaders as they develop and implement their conversion plans.
4. Collaborate with internal education to establish the necessary education and resources.
5. Direct and guide the actual implementation of self-directed work teams.
6. Develop necessary assessment and evaluation tools to support the efforts of managers/leaders as they develop self-directed work teams.
7. Monitor the implementation process.

Selecting members of the design team is critical, since its goal is to operate from strength and diversity. Select "star" employees, people who are capable and motivated to produce a successful implementation. If you were a sports coach, you wouldn't play your second string at the championship game, you'd play your very best players. Consider this effort your championship game. This is easier said than done because, most likely, your star performers are already over committed in key efforts in the organization. Organizations too often appoint employees who have time available or whose positions will be eliminated or consolidated in the future. In neither case is this the best recommendation for assignment to such an important project.

Include representatives from key areas of the organization and from as many levels as possible. Limit membership to no more than 12 people. An employee who has been responsible for the team educational effort should serve on the design team. Include at least one current manager and assign an executive to serve as an advisor or external team leader. This executive's responsibilities will include coordination of communication to upper management, problem-solving resources, and advocacy for the design team.

The scope of the project determines whether participation on the design team is a full-time or part-time assignment for members. The advantage of full-time assignment is obvious: Members are not distracted and their efforts are not fragmented by other work assignments. Bob Waterman, in *Adhocracy* (1990), points out that our ability to create fluidity and resilience in our organizations is directly related to the ease with which we are able to move our key employees in and out of major assignments such as this.

Before selecting members, determine the characteristics and attributes members will need to be successful. These include at least the following:

- ability to tolerate high levels of ambiguity
- self-directed behavior and demonstrated initiative
- good communication skills
- being a creative thinker and continuous learner
- great curiosity
- ability to interact effectively with employees from all levels of the organization
- demonstrated belief in the concepts of employee involvement and empowerment

Implementation issues for which the design team is responsible are numerous. The first is the actual design of teams. This issue is extremely critical to the success of this effort and was covered at length in Chapter 2. Once the teams are designed, other issues to be addressed by the team include:

- roll-out time frames
- systems requiring modification
- educational and training support for team members and key stakeholders
- organizational barriers to change
- gaining organizational and personal commitment
- measurements of progress
- communication strategies
- transition support
- conversion process

Let's examine each of these issues more closely.

Roll-Out Time Frames

Information gathered from the assessment and the feasibility study will assist in development of reasonable time frames. Organizations whose employees already participate in decision making are able to move rapidly toward implementation of teams. Those with a fully implemented and successful total quality management (TQM) effort and employees experienced in serving on quality improvement teams may also find it easier to convert to a team-based structure. Nursing departments with widespread primary nursing or a shared governance model will have staff members accustomed to accepting responsibility and higher levels of authority. These are advantages. On the other hand, similar failed efforts may reduce employee willingness to commit to yet another change initiative. If previous initiatives such as quality, shared governance, or primary nursing failed to achieve their goals, employees may cynically view the new initiative with a "been there, done that" attitude.

Setting realistic roll-out time frames is difficult. Often, teams are regarded simply as a new structural way to organize employees within their work groups, but teams are a totally different way of driving decision making in the organization. Structures can be changed quickly but it takes employees much longer actually to incorporate team concepts into their daily practice and behavior. Each department that converts to teams will consume significant resources in its early stages. These resources include the necessary time to become a team and to educate and train members, and the time and energy of leaders who serve as coaches. For these reasons, it's important to consider carefully the number of teams that can be realistically initiated at any given time. Further discussions related to the pace of change may be found in Chapters 6 and 12.

Health care organizations implementing teams have run the gamut of approaches. Some began with one pilot team in one department. Based on the team's proven success, subsequent implementation was undertaken throughout the organization or department. The chief advantage of this approach is that resources can be committed and care taken to ensure the success of each individual team. Teams can actually progress through their early stages of development before the manager's attention is diverted to another team. On the other hand, some organizations have implemented teams so slowly that the effort became fragmented and failed to build enough momentum to overcome normal resistance to the change initiative. Employees who are impatient and anxious to embark on the change also can quickly become disillusioned by perceived inaction. Another disadvantage with this approach is the danger of isolation and exposure faced by pilot teams and their difficulty in interfacing with nonteams.

Organizations that attempt to convert their entire structure or create multiple teams in a department often underestimate the required resources. The worst case scenario is to assign a department manager new to the management role or department the job of initiating eight or ten teams at the same time. The odds are overwhelmingly negative in this situation because of the excessive amount of managerial direction, support, and coaching required.

Systems Requiring Modification

The design team is instrumental in identifying organizational barriers needing modification to ensure the success of conversion to teams. Chapter 12 will explore these barriers in detail but, in short, these barriers often include information systems, reward and recognition systems, and methods of communication as well as the hierarchical structure itself. If full-scale implementation of teams is anticipated, this function of the design team becomes more critical than if only a few teams are being implemented. Be aware, however, that the impact of these barriers on a team is just as devastating for a single team as it is for multiple teams. The simple fact is that the organization's motivation for making major modifications is much lower for one or two teams.

Educational and Training Support

Converting an entire organization to teams requires a massive employee educational effort. A curriculum for initial and ongoing team and leadership training is a must for the initiative to flourish. Due to the crucial nature of educational and training support, Chapter 11 is devoted entirely to this issue and there is a further discussion of retooling educational capabilities in Chapter 12. The design team is involved in the original design and implementation of a self-directed work team curriculum, but must continue to identify additional learning needs throughout the entire implementation process.

Organizational Barriers to Change

As an instigator and initiator of major change, the design team's critical work occurs at the key interface in the organization where the "rubber hits the road." This unique position presents a rare opportunity for the team to uncover previously unnoticed barriers to change in its organization. These barriers appear in many forms (see Chapter 12 for some guiding principles to help identify these barriers), including some of the following:

- Influential people who appear to be "on board" but who have not yet accepted or internalized the concepts
- Unwritten "rules of the game" and institutional norms that are unspoken and unrecognized but are in opposition to the desired change. For example, even though it may be stated that management wants em-

ployee input, the unwritten rule may be that it is not okay to contradict or disagree with the manager.

- Information structures that deny teams needed access to information essential for completion of their work. For example, if financial reports are divided only by departments or cost centers, it will be nearly impossible for teams responsible for their own financial management to monitor their finances or prepare an accurate team budget.

The design team needs a respected and accepted executive-level sponsor who either coaches them in removing these organizational barriers or who uses his or her own influence to do so. The design team apprises the steering committee of such issues and their impact on the project.

Gaining Commitment

Gaining commitment of employees and managers affected by these changes is another key issue for the steering committee and design team. Teams don't just happen because the CEO declares the organization will now be team-based. Individuals in the organization must change before the organization itself can change. The organization is no more than the people within it. Employees have to buy into and be committed to the team concept before they will be willing to undergo the sometimes painful and difficult process of change.

By involving employees in the process of designing teams and resolving implementation issues, a higher level of commitment can emerge. Another key role of the design team is coaching managers and leaders on appropriate ways to involve employees in these decisions. Employee participation succeeds only when employees have adequate information, knowledge, and skills related to these decisions. Managers and leaders must develop a positive, proactive attitude toward open sharing of information.

A plan also needs to be developed for gaining the commitment of other stakeholders, such as patients, physicians, third-party payers, and vendors. Block (1987) advocates an approach used by one organization that entails identifying the key stakeholders and distinguishing the allies from the opponents and the bedfellows from the fence-sitters.

Measurements of Progress

Milestones and checkpoints provide ways for the design team to measure its progress. These may be as simple as time frames established or as specific as the number of teams designed and the developmental progress attained by these teams. When key milestones are missed, the design team investigates reasons for the deviations and determines if self-correction is needed. Periodic measurements of individual team progress including team effectiveness and team development are also useful in assessing progress. Merely counting the number of teams in place or that have completed the educational curriculum cannot adequately measure the effectiveness of the transformation process. Better to measure the additional responsibilities teams have accepted, how many team members are capable of accepting their responsibilities, and whether teams are attaining outcomes related to their responsibilities.

Communication Strategies

The design team reports its progress to at least three different audiences: the steering committee, the organization as a whole, and internal management staff. The relationship of the design team to the steering committee is one of direct reporting. Steering has a firm grasp on the overall direction of the initiative and is fully accountable for its implementation in the organization. Although the design team reports directly to steering, the relationship between these two groups is really a partnership with open dialogue and much give and take to ensure that decisions made are sound and the project stays on track.

Equally important, management staff need to hear about and see examples of progress with this initiative. A manager in the midst of implementing teams may be too close to the process to maintain a clear perspective. In our experience, involved managers often miss signs of progress or small victories that an external observer would note immediately. In one department, for example, a manager believed a team was deteriorating because of disagreements and bickering among the members and frequent challenges to the manager's opinions and ideas. This manager failed to see that the team was making significant developmental progress by opening up to this level of discussion. Before becoming a team, these employees were passive, quiet, apathetic, and never disagreed with anyone. What the manager interpreted negatively was actually a sign of increased involvement, commitment, and movement toward independence and mutual cooperation.

Communication about learning points and progress achieved develops momentum in the organization when these are shared widely. Excitement about results stimulates interest, enthusiasm, and positive inclinations from employees not yet involved in the effort. The design team may not actually be responsible for dissemination of this information, but at least can feed examples and ideas to whomever is responsible. The education team may often be better positioned to provide these updates and some should come periodically from the executive level. Newsletters or bulletin board postings can be used to create a sense of excitement and continuing interest in teams.

Transition Support

A successful change effort of this magnitude results in an organization in transformation. Employees and leaders alike are being asked to learn new methods, to behave in different ways, and to adapt to new situations. Adapting to change demands energy and usually involves giving up old ways to make way for the new. Large portions of the organization actually may be going through a grieving process at the same time. This has the makings of disaster unless leaders recognize the need to support employees who are in transition. This issue will be discussed more thoroughly in Chapter 8.

Conversion Process

Designing a conversion process for the implementation of teams is an important role of the design team. Clarifying boundaries and separating the responsibilities of the design team from those of departmental managers is part of this process. Once teams are designed, when does the manager assume responsibility for conversion? Does the manager have the authority to make team design changes if things aren't working out, or is the manager expected to use the design team to do so? How much input does the design team have into the manager's conversion plan? If a manager has established unreasonable expectations for transferring responsibilities to the team, what is the appropriate response and role of the design team? How will the design team position itself so it isn't considered Big Brother or the bad guy in this major organizational change?

Another issue relates to ownership and accountability for the actual conversion process. How will individual managers be held accountable for outcomes? The design team? What resources can the manager access? Does the manager feel ownership for this process or has the manager abdicated that responsibility to the design team or the education department? The latter happened in one organization whose education department was instrumental in developing a curriculum and teaching employees about teams. Individual managers treated the education for employees as someone else's responsibility, and did not become actively involved with their teams until they completed the educational process. As a consequence, managers felt little ownership of the process and their teams were not successful.

Members of the design team are instrumental in implementing teams in the organization. Serving as a resource to managers, leaders, and employees, they guide the process of operationalizing the team concept in the uniquely different ways required by each organization. The most effective design teams work in partnership with managers and employees in all departments and areas affected.

The design team is the entity that can project financial expenditures needed for implementation. Through developing a budget for the conversion process, the design team can assure that financial resources are available to support the implementation through the typical transitional inefficiencies. Common inefficiencies include the need for extensive managerial coaching and support for newly formed teams, the massive amounts of education needed by team members and managers/leaders alike, and the expense of running dual systems (both a centralized department or function as well as redeployed functions).

Summary

There are several commonly experienced pitfalls within these implementation steps. The most common we have seen is that the organization begins with step five—making the implementation decision—rather than laying the necessary foundation in the first four steps. The result: Restructuring and redesign have begun, teams are emerging, and executive leadership starts to feel like they've just opened Pandora's Box. Or, the teams simply aren't coming together even though initially it sounded so easy.

Another common error is not establishing a solid design team or a team of people specifically skilled, responsible, authorized, and accountable for the numerous implementation issues identified in the previous section. The responsibilities identified here for the design team are often fragmented or not even considered until problems occur. Another pitfall occurs when the entire executive group becomes the steering committee. This is usually unnecessary and bogs down the process because there are too many busy people involved. A final pitfall is slapping together existing jobs, rather than designing the design team with its work in mind.

DEPARTMENTAL IMPLEMENTATION OF TEAMS

Teams may not be implemented organizationally, but rather by individual managers and leaders. At the departmental level, many of the issues are similar and steps discussed for housewide implementation also apply if the scope of the project is just a single department. The resources available may vary considerably, however. If teams are being developed in one department, the manager must first learn everything he or she can about teams and the potential impact of teams within a department. A departmental assessment will give the manager information about the current culture and possible barriers that exist. An informed decision can then be made about the desired level of employee involvement and compared with the present level of employee involvement to determine the next steps. In some departmental groups, employees and managers together may decide to restructure into teams.

Whether or not the entire organization is converting, these are steps for managers at the department level to consider:

- building employee awareness
- developing a conversion plan
- establishing the teams
- coaching the teams

Let's look closely at each of these steps.

Building Employee Awareness

There are two basic approaches to building employee awareness. The first entails communicating the management decision to convert to a team-based organization or department and discussing with employees how this will affect their work lives. A second, more powerful, but more challenging approach involves identifying problems in the department, facilitating the group through a visioning process that creates an idealized future, and coaching employees through the design of structures that will achieve this idealized future. The assumption is that in most organizations, the structure most likely to assist in achieving an idealized future will involve teams.

Let's start with the first approach. If the decision to convert to teams was predominantly a top-down decision, employees ideally will learn about teams from their immediate supervisor. Information is shared and discussions are held about advantages of teams and how they will work. Reasons for shifting to teams, the process for selecting team members, and the impact of teams on compensation, hiring, and job security can be discussed. Expect varying reactions to the team concept. Some employees will want to know why teams can't be started now and others will see it as the latest management fad. Not all people react positively to the idea of more responsibility. In the past, individual responsibility acceptance may have led to blame and punishment when things didn't proceed as expected. Some staff members, like those described by one manager as "having a production mentality," just want to put in their eight hours and go home with no additional worries.

At this juncture, managers need to talk openly about their own new roles in a team environment. Expect to be challenged by employees who say, "If we begin making decisions about our work or take on your supervisory responsibilities, what will you be doing?" The manager needs a clear and positive response about his or her future role, such as, "I will be responsible for coaching and teaching you as you take over these responsibilities. I will be responsible for coordination between the teams and the rest of the organization." Other common employee responses include, "Why should we do the budget? That's what you get paid for!," or "How much more are you going to pay us if we take on this additional responsibility?" Thinking through positive and honest answers to these questions and actually role-playing your responses with another colleague can reduce the discomfort you'll experience when these remarks are made.

The second approach suggested is one in which employees actively participate from the beginning of the process. This may be likely when individual departments and their leaders are considering the team alternative rather than the organization as a whole. In a department, this approach can be more closely and carefully facilitated. This method of involving employees and developing awareness about teams begins with discussion about current problems within the department as perceived by employees. Generating lists of issues is only the first step. The leader then facilitates a visioning process during which only the ideal future state is considered. No deficiencies or problems are discussed. Questions are asked, such as: "What will we look like? How will we work together? How will we interact with the rest of the organization? How will we communicate with each other?" Once this ideal future is thoroughly and specifically described, the group, or a group from within the staff, determines structures that would help realize this idealized future. The structure often identified is a team or teams with significantly increased employee participation.

Developing a Conversion Plan

In the absence of a housewide initiative, departmental leadership develops a preliminary conversion plan that outlines:

- probable team structures and design
- possible needs and avenues for multiskilling
- the process to be used for selecting team members
- probable time frames for the sequential transfer of responsibilities to the team
- resources needed for implementing teams

Individualized plans for departments are far more successful than any cookie-cutter approach. At this point, however, this is only a preliminary plan. The best of these plans are developed with the further input of employees and the manager's immediate supervisor. A sample sequencing of responsibility transfer is included in Table 4–2.

Table 4–2 Sample Transfer of Responsibility Plan

EXPECTATIONS/ OUTCOMES	YEAR 1	YEAR 2	YEAR 3	YEAR 4	YEAR 5
Work of the Team	The team will: 1. Do the clinical/ technical work of the team. 2. Be fully trained with the necessary technical skills. 3. Clarify roles and responsibilities for each team member. 4. Identify its purpose (congruent with the organization's mission). 5. Develop a vision of what it will be in five years (first developed by the leader and shaped with input from the team). 6. Identify customers and their needs.	1. Continually seek ways to improve its work and the value to customers. 2. Accept responsibility for follow-up with risk management for unusual occurrences. 3. Establish a plan to meet customers' needs and to improve customer service. 4. Follow established parameters for customer service recovery.	1. Accept responsibility for assigning work and scheduling team members. 2. Use data and research methodologies to improve the clinical/technical work. 3. Manage relationships with key customers (i.e., physicians, administrators, other department heads).	1. Manage relationships with outside vendors.	

continues

Team Dynamics			
1. Establish and share expectations among • team members • team members and team leader • the team and any group it works with frequently 2. Establish healthy (direct and open) communication patterns within the team. 3. Handle change and transitions in a healthy manner, openly and supportively among team members. 4. Use good listening skills. 5. Develop beginning group problem-solving skills. 6. Participate actively in team meetings.	1. Establish new and renegotiate old expectations as needed. 2. Apply principles of conflict resolution and negotiation. 3. Be responsible for resolving conflicts within the team using a win–win approach. 4. Assume responsibility for agenda preparation, scheduling, and facilitating team meetings. 5. Participate on housewide committees.	1. Accept responsibility for assigning team members as representatives at housewide committees. 2. Apply principles of negotiation with other teams and departments. 3. Willingly provide assistance and support to other teams in the organization.	1. Recognize and support the work of the entire unit/department.

Table 4–2 continued

EXPECTATIONS/ OUTCOMES	YEAR 1	YEAR 2	YEAR 3	YEAR 4	YEAR 5
Management Human Resources	1. Orient new members as needed. 2. Identify team needs for additional training or educational support. 3. Provide needed in-services for fellow team members. 4. Require that each team member accepts responsibility for validation of institutionally-required competencies.	1. Use principles of adult learning when teaching others. 2. Identify ongoing competency verification needs. 3. Identify critical characteristics and/or competencies for new team members. 4. Give each other feedback and coaching on performance issues. 5. Provide peer input for evaluation process.	1. Participate in educating other teams and in educational efforts within the organization. 2. Interview and select new team members. 3. Coach fellow team members on performance issues. 4. Participate in recognition of team members.	1. Be responsible for meeting learning needs. 2. Accept responsibility for ongoing competency validation of team members. 3. Assume responsibility for peer evaluation process. 4. Accept responsibility for discipline issues or team member performance problems. 5. Participate in recruitment activities.	1. Assume responsibility for evaluation of team. 2. Make recommendations for team compensation issues. 3. Accept responsibility for recognition of team.
Planning	1. Establish team goals.	1. Establish team goals.	1. Provide input into annual strategic plan for the team.	1. Assist in the development of the annual plan.	1. Share the responsibility of long-range planning for the team.

Planning (continued)	2. Monitor and measure its performance against established goals. 3. Determine actions to meet its goals.	2. Determine actions to meet its goals.	2. Monitor performance against the long-range plan.	2. Monitor process toward attainment of long-range goals. 3. Assist in development of action plans.	2. Assume responsibility for initiating self-correcting action as needed.
Financial	1. Provide input into annual capital budget. 2. Participate in identifying appropriate cost containment measures.	1. Provide input into annual operating expenses and personnel budget. 2. Participate in monitoring operational variances.	1. Participate in preparing annual operating, personnel, and capital budgets. 2. Share responsibility for monitoring variances. 3. Provide input into decisions regarding expenditures. 4. Initiate appropriate cost containment efforts.	1. Accept responsibility for preparation of annual operating, FTE, and capital budget. 2. Monitor financial performance and initiate corrective action as needed. 3. Accept responsibility for expenditure decisions within financial parameters.	

Source: Copyright © 1994, Jo Manion, Manion and Associates, Altamonte Springs, Florida.

Establishing the Teams

Establishing teams is the next step, which includes selection of team members as well as clarifying expectations and boundaries. In some instances, there is no true selection process. Employees within the department are simply placed into teams. This creates a significant disadvantage in that it can perpetuate preexisting patterns of entitlement. "You're owed a team position because you are an employee in this department." Some employees have no intention of becoming a team player. They've never evidenced this behavior before and are often quite proud of it! However, if a manager has no real choice about the employees who will serve on the teams, this redesigned structure can be used at least as a means to set new performance expectations as they relate to working within the team. Work with human resource experts to be certain your expectations will stand up should you need later to terminate an employee for nonperformance of the expected behaviors.

Assuming there is some degree of choice, we've seen two very different approaches work for team member selection. The first is to select the internal, within-the-team leaders, who then select their team members. This approach is more hierarchical and less participatory. A second approach is to select team members first and coach them to identify what they need from a within-the-team leader or coordinator. They can then select their own internal team leader. In either case, determine the process for selection of team members. Consider selection criteria such as skills and experience, interest in participation on a team, ability to handle ambiguity and new responsibilities and to learn and apply new skills. Be as clear as possible about skills and attributes teams should be seeking. Get employee and immediate supervisor input on these criteria before presenting them as final.

It's important to clarify performance expectations of the team and existing team boundaries. Expect the team over time to earn increased authority over its own activities. Even the most empowered teams, however, operate within firm and clear boundaries. Consider fiscal, legal, quality, and service standards, regulatory standards, and organizational policies when clarifying parameters. For example, even if team members have learned interviewing skills and are very motivated to select a replacement team member, they must fully understand and comply with equal opportunity standards.

From the beginning, be alert to the team's reactions to these parameters. Most employees have a limited understanding of the constraints managers deal with in carrying out their responsibilities. Transferring these responsibilities to a team dismantles some of the past mystique that has surrounded the management role. Employees begin to realize that management is a different role and one that they can learn. This can be a difficult change for traditional managers who expect employees to respect and defer to them because of their positional authority. A serendipitous benefit of teams assuming traditional supervisory responsibilities is greater appreciation for the manager's role.

Coaching the Team

Whether teams are being implemented organization-wide or within a single department, the actual discipline for developing a team is the same. Using these key principles to create a team transcends the superficial team building activities of the past. Because of this increased complexity, the coaching role of the manager becomes a critical factor in the success of teams. The managerial time investment and coaching commitment must increase when new teams are formed. Chapter 7 explores the coaching role and Chapter 3 outlined a discipline for building newly formed teams.

CONCLUSION

Whether you are a manager interested in implementing teams in your department or an executive seeking much broader implementation of teams, the issues you face are the same. Learn all you can about teams and what makes them successful. Conduct an accurate and excruciatingly honest organizational assessment. Consciously make decisions about the level of employee involvement you are seeking. Take the time to conduct a feasibility study before making a decision. Finally, create a leadership structure that will help you attain your goals, specifically in the form of executive support and a team of internal experts who serve as a resource team.

Departmental implementation of teams begins with creating awareness among employees and developing a conversion plan. Actual team formation includes the selection of team members and an internal team leader. Coaching the team and providing adequate resources for the team then become an ongoing function.

PART II

Challenges for Leadership

CHAPTER 5

Health Care Teams: Perils and Pitfalls

Team language has been used widely in health care over the years, but there has been limited experience using teams as the basic structural unit of the organization. Operating suite and emergency department teams, as well as multidisciplinary rehabilitation teams, are examples of entities that most closely meet the definition of teams suggested in Chapter 1. As discussed earlier, at least two major errors are often made when developing health care teams. The first is team design that poorly or inadequately matches the work the team needs to accomplish. The second is lack of a specific discipline to be used for developing the team. A less frequent error occurs when the wrong kind of team is used for the work that must be accomplished. The clearer the understanding of different types of available teams, the more likely the appropriate type will be used and problems with team development prevented.

This chapter explores three different types of health care teams and their characteristics, challenges, and pitfalls: (1) primary work teams, (2) executive or management teams, and (3) ad hoc teams. Common perils and pitfalls unique to each will be illustrated by concrete, real-life examples.

PRIMARY WORK TEAMS

Primary work teams comprise the basic structural unit in a team-based organization. When people refer to self-directed work teams, they usually mean a primary work team. As pointed out in Chapter 1, any team can be self-directed about its work, but in a team-based organization, primary work teams predominate: most of the employees are organized into such teams and they perform nearly all of the organization's basic work. Many organizations define the work of the team broadly enough to include some traditional managerial responsibilities.

Unlike the executive and managerial leadership teams, primary work team members are selected because they possess skills and talents needed to help this team do its work. Team members don't have another primary job—this is their work. These teams differ from ad hoc teams in their permanency, whereas ad hoc teams have a temporary life span. Conversion to a team-based organization doesn't happen simply by reorganizing employees within departments and telling them they are now a team. Forming primary work teams requires application of a data-driven design process and constant coaching and development.

A fundamental subject of this book—primary work teams—has already been defined. To recap, key elements of successful primary work teams include:

- small consistent membership
- a common relevant purpose
- a common working approach
- complementary and overlapping skills
- specific team goals and outcome measures
- mutual accountability

Furthermore, primary work teams evolving into self-directed work teams possess all essential capabilities, responsibilities, and authority required to do a whole piece of work. These same elements describe the essence of executive/managerial and ad hoc teams as well. But those types of teams don't form the basic work structure of the organization as primary work teams do.

Primary work teams in health care face seven potential problems. These commonly experienced perils and pitfalls include:

1. assigning, not designing teams
2. confusion about the team's work
3. lack of real authority and responsibility
4. lack of structural team-building work
5. dysfunctional team behavior
6. lack of team-based outcome measures
7. inadequate or inappropriate coaching

Let's examine each of these.

Assigning, Not Designing, the Teams

Hospitals and health care organizations are replete with examples of the consequences of this pitfall. Teams are now the latest trend, the bandwagon everyone wants to ride. Yet institutions and departments jump on without understanding the true nature of teams as a specifically designed structural unit. Instead, a manager determines arbitrarily to divide and "team" up employees in his or her department. Reasons are formulated that make sense at the time, such as "they work the same weekends," "they are all day-shift employees," or "they all do the same kind of work." One of the worst examples was a department manager who chose employees for a team simply based on their membership in previous quality improvement teams. Employees got the message, "He thinks this is just like the quality process, so he doesn't really understand teams." Along the same lines, but one that makes more sense, is the example of a small department with 10 to 12 employees, which forms a departmental team.

Designing the team involves a conscious process that is fact-based and data-driven. It requires scrutiny of the work to be accomplished, the frequency of this work, and any licensure or skill requirements *before* making decisions about team design. Chapter 2 is devoted to the pivotal issue of initial team design. Just as important is ongoing assessment of the appropriateness of any team design. Does the design work in actual practice? Were the design assumptions correct? Does the team's design need to be modified to work better?

Designing the team also creates an opportunity for selection of appropriate team members. Instead of simply shifting employees into team positions, using a selection process to match employee skills with the team's needed competencies results in a stronger team. If managers have little choice but simply must transfer employees into a team, they can still establish new expectations for performance or skill development along with appropriate consequences if employees don't meet these expectations within a specified time period.

Assigning employees to teams without carefully considered reasons raises a red flag with employees. "Nothing has really changed, we're just calling this a team now." It's "program du jour," the latest management whim, rather than a serious organizational undertaking. Most important, assigned teams rarely work out because there has been no basic redesign of the work. Employees are functioning in the same ways they did as individuals, only now they are called a team.

Extensive specialization and compartmentalization in health care has resulted in multiple handoffs between departments, increased errors, and extensive communication problems (Watson et al. 1991). It is currently a rare team in health care with responsibility for a whole piece of work. Most teams define the whole piece of work very narrowly—for example, as nursing care needed by the patient between the hours of 7:00 A.M. and 3:30 P.M.

Health care teams must be consciously designed to ensure their effectiveness and achieve their potential for self-direction. Organizations undergoing massive restructuring projects find that deploying employees from central departments to patient care unit-based teams is a positive way to bring needed services closer to the patient. Such deployments certainly go beyond the assignment approach of dividing up the department into teams. Compare the decision by an environmental services manager to divide the department's employees into teams to a decision to transfer a portion of these employees to teams in the patient care units. The first merely changes the organization chart, the second changes the organization to meet customer needs. A departmental manager must consider organization-wide restructuring and design plans when redesigning department work so that team design is congruent with the overall change initiative. An example of this occurred in a medical records department, whose manager designed teams, ignoring the organization's move to redeploy certain medical record functions to the patient care departments.

Confusion about the Team's Work

Most primary work teams are clear about their basic work—understanding and providing their technical or professional service to customers is not usually at issue. Confusion often lies, however, in the subtleties. What is the team's level of authority in performing its work? Is managerial approval or input needed before the team can decide upon a course of action? About what issues or situations does the team need to inform the manager? These and similar questions are often not discussed until a problem arises. Then it becomes apparent that the team assumed either a higher or lower level of authority than was intended.

Confusion also reigns over leadership and managerial responsibilities for the team. What is the manager's role and what responsibility does the team accept? When the work of the team is originally defined, does it include team development? Who is responsible for this? What are the roles of the manager and the team in this process? As the manager transfers responsibility for specific managerial functions, such as staffing, interviewing, and financial monitoring, is it clear exactly what the teams' responsibility is?

Many organizations have converted to so-called self-directed work teams and, in the process, are combining and eliminating management positions. Employees are placed into teams and expected to accept greater responsibility for managerial functions. While employees have the capability for this transfer of responsibility, the time required to learn new responsibilities and to fulfill them on a day-to-day basis often isn't built into team designs or expectations. This creates a no-win situation for both employees and the organization. Who is responsible for team performance? For an individual team member's nonperformance? Is it the manager or team? Who is responsible for customer service recovery issues? What are the parameters within which the team can make restitution to an unhappy customer?

Lack of clarity about key aspects of the team's work can lead to confusion, conflict, resentment, frustration, apathy, and/or lowered productivity. Primary work teams and their external leaders continually will need to discuss these issues and resolve differences. Recognizing this potential pitfall is the first step.

Lack of Real Authority and Responsibility

Reorganizing employees into teams that are well designed without granting them the appropriate authority to carry out their responsibilities inhibits employee commitment and emotional engagement. If managers merely pay lip service to the idea of relinquishing control, employees become disenchanted and cynical about teams, and one of the essential benefits of true teams will not be realized. Making this mistake damages the credibility of the entire team effort in the organization.

As discussed in Chapter 3, the nature and assignment of responsibilities must be crystal clear, otherwise there will be gaps, overlaps, confusion, and conflict that impede team development and diminish the quality of service provided. The transferal process means clarifying specifically what is the team's responsibility and what is the manager's. Managers who find it difficult to relinquish control will find this very trying. Managers who continue to make decisions about the technical and professional work of the team, as well as about managerial issues, simply will have failed to empower effective work teams.

A team in a maintenance department ran into precisely this problem. As a department in a 400-bed community hospital, they had recently formed into teams. "Don," a supervisor with 30 years of supervisory experience, mostly as a career military officer, was responsible for coaching three of these newly formed primary work teams. Team members were excited about accepting more responsibility and making final decisions about their work. The teams believed this was a way to get out from under Don's micromanaging approach. During a construction project, one team made a decision about the location of computer monitoring equipment. Their decision was promptly overturned by Don, who wanted the equipment placed elsewhere. The team was furious. Not only was their decision disregarded, but Don's decision ignored several key factors necessary to smooth operations. Talking to Don was unproductive, as was discussing the issue with the team's department manager. To ensure a suitable decision, the team communicated directly with the manager of the department for whom they were doing the work. She insisted the equipment be placed according to the team's original recommendation. Although finally, the team's decision was accepted, it lost all confidence that the supervisor truly intended to transfer any responsibility to the team.

Not only must responsibility be clearly assigned and understood, but appropriate levels of authority must be granted and the existing parameters defined. Many people believe that being empowered means always making the decision and taking action. Empowerment, however, actually occurs when the level of authority is appropriate for the responsibility accepted. If the team is not totally responsible for a function, it doesn't need a high level of authority. At least four levels of authority have been identified (Miller and Manthey 1994), with the first level being the lowest.

Level 1   The authority to gather data or collect information to be shared with the person granting the authority, who then makes the final decision

Level 2   The authority to gather data or information and to make a recommendation to the person making the decision

Level 3   After collecting data or information and making a recommendation, the recommendation is discussed with the person who has decision-making authority. Once agreement is reached, the team acts on the decision.

Level 4   The authority to decide and take action without first communicating or obtaining approval

For some responsibilities, such as carrying out the patient admissions process (by an administrative team) or cleaning a carpet stain (by an environmental service team), the team clearly has Level 4 authority—Team members don't require discussion, permission, or approval. In fact, dependent team members who require continual direction because they are uncomfortable acting independently create problems for effective team functioning and can become a performance issue. As teams gain experience with new responsibilities, higher levels of authority are granted. When a team initially accepts responsibility for interviewing and selecting a new team member, they may have Level 2 authority. As they are successful in subsequent interviewing and selection processes, the level of authority is increased. Ideally, the level of authority should be agreed upon before the team begins work.

Accusations that the manager is not relinquishing control often are the result of confusion about levels of authority. Teams that assume a higher level of authority than they have been given are sometimes referred to as renegade teams.

Discussing and defining existing parameters is another essential key for effective transfer of responsibility. Experienced managers understand the many parameters involved in interviewing and selecting new team members. There must be compliance with human resource policies and fair labor standards. An important managerial responsibility involves identifying and communicating these applicable parameters to team members who assume this responsibility. Sometimes, parameters may involve time frames (respond to patient complaints within the shift in which they occur) or financial limitations (a team can order supplies costing less than $250).

Not establishing the parameters can quickly cause problems. Patient care teams in a general surgical department of an 800-bed medical center were responsible for customer service satisfaction levels, but performance expectations and levels of authority had never been discussed. The manager, whose operating style was laissez-faire, was confronted one day by a physician who demanded a new team. The physician claimed she had tried to work out issues with the team, but found it unresponsive to patient care problems that concerned the physician. After the manager stepped in to resolve the problems, she was appalled at the team's lack of action and misunderstanding of their responsibility. The problems centered around the interface with another department and had continued for more than a year. In analyzing the situation, several mistakes became apparent:

1. The team did not identify all its customers. It saw the patient as the first and only customer. The physician's problem was not viewed as a priority even though it directly affected patients.
2. There was no discussion about measuring customer satisfaction, about what it meant, or how to determine if it was achieved.
3. Team members assumed they lacked the authority to make system changes that the physician requested and basically ignored her requests, believing that nothing could be fixed.
4. The manager took over the process and assumed responsibility for its resolution, rather than helping the team solve its own problem. As a result, the team learned little about resolving the problem, except that they needed the manager to do so.

A similar example involves an implementation team planning the restructuring of a traditional patient care unit. One of the team's decisions concerned the linen requirements for the newly redecorated department. The team selected and purchased bedspreads, draperies, and other linens. The linen services manager then discovered that the fabrics selected by the team could not be laundered with present equipment. Here we have a team being assigned or assuming a level of decision-making authority for an area in which they were not technically knowledgeable. Parameters for cost or for fabric composition had not been shared with the team, nor had it requested them. The team's failure was simply due to an oversight in setting parameters, yet this became a powerful example in this organization of why empowerment of teams "doesn't work."

A subtle difficulty arises when responsibility is transferred to the internal team leader, rather than to the team as a whole. Although this may be appropriate in early stages of team development, over time it can cloud the essence of the internal team leader's role, which is to develop the team and increase the team's ability to handle additional responsibilities. The reward and recognition system in the organization must take into account the true nature of the internal team leader's role. If only the team leader assumes extra responsibility, the organization has simply duplicated its old supervisory hierarchy in the new team structure rather than increasing responsibility acceptance by all team members.

Avoiding this pitfall is simple, but not always easy. The first step is to discuss and establish clear expectations, parameters, and appropriate levels of authority, which will prevent many problems. Second, plan the transfer of responsibility to the team so it occurs gradually as the team becomes ready to assume additional responsibilities as described in Chapter 4.

Lack of Structural Team-Building Work

Primary work teams are often formed and begin working immediately. Seldom are all the structural elements of a team in place before it is expected to begin performing. These elements, such as clarifying purpose, discussing expectations, defining the work, and establishing goals and outcome measures, instead are established as the team conducts its primary work. The urgencies of day-to-day operations, however, require the entire focus of the team; there is seldom any time or energy left to devote to becoming a team.

To compound this problem, early attention to team building prior to team formation usually focuses on the interpersonal aspects of teams. While important, this sequencing is like putting up the walls for a new house before pouring a foundation. Interpersonal team dynamics thrive better when time is taken first to establish these foundational elements. When done early in team formation, establishing expectations and identifying team roles can markedly reduce the number of interpersonal conflicts in these areas.

Team researchers Katzenbach and Smith (1993) observed the same tendency to focus initially, and sometimes exclusively, on the interpersonal relationship side of building teams. They note that when a team is not doing well, the response usually is to recruit a charismatic speaker to do team building—not a bad idea, but it doesn't treat the real problem. Refocusing the team on its purpose, setting clear expectations, and challenging its performance is usually far more effective. Other students of teams agree. Larson and LaFasto (1989) discovered that whenever they identified a poorly functioning team, the team's ineffectiveness involved the team's purpose—it had become unfocused or politicized, had lost a sense of urgency or significance, or had become diluted by too many other competing goals. Establishing clarity of purpose is part of the structural work of becoming a team. To achieve this, carve out time for teams to work on becoming a team. Provide experienced facilitators who understand this many-faceted process. If a team is floundering, assess the status of its structural elements before assuming the problems are interpersonal.

Dysfunctional Team Behavior

Dysfunctional interpersonal relationships have become such a hallmark of health care organizations that employees may believe these dysfunctional behaviors are normal. Indirect communication, passive-aggressive behavior, blaming others for mistakes, swallowing hurt feelings rather than addressing co-workers' behaviors, caretaking rather than caregiving behaviors, and not accepting responsibility for one's own feelings are just a few examples of commonly observed dysfunctions. A first step in changing these behaviors is to state clearly the team's responsibility for maintaining healthy relationships with their co-workers, both within and outside the team. Don't assume team members know what healthy relationships are.

Teams first need to know what is meant by healthy interpersonal behavior. Then they need both the opportunity and the expectation to develop needed skills such as addressing conflict, giving honest and direct feedback, negotiating win–win solutions to differences, and actively listening to another party's point of view. Expectations must be articulated and negotiated. It is unacceptable for team members to not address a teammate's potentially destructive interpersonal behaviors. Early in their acceptance of this responsibility, the manager or a resource person may need to coach participants. If left unaddressed, interpersonal conflicts can become severe enough to destroy the team. The good news is that when employees know they will be teamed together indefinitely, they are more likely to work out problems. The level of commitment to problem solving resembles that found in a marriage rather than in a sporadic dating relationship.

Lack of Team-Based Outcome Measures

This is a serious pitfall. A team cannot hold itself accountable if it has not established outcome measures. How will it know whether it is accomplishing its intended purpose? How will it measure its success? Its progress? How will the team know when to celebrate its successes? There are really two issues in question. First, the team must establish outcome measures based on its work. What is to be accomplished, to what standards, and within what time frame? Measures must address not only the technical or primary work of the team, but also its progress in becoming a team. Teams often will focus on the first and not the second.

A second issue involves obtaining data measures on a team, not a departmental, basis. Most outcome measures available in traditional organizations—patient satisfaction scores, financial performance data, quality improvement outcomes—tend to be departmental rather than team-based. This makes it difficult for the team to measure itself. This topic is addressed more fully in Chapter 12. Holding the team accountable for outcome measures is possible only if it has continuity of customers. This issue has been addressed before but is critical enough to reemphasize. Consider a patient care team. How can you hold a team accountable for specific patient outcomes, such as reported satisfaction levels or lengths of stay, if the team shares this responsibility with all other employees in the department who only occasionally may have been assigned to the same patients?

Inadequate or Inappropriate Coaching

This peril related to team leadership will be discussed further in Chapter 7. It is mentioned here because it is a pitfall that can prevent the team from realizing its true potential. Rarely will teams develop in spite of or in isolation from the manager. Most newly formed primary work teams depend heavily on the manager for direction, suggestions, feedback, and monitoring. Serious difficulties arise when the manager is unable or unwilling to modify his or her usual coaching style to match the needs of the team in its present developmental stage. For example, the manager may "let go" prematurely, believing the team can make its own decisions without direction. This leaves an immature team feeling stranded. Or, the manager may continue providing structure and supervision far beyond the team's need for it, thereby irritating and annoying team members and stunting the team's growth.

Managers who meet with their teams and talk through their coaching role are usually more effective coaches. New primary work teams will sometimes have an inflated sense of their abilities. "We're self-directed, so just get out of our way!" Managers of such teams need to clarify their roles and give examples of areas in which direction or specific parameters would be helpful. For some responsibilities the team may be very self-directed, but in other areas, where it is accepting a responsibility for the first time, it needs direction and structure. The most effective coaches will work in partnership with their teams throughout the learning continuum.

This pitfall is a serious problem for teams and one that requires a high level of leadership skill to avoid. Managers will often need added coaching skill development to coach teams successfully. Assessment and diagnostic skills are needed in addition to versatility in coaching styles. These seven common pitfalls are serious and can undermine team development. They can be avoided if understood. Let's review two case studies illustrating some of these issues.

Case Study: "The Self-Directed Work Team That Wasn't"

This group of employees worked in the communications department of a large, urban, tertiary medical center. They became a team when their manager, Valerie, resigned. The organization was planning considerable managerial downsizing and found this to be a good opportunity to conduct a trial with a self-directed work team. One day, without its prior knowledge, input, or readiness, the group became a "team." It was determined that all 15 members of the department would be on the team regardless of part-time, full-time, or on-call status. Team members were simply informed they would take over the management responsibilities that Valerie previously carried out.

Their "coach" was Bob, the vice-president to whom Valerie had reported, and an individual who, in the current restructuring endeavor, would assume responsibility for an additional five departments. Bob had worked his way through the hospital ranks, previously holding the position of director of environmental services. A no-nonsense, "do what you need to, but get it done" kind of person, Bob was feeling overwhelmed by his increased responsibilities but was confident he could handle this transition. He was feeling added pressure because he was responsible for the only pilot self-directed work team in the organization.

Bob met with the group and told them that they were now officially a self-directed work team and as such they were responsible for all elements of Valerie's job. He encouraged them to buckle down and pull together, exhorting them to handle this like a team. When they asked how they would learn all these new skills, Bob assured them he would help. When they asked how they would find the time to do these things, he responded that they would just need to be more efficient, and "work smarter, not harder." To give this group of employees credit, they did work together to decide how to divide up Valerie's work, or at least the elements of her work that they understood.

Periodically during the next several months, Bob met with the group to share information, answer questions, and monitor their progress. The department's work was being completed but recently Bob had been contacted by other managers who were experiencing problems getting this group to respond to special requests or to solve existing problems. The group was making many decisions about its work, they just weren't always good decisions. In some cases, members of the group had simply declined to respond to a request. The team had no established expected outcomes, nor had there been any discussion of parameters, levels of authority, or a definition of the team's work.

The group reached a crisis point when time came to appraise the performance of a particularly difficult group member, Jane. Jane was the center of most interpersonal difficulties in the group. She arrived late at least twice a week, creating significant problems for the departing shift. Her absenteeism rate was higher than that of the rest of the team combined and part-time employees were repeatedly required to change their plans at the last minute to cover for her. Other group members frequently did Jane's work to keep her out of trouble. Her poor performance had never been addressed and now it was the team's responsibility to appraise her performance. Some group members thought Jane should be terminated, while others disagreed or were afraid to discuss the issue. When Bob was asked to step in and assist, he was in the midst of a crisis in another department, and responded by offering general guidelines and assurances that they could handle this.

It was handled all right! The appraisal was watered down but still critical. Jane felt the others were ganging up on her and from that point relationships in the department deteriorated badly. Bickering and complaining reached new depths, occurring in front of employees from other departments. Work performance slipped markedly with complaints coming from both inside the hospital and from customers trying to access the switchboard. Within a six-week period, 8 of the 15 employees resigned. Self-directed work teams were deemed ineffective and the organization decided not to use them.

This team actually hit all of the potential major pitfalls, dooming its viability. Neither its coach nor the leadership in the organization understood the nature of teams, nor did they attempt to learn. The reason for this "team" conversion was to eliminate a management position and turn over important responsibilities to a group of employees. In this case, the employees were ill-equipped to handle them. At a time when they needed to learn new skills and ways of working together, they were offered less managerial coaching than at any time in their previous history. All due to the mistaken assumption that an unmanaged team is a self-directed work team.

Case Study: "The Star Team"

A patient care team is the focus of this second case study. Often difficult to form because of the critical design issues, this team is a prime example of a highly functioning self-directed work team in a hospital. Formed during a restructuring project in the organization, this team was carefully and thoughtfully designed. Part of the initial design work included reaggregation of patients and specific team designs to meet the needs of these unique surgical patients.

Members of the team were selected based on skills, competencies, and personal attributes and included employees interested in serving on the team. Two team members—an RN and a respiratory therapist—worked the day shift, two—an RN and LPN—worked evenings, and one—an RN—worked nights. On the weekend, there were two caregivers on the 12-hour day shift (an RN and a patient care technician) and one RN worked on the night shift. Their skills represented the many competencies required for providing patient care and all team members were cross-trained and multiskilled. Work in the department was redesigned and professionals from other disciplines were redeployed to this patient care unit. A unit-based pharmacist, medical technologist, registered dietitian, social worker, and radiology technician worked closely with the patient care team.

A remarkable attribute of this team was the consistency of its membership. In the first three years of its existence, only one team member left to relocate to another city with her spouse and family. Otherwise the original team remained intact. Consistency was also a key factor with members of the ancillary disciplines and the medical staff. Working closely with the same unit-based professionals on a day-to-day basis resulted in better communication patterns, more sharing of knowledge, and a feeling of camaraderie that had not existed previously. The team provided care for the patients of only two physicians, which gave it the ability to collaborate more fully with physicians than ever before.

During the first year of team formation, many responsibilities and functions were assumed by the internal team leader rather than by the team. Team members were busy learning their new clinical skills and becoming comfortable working as a team. Gradually, however, the team accepted and integrated managerial and leadership responsibilities within the team. The team reviewed all work needing to be done, determined how to share it, who would accept various team roles, and clarified its expectations of fellow team members who accepted these responsibilities. Within the first two years of its existence, the team accepted full responsibility for interviewing and selecting new team members, staffing and scheduling, continued professional development and continuing education needs, and intra- and interteam interpersonal work relationships. It had specific goals and identified outcome measures which it celebrated when they were achieved. The team asked its manager for assistance whenever it was needed.

Becoming a team wasn't easy; there were difficulties to overcome. But this team matured as it navigated rough waters and conquered these difficulties. The results were impressive. Patient and physician satisfaction rates skyrocketed. Responding to a survey question "What can we improve?," one patient wrote that she had to use her call light once! These team members were in the rooms with their patients or immediately adjacent to their patients almost 100 percent of the time. Critical patient incidents such as hemorrhage and cardiac or respiratory arrests were almost nonexistent because caregivers responded to changes in patient conditions in their earliest stages. Fewer missed communications occurred because caregivers on the day shift reported to the same caregivers on the evening shift every day. Problems with multiskilling were minimal because of the consistency. Team members helped teach each other. Their long-term assignments resulted in extraordinary commitment to one another and knowledge of each other's skills, talents, and limitations.

The team reached a crisis point about 18 months into its existence when Sally, one of the night-shift caregivers, shared her plans to resign. She and her husband were having marital difficulties because she worked the night shift and they mutually decided Sally needed to find another job for the sake of their marriage. The team was initially devastated at the possibility of losing a team member. It quickly mobilized and generated several possible solutions. The team discussed options with Sally such as other team members rotating turns on the night shift so Sally could work days rather than leave the team. Any manager who has ever experienced the resignation of a key night-shift caregiver knows how remarkable this response is! Sally stayed on, now working days. This continued for the next year and was working well when Sally's husband accepted a job offer in another state. Sally left the team, but both she and her team had experienced the synergy, extraordinary level of commitment, and support that results from a true team.

During the process of interviewing for Sally's replacement, the team again demonstrated its strength. One of the candidates, Dave, was exceptionally strong in terms of clinical skills, but several of his references indicated he also had a "strong" personality, a euphemism for being personally difficult. The team talked openly with Dave about this issue and they mutually agreed to certain expectations. The team decided to take a chance on him because it needed a clinically strong individual on the night shift. Although there were some tough times, Dave, with his personality quirks and sometimes difficult behavior, was ultimately integrated into the team. Again, this is remarkable when you consider the traditional scenario that results when a manager makes a decision like this for the work group. Because this was a team decision, the entire team was committed to helping Dave make it.

Effective primary work teams in health care provide unparalleled possibilities. Creativity in quality improvement processes abounds, higher responsibility acceptance on the part of employees is evident, and satisfaction levels of employees are greater. But these teams can be disastrous if you don't anticipate and prevent the most common pitfalls, or, at least recognize when a team has fallen into one! Let's next explore the second type of team common in health care—executive and managerial teams.

EXECUTIVE/MANAGEMENT TEAMS

Consider Hospital Trendy (name is changed to protect the not-so-innocent!). Ralph, the CEO, returned from a nationally sponsored meeting for health care executives where he attended several sessions on teams in health care. Excited about the possibilities teams could bring to his beleaguered organization, he added the topic to the next department head meeting. At the meeting, he exhorted department managers to begin thinking "team" and to start looking for opportunities to create teams. He shared examples highlighted at his conference and implored managers to duplicate these efforts and results. Commitment from the organization was strong, he said, and extensive resources would be available to ensure appropriate team design and education of employees. With exception of a few naysayers, who seemed to be negative about everything, people left the meeting excited and optimistic about implementing teams.

During the coming months, Ralph kept his word. An external organization experienced in designing health care teams was engaged, as well as consultants who specialized in team education and cultural change. A small cadre of employees with special interest in working with teams was identified and began developing their knowledge and skill base as internal consultants. A team curriculum was established, and after the teams were designed, all employee teams began their education. Enthusiasm built and preliminary results were positive.

Forward movement came to a halt about six months into the effort. Teams floundered and managers, despite their earlier enthusiasm, were reluctant to relinquish responsibility for important elements of their managerial work. Some managers openly questioned, "If I give the team my work, what will I do?" Managers and executive leadership increasingly expressed the attitude "You're a team, just go do it." Managers and executives were hampered by their lack of knowledge about the struggles of becoming a team because they had not been through the process themselves.

It was also becoming apparent to employees who were working hard at becoming teams that the managers and executives with whom they worked were not functioning as teams. Repeated handoffs, passing the buck, miscommunication, and bad feelings were growing among departments and divisions. Employees were heard to remark, "They aren't a team, why should we work so hard to become one?"

The diagnosis was clear: Effective team behaviors were not being modeled from the top. Worse, managers and executives underestimated the struggles involved in developing into a high-performing team. Both problems could have been prevented by forming teams at the top, prior to initiating the organizational effort.

Ralph and his colleagues learned the hard way that executive and management teams are crucial in an organization converting to a team-based structure. If senior management and executives cannot function as a team, the credibility of the entire effort is at risk. When organizational leaders are not expected to function in real teams, the message conveyed to employees is that "we're not really serious about this." The best preparation a manager can have for leading and coaching teams is to have experienced the developmental process and challenges first-hand.

The primary purpose of executive and management teams is to provide management and leadership at some level in the organization. They are usually a relatively permanent or stable structure, unlike ad hoc teams that disband when their purpose is accomplished. The exception is ad hoc leadership teams that form to provide leadership for a particular effort, such as organizing and implementing a special fund drive in the organization, leading the construction of a new facility, developing a new service, or merging two organizations. Ad hoc leadership teams are temporary in nature.

Members of executive leadership or management teams often have other primary work in the organization and may be members of many teams. At the executive level, vice-presidents or executive leaders serve on the executive team. They may also serve as the "external team leaders" for a leadership team composed of the department or service line managers who report directly to them, as depicted in Figure 5–1. They are also likely to serve on various ad hoc teams in the organization. The department manager is a member of the divisional leadership team and is also the external team leader for the department teams. Along with internal team leaders, this leader serves on the leadership team for the department. Each of these leaders, from the executive to the employee, has other primary job responsibilities. The executive leader or vice-president is responsible for managing the division, the depart-

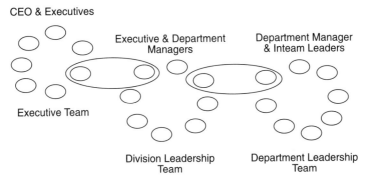

CEO & Executives

Executive & Department Managers

Department Manager & Inteam Leaders

Executive Team

Division Leadership Team

Department Leadership Team

Figure 5–1 Leadership Teams

ment manager is responsible for the department, and the internal team leader functions as a full-fledged team member, doing the work of the team.

Holding membership on multiple leadership teams is not necessarily a problem because it is unlikely that functioning as a team member requires a high percentage of an individual's time. This is similar to ad hoc teams, but very unlike primary work teams, whose members spend more of their time functioning as a team. The amount of time spent in collective teamwork depends on the nature and purpose of the team (see Figure 5–2). Juggling multiple team memberships requires clarity of purpose and a tight focus on each specific team's work.

Perils and pitfalls confronted by executive and management leadership teams are numerous. When difficulties are encountered, finding a high-performing executive or leadership team to use as a learning example is often next to impossible (Hart 1995). Special problems faced by these teams include:

1. inadequate design work
2. confusion over purpose
3. lack of clarity in defining the work
4. historical preference for individualistic approaches
5. inadequate developmental time
6. persistence of hierarchy

Let's examine each of these in detail.

Inadequate Design Work

Few leadership teams are designed or their members selected strictly because this combination represents the best team for the work to be accomplished. Instead, managers and executives are usually selected for their abili-

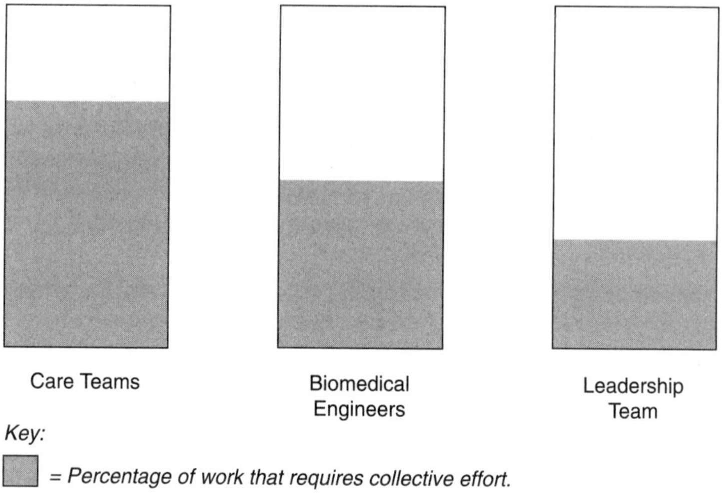
Care Teams
Biomedical Engineers
Leadership Team
Key:
= Percentage of work that requires collective effort.

Figure 5–2 Time Spent in Collective Work. Teams will meet to do work related to their common purpose, which may consume differing percentages of their time.

---

ties to manage or lead a particular department or function in the system. Superficial consideration may be given to whether these personalities will blend and work well together, but concrete analysis of the team's work seldom focuses on establishing criteria for team member selection.

Managers or executives in specific positions may be included on the team whether or not the team needs them to complete its defined work and regardless of the team's commitment to work together. If executive teams are formed, usually all vice-presidents are considered members, whether or not there is a reason for them to be a member. This is also true at the management level. Directors of departments with no team members reporting to them may not need to belong to the division leadership team, yet they normally are included. Executives and managers with no clear contribution to the team's work may not be constructive additions to the team. Katzenbach and Smith (1993) note the assumption that individuals must not be excluded is invalid. Each member of the team must contribute directly and concretely to the team's work. Executives or managers not included can still be valued and can contribute in other ways, however, this needs to be designed carefully and well supported by their managers.

Confusion over Purpose

Leadership teams often confuse the overall purpose and mission of the organization with their mission as a team, missing an opportunity to define clearly their reasons for existence *as a team*. Although ultimately a team's purpose must be congruent with the organization's mission, the two are not synonymous. Clarity of purpose affects day-to-day decisions and behavior. One divisional leadership team defined its purpose in the following way:

> To provide consistent leadership for employees and teams within the service line through coaching and mentoring of employees, by continually challenging the status quo and seeking quality improvement, and by creating an environment where blaming is nonexistent, mistake making constructive, and risk-taking encouraged.

Members of this leadership team changed their approaches and behaviors remarkably after clearly defining their purpose. Previously, if external customers complained or were unhappy with service, the manager was expected to get involved and solve the problem. If problems reached the CEO, the immediate response was to call the manager of the department for action. With this new definition of purpose, managers began coaching employees and teams on solving customer service problems, before they reached the manager. When managers were notified about a problem, they contacted the employee team involved and coached that team in resolving the issue. Within several months, managers were hearing fewer complaints because employees were solving problems and issues as they occurred. Because the teams felt more ownership and responsibility, they were taking corrective action to prevent reoccurrence of many problems.

Lack of Clarity in Defining the Work

What is the actual work of the team? How does it spend its time? Is its focus on issues such as day-to-day operation or on strategic leadership? Hart (1995, 15) expresses the following view on this pitfall of management teams:

> By their own admission, leadership teams often work on the wrong things. They find themselves driven by urgency, not importance of issues. They spend too much time on managerial issues and not enough on leadership. They plan and budget, deal with staffing, and solve problems. But they rarely create views of the future, articulate strategy, chart ways to align and mobilize people, or build a framework that will keep them on the path to the future. In short, they put out fires but seldom light any.

Work of individual team members and the work of the team must be clearly differentiated. Which decisions are made by individuals and which are reserved for the team? When is an individual member expected to inform the team of a decision? Confusion sometimes results from the perceived overlap of responsibilities. As an example, effective leaders have a vision for their area of responsibility that creates excitement and commitment among followers. As a leadership team member, part of the team's work may be to develop a challenging vision for the entire division or the organization. Thus, both the team and each individual member may be involved in parallel visioning activities, but it is the scopes of these visions that differ. The individual leader may be developing a collective team vision yet must also have an individual vision.

According to the purpose statement of the leadership team cited earlier, "providing consistent leadership" for the division is a reason for its existence. Ramifications of this statement for day-to-day decision making and leadership behavior abound. Members of this team agreed that developing employees to accept higher levels of responsibility would be a major goal for the following year. From the interactions between employees in two different departments it became obvious that one manager was relinquishing control and granting higher levels of authority based on employee capability while another manager in that same division still expected employees to consult with her on any decisions involving another department. This second manager had no intention of changing a very controlling and directing style. This behavior did not fit the team's mission and was addressed by her teammates, a situation that forced the team to recommit to its original purpose. Her behavior impaired the team's success and was no longer acceptable. Team members coached their colleague to modify her approach.

Historical Preference for Individualistic Approaches

Often those in executive and management positions are self-confident people recognized for their ability to accomplish results. Although everyone understands that one doesn't accomplish results alone, in the past most leaders have been rewarded as individuals for their accomplishments. The employees with whom they worked to attain the results were neither promoted nor rewarded as a team. Leaders have experienced years of reinforcement for such individualistic performance.

Their first real experience of shared accountability with a team can be anxiety-producing—if one team member fails, the entire team fails. If the vice-president of human resources implements an unsuccessful program, the entire executive team has failed. If the controlling manager in the earlier example fails to develop her employees and they remain dependent on her for decisions, the entire divisional leadership team has failed. Many of us, whether at the leadership or employee level, don't feel entirely comfortable relying on others for the quality and success of our performance.

On the other hand, truly sharing responsibility as a team can be liberating and a powerful experience. An executive team whose organization underwent restructuring decided to share responsibilities differently. In the new structure, each executive's responsibility included patient care departments. The nurse executive, months later said, "This is the first time I felt the responsibility for patient care was not mine alone. A tremendous burden has been lifted from my shoulders." (Voluntary Hospitals of America 1994) The executive team actually shared responsibility and accountability for patient care in a very concrete way.

Finding a common approach to the team's work is the essential element in avoiding this pitfall. If a team member has a unique way of approaching problems, he or she may be unwilling to agree to the team's problem-solving methods. Yet if the team requires a common approach to be effective, and all team members consent, significant performance variations will have to be addressed.

Inadequate Developmental Time

Inadequate developmental time is often a more severe problem at the executive and leadership levels. Virtually any team has difficulty finding time to develop itself as a team. Extracting time from the day-to-day work of the group in order to focus on "becoming" a team seems almost impossible at times. Unfortunately, the higher the team is in the organizational hierarchy, the stronger the belief that this work isn't really needed. "We all know all this stuff, right?" Beckhard and Pritchard (1992) say it best: "A paradox of today's world is the increasing need for leadership to become involved with creating an organization that is actively moving toward its potential, while at the same time solving today's crisis or emergency." Although referring to general organizational leadership issues, this concept applies to individual teams as well. Too often, the daily urgencies eat up the time required for becoming a team; the team focuses on operational rather than leadership work. For executive and managerial teams, applying a specific discipline to becoming a team may seem too simplistic, something they can do later. But, the high visibility of leadership teams is the critical reason for these teams to commit the time needed to become an effective team before asking their organizations to follow. Committing the time not only ensures more effective team functioning but clearly communicates a respect for the process to the rest of the organization.

Based on their research, Katzenbach and Smith (1993) conclude that no potential team will become highly performing unless it does this initial work. This means taking the time to work through the developmental stages of becoming a team. It means addressing nonperformance and dealing with conflicts within the team. It also means respecting the process and not hurrying it along.

The Persistence of Hierarchy

Hierarchy and teams can work well together. Katzenbach and Smith (1993) note that teams are an organizational structure that supports the organization's hierarchy by developing a common sense of purpose among many diverse employees. Hierarchy within a team, however, can possibly destroy the team, or at the very least, reduce team effectiveness.

Hierarchy within a team may be as subtle as a team member with higher positional authority who always sits at the head of the table, or team members who call each other by first names but defer to the chief executive by full title, i.e., Dr. Jones or Ms. Smith. The danger of hierarchy within a team is the corrosive effect of these practices. Hierarchy results in deference being given to a single team member's opinion, and reluctance of team members to disagree or to state an unpopular viewpoint because they know it differs from that of the team member with higher positional status. Lost creativity and inferior decisions are prices of these behaviors.

Executive and management leadership teams are more likely victims of hierarchy than most ad hoc or primary work teams. The problem lies with traditional management behavior rather than any individual team member. In other words, it is not so much due to the person with the positional authority but because other team members defer to him or her. In comparison, when hierarchy is a problem within an ad hoc team, it more likely comes from an individual team member who may expect to be the leader and is given deference because of organizational position.

Perhaps as traditional members of the organization's hierarchy, executive or managerial team members have learned to respect or value positional authority. They may think their teammate with more authority expects deference because of position. On one executive leadership team the CEO suggested that the role of internal leader rotate among team members. The CEO didn't believe she needed to be the team's external as well as internal leader. Some team members were very uncomfortable when they served as the internal team leader in the CEO's presence. In comparison, some executive teams wouldn't have even considered someone other than the CEO being the team leader.

Few executive or management leadership teams will find it easy to realize the true benefits of team. It takes hard work and commitment to spend time becoming something that is unfamiliar. If they simply meet to read each others' reports rather than review recommendations and make team decisions, they will not realize their potential as a team. Asking difficult questions to address and resolve conflict is essential for the group to function as a team. Besides creating chaos at the top, "Managers who can't get along paralyze the lower ranks of hospitals and health systems, where ideas from the top are supposed to be put into play, where real change must happen" (Lumsdon 1995, 25).

Let's look at two actual examples of executive and management leadership teams and see which pitfalls they encountered.

Case Study: "An Executive Team in the Making"

An executive leadership team was formed at a hospital after a major restructuring of the hospital management. Self-directed work teams were implemented in all departments and work redesign efforts in patient care areas had begun. The CEO, an inspiring individual, came up through the ranks in the organization. Members of the executive leadership team included a chief operating officer (COO), five vice-presidents who had composed the previous executive team, and an additional four vice-presidents who were newly appointed executives. All had been promoted to their executive positions from within the system.

The team enjoyed the advantage of having some baseline knowledge about teams and team-based organizations. The hospital's previous experience with employee teams gave these executives an advantage other executive teams often lack. This knowledge proved a disadvantage as well because team members confused their intellectual knowledge about teams with actually functioning as a team. When members realized that calling themselves a team did not determine their ability to function as one, they committed to performing as a true team.

The discipline of building a team as presented in Chapter 3 worked well for them. They met on a quarterly basis, devoting a full day every three months to their work as a team. Over a three-year period they became a true executive team. Visioning, strategic planning, agreement on operational strategies, and financial planning for the organization are examples of work they now do as a team. Currently they are undertaking the expansion of their health system to include all elements of an integrated health network.

Two major issues this team faced and resolved included deference to hierarchy and dealing with nonperformance of a team member. The CEO is highly respected by all team members but is personally intimidating to others who have less self-confidence. Her decisive approach to issues and well-formed opinions often caused the team to acquiesce prematurely to her viewpoints. This behavior gradually decreased over time as a result of clear expectations about dialogue and consensus from the CEO and of continual evaluations of team outcomes. As the new executives gained more confidence in their roles, they began participating fully and functioning as true team members. In addition, the CEO declined the role of inteam leader, thus paving the way for other team members to assume and share leadership responsibilities.

Dealing with inadequate performance of a team member was an issue that threatened the viability of this leadership team. In this case, the executive, Tom, was a long-term employee whose position was key to the success of teams in the organization. Not only was he making poor decisions and performing poorly, but he was actively sabotaging fellow team members and their implementation effort. This behavior was apparent to several team members when their team was established. They first addressed the behavior with Tom, who, in response, increased his sabotage of those team members, creating a very uncomfortable situation. With further occurrences, the team members being sabotaged discussed the situation with the COO to whom Tom reported. To support Tom, the COO coached him and worked hard to help him become successful.

Over an 18-month period that saw little improvement in the situation, team members began questioning the COO's credibility. Other employees in the organization noticed Tom's problematic performance. Managers were heard to say, "If they (the executive team) can't handle their performance problems, why should I worry about the ones in my area?" The executive team was rapidly losing credibility throughout the organization and among its own membership.

The cost of nonperformance was becoming astronomically high: the potential destruction of the team. In this organization, which was implementing teams housewide, the success of the executive team was critical. If the executive team had failed, the rest of the initiative would have been fatally crippled. Years of effort to gain improved levels of trust between employees and executives would have been lost. In this case, it was not the team that directly removed Tom, but his direct supervisor. This action was appropriate for the stage of development of this team. Over time, the issue has been viewed less as a problem with the executive's team performance and more his individual poor performance.

Case Study: "A Managerial Team on the Rocks"

This brief case is a dramatic example of what not to do. It happened in an organization where the vice-president for patient care services resigned. Her effectiveness as a chief nurse executive was hampered by her strong need for control and a tendency to micromanage the department, behavior which had caused many problems over the years. With her resignation, the CEO converted the group of nurse managers into a "self-directed work team" that would manage the division of patient care services and also function as chief nurse executive for the organization. He pulled the group of managers together, shared his idea, offered support, and told them that they were now a team. The group proceeded to encounter painfully most of the above-mentioned pitfalls.

The main problem with this nurse managers' team is that it had no design whatsoever. Those in nurse manager positions were automatically on the team. The skills and competencies represented by members were woefully inadequate for the team, through no fault of their own. Several of the managers were experienced, but under the previous vice-president's regime, their nurse manager roles were more like clinical shift supervisors than managers in a broader context. So, although clinically experienced, these employees did not have the skills and competencies necessary for a nurse executive position. By their own admission, at the time of this conversion, these managers also depended on the vice-president for virtually all decisions and direction.

The team was relatively clear about its purpose, which members described as "managing the nursing department" and "functioning as the chief nurse executive." All group members articulated this purpose, and in fact, thought it was a relevant and important function for the organization. This pitfall, however, displayed itself in subtle ways. First, these well-meaning professionals were clueless about the differences between managing and leading. To have their purpose identified as managing the nursing department significantly limited their scope. They simply proceeded to perform the previous nurse executive's job in much the same way she had done it. When asked about their plans for developing their employees to assume further responsibility, they drew a blank. They envisioned nothing beyond day-to-day management requirements.

The second stated purpose was to "function as the nurse executive" for the organization. This sounded clear, but the group as well as the entire organization had little concept of what this role should be. Their recent role model had left because of her ineffectiveness and lack of vision in carrying out this role. The group conducted a team meeting and listed the responsibilities of the nurse executive, as it viewed the role, but failed to consult with nurse executives in other hospitals or with the American Organization of Nurse Executives, which might have helped the group clarify this role.

The rest of the organization was also very unclear about this group's purpose. The CEO purposely elected not to inform other department managers about the formation of this team because he wanted to "let it grow some first." Other executives were informed, but, when asked, expressed confusion about the team's real purpose. This cloak of secrecy alone made it almost impossible for the team to be effective. Although the "team" was collectively functioning as a nurse executive, it continually had to renegotiate its relationships with every manager in the hospital every time an issue or conflict arose.

Taking a group of first-line managers and calling them the nurse executive for the organization proved very difficult. The "team" and its external team leader, the CEO, did discuss decisions it could make and its level of authority. In fact, the high-level sponsorship of the CEO and his commitment to the team was one of the few factors in its favor. The group was continually challenged as it faced resistance from virtually every area in the organization. Typical committee assignments were closed to them because they were not executives but first-line managers. A year into this process, the team leader was finally invited to medical staff meetings and began attending executive staff meetings on a regular basis. Yet, as identified earlier, no one in the organization was clear about the work of the nurse executive.

Surprisingly, this team did relatively well at the outset. The hospital was anticipating an accreditation visit by the Joint Commission on Accreditation of Healthcare Organizations six months after the team was developed. Within the group, each individual was clear about the need to ready their department for the visit. They believed that if the hospital failed because of the nursing department, it would be their individual and collective failure; thus they worked hard to make the visit a success. Once this hurdle was passed, however, the group began to disintegrate and exhibit signs of dysfunction. No wonder! The challenge of preparing for the Joint Commission had pulled them together and required significant performance from each member. Once this challenge was met, the lack of structural development toward becoming a team became apparent.

An external trainer with team experience in other industries was hired to assist the group with some of the early team development steps. There was no one internally available to help them become a team, however, and no good model of team in the environment. Long-term consistent coaching was unavailable because of the perceived cost in time and money and an underestimation of the work it takes to become a team.

The group was demoralized and felt like a failure. The CEO felt pressure because his colleagues in hospitals around the state were closely watching his "experiment." Most important, the department itself experienced a slow decline in quality of service.

AD HOC TEAMS

The third type of health care teams are ad hoc teams. These are temporary teams that are formed to meet a specific purpose. When the work is finished, the team disbands. These temporary teams may exist for years, but they are not permanent organizational structures. Waterman (1990) suggests that "adhocracy" itself will become an organizational structure in the future.

Adhocracy is broadly defined as any organizational form that challenges the bureaucracy in order to embrace the new. Bennis (Waterman 1990, 18), in the mid-1960s, similarly argued the need for "adaptive, problem-solving, temporary systems of diverse specialists linked together . . . in an organic flux." Both of these respected authors agree that an organization's ability to use ad hoc teams effectively will be largely responsible for its success in the fast-changing environments we are beginning to experience.

Ad hoc teams differ from executive and managerial teams in several ways. First, they are usually designed and their membership selected based on work at hand. Second, the purpose is usually defined for the team, rather than by the team. Finally, they disband when the work is completed, unlike executive/managerial or primary work teams, whose work assignment rarely ends because it is never finished.

Health care organizations offer many examples of ad hoc teams, such as quality or problem-solving teams, project or development teams, or integration and implementation teams found in work redesign initiatives. Ad hoc leadership teams may enjoy a short-term existence to lead an acquisition or expansion effort, to develop a new service, or to guide a merger. This ability to form effective ad hoc teams improves the viability of any system.

These teams face several unique perils and pitfalls including:

1. quick start-up
2. membership issues
3. assigned purpose
4. the handoff
5. inadequate resources
6. lack of outcome measures
7. disbanding the team

Let's explore each of these.

Quick Start-Up

This peril directly relates to the temporary nature of these teams. An ad hoc team, depending on the scope of its work and purpose, often has to "hit the ground running." Teams pulled together to manage an organizational crisis or teams under tight deadlines must be able to function effectively almost immediately. Team members must have all the necessary skills to gel instantly as a team. A solid understanding of the discipline for developing teams and experience with being a team member are essential.

For example, a planning team was assembled to develop the educational plan for an organization undergoing major restructuring and work redesign.

This plan was needed quickly to integrate with the organization's imminent budgeting process. Precious time was lost in the beginning because the team's purpose was not clearly identified, roles of various team members were not clarified, and expectations of team members were not discussed. At the second meeting, it was obvious the team needed to accomplish this foundation work before it could proceed. Two weeks of a five-week schedule had been lost, unnecessarily loading team members with extra stress.

Membership Issues

In determining membership for an ad hoc team, it is crucial to consider the work to be accomplished. What skills and competencies must be represented? Most ad hoc teams are formed for a specific, urgent or important reason. Some organizations assign people with time on their hands to serve on these teams rather than find the most qualified candidates. One hospital began its three-year restructuring effort with a project design team composed of managers and employees who were going to lose their jobs in the restructuring. Starting a major initiative such as this with your "B" team players is no way to win the championship!

Key membership considerations identified by Waterman (1990) include:

- make membership an honor
- team size is important
- team composition is important
- full-time membership
- team leader is not the expert
- recruit people with process skills

Make Membership an Honor

It will be easier to attract star performers if team membership is an honor. If membership is seen as a penalty or as a temporary placement because your job is being eliminated, the team will not be able to function in a successful manner. Its recommendations will be more readily accepted if the team is credible and respected.

This suggestion can backfire. If the project is unpopular in the organization, yet members of the ad hoc team believe it is an honor to serve, friction can erupt between the team and the rest of the organization. Any hints of arrogance on the part of the ad hoc team can result in damaged relationships in the organization. This happened to a restructuring project team in one hospital. Employees in departments to be restructured were not thrilled with the idea and the pride of project team members (interpreted by others as arrogance) resulted in friction and outright conflict.

Team Size Is Important

Team size was discussed in Chapter 1 and it is important for any ad hoc team. Members are drawn from key constituencies affected by the change. The team must be large enough so no key stakeholder group is neglected, yet small enough that it can do its work efficiently.

One project team in an organization converting to teams included 18 people at its zenith. It was difficult for this team to agree on anything. Simple logistics hampered the team in accomplishing its work. As members were absorbed back into the organization, the team reduced its size to about 12 people and regained its effectiveness.

Team Composition Is Important

The general rule is to match the team to the issue at hand. Select team members who collectively reflect the breadth, nature, and complexity of the problem. If team design is part of the project team's work, members with analytical and computer skills are essential. Members with clinical backgrounds who understand the health care environment also are helpful. New quality teams often have members who have served successfully on previous quality teams.

This principle of matching team with task also holds true when forming ad hoc teams in a department. Consider the purpose of the team and include members who come from different shifts, disciplines, or job categories. Find all the skills needed for this particular piece of work. Consider technical, problem-solving, and interpersonal as well as project management skills.

Full-Time Membership

Waterman (1990) strongly advocates adequate resourcing of the team and this applies particularly to membership. The size of the team is not as important as the full-time nature of the membership. Full-time appointment to an ad hoc team is important if the scope of the team's work is of significant magnitude and complexity. Design teams for restructuring efforts are often composed of full-time members. This allows for a clear focus on the work at hand and avoids the distractions that occur when team members retain their original responsibilities. Some organizations now are using department-based integration teams to design the new structure and implementation. Staff members may have full-time responsibility to the team for the duration of the project and then return to their original positions when their work is done.

For projects of smaller scope, full-time membership is not important, however, release time from daily work in order to accomplish the team's work is a necessity. Before decisions are made regarding membership, realistic time requirements must be established.

Team Leader Is Not the Expert

If the team leader is also the expert in the assigned team work, the team may begin deferring to the leader rather than collectively working as a team to make decisions. Also, if the team leader has the highest positional authority within the group; team members may defer to the leader's opinion and expect the team leader to make the important decisions.

Recruit People with Process Skills

Ad hoc teams need strong process skills at least as much as they need technical expertise. Without process skills, the ad hoc team will not succeed. These skills include:

- planning and conducting an effective meeting
- establishing schedules
- assigning responsibility
- keeping things on track
- establishing and measuring outcomes
- ensuring that work is done between meetings
- getting input from all team members
- openly communicating
- addressing conflict
- listening
- gaining consensus

Although these sound simple, many people don't possess these skills, or if they do, forget them when they start a new team. The team may need education about these skills early in the process.

Assigned Purpose

Because an ad hoc team is established to accomplish a specific purpose and then disbanded, it is likely that its purpose is defined for it by the external leader. This may or may not be a pitfall. Usually, only people who are interested in the project will seek participation on the team. Team members, however, may be less than fully engaged in the process if their mission is handed to them. If this is the case, it helps to have the team discuss and make slight modifications in the purpose to promote shared understanding and commitment to it.

The Handoff

Almost all ad hoc teams are charged with creating something new, solving a problem, or improving an organizational process. A major predicament occurs when the team responsible for creating the innovation or finding a solution is not the same team responsible for implementation. Success rates are higher if the team is responsible for both design and implementation. This has been a common complaint of quality improvement teams for years. After making recommendations, they may have no more involvement or even knowledge of the outcome of their recommendation.

The problem is that people who have done the creative work can't transfer their knowledge or understanding completely to others not involved in the planning. The level of enthusiasm experienced by creators rarely exists in implementors. And, members of the ad hoc team are simply more responsive, focused, and practical if they know they will have to live with whatever they've recommended (Waterman 1990).

Hospitals involved in major restructuring often use integration teams (as pointed out earlier) including employees and managers who actually will be implementing the changes designed. Ideally these teams also have members with specific expertise in restructuring and work redesign so they have a sufficient knowledge base. Such a combination of employees experienced in restructuring and employees who will actually implement the design is powerful.

Inadequate Resources

Ad hoc teams often lack resources unless these are specifically allocated. Resources include adequate equipment, secretarial or clerical support, space, time, and executive sponsorship. Adequacy of resources may depend on the type of ad hoc team and its purpose. Quality teams composed of employees from various departments often don't have a specific budget or a source of funds. Manager team members may have access to a secretary, or the person in the organization who coordinates quality improvement initiatives may be available for support.

Specific resources need to be allocated when the scope of work is broad or when the ad hoc team is a long-term structure, such as a development or project team. Space is important. If the team has no regular meeting place it can become distracted and frustrated from time wasted finding a place to work. Spontaneous synergy is unlikely to occur if team members are physically spread throughout the organization. This doesn't mean it won't happen; but instead it may be confined only to meeting times rather than part of the day-to-day work.

Equipment needs must also be considered. Networked computers with electronic mail and a shared workspace for documents help people work more efficiently. Facsimile and copy machines improve productivity. If data analysis is part of the team's work, the ability to access databases may require special software. Supplies needed for accomplishing the work are also important, including items such as flip charts and markers.

Executive sponsorship is another critical resource. Ad hoc teams tackling major organization issues will need consistent and visible executive support. Executives need to meet periodically with the team, report on the team's progress at organizational meetings, stay informed of progress, and generally be accessible to the team. Allocating resources to teams that are producing results or working on important projects is a visible sign of organizational support.

Lack of Outcome Measures

Any team can experience the lack of outcome measures as a pitfall, but given the temporary nature of the ad hoc team, this point is especially crucial. If outcome measures haven't been established, neither the team nor its sponsors can determine its ultimate effectiveness. Ad hoc teams run off track more easily than other teams, perhaps because they are not part of the organization's normal structure. Good ad hoc teams establish milestones, predict results, and measure themselves continually against these standards and expected outcomes. When they don't achieve their expected results, they reevaluate to determine where and why the variance occurred.

Effective ad hoc teams have an established mechanism for reporting results. It may be to an executive sponsor, a department manager, or a steering committee. At regular intervals, the team reports what it achieved and what it expected to achieve. It identifies the next milestone and what is expected to be achieved. In some cases, teams review their budget and actual expenditures.

Missing milestones or taking longer to achieve results is not critical as long as learning has occurred and progress is being made. Real problems occur when nothing is being measured and no one is managing the team's progress, or lack of it.

Disbanding the Team

All ad hoc teams need closure when their work is finished. Allowing the team to just fade away is disrespectful of its contribution and destructive of the motivation to participate on future efforts. Quality teams often make recommendations but may not reconvene to hear the outcome of their recommendations or to debrief and evaluate their effectiveness as a team. Thus, they may not benefit completely from the learning that occurs from serving on such a team. Worse, the learning from one team isn't imparted to the next team.

Ad hoc teams of long duration may experience difficulties when disbanding. If employees or managers left their full-time positions to serve on the ad hoc team, they may not have positions to which they can return. Their skills or experience may not be required by the next major ad hoc team. This is described by Waterman (1990, 26): "Today's companies need, but seldom have, the ability to move seamlessly from bureaucracy to adhocracy and back again. Today's managers need, but seldom have, the skill and security to leave their posts for a while and become effective members of project teams. But without that ability, companies and people go on making the same old mistakes. They do not learn. This is the Achilles' heel of corporate America."

Employees and managers who serve successfully on ad hoc teams grow tremendously through the experience. Their value to the organization increases with their new skills and competencies and finding new places for them only makes good business sense. This may mean creating temporary special project positions to avoid losing these employees permanently.

Case Study: "A Restructuring Resource Team: Lost in the Trees"

A metropolitan medical center had undertaken the task of completely restructuring itself and becoming a team-based organization. An experienced and respected manager from within the system was hired as a full-time project leader to guide this effort. Other employees were brought in gradually as full-time members of this resource team. The team had been operating for only six months when it experienced serious difficulties. Let's explore a few of them.

Although intentions were good and the team members were committed on a full-time basis, the team got off to a slow start. In fact, it didn't get started at all. After six months, it was still floundering, trying to define its purpose. Team members were uncertain whether they were supposed to be experts in redesign, take an active role in coaching their managers who were going through restructuring, or serve as resource people or trainers as teams were implemented. This confusion about purpose made it difficult for the team to work with those doing design work for the departments being restructured.

There were also unresolved issues related to membership. Team members were not selected from the best and the brightest, but instead from a group of employees who were being displaced in the organization. They needed to find jobs quickly and this opportunity was a godsend. While they certainly weren't poor employees, the majority had limited presentation and process skills. Their credibility with managers suffered as a result and their self-confidence wavered.

Without a clearly defined purpose, it was virtually impossible to define outcome measures. This team had no specific deadlines or milestones. They knew they should be doing something as the date for conversion of the first restructured department loomed closer, but they didn't know what. This was clearly a team without direction, without a rudder.

Case Study: "A Restructuring Resource Team That Sees the Forest"

The second example is a design team involved in a restructuring project in a 625-bed community hospital. A steering committee composed of senior executives envisioned the work required and assembled a team that represented the needed skills. Positions were posted and applicants were selected based on their skills and experience. There were three project leaders, three data analysts, and three team members who served as facilitators. Another team member was experienced in building teams and managing change. These 10 people represented different clinical disciplines and business functions in the organization and were considered some of its brightest and most creative employees. Five had managerial experience as well. Two had some team experience in industries outside of health care.

Although given a purpose and direction by the steering committee, this team reviewed what they understood its purpose to be and made minor modifications. What was important for all team members was the opportunity to discuss and revise the purpose until all were fully committed to it. The team quickly mobilized itself, discussed various roles, identified expectations of each other, and the expectations each had for the internal and external team leaders. It agreed on a common approach to work and necessary team roles. Throughout the three-year life of this team, these issues were periodically reviewed and modified as needed with all team members participating.

Resources necessary for accomplishing the work were provided. The team was housed in a suite of offices with adequate space and a generous conference room. Equipment and supplies were made available and a team secretary was employed. The team's external team leader was the executive responsible for the restructuring effort. He attended team meetings and was readily accessible to the team. Milestones and time frames were routinely established with frequent reviews.

The one major pitfall encountered by this team was in the area of the handoff. As a mature ad hoc team, boundaries were clearly established with each project. The team was responsible for the design of the newly restructured department with input from employees, managers, and other key stakeholders. The facilitators supported the initial conversion of each restructured department, but then transferred responsibility for long-term implementation to the department manager and employees. Although the restructuring project continued at a fairly rapid clip, the design team was hampered in its learning because it was unable to remain involved beyond initial implementation. It observed what worked and what didn't only from comments and criticisms received from others. Over time the organization developed a fairly strong "we–they" attitude between the operational managers and the members of the design team because of this lack of long-term follow-through.

CONCLUSION

All teams face unique challenges based on their characteristics, purpose, and membership. No team becomes a real team without hard work and constant attention. This chapter has described three kinds of teams commonly seen in health care organizations: primary work teams, executive and managerial leadership teams, and ad hoc teams. They all face significant, if sometimes unique, challenges. A team-based organization has all three types of teams and, as a result, has many employees who are able to mobilize quickly into new teams when needed.

Primary work teams that flounder and fail to meet expectations often have one of these pitfalls to blame: assignment of team members, no team design, confusion about the team's work, inadequate delineation of authority or responsibility, a lack of team building around the structural elements of a team, or unaddressed dysfunctional interpersonal behaviors within the team.

Major pitfalls for executive and management teams are similar although unique to teams responsible for leading others. They include a team that wasn't designed, confusion over purpose, a lack of clarity in defining the team's work, a historic preference for individualistic approaches, inadequate time spent in developmental work, and the persistence of hierarchy within the team.

Ad hoc teams are characterized by a relatively short life span and, consequently, face different problems and issues. These include a need for quick start-up and rapid results, finding the right members, having an assigned purpose, accomplishing an effective handoff to those implementing its recommendations, inadequate resources, lack of specific measurable outcomes, and difficulties disbanding the team.

The good news is that these perils and pitfalls can be avoided if they are anticipated. But there has to be a willingness on the part of leaders to learn from the experiences of others and not to repeat their painful and difficult lessons.

CHAPTER 6

Leading the Cultural Change to Teams: Six Key Elements

For many if not most health care organizations in the United States, their structural antecedent is the military model of vertical hierarchy. The top spot is held by a general officer, responsible for results produced by the entire organization and answerable only to the board of directors. Below him or her, a small group of lesser officers is given authority over operational and support areas as well as major employee groups such as nursing and relations with the medical staff. Below this come the ranks of managers, sometimes three or four levels, followed by those who perform the hands-on work.

It is no surprise that this model persists. It has been carried over from earlier centuries when military hospitals or church hospitals (also organized on a similar hierarchical model) were the only sources of medical care. For mobilizing the largely illiterate and untrained workers of those days and ensuring they did exactly what was needed, this system worked. At a time when most people were born, survived their illnesses or accidents, and died at home, these early hospitals were sufficient for public health needs. For meeting the medical challenges of substantial battlefield casualties or wards filled with victims of widespread epidemics, this organizational structure also sufficed. This model was reinforced as recently as 1945, when a whole new class of hospital administrators—graduates of U.S. field hospitals during World War II—left the military services. When they were demobilized at the war's end and headed off to run health care organizations across the United States, the same structural model of health care went with them.

The only real surprise may be that this top-down model is still with us in the final years of the twentieth century, when so many of the factors demanding, supporting, and rewarding hierarchical hospital structures have disappeared. At the end of a long century filled with great wars, hospitals now finally have been forced to step back from a war footing in which cost-plus became a way of life and more was always better. Dramatic changes in society's needs and customers' demands require profound reassessments of the structures and cultures of our health care organizations. True leaders will be up to this challenge; those who are only managers of the status quo need not apply.

A favorite philosopher and ice hockey legend, Wayne Gretsky, once explained his athletic greatness in these terms: "I just skate to where the puck will be." His point of view reflects the profound difference between leaders who see beyond current situations to create a future when it is needed, and today's managers who can only see, and therefore only recreate, the present (they skate to where the puck *was*). This contrast has become critically important in the health care industry. For organizations that have chosen to travel the team-based route to their futures, this distinction is crucial. The journey to teams is difficult or impossible without visionary, proactive leadership at the helm. Within team structures, unlike in traditional hierarchies, there are significantly more demands for strong, determined leadership and significantly fewer places for weak, unfocused management to hide.

KEY LEADERSHIP ELEMENTS

Six leadership elements are keys to success or failure:

1. modeling change
2. establishing trust
3. setting the pace
4. creating the vision
5. focusing the organization
6. building commitment

This chapter will discuss these leadership elements in depth, examining each as it relates to executive leaders, external team leaders, and internal team leadership.

Executive leaders are members of the top management group who have overall responsibility for direction and management of major divisions of the organization. Throughout the transformation to team structures executive leaders play important roles. Initially these center around formulating and clearly communicating about the new environment. Ultimately they involve "staying the course" and monitoring and rewarding positive changes.

External team leaders are those people who provide the direct support for teams during their transitions. These leaders are normally recruits from the middle management ranks who have demonstrated an ability to coach and guide work groups effectively throughout the many changes necessary to becoming real teams. Holding transitional positions, these people must expect to work themselves out of their assignments over a period of several years. Their goal is to create strong teams that, in the end, can function with minimal management.

Internal team leaders are members of the team. The team periodically reassesses its need for leadership and appoints the leaders it needs. In best-case scenarios, the inteam leader serves for a limited defined period (one to two years) and then the role rotates to a well-trained successor. Since growth in leadership capabilities of the entire team is a major goal, no permanent job is created for a team leader and no pay differential is offered. This leader takes on a role defined by his or her teammates; a role designed by the team to meet its unique needs at that particular point in time.

MODELING CHANGE

In the mid-1700s a resident of Philadelphia by the name of Benjamin Franklin became convinced the city would be improved by lighting the city's streets at night. In the dark streets, pedestrians were commonly injured in accidents or accosted by criminals bent on robbing them. Now, Franklin might have drawn up a plan (including cost-benefit analysis) showing how the city could provide lanterns for major thoroughfares and then submitted it to the city fathers. And if the city proved slow to act he could have gathered supporters and petitioned for its compliance to the people's will or even written one of his famous, widely read pieces for the newspaper. Instead, he simply hung a single powerful lantern on a long pole from the front of his house and every evening at dusk faithfully lit the wick. The idea caught on. People soon noticed that they stumbled less on that particular street and experienced fewer robberies. Before long, Franklin's neighbors began lighting lanterns above their front doors and within a few years Philadelphia became a city of lighted streets.

Franklin had chosen to lead major change rather than to manage this change. The concept of lighted streets was new to the British colonies (although many European cities had been publicly lighted for years) and someone needed to demonstrate dramatically the benefits of this new concept. So, Franklin led by example, and created a new paradigm. This is an example of what Joel Barker means when he says, "Leaders lead between paradigms, managers manage within paradigms" (Barker 1993). In other words, the function of a leader in times of major change is very different from the roles we traditionally ascribe to managers. The more major the change, the more significant the differences. To get a better handle on these differences, let's contrast the characteristics of managing and characteristics of leading.

Characteristics

Managing	Leading
directing	coaching
ordering	mentoring
commanding	enabling (freeing)
controlling	empowering
dominating	teaching
taking charge	developing
overseeing	encouraging
presiding	catalyzing

In these lists you can see dramatic differences between the command and control approaches of managers working in a military-like power hierarchy and the empower and coach style of leaders working with well trained, semi-autonomous individuals and groups.

We should be reminded of Ben Franklin's story whenever we hear of health care organizations attempting to become team-based from the ground up, without simultaneously working to become team-based from the top down. Executive management in such organizations seriously underestimates the scope and challenges of the anticipated changes. They are attempting to steer an ocean liner with a paddle. The message they send employees is, "You make all the changes; we'll lead." Rather than capitalizing on the leverage of their prominent roles by modeling necessary changes, they essentially abdicate leadership at a critical time in the life of their organization. The role of executive leaders in such situations is to lead by example, not to follow or wait to see how others cope with difficult changes.

Leaders unwilling to set an organizational example are unlikely to maintain leadership credibility. Earlier, in Chapter 5, we took a close look at the many real pitfalls that can hamper those trying to create true leadership teams, especially at the executive levels of organizations. Despite these challenges, leaders are always in greatest peril when they try to avoid leading by example.

As a major transitional support element for teams, external team leaders share the same downside risks as executives. They are usually likely to feel the more immediate consequences of modeling or not modeling change, however. As the leaders in the middle, they are carefully watched by both sides. For example, a supportive external team leader with an unsupportive executive is in a no-win situation, pressured from below by teams with real, pressing needs for assistance and yet handicapped from above in trying to extend this help. Other combinations are equally disastrous, save for one. (See Figure 6–1.)

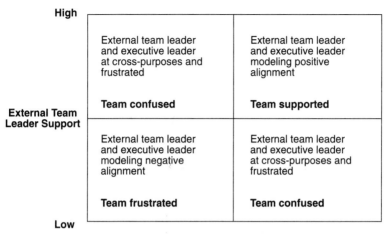

Figure 6–1 Levels of Leadership Support Affect Team Development

Both high executive leader and high external leader support is required to model positive alignment and provide coherent and coordinated assistance to teams. The other permutations merely frustrate and confuse people. Some organizations have tried to solve these alignment problems by combining executive and external team leadership in a single person, but with many divisional teams needing simultaneous support, such a load quickly becomes too heavy for one individual.

External leaders are probably in the toughest position in terms of modeling because of their central position. They are neither executives (who are often granted greater license to be themselves by work teams) nor team members (who may also be given latitude based on crucial roles or long association). For this reason it is not unusual for work teams to be more immediately critical of their external leaders than they are of anyone else, including themselves. Such close scrutiny also may account for the flip side of this phenomenon, when an excellent, highly skilled external leader is considered by his or her teams to be an absolute paragon. Rarely are such extreme negative or positive evaluations totally accurate. They also are never arrived at objectively. All of which shows that the external leader position carries a unique charge—a special power for good or ill—and a particular responsibility for effectively modeling desired changes.

The inteam or internal team leader is first a member of the team, and second a leader. This leader is chosen by the team to meet needs it has identified. For example, a team in early stages of development may choose a leader who is comfortable and skilled in team formation activities such as determining roles and responsibilities or clarifying team boundaries and goals. A more mature team might pick someone who is particularly good at facilitating boundary negotiations with other teams or upper management. In any case, the team decides what responsibilities the inteam leader will assume. In most high-performing teams, the inteam leader position is seen as a role, not a job. This status allows the responsibilities of the role to rotate, building team capabilities, and enlarging capacity whenever another member takes his or her turn as leader. Modeling at this level is certainly important because of the message it sends to teammates about appropriate leadership behaviors. However, this position is usually not as highly "leveragable" as those of other leaders, most especially the external leader.

Teams have immediate recourse with their inteam leaders. One who cannot appropriately model the changes required by the team can be moved out of the leadership role more quickly than if this change had to pass through bureaucratic performance review and placement processes. For example, a team in an information services department started up with a leader who seemed to know more about forming teams than any other member. Soon, this individual very aggressively began promoting the team's "rights" of autonomy and decision-making power. Within six months this behavior had caused several problems for the young team. So the team, after several open discussions about how this individual was moving too far too fast, replaced her with a more moderate, slower-paced leader. The change provided all team members with valuable lessons about becoming a team and along the way substantially clarified their leadership needs at this phase of their development.

Probably too much has been written already about "walking the talk," but the record is very clear—executive, external, and inteam leaders only earn the right to "talk the talk" by walking the talk. In the final analysis, those who eagerly model the changes they're expecting to see from their organization and their staffs will succeed; those who don't will fail.

ESTABLISHING TRUST

Case Study: To Kill a Team

Gary, an external team leader who had previously been a manager in the physical plant area, was having persistent trust problems with his teams. Early in the hospital's move to teams, Gary had been openly hostile to the idea, but his immense knowledge of the workings of the hospital and his involvement in the organization's many ongoing construction projects made him almost "fireproof." Finally, his first team was formed and began team training. But, when it came to him with a problem, Gary's initial irritable response was, "You're a self-directed team now; fix your own damned problem!"

His executive leader, a younger man, worked hard and long to change Gary's behaviors and over the first year or so a great deal of progress occurred. Gary began to see that self-direction could offer him some benefits, including greater opportunity to focus on his time-consuming construction projects. He still had real problems understanding why any group of workers in their right minds would want to assume their own management. Due to the changes they saw, his teams tentatively began to believe that Gary was letting go of his old command-and-control mentality.

Late in its second year of existence, one of Gary's maintenance teams was surprised to learn it was being reconfigured and reassigned. Right in the middle of a number of big construction projects, Gary had learned the hospital was taking over maintenance responsibilities for a new clinical services building. Without informing or consulting the team, he published job openings for two new team members and unilaterally divided the team between the two facilities. The team was crushed about not even being consulted. The fragile framework of trust they had built collapsed.

The subgroup of team members sent to the new clinical services facility survived as a team, reforming quickly now that they were out from under Gary's daily rounds. They decided they had been cut loose. They were helped by the fact that demands on their subteam were very high and required a lot of autonomous decision making and interdependency. Those members assigned to the hospital almost immediately returned to their dependent behavior of two years earlier. They no longer trusted Gary to give up any control over their work. Even though several of these employees had been with the organization for decades, the entire hospital subteam regressed to the self-confidence level of its two newest members! With this, team development had stopped dead.

We live in a time of great paradoxes regarding trust. As solutions to political, economic, and social problems become increasingly complex and more difficult to achieve, our trust and confidence in our leaders' abilities to find these solutions has reached all-time lows. In Washington, D.C., these days it's said that all the nation's easy problems have been solved; only the thorny ones remain. Yet, if you ask most people how much trust they're willing to place in our elected congressional representatives, they'll put them dead last (right after used-car salesmen).

Warren Bennis (1989) has suggested that our trust in our leaders varies directly with the presence or absence of three characteristics: (1) competence, (2) constancy, and (3) congruence. Let's look at each of these.

Competence is the skills and ability to do the job. In the case of the U.S. Congress for example, many Americans seriously doubt their elected representatives' capability to solve complex problems such as health care reform or the budget deficit. This is probably worsened by close media coverage of the legislative processes surrounding such important issues. As Mark Twain once suggested, both making sausage and making laws are activities that don't bear close scrutiny. Today, many of us trust the competency of machines more than we are willing to trust other people, or even ourselves. Most air travelers are heartened by the fact that a Type 3 airliner like the Boeing 757 can literally land itself, unassisted—this means they have to depend less on the fallible human crew. Many others are completely willing to turn over the tracking of their personal finances to a bank's computers. Most of the people you know probably gave up balancing their checkbooks years ago, figuring the mainframe at First Trustworthy is more likely to be accurate than they are.

Constancy is another important element of trust. We expect to be able to predict, more or less, where a person we trust will stand on any given issue. According to Bennis (Flowers 1990) a national survey reported that a majority of people prefer a predictable (constant) leader, *"even when they disagree with their viewpoint,"* rather than an unpredictable leader with whom they generally agree. Unfortunately, our desire for such predictability in the face of difficult, fast-changing situations often elevates single-issue leaders or demagogues.

A preferable method for building a basis of trust is to do it over time. This requires more personal disclosure and mutual discussion about how decisions are made than many leaders are accustomed to. The payoff comes, however, when people recognize that there are consistent themes, values, or ethics informing each decision this leader makes. When others believe this foundation always underlies a leader's decision making, that leader will have achieved constancy in their eyes.

Congruence exists when a leader's behavior matches his or her actions. It also refers to a high degree of similarity between a leader's view and that of followers. We tend to trust leaders with whom we agree. If you believe this health care organization exists to provide excellent patient care and see this belief reflected daily in the lives of leaders, you'll tend to trust them. But if decisions are made or actions taken that work against this purpose, you will begin to lose trust. Incongruent behavior by leaders at any level nearly always has a serious corrosive effect on their organizations. Lack of trust in leadership erodes once-strong linkages among team members, between people and their leaders, and ultimately between individuals and the organization itself.

Perhaps the greatest paradox is that while so many of us are unwilling to place much trust in our leaders, most of us, at the same time, are yearning to find a leader whom we can really trust. This phenomenon may explain the immense popularity of the leading presidential noncandidate for 1996, General Colin Powell, who took a lead in the public opinion polls well before he made any of his opinions public. This is the paradox facing all potential leaders today: a terrific desire for competent, constant, and congruent leadership versus high skepticism and tremendous fear of disappointment. In this opportune but dangerous situation, a leader who understands the importance and fragility of the people's trust and conscientiously works to earn their trust, can and will be trusted.

A hospital CEO we know beautifully demonstrates this capacity for trustworthiness. She is a firm believer in "LBWA—leading by walking around," and on any given day can be found anywhere from patient care centers to the boiler room. Wherever she goes she engages people in conversation, whether they are staff, patients, visitors, or suppliers. She asks them questions and carefully listens to their answers. She's rarely too busy to respond to their questions or listen to their opinions. But when she disagrees, she offers her opinions straight up, so people generally know where she stands.

As a nurse and former director of nursing, she has credibility with clinicians as well as with nonclinicians and can engage staff very knowledgeably on most issues. But this is a real person and occasionally she forgets to use her managers, slipping back from LBWA into MBWA (managing by walking around—that direct problem-solving mode she used so effectively in her years as head of nursing). In several situations, she's seen a problem on a nursing floor or somewhere else in the hospital and simply directed people to fix it right then and there. Or, she's heard a staff member's concern and taken remedial action without first consulting the appropriate manager or team members.

This firefighting behavior is not particularly unusual among former line managers, but the most interesting thing is the reaction from her management staff. Typically, the affected manager will, as soon as possible, talk directly with this CEO, reminding her of the importance of involving managers in problem solving within their own areas. This is done without rancor and without blaming. It is offered and accepted as feedback, not as a threat or indictment. Fear is missing from this relationship and that is because of a deep sense of mutual trust.

This CEO trusts her people to lead appropriately and generally models trusting leadership. Her infrequent lapses are seen as just that rather than as a lack of trust in her staff or a breaking of the trust relationship. Her ability to accept direct feedback on these errors actually strengthens the loyalty of her people. This deep loyalty has allowed her to lead her organization through an amazing number of difficult changes.

Trust need not be a fragile thing. In the above example it is remarkably strong and pliable, but it also should be noted that this is based on more than 30 years of interaction between this leader and her organization. Particularly when entering into a major organizational transformation, experienced leaders at every level need to ask themselves, "How have we broken trust with employees in the past?" They also need to ask employees for feedback on this key issue. Ignoring examples of this problem only increases the likelihood that trust will be violated again. Directly facing this issue sends two important messages: (1) strong trust is vitally important to leaders and to the organization, and (2) when fallible people break trust (as they inevitably will, on occasion) this situation is reparable.

But what if leaders are new to an organization or a team, or just new to a situation they've never before encountered (like organizational restructuring)? What can they do to establish trust with the people they are trying to lead?

Look Around, You're in the Limelight

First, recognize that you are in the spotlight, and that spotlight is always on. For example, at the beginning of a relationship, with no historical or experiential basis for trust, everybody following you is trying to answer a single, important question, "Why should I trust you?" They are closely watching not only how you treat them individually, but also how you treat others. Are you abrupt with secretaries but deferential with doctors? Can you make decisions and then stick to them, or do your opinions swing with the breeze? Do you talk about others' shortcomings when they aren't present? Will you address tough issues directly and openly?

Being the new leader at any level in the organization is like fictional TV psychiatrist Bob Newhart's old joke about the first session with your psychiatrist—everything counts! You must watch what you do and say, and what you don't do and don't say. Like it or not, you are being watched very carefully and are being judged by the watchers. If you are feeling vulnerable and exposed, you are probably right! Seek out trusted leaders among your colleagues to serve as mentors during this difficult adjustment period. Periodically ask your people how you are doing and take action on their suggestions.

Capitalize on Your Newness

Steven Covey (1989) suggests a useful analogy for trust—a bank account. In a new relationship, each party begins with a small amount deposited (let's call it the "benefit-of-the-doubt" account) and subsequent behavior determines whether this account grows or shrinks. If you are trustworthy and prove yourself dependable, over time this account will grow. If, on the other hand, you're perceived to be dishonest or unreliable, your account will leak trust until one day you discover it is all gone.

One difficulty is that both trustworthiness and its opposite are based on the perceptions of others. Rarely do people consider themselves dishonest. This is why it is so important regularly and explicitly to check out trust levels with other people. When one new executive leader did this he was surprised to learn that while people at the division's team level trusted him, his group of department managers (now external leaders for their own teams) had serious trust problems. In several instances he had overruled members of this group when he saw old management practices being performed. He also was actively urging this group to transfer real responsibilities to its teams. Some members saw this as undermining their authority.

Thinking he was perceived as unsupportive because these external leaders were unclear about their new roles, he immediately stepped up efforts to develop his leadership team. He enrolled this group of managers (and himself) in education sessions on an expedited schedule. The plan was to get them out ahead of their teams, rather than lagging behind. He asked individuals to "shadow" external leaders in other areas who had advanced further on the learning curve. As these leaders began to understand their new responsibilities and the roles necessary to carry them out, trust returned. Ultimately this group became a true leadership team sharing the common purpose of developing all its teams. When they finally learned to share mutual accountability for achieving this goal, trust among the team hit an all-time high.

The challenge for a new leader is to capitalize on your "benefit-of-the-doubt" account, using methods that will connect you quickly with others in your group. By expressing your goals and aspirations for the team and carefully listening to those of the other members, you can establish a foundation of commonalty and model mutual respect. This also initiates an open sharing of ideas and opinions that will continue to pay dividends for everyone. This open approach is also an important step toward creating a shared vision—something we'll discuss in depth later in this chapter.

Serve the Team

Regardless of whether you were elected by your teammates, appointed by the organization, or brought in from outside, you have been asked to *serve* as a leader. The best leaders take this word literally. There are a number of good books written on servant leadership and reading any one of them would be a great place to start. The premise of all of them is the same: that somehow we've slipped into believing that the people who do the work—deliver the services, care for patients—are working *for* the manager. In today's workplace, this belief is way off the mark.

If you ask most hierarchically organized hospital staff who they are *working for*, they'll nearly always name their boss. Traditional bosses will reciprocate by telling you how many people "report to him" or "work for her." These pyramidal relationships have been supported by our use of terms like "supervisor" (which is a kinder, gentler version of "overseer" with its dark echoes of the plantation), "superior" (meaning above or greater), and "subordinate" (defined as belonging to an inferior rank, grade, class, or order—a subordinary person).

In our society the tide is running in the opposite direction. Members of our highly educated culture every year demand more egalitarian treatment. Our technologically sophisticated industries require employees to achieve ever higher skill levels just to retain their present jobs. So, in hospitals, which need increasing productivity to survive in today's fast-changing markets, archaic vertical distinctions have become barriers to success. Enter the servant leader.

This new servant leader, regardless of position in the organization, recognizes she or he is part of a larger team, and not necessarily the most important part. For many executives and long-time managers this will be a humbling experience. If the servant leader asks teammates who they work for they'll include all their teammates in this list, pointing out their need to serve one other as well as their other customers.

If an inteam leader, then the servant leader is one of them—a member of the team—but his or her focus is different from that of other teammates. The servant leader is the one chiefly responsible for the team's teamness, that essential but often elusive element that creates something like a fusion reaction in which more energy is created than consumed by the group. This individual is there, first and foremost, to serve the team and its goals—not individual members and not management—but the team itself.

If an external leader, the servant leader is there to serve one primary customer—the division's teams. This is often a role for expert and creative jugglers since the needs of these teams are often out of balance or synchronization. External leadership is concocted of integration, protection, and reconciliation, with more than one dash of courage. The Flying Karamazovs come to mind—simultaneously juggling a kitten, a bowling ball, and a screaming chainsaw.

When newly selected leaders recognize their responsibilities to model appropriate behaviors, capitalize effectively on new beginnings, and serve their team's needs and goals above all else, leadership credibility and trust will grow.

Repair Trust

What if trust has already been broken or at least badly bent out of shape? Here's the bad news: There is no magic pill, no super glue, no quick fix to repair a broken trust relationship. Again, the bank account metaphor applies. When a leader's account has been built up over many years, minor trust problems are easily repairable. In fact, with enough trust in the "bank," many lapses (like those of the CEO in the earlier example) won't ever be considered as trust issues. But even accounts built up over decades can be bankrupted by major problems such as unethical or criminal behavior and, in the case of new leaders, much smaller blunders can quickly drain their relatively tiny trust accounts.

Trust is a lot like oxygen: easily overlooked when abundant and awfully hard to ignore when it's depleted. So, what can you do? Basically, only three things:

1. Acknowledge the lapse.
2. Apologize.
3. Make reparation.

Doing these three things and then staying the course of rebuilding trust are the first steps on the long road back.

SETTING THE PACE

In a study investigating the impacts of major restructuring initiatives on the roles of hospital executives (Voluntary Hospitals of America 1994), more than 40 executives in 17 hospitals nationwide were interviewed. One of the surprising findings was that the price of timidity was generally higher than the price of boldness. Organizations in which leadership made small, incremental operational changes rather than larger, more sweeping alterations in structure, culture, and operations were regularly frustrated in attempts to transform their hospitals. Some of the lowest levels of change researchers encountered prompted the highest levels of resistance from all sectors of entrenched subcultures. As expected, leaders in hospitals undergoing moderate changes encountered more moderate levels of resistance. But hospitals taking the boldest change initiatives experienced the lowest internal resistance to change of all three groups studied.

When pressed to explain this phenomenon, these executives responded with statements such as, "We're all too busy changing to spend much time or energy resisting the changes." In other words, the pace being set was so challenging, it virtually eliminated opposition to change. People who most likely would have dug in their heels over the change of just one word in their department's name were being swept into the collaborative energies of major reorganizations—reorganizations that often merged entire divisions and rewrote everyone's job descriptions. It is a challenge for a hospital's leadership to decide how much change the organization can tackle while still remaining healthy and whole. The experience of several early adopters of team-based restructuring indicates that a great challenge is preferable to not enough challenge.

In her book, *Danger in the Comfort Zone*, Judith Bardwick (1991) argues that institutions and organizations immersed in entitlement due to historic paternalism or managerial ossification normally require a major shock before they'll begin moving toward interdependence and greater productivity. A challenge requiring significant amounts of organizational stretch is an effective means of administering this shock and cracking the tired old shell of entitlement thinking. It can open up the organization to a whole set of new realities.

Case Study: "The Hurry-Up Defense"

A medium-sized tertiary care hospital located in an established suburb of a large city had ignored its changing environment far too long. While it slept, HMOs were gaining major footholds in its service area and it had become the high-cost provider for several services. Its medical staff and referral network aged and its historical base of loyal clients changed as people died, retired, or moved out of the area. Census in the obstetric and pediatric areas had steadily declined for several years.

The Shock: A new top management team from the hospital's system headquarters arrived to turn this organization around, with a four-year time frame in which to accomplish this feat. Targeting the patient care areas for major restructuring, management hired a consultant with experience in health care redesign and laid the following challenge before the organization: "Our new clinical approach will be patient-focused care. We will completely restructure all patient care areas to new models based upon clinical teams. All staff in these areas will be expected to reapply for positions in the new organization and there will be fewer jobs available in this 'new' hospital than there were in the old. We will complete this entire clinical transformation within a period of five months."

This announcement got the organization's attention. The first group to learn of these plans was the nurse managers during an off-site closed session and their reaction was predictable: shock, panic, and blame. Shock that the hospital's fortunes, gradually declining for years, had finally become a cause for top management action. Panic when they realized this meant adjustments in their work lives and those of their staffs, or possibly NO JOB! And finally blame, as a search for the elusive scapegoat began to gather momentum.

To their immense credit these middle managers appeared to recover quickly and a day or so later were already hard at work developing plans and gathering resources for the new structures. Where a lesser change probably would have resulted in jockeying and infighting, this major challenge completely changed the game and focused everyone on the fundamental tasks of organizational reinvention for survival.

Rewards for their efforts were simple and clear: Help make this change happen and you may well have a job in the new organization— otherwise you won't.

Samuel Johnson once said, " . . . when a man knows he is to be hanged in a fortnight, it concentrates his mind wonderfully" (Boswell 1970). While we don't recommend the threat of no job used by the above leadership team as a standard opening gambit, there are cases in which it is not only appropriate, but absolutely necessary for survival of the organizational mission. The point is, a truly major challenge to the organization and a fast pace for change can and will direct attention to critical issues.

Organizations and teams sometimes can be torn apart by too much of a challenge, too fast a start, or too hard a turn. More often than not, however, they simply rust out, destroyed by sitting too long in one place. One hospital, for example, was openly proud of the fact that it had taken 10 years to design and build a new operating room service. What chance does such a relaxed time frame have in today's health care climate? The key skill for setting the proper pace lies in finding the right level and intensity of challenge for the organization as a whole and for each team and individual within it. Executive leaders are responsible for the former, external and inteam leaders for the latter.

Here are some typical warning signs that organizations might use to assess whether the pace of change is too fast or too slow:

Too Fast	**Too Slow**
▪ confused or fearful organization	▪ turf staked out
▪ stressed out staff	▪ self-congratulatory complacency
▪ declining quality	▪ little job mobility
▪ strained resources	▪ overspecialization of tasks
▪ high turnover	▪ good people leaving, citing need for challenge
▪ large and growing training backlog	▪ "automatic" annual budgets

CREATING THE VISION

Recently, an e-mail message circulated through a "Women's Network" at the U.S. Forest Service. The individual who sent the message had given a talk at her child's elementary school and saw this list on the blackboard. When asked how the list was compiled, the teacher said the sixth graders created it after learning how to work in teams.

What We Learned about Team Building

Ways to work successfully together:

1. Plan your strategy.
2. Include EVERYONE!
3. Be patient with your group.
4. *Listen* to each other.
5. Cooperate with one another.
6. Trust your group members.
7. Share/change responsibilities.
8. Build self-esteem in each other.
9. Don't be afraid of failure— REPLAN!
10. Perseverance!

There are two pieces of good news here: (1) At least some schools are actively preparing children for a future composed of teams at work, and (2) these clear-eyed kids cut straight to the heart of what really makes teams work. Leaders of teams must have a similarly clear vision of team success and be able to communicate it effectively, since without this vision (as the Good Book says) "the people will perish."

Warren Bennis in his book, *On Becoming a Leader* (1989), refers to this leadership competency as "the management of attention." Indeed, the first job of team leaders at any level is to help crystallize their teams' visions into a living picture of organizational success. The key words here are "help crystallize" and a "living picture."

In his video, *The Power of Vision* (1993), Joel Barker says that vision creation is a "leadership function." He defines vision as a "compelling image of the future shared by leaders who then act in partnership with followers to make it a reality."

In a team-based organization, however, leadership and followership are less often determined by levels in a hierarchy and more likely to be interwoven, changing roles within a team structure. So who actually has this leadership responsibility to crystallize vision? Ultimately everyone shares this responsibility, but the "formal" leaders must initiate a collaborative visioning process. In an organization structure largely made up of teams, the vision ultimately must resemble a cascade (Figure 6–2), linking divisions with their executive group, teams with their divisions or departments, and individuals

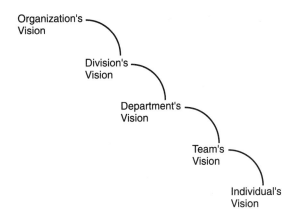

Figure 6–2 Vision Cascade

with their teams. Because this vision cascade requires unbroken continuity as well as an ability to develop, modify, and realign itself, we believe the basic skills required to continue the visioning process and broaden this vision over time must be shared by all who would lead, at any level of the organization.

Initially, from the very top of the organization a clear and compelling picture of the future must be expressed and delineated. This vision then cascades to the next level where it is reexamined, reinterpreted, and renewed with insights and answers specific to that new level (while simultaneously feeding back upward any ideas for improvement) and so on, throughout the entire organization.

There are four key steps in the visioning process:

1. developing the vision
2. clearly articulating the vision
3. establishing support
4. gaining commitment to the vision

Let's examine how this might occur in a hospital.

Developing the Vision

Through their planning processes, the hospital's executives, in consultation with their board of directors, once again review their mission to deliver caring, high-quality, and cost-effective health services to consumers in their largely rural regional market. Through their deliberations they become convinced that in five to seven years their market will be able to support the current tertiary-care hospital facility only if it is integrated as part of a larger health services network.

Their strategic investigations further indicate low probabilities of increased patient competition from new entities such as for-profit hospitals, but a significant potential for increased pressures from out of region or out of state clinical specialty programs. Through newly enacted state health care legislation and the action of the region's larger corporations, growing numbers of people are being moved toward HMO delivery models and similar capitated payment systems.

The hospital makes a strategic decision to develop a regional integrated service network with the hospital as both prime mover and as the financial/organizational hub for these development activities. Additional decisions involve strengthening clinical areas and expanding the hospital's small HMO to provide more attractive options for employers.

Financially, the hospital's revenues are projected to remain adequate through the first three to four years of this conversion (scheduled for a seven-year period.) Unless employee productivity increases over this same period, however, the hospital's growing operating expenses will begin eroding investment capital necessary for building the larger service network. Operationally, the hospital should be able to accomplish all network creation functions if several key managers at various levels can be freed from their current duties to focus full-time on these larger development activities.

Another strategic decision is made to restructure the entire organization to fulfill needs of the future integrated service network proactively. Top decision makers settle on a design that aims to reduce hierarchy (and thus free up the necessary development resources) by implementing self-managing teams wherever this will result in two outcomes: (1) improving customer outcomes and (2) increasing organizational productivity.

Clearly Articulating the Vision

The outline of a challenging yet very practical plan is completed through a series of meetings at the highest levels. The board and the hospital executives have contributed and now share a common, detailed vision of where the hospital is headed, but nothing beyond a few vague mentions of possible "future changes" has been shared with the larger organization or the community.

A task force is assigned the responsibility for planning and implementing the introduction and dissemination of this new vision. It carefully reviews the needs of each stakeholder group—from patients to local and state politicians to staff to suppliers—and determines how best to communicate the vision and address those specific questions each group will want answered in the process.

Board members are provided with scripted remarks and scheduled to speak with key civic groups. The CEO is scheduled to address division and medical staff meetings and his speech is videotaped for distribution to other shifts and internal groups. For several months he conscientiously seizes every opportunity to talk about the vision, describing the future integrated service network and the hospital's role in it in precise detail. A monthly newsletter reporting on the plans and progress toward this new vision is initiated and distributed housewide. As the internal communication goals are being met, the hospital's external marketing efforts are also synchronized with the new vision.

The hospital's executives take this work very seriously. At every executive staff meeting "vision" is on the agenda. They recognize its living, ever changing nature and their duty to reframe and recrystalize it continuously for the trip down the "vision cascade." As tough questions and wild rumors crop up, this group determines how each should be addressed and coordinates its members' messages, so the organization will continue to receive a coherent, consistent picture. At least once a quarter they dedicate group time to brainstorming about their evolving vision of the future. This is done to counteract the dangerously constricting forces of group think and to inject new life and relevance into the process. They recognize the clear dangers of getting so caught up in their daily work that they lose perspective.

Establishing Support Structures

Having this clear vision of the future is not enough. Structures supporting the new vision must be established.

The hospital restructuring initiative provides all managers an opportunity to reconsider how care and services should be delivered in light of this new vision. The new perspective of the hospital as critical care and network support hub for a regional, collaborative service entity, along with the revised clinical focus and the implications of more HMO clients, challenges old assumptions and old expectations.

As the hospital's divisions are reshaped and recast better to serve the new vision, their departments are also modified and melded together into new configurations. Senior managers work closely with their middle managers to translate these new elements of the hospital's vision into consistent and detailed departmental visions.

While clinical and operational teams are being designed and formed, those senior and middle managers identified as executive or external leaders receive additional training specifically to support these teams through the difficult start-up period. Vision creation also figures prominently in this education.

Gaining Commitment to the Vision

These leaders learn that changes of this magnitude require both high management and high leadership skills. While fast-developing teams will require a good deal of how-to information, their foremost need will be to know the whats and whys of this new vision. They will need a context for the changes they are being asked to make. They will need to trust that these changes are both necessary and sufficient to create a better future. Above all, the teams and all their members will need to own a piece of this future vision to ensure that it receives vital personal individual commitment.

Executive and external leaders work closely with the new teams, facilitating their collective creation of exciting team visions that inspire and challenge the groups to tackle tough team-building issues. All major elements of each team vision are directly linked up the cascade to the departmental, divisional, and organizational visions. They are like a continuous cable connecting all levels and units of the hospital together in what Joel Barker calls "the vision community" (Barker 1993).

This continuous connectivity results in an organization that remains in better alignment, contributing to a stronger foundation of trust. Counterproductive side issues and rumors are minimized and more energy is focused on creating the vision, instead of wasted on fighting unnecessary fires caused by confusion or mistrust. Led by its compelling and living vision, our fictional hospital is prepared for success.

The late Walt Disney once said, "If you can dream it, you can do it." The Disney entertainment empire is an eloquent testimonial to the success of his philosophy. But beneath this simple statement lies a profound understanding of the role of vision in leadership—the recognition that most people not only desire, but require, a reasonably clear and complete picture of their organization's future in order to do their best work. This is particularly true when we ask them individually and collectively to make this picture a reality.

In their book, *TeamWork: What Must Go Right/What Can Go Wrong*, (1989) Larson and LaFasto found a clear correlation between the success of teams and a "clear, elevating goal." Everyone on the team must connect a goal to something deep within themselves and then reach outside of themselves to achieve a greater good. It must be possible to live this goal individually, on a daily basis. In other words, some part of it must be owned in a very real, personal way by each participant. Such a goal is the absolute core of the vision. Without this level of commitment leaders will receive mere compliance, if that.

Let's briefly compare compliance with commitment.

	Preparation	**Implementation**
Compliance		
Commitment		

Perhaps it is just human nature, but when times get tough it's often tempting for leaders to think, "I'll just tell them what they have to do." Problem is, this almost never works—at least not in this life. Simply telling the organization, a team, or an individual what they have to do does have the benefit of a relatively fast start-up, without a great deal of leadership planning or preparation. You don't need to think through all the ramifications of this action for every participant. You don't have to ask for opinions or suggestions. You just tell them what to do and they comply! The problem with compliance doesn't hit in the preparation stage, which happens quickly, but it comes when you have triggered compliance in your people and then expect to see implementation. It often doesn't happen. People drag their feet. They show no enthusiasm. They come up with all kinds of reasons why this won't work, or worst of all, keep coming back at every opportunity to ask what they ought to do next. Your implementation phase can, literally, be endless.

On the other hand, where a clear and compelling vision has been shared with others, their contributions solicited and used to develop this picture further, and where others have accepted ownership of pieces of the solution, implementation of the vision is smoother, faster, and much more likely to occur. This deliberate focusing of organizational attention clearly pays off. Wellins and his colleagues (1991) found that vision-driven organizations outperform others by 55 percent! Building solid commitment to a common vision is a pay-up-front, or pay-much-more-later-on proposition.

FOCUSING THE ORGANIZATION

Case Study: "Death by Beeper"

The executive staff of a large metropolitan hospital system had perfected the art of fire fighting. Every member of that staff had achieved his or her current position by possessing the "right stuff," enabling them to solve problems on the fly and make a higher volume of decisions per month than their direct reports. The new CEO, recently promoted from COO upon the retirement of his predecessor, had comfortably assumed his mentor's role as chief workaholic. His management staff gloried in their considerable abilities to manage the organization at almost every level. The only level they didn't handle well was leadership—they were too busy fighting fires!

During planning retreats it was nearly impossible to create the continuity of dialogue necessary for truly interactive deliberations. Their beepers and cellular phones were ringing continuously, pulling them out of discussions. Extensive time was spent constantly recapping for executives returning from phone calls. When the CEO was the one "on the horn" a whole roomful of expensive talent sat around waiting to continue the discussion and unwilling to forge ahead without him. Agreements to limit calls never succeeded because of the shared belief that these communications represented the real work of the organization and were high priority.

This group clearly lacked a central leadership focus. In lieu of this, these leaders simply defaulted to their old management habits; they kept busy and filled their days with directing, controlling, allocating, and trouble-shooting. Precious little of this activity represented what they were being paid to do—lead the organization. The executive staff had fallen into a trap once described by Ernest Hemingway, when he said, "Don't confuse motion with action." What's worse, they unwittingly were creating similar counterproductive dependencies among their staffs. Rather than developing lean, muscular divisions, their staffs got fatter and slower always waiting for the word from above.

Fortunately, new competitive realities recently shocked this group into an entirely new sense of leadership responsibilities and changed many unhealthy habits. But without such a major challenge (coming from outside the organization), the mind of this hospital system might never have become focused, until it was too late and their organization far too debilitated by micromanagement to respond effectively.

Focusing the organization is not normally a single event but rather a carefully planned and executed series of congruent leadership statements and actions occurring over an extended period of time. For example, a hospital wishing to redefine itself from a local to a regional player will have to use this new vision as a tool for both internal and external change. As it begins to reshape the external marketplace it will have to build or convert internal resources to support this broader perspective. The vision cascade will be utilized to inspire and inform divisions, departments, teams, and individuals to redefine and refocus themselves on the new regional objectives.

Internal resources will have to be redeployed, inevitably raising questions and posing potential dilemmas. In one hospital, for example, the biomedical department found it impossible to service an emerging regional network and the hub hospital simultaneously using existing personnel and existing work structures. The task of defining solutions was assigned to the biomed work team by its external leader with no attempt to clarify decision parameters or levels of authority.

This project rapidly went awry. The team, personally feeling the considerable pain of its internal and external customers and seeking a rapid resolution, decided the best solution lay in staffing a new external service team. This group would focus entirely on meeting the needs of customers in the regional network. But the external leader now felt a pinch as he realized the implications of adding another team to his already heavy coaching load. He expressed his concerns, but some of the 'biomeds,' having assumed they had decision-making authority, had already envisioned their spots on this new team and interpreted his objections as a lack of management support for teams.

About this time the finance department got wind of the team's decision and issued a "cease and desist" memo stating that neither the team nor the department had the authority to add FTEs. Several biomed team members saw this as an inappropriate intrusion into their team's work. Finally, after several executive-level meetings and the direct intervention of the executive leader working with the team and its external leader, the problem-solving process was restarted with clearer expectations and guidelines. The solution that emerged combined redeployment of some current tasks to other teams, outsourcing of some periodic maintenance, a restructuring of the team to cover both internal and external customers without resource competition, and the addition of one new technician paid for by a small increase in customer charges and by expanding coverage to include two nursing homes. It's important to note that this second-round solution would never have emerged without a refocusing effort. The key difference between the first and second attempts to solve the problem was the clearer delineation of acceptable parameters.

In order to focus their organizations, leaders at all levels must take the time and make the efforts necessary to predefine the boundaries of every delegated recommendation, decision, or responsibility. This is particularly true in the early stages of developing team problem-solving and decision-making capabilities. These boundary definitions are absolutely crucial to the success of both teams and their leaders. Without this predefinition step the organization will rapidly lose its focus on the vision and goals. Trust will evaporate. The pace of change will bog down into meaningless squabbling. Perhaps most important, the quality of decisions at all levels of the organization will significantly deteriorate as the number of problems rises.

Predefining the boundaries is a discipline for which leaders can and must hold themselves accountable. When the external leader learns he is expected to carry out new initiatives for customer service improvements, he must ask questions of the executive leader. The goal is to understand completely the scope and limits of his responsibilities, authority, and accountability. He must also know his own abilities and what resources will be made available to him. Until he knows all this he is unprepared to delegate any elements of this job to others.

The executive leader initiating this program, however, cannot simply rely on her external leader's questioning skills. She must define all key elements as clearly as possible, check out what support resources will be available, and build in sufficient meeting time for the handoff to be completed.

The same process of preparation and questioning must occur when any responsibility is transferred from external leaders to their teams. With a mutual dedication to preparation and the discipline to follow through, leaders can keep their organization's vision in focus. They can align their own actions, establish new standards for creative problem solving, and empower their teams to higher levels of performance.

BUILDING COMMITMENT

Around the year 1850, the French word, "solidarité," found its way into the English language. It's a word that describes a sense of community and means "being at one or united in some respect, especially in interests, sympathies, or aspirations" (Oxford English Dictionary 1971). In the years since, the word solidarity was misused by communists and has been overused by trade unions and other interest groups often in adversarial situations. It is now a problematic word, particularly so in management circles.

These negative connotations are regrettable because they limit further our abilities to describe the vital sense of community needed for teams to thrive. As leaders our role is to support solidarity—to encourage that critical sense of community within and among the organization's teams. Yet, too often, individual needs and fears rebel at the thought of letting go and giving others any meaningful control. Even among the pioneering team-based organizations in Scandinavia (described later in Chapter 9), one of the greatest problems they faced was a total misunderstanding of teamwork by managers. David Herman, the CEO of Saab, said of his company that even in one of the world's most egalitarian nations (Sweden), "There was a benign neglect by the middle manager who failed to relate to the work force and did not create a team spirit within the company" (Wickens 1993). Neglecting to build their teams' commitment to the company's vision, managers became an obstacle to success. Team spirit cannot be created from above, it is only created from within. Leaders who put themselves above or apart from their team effectively place themselves beyond that team spirit and outside the community that defines the team.

We need to remember that the hierarchies we are trying to restructure are usually no longer competitive. They often are serving their customers poorly. In many cases they misuse their employees, squandering their talents and capabilities through underutilization and neglect or paternalistic entitlements. These old structures have provided hideaways and support for a good deal of incompetent or downright lazy behavior at all levels. For example, a hospital human resource director in the early 1980s insisted that his institution had no need for training, beyond an occasional three-quarter-hour in-service for nurses. "We only hire fully trained, highly qualified individuals here at Memorial," he said. His stolid self-satisfaction was breathtaking—and ultimately deadly for all those human resources he was supposedly developing.

The old structures separated people and subdivided work groups, creating sub-subspecialists, fiefdoms, and "not-my-job" mentalities. They rewarded competitiveness, supported separateness, and reinforced the divisions between even functionally interdependent parts of the organization. Organizational power and rewards were linked to levels and titles, sometimes bearing little relationship to any tangible contributions to the hospital's mission. Managers got more power and rewards than staff simply because they were managers. Technical specialists got more than generalists just because they were specialists. It's very possible the only thing that kept everything afloat was a rising tide of regular, annual, double-digit cost increases in health care that "lifted all boats." Then the happy music stopped.

It's against this backdrop of our industry's history that we are now trying to promote change and rebuild structures and cultures to work in a new and progressively more constrained marketplace. Vestiges of the past, such as the old reward and reinforcement systems, will need clear-eyed scrutiny and major and dramatic change. No system designed primarily to support and reward individual performance should be expected to do anything else (Table 6–1). Applied to team-based structures and cultures, these competi-

---

Table 6–1 Comparison of Competitive and Collaborative Organization Characteristics

Characteristics	Competitive	Collaborative
structure	pyramidal	circular
communication	vertical	horizontal
decision making	top-down	consensus
problem solving	individual	group
authority	concentrated at top	allocated/shared
responsibility	concentrated at top	allocated/shared
rewards	concentrated at top	allocated/shared

tive systems will undermine commitment to the organization's collaborative vision and trust in leadership. They destroy teams.

Life on a mature, smoothly coordinated team is an inherently rewarding activity. Medical emergency teams often personify this characteristic. Working like the powerful coordinated limbs of some Saturday morning cartoon superhero, they calmly deal with nearly impossible situations and routinely succeed in defying death. Like most high-performing teams, they often consist of a self-selected group of highly trained and thoroughly interdependent individuals. Each member knows his or her own strengths and limitations and how these support or are supported by their teammates.

Unfortunately, no team begins its existence at this point of maturity. Teams typically go through conception (planned or accidental), gestation (with periodic nausea for the parent), birth (often noisy and overwhelmed by expectations), and development (complete with adolescence) before reaching any level of stable maturity. This often lengthy and tumultuous growth process is where the team's needs for rewards and reinforcement are most critically felt. To assuage the pains of growth and underscore the message that "this is necessary for the team's good," rewards must be consciously and carefully tied to team outcomes.

In organizations that are newly implementing teams, the performance and compensation systems are sometimes allowed to lag behind team implementation. A common excuse is that designing such new systems is complex and time-consuming work. If NASA had used this same reasoning, its complex, liquid-fueled, first-stage rockets would have lagged behind implementation of the simpler, solid-fuel, second-stage rockets. Problem is, only the liquid-fueled boosters were powerful enough to overcome the inertia and force of gravity at sea level. Solid-fuel alone could not have lifted the necessary payloads required to orbit spacecraft.

Launching teams is a lot like launching spacecraft. The older and more hidebound a hospital's hierarchy, the more inertia or organizational gravity is resisting this launch and the more powerful any launch vehicle will need to be. Focusing the mission, building the launch pad, and keeping the rocket on course once launched are all important, but actually getting it off the ground requires a complex, powerful first-stage booster. Team-oriented performance and compensation systems can provide this powerful lift.

Because development of such systems is time-consuming, this work should begin the moment your organization decides to move to team-based structures. The good news is that team-based compensation systems are no longer rare in American industry and there is a growing supply of consulting expertise available for design and implementation. A brief overview of developments in this area is provided in Chapter 9 and a longer discussion can be found in Chapter 12.

We have experienced a few special circumstances where pioneering hospitals successfully launched teams without the support of team-based compensation systems. In each of these instances, however, rewards and reinforcement remained a point of dissatisfaction for most team members until those systems were changed to reflect the new realities. The discontinuity between individualistic reward systems and the new demands of life within team structures just added another obstacle to teams achieving high performance, not to mention high job satisfaction.

Leaders have a responsibility for creating rewards and reinforcements that are fundamentally congruent with the desired structure and trajectory of their organization. Therefore, a hospital moving to teams will need to develop new rewards and reinforcers for members of emerging teams that are equitable with those available for individual performers. Over time, as the organization builds more team-based structures, this may become the predominant reward system, but individual performers (who don't fit into any team) will probably continue to exist in virtually every hospital and therefore parallel systems will be needed indefinitely.

Manager rewards also need close review. In other industries that have already switched to teams, many types of managers (foremen, supervisors, etc.) have virtually disappeared through restructuring. Upper managers have found their jobs and roles greatly enlarged in terms of span of control, with new responsibilities for leading hundreds, rather than 40 or 50 associates. Yet, even the phrase *span of control* is outdated because it is self-management by these teams of people, rather than increased *control*, that makes such broad spans possible. At the same time, self-management itself fundamentally changes the meaning of management control. Transformed management jobs must be reexamined to determine both their new organizational responsibilities and their realistic levels of worth to the organization. For example, team-based corporations in other industries commonly assess leaders based on the developmental levels achieved by their teams.

Putting responsibilities and rewards of managers and self-directed teams into balance based upon their contributions to the hospital's mission will go a long way toward building commitment and reestablishing organizational solidarity. But an entirely new relationship also needs to be forged between the leadership and its associates. This may require fundamental cultural changes.

Back in the late 1970s many industry consultants were struck by the high levels of formality encountered in hospitals. It seemed that people in health care were normally and almost ritualistically referred to as Doctor, Mister, or even Miss. This jarred against ears accustomed to the far less formal cultures found in business, even at very hierarchical companies such as AT&T and IBM. Today, even in very informal gatherings, we hear similar levels of formal address within hospital executive groups, even among people who have worked together for more than a decade. Trivial social artifact? More likely an unconscious indicator of the tenacity of the hierarchy and a telltale pointer to the way people currently think. Considering that long tenure is a fact of life in most hospitals, it is likely that the old culture is never far away.

Health care leaders, especially those with decades of industry experience, need to examine their own cultural baggage. Deciding what to keep, what to dispose of, and what to add may be easier if done in light of Table 6–1. Once these choices are made, leaders must create a strategy for changing the culture by getting others to share their commitment.

The story is told about Roger Milliken, head of the large carpet and textile company that bears his name. He recognized his firm's old paternalistic culture was not only represented in the organizational chart but also in the design and construction of his executive offices. He personally and organizationally supported a policy of openness at the top to any company employee. Yet his corner office in the executive suite was imposingly inaccessible to all but a small circle of top management colleagues. So one evening he had carpenters come in and entirely remove his office walls, leaving his desk standing in the middle of an open space. Whether or not this ultimately gave employees more access, an important symbolic step was taken and many walls, both physical and mental, soon came down throughout his organization. As they began to share a common commitment, Milliken, his leadership team, and others throughout the organization continued to remove obstacles separating leaders and their followers. Employees at Milliken still point to this act when they talk about the new culture of the reinvented company.

Unfortunately, a more common approach to reinvention was taken recently by our 104th Congress whose reforming zeal wavered slightly when it considered giving up the private Legislators Parking Lot near the entrance to Washington, D.C.'s National Airport terminal building. Their classically political solution: Change the sign to read Restricted Parking Lot and add a 24-hour gatekeeper. Merely changing the signs is no longer sufficient to lead changes in a work culture. The current work force is too sophisticated to be fooled by empty gestures or phony promises. Real actions leading to real changes are required to build people's commitment.

In the nationwide survey mentioned earlier (Voluntary Hospitals of America 1994), one of the challenges most often mentioned by hospital executives involved in leading major change was letting go. "Letting go of what?" you may ask. These executives were speaking mainly about control over necessary changes and their struggles with delegating real responsibility and authority to others. Loosening these historical reins of power and preparing teams to accept new responsibilities for work design, budgets, performance measures and reviews, and even team member selection and firing, was a slow and agonizing process for many leaders. This is a tremendously important issue. Truly empowering teams to own their own work is the central skill in building commitment. It must begin at the executive level and continuously extend through external team leadership. Inteam leaders also need to be empowered and empowering of their teams. Only when the last person in the final team feels truly empowered is the job done.

CONCLUSION

Modeling change behaviors, building a base of trust, setting an appropriate pace for the changes, creating a compelling vision of success, focusing the organization's many resources, and consistently building commitment and solidarity between leaders and teams are keys to leading organizations successfully through the major transformations facing health care today.

CHAPTER 7

Meeting the Challenges of Teams: New Leadership Roles and Responsibilities

Although this entire book is concerned with defining the new leadership required today, this chapter briefly reviews specific changes and their impacts on each of three levels of team leaders. It is a common reality that health care organizations tend to view restructuring and reengineering as activities that result mainly in changes for their staff-level workers. Both a review of the literature and extensive field experience belie this point of view. Most failures of team-based restructuring efforts are ultimately traceable to management's strategic or tactical errors rather than to problems at the team level. This is a bad news/good news message. Executive management has responsibility for any lack of success, but it also has the power and resources necessary to improve any poor outcomes.

How to meet this challenge is the subject of this chapter. We will identify concrete leadership roles and responsibilities at the three levels: (1) executive, (2) management, and (3) team. We will explore examples of these behaviors in action. Finally, we will extract several key principles for new leaders to follow as they institute changes to meet the challenge of teams.

NEW EXECUTIVE LEADER ROLES AND RESPONSIBILITIES

In the previous chapter we discussed the immense leverage executives wield and the corresponding weight of responsibility that such leaders must learn to carry successfully. Perhaps Rensis Likert, the father of participation management (Likert 1961), captured this best when he noted that until management behavior changes, nothing really changes.

Four key aspects of executive management are critical to understanding how new executive roles and responsibilities can promote organizational restructuring (Hout and Carter 1995):

1. Executives alone have a broad enough strategic view to direct major tactical modifications.

2. Executive-level managers can cut through multiple layers of the old hierarchy.
3. Management is uniquely positioned to solve political or process problems.
4. Executives control their own effect on the organization.

Let's examine each of these issues more closely.

The Broad Enough View

Restructuring initially requires two things: (1) a fresh review of the core purpose of the organization and (2) a redesign of existing structures and cultures to meet this identified purpose. In earlier chapters, we outlined various processes and methods to accomplish both these goals. In the real world, however, design teams often find themselves focusing exclusively on primary work teams. Who does the higher level redesign work? Who designs the leadership teams? Who ensures that the overall organization is better structured to fulfill its strategic purpose?

In the days before continuous improvement and organizational re-engineering the unwritten policy on such questions was something like, "Don't ask, don't tell." It was generally assumed that top management had already looked at the current structure in light of then current strategy and either found it good or was proceeding to move in the right direction. Today, we have educated, trained, and encouraged our staffs to look critically at *all* structures and processes. We've told them to *not* take the status quo for granted. They now ask, and leaders need to tell whenever possible.

The broad enough view encompasses all the key strategic knowledge necessary to make accurate, appropriate, and timely decisions about high-level restructuring. As we demonstrated in Chapter 2, careful design can eliminate major problems and wasted efforts by the rest of the organization. For example, one executive leader in a senior care organization found it necessary to redirect restructuring work in laundry services better to fit the needs of an upcoming—but unannounced—merger with a multihospital system. To discover and determine clear parameters for the design team, he had to conduct careful fact-finding and perform several delicate negotiations, all the while maintaining strict confidentiality. This was not a task that could have been readily or responsibly delegated to other staff members at lower levels in the organization.

Cutting through the Hierarchy

Significant changes in the restructuring process often need to cut vertically or diagonally through the organization. The multiskilled, multidisciplinary patient care team required for patient-focused care is the classic example. Employees from several traditionally separate departments and disciplines are combined into new mutually accountable work units. Only executives have the positional authority to propose this major structural surgery *and* the clout to carry it out. Vertical changes through a division may be authorized by that area's executive alone (although in the interest of organizational cohesion and effective communication such moves are rarely made without the advice and counsel of other members of the executive group). The entire executive council normally is involved in strategizing, negotiating, and planning when diagonal, cross-divisional modifications are proposed.

A design team at any level below the executive usually would not propose such major changes, even if it accurately identified the need for them, simply because these would exceed its normal horizons of authority. Staff-driven recommendations calling for cross-divisional restructuring often are perceived as dangerous to the group making them—likely to result in dead messengers, shot from at least two sides!

Case Study: "Higher Vision"

During an executive retreat, management identified serious problems with several internal service functions including word processing, computer support, and telecommunications.

Historically, each of these areas had developed in isolation from the others. Word processing currently reported to the office of the executive. Telecommunications was located in the materials management division (placed there because the telephone switch originally was located in the warehouse). Computer support was keeping a low-to-nonexistent profile somewhere inside data processing.

As might be expected, these functions shared no common service vision. Time that might have been better spent serving internal customers was used instead to protect fuzzy departmental boundaries. Quarrels about overlapping and conflicting areas of responsibility and a lack of coordination resulted in lost productivity, finger pointing, and a great deal of frustration throughout the organization.

Executive management brainstormed potential solutions. At one point in this process, the COO suggested creating a new area of information services to unify these functions into a new group and refocus them on their internal customers. Someone else suggested this group could be designed to set a whole new standard of service excellence. This idea caught the imagination of the retreat group. Several weeks later, a small task force completed a structure and work design for this new organization. The executive group reviewed and agreed to support this new structure and the proposed new standards. They also jointly pledged to begin moving their areas of responsibility toward applying these same standards.

Such major restructuring and commitments could not have emerged from lower levels in the organization. These outcomes required a level of insight sufficient to identify potential positive and negative impacts on the organization as a whole. It called for the involvement of people able to cut through the structure vertically, horizontally, or diagonally as necessary to solve problems.

Solving Political or Process Problems

There is a law of organizational dynamics that may be worthy of Sir Isaac Newton. Let's state it this way: "The more significant and meaningful an organizational change, the larger the political or process problems facing that change." Although there are many corollaries to this law, let's focus on the inherent cause and effect relationship. Major changes are, by definition, unsettling to the status quo. Those as fundamental as restructuring will question and modify the organization's focus and may even change its purpose. They ultimately may have noticeable effects on virtually everyone in the organization. People instinctively recognize this likelihood and equate major change with heavy-duty stress and anxiety. Even executives are not immune to fight-or-flight responses when confronted with such perceived dangers.

As a result, the most important, rule-changing, breakthrough ideas are not just *sometimes* met with resistance—they are nearly *always* met with serious resistance. This is because cross-organizational, cross-divisional, and cross-departmental solutions invariably rip up lovingly tended turf and stomp on carefully manicured toes. Let's use a football analogy: If the NFL still played entirely on natural grass, and groundskeepers ruled the league, cleats would surely be banned. Blocking, tackling, and quarterback sneaks also would be forbidden because of their harmful effects on the turf. Imagine a football game played first to protect the field and only second to outscore the opponent.

In organizations out of touch with today's economic realities, the game *is* being run by the groundskeepers. For these organizations, it's not quality patient care, or the mission, or even the bottom line—it's the turf, stupid! Top management has fostered specialist-dominated fiefdoms or at least allowed them to develop more or less unchecked. Now, only the executives can overthrow them—by dismantling them and/or stripping them of their organizational power.

More often than not, process and political problems are found to be the flip sides of a single issue. For example, one hospital's inability to deploy respiratory care services successfully to patient care teams was initially attributed to the inherent complexity of the procedures combined with the organization's so-called unique patient mix. Soon after, when a competing institution accomplished this supposedly impossible feat it was discovered that the "process complexity" problem was really a political power struggle between the manager of the respiratory services department and several nurse managers. Solving these game-stopping process and political problems is a key role for executive leaders, because only they are equipped to deal with them forcefully and directly.

Managing the Effects of Top Management

In the previous chapter we discussed the enormous leverage wielded by upper management, both for good and ill. This multiplier effect is heightened in times of major uncertainty because leaders are watched even more closely by anxious followers. So, the effect of executive decisions must be carefully managed to assure alignment with the organization's mission and congruence with its high-priority outcomes.

Executive self-regulation is commonly required during major change efforts. For example, a hospital vice-president in charge of human resources disagreed so strongly with the hospital's strategic restructuring plans that she began actively and secretly working to undermine this initiative while publicly voicing support. After many subtle attempts to derail the emerging team-based designs, she recognized that a growing momentum was overwhelming her efforts. In frustration, she began working more blatantly against the restructuring and in the process tipped her hand. When the CEO confronted her, she finally admitted she did not share upper management's team-based vision for the organization and resigned on the spot. Her resignation was accepted.

The staff and managers who reported to this vice-president had known for years about her mistrust of team-based structures and processes. During her five-year tenure they watched her assume control over and micromanage every department reporting to her into a state of absolute dependence. As the executive group implemented strategies for restructuring the hospital based on teams, her staff witnessed an ever-widening gulf between the public vice-president of human resources who talked the talk and their private boss who took frequent aim at these "harebrained" ideas.

Due to the seriously mixed signals their boss sent them, these managers of several human resources functions crucial to the change operated under a caution light. As a result, the entire organization's efforts were hobbled. Direct executive intervention was required to resolve this situation. No other levels of the hierarchy possessed the positional or personal authority required to deal effectively with the problem.

Fortunately, most organizational effects of upper management normally don't involve acts of bad faith requiring dramatic confrontations. More typically, problems are caused by honest mistakes and miscommunication, and are solved straightforwardly in face-to-face discussions between peers. In practice, ill-advised executive actions or decisions will rarely be dealt with by anyone other than the top management group (boards of directors are occasionally forced to act).

One of the challenges for executive leaders is to establish and maintain good feedback channels. Mirroring the realities of position and power, that old hierarchical communications habit—bad news down, good news up—is pervasive enough in most organizations to assure an ongoing need for accurate executive self-examination. The key question, "How are we doing?" must be asked regularly. Trusted and trustworthy sources for both the good *and* bad news must be found and cultivated. Some executive groups periodically will use consultants, in addition to internal indicators, to help assure objectivity. Most will employ regular, tightly focused organizational assessments and use longitudinal monitoring methods such as climate surveys and exit interviews.

Summary

Major organizational transformations need to be guided by executive leaders because they alone have the broad strategic view of organizational requirements, market imperatives, and industry trends required to develop high-level work redesigns. The focus of change must be on what is best for the organization and its mission, unimpeded by low-level territorial or procedural issues. Implementing these changes calls for decision making and problem solving across traditional structural lines. Executive leaders need to clear a path through this minefield of explosive political issues in order for the rest of the organization to follow through on the desired outcomes. Perhaps most important, the powerful impacts of upper managers themselves will require constant monitoring and frequent modification, based on accurate timely feedback from a broad variety of sources.

NEW MANAGEMENT LEADER ROLES AND RESPONSIBILITIES

There is normally a direct relationship between the success of middle management leaders and that of their teams. When aided by empowered managers (who understand that their roles and responsibilities are fundamentally and permanently changed by the new structure), teams will thrive.

Handicapped by traditional command and control management, teams struggle, shrivel, and die. Middle management roles and responsibilities during this conversion are absolutely critical to team success, yet many organizations don't understand or acknowledge this crucial interrelationship.

The danger is particularly strong for those organizations tightly focused on reaping significant savings by removing the middle management layers. They may believe that the earlier they get managers out of the way, the sooner their teams will coalesce. The opposite usually proves true. As we've outlined in preceding chapters on design and implementation, teams require a great deal of attention and assistance. This is especially true in their early stages. If middle managers are already removed (either physically or psychologically) who will do this important work?

Five key roles emerge for these managers/coaches:

1. protecting teams from becoming disenfranchised
2. ensuring that leaders and teams receive needed training
3. modeling empowering behaviors
4. rewarding empowering behavior
5. coaching leaders and teams in empowering skills

Protecting Teams

You might think of your initial teams as viruses invading a body. Immediately alerted, the body's defense system sends out a wave of antiviral attackers to isolate and destroy the invaders. Health care organizations generally have well-developed immune systems. If allowed to operate freely without suppression, these defenses will usually succeed in killing the teams. New teams, particularly those formed early in an organization's restructuring process, face daunting challenges. Some we've seen include:

- shunning behaviors from colleagues
- sabotage based on envy or spite
- deliberate slowdowns by internal suppliers
- negative gossip and rumors
- multilevel obstructionism

Teams need to have recourse when they run into nonsupportive colleagues or managers and rightfully look to their coach(es) for help. Early in the organization's transformation, clearing away internal and external obstacles may be a large part of the manager's job. For example, it may be necessary to negotiate with the executive leader about assigning a team leader to a key information-sharing committee. Initially the coach may need to attend meetings with this person to ensure acceptance by the group.

Ensuring Training

The health care industry historically hasn't been a leader in employee training. A very common attitude until quite recently was, "We hire only well-trained people, why train them further?" Teams, however, require extensive education. (See Chapter 11 for curriculum suggestions.) Managers/coaches often must fight for the funds and the time necessary to train their teams. Even when dollars and hours are available, these leaders still have to guide their novices through the initial obstacles. Just arranging attendance by a multishift patient care team for a single day of training is an amazingly daunting activity, often requiring a manager's power and connections.

On the other end of the learning curve, managers must make certain that team education doesn't end too soon. Teams need encouragement to stick with the program even if the patient census skyrockets or new construction projects intrude. Work-related obstacles to training will need to be managed. At the top, the organization may even suffer from the "marathon effect." This is when leadership, which earlier began the team-based restructuring, forgets that its group was among the first runners. Although they may view the race as already completed, many teams may have just left the starting gate or are waiting to begin. The coach makes sure these teams have a chance to finish.

Modeling Empowering Behaviors

This aspect of leadership was covered extensively in the previous chapter, but an example at the middle-management level would help reemphasize its importance.

Case Study: "The Laboratory Laboratory"

A laboratory manager created a design team consisting of department members. Among its first projects, this group was charged with creating descriptions of the self-management responsibilities that lab teams would own within two years, five years, and seven years. The manager became an on-call consultant to this team, assisting it in creating initial lists of current management functions, joining in joint visioning efforts, answering many questions, and referring it to other information sources. Department members were consulted extensively and regularly informed about progress.

The design team's first work product was a complete list and proposed seven-year schedule for implementation of transferred responsibilities covering the laboratory team's development. Design Team members presented this plan to the newly formed teams who accepted it as an accurate and helpful guidance tool. Teams were encouraged to use this document as a guideline and were given freedom to take on tasks earlier than projected if required by their individual needs.

The level of responsibility and autonomy given to the design team by its manager sent a strong empowering message to all teams. Also, as department staff members watched the manager work in a coaching role with the design team, old stereotypes were broken and new practices and behaviors modeled.

Rewarding Empowering Behavior

The laboratory manager rewarded those behaviors he wanted to increase. He gave the design team a whole piece of important work to do. Early on, as the team recognized its shared talents and capabilities, he clarified the parameters of its charter or purpose. He noted that the team's decisions were important to all lab teams, affecting the work lives of everyone in the department. While he gave it a good deal of scope in decision making, he also offered his advice and support. In some instances, issues and problems were brought to him that really should have been directed to the design team. He consistently referred these back to the team, recognizing that the team would ask for help if needed.

Giving the team this level of autonomy required significant levels of trust on both sides. The laboratory manager trusted his design team to make good decisions; the team trusted its coach to be available for advice and support. This relationship was mutually rewarding. The team was proud of its work product. The manager was proud of his design team and said so at the plan's presentation.

Coaching Others in Empowering Skills

For teams to work, all team members ultimately must learn how to empower each other. Empowerment is one of the key management responsibilities that must be transferred to the team and it is one of the most difficult to accomplish.

An image that springs to mind is a high-wire act. Envision the manager on one end of a tightrope and a team at the other. The challenge for this leader is to pass several heavy and bulky responsibilities over to the team while all balance together on the shaky wire. Things passed too early may cause everyone to lose balance. Things passed too late force the team to seize responsibilities, toppling everyone. Developmental activities by the team and its coach must be continuously and carefully coordinated. The relationship between managers and inteam leadership is especially important in helping maintain this sense of balance. In the next section we will discuss this area in more depth, examining many specific challenges facing inteam leaders.

Groups unaccustomed to having decision-making authority or owning any real job responsibilities will require a weaning process to change their old pass-the-buck-up habits. They'll also need time to practice making their own decisions and living with the consequences of those decisions. These people will need coaches who are aware of these needs and who will actively seek opportunities for practice where the cost of mistakes will be relatively low.

Summary

Coaching is a central role for middle managers. It is critical, particularly in the formative stages of team building. Managers who have made the important personal transition from hands-on supervision to hands-off coaching are worth their weight in gold. Such leaders accomplish what is arguably one of the most difficult tasks we have ever asked of managers—turning over major management responsibilities to their teams in a timely, clear, and conscientious manner. As Beverly Geber, Special Projects Editor of *TRAINING* magazine, says, "The transition from manager to coach is probably the most difficult of all the individual changes that must take place to bring work teams into being" (Geber 1992, 25).

INTEAM LEADER ROLES AND RESPONSIBILITIES

In Chapter 3, while discussing team roles and responsibilities, we briefly touched on the important role of inteam leader. Whoever takes on this role assumes several of the key leadership responsibilities required by the team. Since each team delineates and negotiates the unique combination of responsibilities it requires of its inteam leader, it is difficult to precisely define this role. Typical responsibilities involve setting team meeting agendas, scheduling and running these meetings, monitoring team goals, attending organizational meetings, and communicating with other leaders.

The Balancing Act

Particularly among new teams made up of people accustomed to multiple layers of management, this role can be a balancing act. This person is not the new supervisor and must continually resist being miscast as one. He or she is a team member whose responsibilities are always defined by the team. He or she is accountable first and last to the team. Leadership external to the team must recognize this bond and work to keep it strong and viable. In no circumstances should the inteam leader be co-opted by management into a supervisory role, such as being asked to do performance reviews of team members alone or being paid an additional increment for taking on the leadership role.

Where the inteam leader is accountable for carrying out designated leadership responsibilities, the team is correspondingly accountable for the success of its leader. Because an inteam leader is a player/coach, the team should carefully build a doable role, including only those responsibilities that reasonably can be accomplished when added to this person's regular job. As the team develops, its needs will change and its leadership roles and responsibilities will require some revisions.

Role Rotation

The importance of this role leads us again to advise strongly that it be rotated on a scheduled basis, for example, initially every one to two years. This rotation serves several purposes. Teams seeking to develop all members' leadership skills will seek to rotate all positions. A limited period of leadership service will be easier to sell to qualified team members than an open-ended one. If rotated, the role of inteam leader is less likely to be confused with the job of supervisor. Setting an expectation of changing roles will better match the fluid needs of developing teams and make it easier for a team to rectify any mismatch situations.

Leadership Challenges

Regardless of how it is defined or its term of service limited, the inteam leader's role will share three challenges with other leadership positions. The essence of success lies in striking the right balance between:

1. providing guidance and giving up control
2. doing difficult things alone and letting others learn how to do them
3. making the tough decisions and letting others make them

Too much leadership command and control over a given task will stifle the capability, initiative, and creativity of the team, but so will too little direction, guidance, and discipline. The right balance will be a carefully considered blend of control and letting go, based on the team's current developmental level in this particular area of its responsibilities.

Any team leader needs to develop capacity within the team. By necessity this involves allowing team members to learn by doing, especially those things they haven't done before. This means taking risks. It means people will make mistakes. The challenge for a team leader lies in supporting teammates through difficult tasks without taking over—coaching through the inevitable mistakes until a person succeeds in learning to do the difficult things. Often some of the hardest to coach will be interpersonal skills such as effectively asserting one's own opinion in a group, directly confronting an unacceptable behavior in another member, or personally saying "I'm sorry" for a rash statement.

The leadership potential of the team requires continuous development. Most of us can recall situations when we felt torn between making a decision for someone or letting that person make the decision on his or her own. Most parents of children about to enter adulthood or head off to college have experienced this dilemma. You realize these young persons will soon need to be making their own day-to-day decisions without your daily guidance. You have invested years modeling sound judgment and good planning. Now you must trust in what they've learned, but first you must get out of their way and let them try out their own decision-making capabilities. Young teams are similar. A conscientious team leader actively looks for good opportunities for developing decision-making skills. Even if it takes the team longer to make a decision that the leader might make in minutes, the team still gets this task. The point of the exercise is leadership development—their decision is often a relatively incidental outcome.

Finally, the inteam leader must never allow individual team members to fail. This does not mean the leader jumps to the defense or lowers any standards of performance. The leader's role is to remind team members as often as necessary that they are all in this effort together. As a team they will succeed together or they will fail together.

Summary

The inteam leader's role is neither simple nor easy. It demands a complex balancing of team member and leadership responsibilities. It must be more responsive than any other leadership position to the sensitivities and needs of the team. But at the same time, it has to hold the team accountable for its performance, without alibis or blaming. The greatest responsibility of the inteam leader is team development. The greatest danger lies in becoming thought of as the new supervisor rather than as a leader among peers.

CONCLUSION

Each level of team management involves unique challenges. These new roles and responsibilities require learning and practice. Organizations expecting current staff members to assume these positions should expend serious thought and considerable efforts in selecting and developing the necessary skills in their new leadership. If a leadership development curriculum currently exists, it should be carefully reviewed for compatibility with team structures and goals. Basic information specific to building, developing, and managing teams should be added. The success of teams, particularly in their earliest stages, will heavily depend on development of knowledgeable and versatile leaders at all levels.

CHAPTER 8

Chaos to Creativity: Leading Change and Transition

Major cultural transformation such as that entailed in the conversion to a team-based organization simply cannot succeed without effective leadership. Leaders with a strong sense of purpose and clarity of vision. Leaders who can articulate that vision with enough enthusiasm to motivate others to embrace the vision and make it their own. Leaders with the ability and the savvy to manage the transformation and patience to cope with the process of transition as well.

Health care executives and managers have been instrumental in creating and managing change throughout their careers. Lately, however, there is growing suspicion that the current pace of change is different from what it used to be. It *is* different. The 1990s is referred to as the decade of transition. With a new millennium nearing, changes are occurring faster than ever before with each major change occurring hard on the heels of previous changes. An organization may institute a quality initiative one year, restructure the entire organization months later only to find themselves acquired by or merged with another organization or system with what feels like breakneck speed. Also increasing is the complexity of change. For example, a health care organization's decision to use a team model as the basic organizational structural unit alters not only the work of its employees but also how they work, where they work, and what the work includes. It may mean blurring the boundaries between disciplines and it certainly results in changing the work the individual employee carries out. A conversion to teams also changes managers' roles and prompts myriad changes in the organization, especially in the area of information and reward and recognition systems. Who makes the decisions changes and employees contribute and participate at a much higher level.

Change today differs in another way as well. The life span of our solutions is shorter than it has ever been, creating a tremendous impact on the organization (Connor 1993). It can be difficult for executives, managers, and employees to be positive and enthusiastic after investing their energy and personal commitment in a change process that turns out to be only the tiny first step of a much larger evolutionary process in the organization.

CHANGE VERSUS TRANSITION

Effective leaders learn to differentiate between the processes of change and transition. The experience of change is one shared by all health care workers. But, how many times are changes made, where something new is started only for the organization to discover that the employees involved never adapted to it? As the change degenerated over time, work reverted back to the way it was prior to the initiative. Successful leaders recognize that change has an important twin—transition—and although closely intertwined, it needs to be managed separately. Effective leaders respect the transition process and accept that it must occur before the change can be anchored in place and fully realized.

Differentiating between the two concepts is essential. Change is an *external* event, like restructuring, while transition is the individual's *internal* psychological adaptation to the change that has occurred (Bridges 1991). Transitions take longer and may not be outwardly evident to others. There are several reasons changes requiring transitions are not managed well in our organizations:

1. *Change and Transition Are Not Differentiated.* If we don't distinguish between change and transition or understand the relationship between the two, it is easy to ignore the needs of people in transition. The two are so closely related that ignoring or dealing ineffectively with either creates problems. Poorly managed change will impair the ease of a transition. If transition is ignored, the effectiveness and longevity of the change will be directly affected.

In one organization, a newly restructured care center was renovated. Multiple delays and construction problems plagued the project, and even though the center opened on time, work on several major aspects of the renovation was incomplete. When staff members relocated to the new center and the first patients were transferred, there were still many problems: linen chutes that couldn't be opened, missing clocks that hadn't been replaced, and a refrigerator that didn't fit in the kitchen. These problems created difficulties in the delivery of patient care and hampered a smooth and easy transition for staff.

On the other hand, the change itself may proceed smoothly but if people have inadequate time to make the internal transitions and adapt to the change, real transformation may not happen. People will revert to their old ways of doing things.

2. *Productivity Decreases During Change and Transition.* Work usually gets accomplished faster and easier by sticking with the status quo. When we ask people to change, it means they will have to learn new ways and take longer to accomplish the same results during these learning periods. Consider how hard it is to break old habits and replace them with new ones. Remember how long it took you to do a project while also learning a new computer software program? Previous levels of productivity eventually return and usually improve once you learn the program.

You can observe this effect during early stages of team development. Productivity decreases as a result of additional time spent in team meetings. Although the work occurring during the meetings (i.e., establishing a clear purpose, well-defined expectations of each other, or clarity of boundaries between the manager's and the team's work) will lead to more effective team relationships and outcomes, it is very time consuming. Collaboratively planning and making decisions takes a team much longer at the outset than it will after it has gained experience and expertise in these processes.

When people in the organization are in the midst of great change and making personal transitions they spend a lot of time and energy talking about it with colleagues. For many people, such dialogue is necessary to the transition process. In coming to grips with changes, this talk takes additional time away from productive work. Formal and informal communication time with leadership also increases during the transition process.

3. *Transition Results in Painful and Unsafe Feelings.* For transition to occur, the individual must first let go of the old way. This can be more difficult than anticipated, especially if it's not by personal choice. Emotions experienced and observed during transition are similar to those of grieving. There may be feelings of sadness, anger, hostility, bitterness, resentment, and frustration. At the best of times, none of these emotions are pleasant, but they can be problematic in the workplace. It may not feel safe to be angry with your supervisor. Likewise, it often doesn't feel safe to express your true feelings about the latest executive decision. Generally, most people are uncomfortable with themselves when they experience what they perceive to be negative emotions such as anger or depression. Most of us don't like it when we are angry and lose our tempers with those around us because we feel out of control.

4. *Although a Change Can Happen Quickly, Transitions Take a Long Time.* Particularly in fast-changing markets and industries, many executives

and managers are impatient when processes take too much time since there is none to "waste." *All* will be lost, however, if people don't take the time needed to navigate their transitions. In one organization, managers were upset and frustrated with the number of changes that they were being asked to make and support. Their behavior showed a lack of trust in and respect for the organization's executives. When they discussed their concerns about the volume of changes with those executives, managers were told that these changes were just speed bumps and they should just get over them. The managers were infuriated by what they perceived as a lack of understanding or respect for their feelings and a lack of executive support. Some became determined to sabotage the efforts of the executive group.

5. *Change and Transitions Are Unpredictable.* As much as we would like to believe that we can manage these processes and, by implication, control and direct them, it just doesn't happen that way. Change rarely unfolds exactly as planned. You can't predict what losses people will feel or who will feel these emotions most strongly. A CEO interviewed for a recent Voluntary Hospitals of America (VHA) study entitled, "Improving Patient Outcomes Through System Change: A Focus on the Changing Roles of Healthcare Executives" (Lorimer 1994), gave two examples of this. The first organizational change made was in the titles of managers from "director" to "leader." He comments that two years later, there are managers who still haven't forgiven him for making this change. He didn't anticipate that managers would perceive the change in titles as a loss. The second example he shared was a new structure for increased physician–employee collaboration and problem solving. He anticipated that this change would take years to accomplish fully and was surprised when significant results were experienced almost immediately. Although one situation turned out better than anticipated and one was worse, the net result of these events was his loss of self-confidence in his ability to predict future occurrences. He was fortunate that this wake-up call came early in his organization's change initiative because from it he learned the need for greater flexibility and resilience.

This chapter will now explore in detail the concepts of both change and transition. A specific process for each will be shared as well as the lessons learned from actual organizations undergoing significant changes.

LEADING THE PROCESS OF CHANGE

Change-management theories of the past have offered insight into how to produce change and how to recognize its various stages. What is needed today, however, are more specific techniques for managing, leading, and coping with the process of change. Past experience barely prepares us for the 1990s, the decade of transition. Although change is unpredictable and can never be completely controlled, applying a logical process to managing and leading it can help us reduce the chaos and increase our leadership effectiveness. Considering change as a developmental process helps us establish order during chaotic times.

As a developmental process, change can be broken down into five phases, based on an energy model adapted for organizations by Nancy Post, an organizational development consultant (*Working Balance,* 1989). The five stages or phases are: (1) preparation (start-up), (2) movement (growth), (3) team creativity (maturation), (4) the new reality (productivity), and (5) integration (closure), as illustrated in Figure 8–1. During the first phase—preparation—major concerns to be managed include establishing the direction or purpose of the change and identifying needed resources to accomplish this change. The work of the second stage, movement, includes dealing with issues such as a decision-making structure and planning for how the change will unfold. Team creativity, the third phase, involves issues of overall coordination and cooperation, priority setting, interpersonal relationships, and communication. During the fourth phase—the new reality—productivity and maintenance of the change are key considerations. Integration, the final

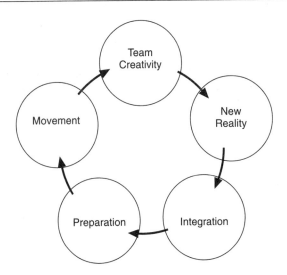

Figure 8–1 A Five-Phase Change Model. *Source:* Reprinted with permission from J. Manion, "Chaos or Transformation," *Journal of Nursing Administration,* Vol. 23, No. 5, pp. 41–48, © 1993, J.B. Lippincott Company.

phase, requires attention to quality and evaluative efforts. These five stages also have been applied to the management of innovation in health care, which is the implementation of creative ideas. (Manion 1993) Each of these phases will be discussed using a short case study and applications to the health care setting. The issues of each developmental phase apply whether you are responsible for large-scale organizational change or change within your work group or department.

Phase One: Preparation

The initiators of change often are anxious to get started immediately; however, smoothness of implementation will be increased by carefully laying the groundwork in early stages. During the first phase—preparation—the exact purpose of the change must be clarified. Why is this change needed or appropriate at this time? Why is it important to patients, customers, employees, or the organization? It may seem obvious but we often overestimate people's understanding of the initiative. How can the organization prepare employees as they undergo or collaborate with implementation of these changes? How is this change congruent with the mission of the organization and goals of the department?

By clearly defining and articulating the purpose of the change initiative, the leader provides a sense of direction for those on whom the change depends for implementation. Clarifying the purpose also focuses people on the change. If, as the leader, you are unable to relate the purpose of the change to something that is meaningful and relevant to those affected, don't expect enthusiasm or support as you proceed. For example, reducing the cost of care still is not as relevant a purpose to many health care employees as are changes to improve quality or increase effectiveness for the customer. Consider what this change means to employees personally. What would be of greatest value or interest to them? Be certain that the purpose of the change initiative is not only congruent with, but strongly supportive of, the organization's mission as this will increase the likelihood of continued support at all levels.

Another aspect of preparation is to secure resources needed for a successful implementation process. Adequate resources must be made available, including money, time, availability of coaches, mentors, and other support people in the system, the skills of employees and managers, and interest from employees. What will it cost to implement this change? Are financial resources available? During the implementation will you need access to people with special skills? Are employees currently dealing with more changes than they can handle? Do employees and managers need to learn additional skills before implementing this new change? Do any of these questions really matter? In other words, is this a change absolutely required for short- or long-term survival, as opposed to organizational demise?

Decide whether the resources needed for implementation match up with those you have available. Peter Drucker, the renowned management expert, says that the real work of leadership today is determining how to provide for and stay focused on the high priority needs with the scarce resources available. It is tempting to become involved in numerous change initiatives because they all seem desirable, but that doesn't mean you should follow through on all. Drucker says, "You have to learn to say 'no' when the temptation is to do good. The secret of effectiveness is concentration of the very meager resources you have where you can make a difference" (Flowers 1991, 53).

It's hard to decline an opportunity to change when you strongly believe in the need for it, but an accurate assessment of resources may tell you it will be impossible to carry out. Too many organizational leaders start down a specific path because it seems the thing to do rather than basing their decision on an actual assessment of resources and the impact of the change on the organization's mission.

Addressing the issues of this first phase is predominantly a leadership responsibility. Employees or other team members have an active role as well, which is to ask questions about the purpose and direction, to assist in further clarifying it and to accurately assess current resources affecting their spheres of influence. Once the purpose has been clarified and needed resources identified, it is then time to proceed to the next phase—movement. A brief example of an ongoing, successful organizational change will illustrate this process.

Case Study: "Trying To Do It Right"

Jane, the CEO of a 320-bed midwestern hospital, attended a regional health care executive meeting and learned about organizational changes in several other facilities involving the implementation of teams and increased responsibility acceptance of employees. Throughout her four-year tenure as CEO, her philosophy and practice of highly involving employees had developed momentum in the organization. She clearly recognized the benefits of establishing teams as the basic organizational unit and as a way to build higher levels of employee involvement into the very structure of the organization.

She decided that a way to prepare her organization for an increasingly uncertain future was to accelerate employees' involvement in decision making and problem solving on departmental and organizational issues. For some time, she had been frustrated with a lack of forward movement toward several long-term organizational goals. The level of employee involvement varied widely among departments and depended on each individual manager's philosophy. Work units were poorly structured and did not enhance productivity or effectiveness. It seemed with each passing month, the organization was being driven increasingly by a crisis orientation that made it difficult to focus on long-term survival strategies for the system.

Case Study/Phase One: Preparation

Jane was anxious to share these ideas with her executive colleagues. For this effort to be successful, she would need the full support and involvement of the entire executive leadership group. Although her first inclination was to begin informal discussions, she decided instead to add this topic to the agenda of the next executive meeting. To prepare she reflected on how a team-based structure would best fit the mission of the organization. She considered the internal culture and challenges facing the organization in the near future. She also identified problems with the system and areas where performance was unsatisfactory.

One area of major concern for Jane involved organizational resources. She considered the following areas:

Financial. Although the hospital was financially sound, length of stays had decreased steadily and revenue had significantly dropped during the last few months. Increasing numbers of patients were covered by managed care contracts which dictated shorter stays and limited reimbursement.

Management Staff. In recent years whenever the manager of a small department resigned, the hospital asked another manager to assume the responsibilities of the departing manager rather than hire a replacement. As a result, there had been some minor reductions in managerial staff; however, more serious trimming was needed. Management staff tenure averaged 12 years and only a handful of new managers had been added in recent years. Management skills were fairly strong, but only a few demonstrated strong, effective leadership.

Educational Resources. Internal education efforts had been impressive years ago, but education department staff had been reduced significantly six years ago during a layoff. Presently, the department provided only mandatory education and training. Because of this limited centralized resource, many departments had developed internal staff to assume responsibilities for education.

Organizational Culture. Employees had been gradually moving from an attitude of entitlement ("You owe me."), to an attitude of earning ("I owe you, so that you will owe me."). Workers' clinical and technical skills were good and pride in their work was rebounding from a dip after the layoff. Although progress was slow, more employees were beginning to accept responsibility for their behaviors and decisions rather than depending on the manager or blaming others when things went wrong.

Among staff groups, two seemingly contradictory attitudes prevailed: the first was a "can do" attitude, and the second was a "wait and see" approach to everything.

Experience with Change. The most significant organization-wide change was the layoff that had occurred two years before Jane's arrival. It had come as a surprise to employees and several key aspects had been mishandled. Trust and respect for the executive team had been restored during the last four years but many employees with long memories remained ready to assume the worst. One serious misjudgment made by the decision makers six years ago was failure to anticipate the emotional reactions of the survivors, the employees who remained. The often publicly expressed attitude of the previous CEO was that employees should be happy they still had jobs!

Timing. Timing was another factor to consider. The hospital was in the middle of the winter season and a high census was straining the human resources of the organization. Employees were exhausted from working extra shifts and overtime. This situation was destined to reverse itself within four to six weeks, however, when the hospital would be entering its slower period.

Jane sensed that change would need to begin as soon as possible if it was to be successful. The rate of mergers, sales, and closures of regional hospitals and health systems was increasing and she knew the effects would soon be felt in this community. Moving to team-based structures promised to increase the resiliency, flexibility, and responsiveness to change within the organization.

At the executive's meeting, Jane introduced the topic of teams by sharing the experiences of colleagues she had met at the regional meeting. The group discussed mutual knowledge and experiences with organizational teams and what they were reading in their professional literature and hearing about when they attended outside meetings. Several executives expressed long-standing interest in the idea. Each agreed individually to explore the concept further. The group scheduled a date and time to revisit the idea.

At the next meeting, the executive team reviewed the mission of the organization and discussed the purpose of a change to becoming more team-based. The actual change was described as "increasing staff's involvement in decision making and problem solving about departmental and organizational issues." Purposes of the change were identified as follows:

- to improve the delivery of patient care and customer service as a result of better prepared and more involved employees
- to create a flexible, responsive structure enabling the organization to respond quickly to new marketplace forces
- to prepare staff for participation in future organizational changes

Resources needed to support this change included:

- training (for leaders and employees) with paid time for educational offerings
- leadership development assistance for current managers
- increased resources within the education department
- commitment from the management group
- support from the board of trustees
- financial resources to hire external consultants to help develop a group of internal consultants
- increased time commitment and involvement for leaders at all levels in the organization
- more open communication systems
- receptivity and trust from employees

Jane and the executive group obtained assistance almost immediately by meeting with and selecting external consultants who were experienced in implementing teams and decentralizing decision making in health care organizations. These consultants were chosen specifically because they were process consultants who would help the organization develop its own solutions and strengthen its internal talent pool. In addition, the executive group began immediately, both individually and with the external experts, to educate themselves as fully as possible. The board of trustees granted the go-ahead for the next phase.

Phase Two: Movement

Structural elements needed for supporting the change are considered during the second phase. What structure do you need to bring about this change? How will decisions be made about the change and who will make them? What kind of committee or task force structure is necessary? How will current employee roles and responsibilities be affected throughout the organization? What changes will be needed in other organizational systems?

Depending on the nature and scope of the change being considered, a vision for the future is important. A vision is imperative if the change requires people to behave or relate to each other differently—often called a cultural change. Asking people to alter their behavior is usually unsuccessful unless the leader can envision future changes, articulate them clearly, and use this vision to gain commitment from the people who must implement the change. In cases of major change, a clearly articulated vision shared by all is usually the difference between mere compliance and true commitment on the part of employees and leaders alike.

A vision is a critical step for planning to be effective, and planning is a key issue for this phase. If you can see your destination it's easier to determine steps needed to reach it. An implementation plan with assigned responsibilities, specific time frames, and estimated costs is fundamental in organizing and initiating the change. The plan is used to communicate with staff members and managers and, in some cases, to obtain needed support from others in the system (i.e., the board, medical staff, community partners) who can influence the initiative. It also provides a means of measuring progress and alerts you to the need for additional resources that you may have missed in Phase One. Overly rigid plans that cannot be modified or updated hamper creativity because innovative change rarely unfolds as planned.

Case Study/Phase Two: Movement

At this point, the executive group worked together to create its vision of the organization for the future. The vision statement read:

"Our organization will be a highly responsive and flexible organization within which employees work in an empowered, team-based environment."

The next step was developing a plan the organization could use to arrive at this vision. A resource team was established to serve as in-house experts for both the design and the development of teams. Reporting relationships, boundaries, decision-making parameters and authority between the executive group and the resource team were established. Selection criteria for resource team appointees were determined as well as the anticipated time commitment. Executive group members began sharing their vision with other employees. This dialogue reshaped the vision in ways that resulted in stronger commitment to it housewide.

"Our organization will be a highly responsive and flexible organization in which employees and leaders work together within an empowered, self-directed, and team-based environment to deliver the highest quality of customer service possible."

Although some employees remained skeptical that certain managers could behave in ways congruent with this vision, they were generally excited by the possibilities.

With assistance from the external consultants, an organization plan was developed which included realistic time frames for each step and clearly assigned responsibilities. Sequencing of departmental implementation was discussed and a preliminary plan approved. The resource team's initial assignment was to establish a process for designing and developing teams. The education department developed an education plan to support these efforts.

Phase Three: Team Creativity

Team creativity is the third phase of change and is usually where the real action begins! Charismatic and dynamic leaders sometimes try to begin the change process here, because the synergy of this phase is seductive. Change progresses more smoothly, however, if the foundation of the first two phases is firmly in place before you reach this stage. Key issues at this point include coordination and cooperation, determining priorities, internal communications, and the interpersonal aspects of the change. Each of these will be examined separately.

Close coordination among internal staff, managers, and leaders is critical for any change initiative to work, otherwise, employees are left with the impression that "the left hand doesn't know what the right hand is doing." Coordination of the actual implementation plan is a major task. Examples of poor coordination abound, but one of the most dramatic is the hospital that restructured, redesigned, and opened a major new care center during peak census period. Just when staff could barely meet service requirements because of volume demand, they also had to learn new processes and work with new team members. The initiative failed and the organization lost months of planning and development time, not to mention credibility with physicians and staff alike.

When there is extensive change occurring, people tend to become "me" focused. Normally cooperative people and departments suddenly seem obstructive and unresponsive. Anticipate and monitor this reaction to mitigate the negative results. Cooperation from staff and managers may be obtained simply by asking for it or stating it as an expectation. Leaders can model cooperation and their expectations for it by openly and frequently sharing information. Better to err on the side of too much information rather than too little.

Staying focused on priorities also helps maintain commitment to the initiative. Reevaluate and restate your priorities as often as needed to communicate continuing support and a sense of urgency for this change. For example, you may be asking people to work in teams and take responsibility for departmental decisions. In the beginning, it may seem that decisions take forever to make. If the workload suddenly increases, or a regulatory agency announces a surprise visit, or some other unpredicted and stressful event occurs, you must resist the urge to revert to the old ways of working. If this change is still a priority, consider adding temporary staff, approving overtime or other alternatives during this difficult period. When people know what the priorities are, they remain focused and thus more efficient. If the new change is "dumped" the minute things become stressful, the message to employees is that it wasn't really a priority after all.

Communication during change is absolutely essential. Leaders must be able to articulate difficult concepts clearly. If the concept wasn't well understood, be willing to try new approaches, explanations, or examples. Key points must be communicated at least seven to eight times before people actually internalize the message. When you are "sick to death" of discussing this change, you may finally be getting the message through. Frustration over having to repeat yourself is ultimately self-defeating. Expect and receive graciously people's questions even if you feel like you've just finished explaining that answer. If they understood, they wouldn't be asking again.

Sharing the purpose of the change during initial stages of the project is important but not an end unto itself. Identify key stakeholders—those who will be directly affected by the change—and target a communication strategy to each stakeholder group to keep it informed about the implementation process as it progresses.

Sharing information through storytelling is an important leadership technique. Stories are powerful motivational tools that not only spread enthusiasm and inspire commitment but are remembered longer than are facts (Phillips 1992). The use of analogies and metaphors is also powerful in helping people relate this change to things they already know. Remember that people simply need much more information during change. Uneasiness, anxiety, and fear are predominant emotions of personal transition and access to clear, current, accurate information is one way to help employees cope with these feelings. Continually sharing examples of successes and experiences of other employees is a way to keep enthusiasm and motivation high. Remember that formal leaders are not the only source of communication and information. Encourage employees to create mechanisms to share information with each other. Some departments have created a weekly newsletter to keep people updated. Discipline-specific governance structures are also an effective means of communication.

A culture that embodies and values open sharing of information stays healthier and fares better during change. In fact, Wilson, George, and Wellins (1994) suggest that more miscommunication results from the manager's attitude than from any particular communication skill. The miscommunications occur as a result of thoughts such as, "This is too much information to share," "They can't understand this," "They're not interested in this kind of information," or "It will make their jobs easier if they are told only what they need to know."

Case Study/Phase Three: Team Creativity

Communication and coordination were major concerns of the executive group and resource team at this hospital. A specific process involving employees had been developed for communicating with the departments undergoing implementation. Specific communication plans and strategies also were identified for key stakeholders. The manager and several employees from the involved department became ad hoc members of the resource team for the duration of their department's design and initiation of teams. They handled communication with the remaining staff.

Meetings were scheduled for staff and departmental leaders. Reactions and ideas were solicited from staff and used to modify the original plans. Although the basic design process didn't change from team to team, by including employees from each department in the design process, the resulting teams accommodated special characteristics unique to the work in each department. Some were skeptical about additional responsibilities delegated to staff and the time it would take for already busy people to assume them. Others doubted whether this change initiative would remain a priority during peak census times. Resource team members and organizational leaders were instrumental in communicating a clear picture of the vision and their personal and collective commitment to it. Before long, several key staff members were also sharing the vision with their colleagues.

Teams were designed with input of staff and based on the needs of patients and families. Rather than have patient-care teams designed by shift or geographical location in the unit, teams instead would be established by patient assignment and geography and would include the entire cadre of direct caregivers assuming responsibilities for the patient. In other words, a team for a small group of patients would include day, evening, night, and weekend shift caregivers. Team membership would remain constant and once it accepted a patient, it would retain this patient throughout that hospital stay. Teams also were designated by physician. Most teams were able to provide care consistently for patients of their primary or secondary physicians.

Once teams were designed and members selected, the work of developing as a team ensued. Most employees and leaders found less understanding of team behavior than they had anticipated. Each team attended educational sessions that helped in developing the basic elements of a true team and refreshed communication and problem-solving skills that would be necessary in working together as a team. Many staff members were somewhat tentative at first about this change, but as they formed into teams a new sense of momentum developed.

Phase Four: The New Reality

In this phase, the true impact of change is beginning to sink in. Stabilizing the change is an important issue during this phase, otherwise people will revert back to previous behaviors. Methods of anchoring this change in the current reality of the organization or department include formalizing structures or processes that were used during a trial period, establishing new routines, or formally communicating the new processes to key stakeholders. Anchoring may also be accomplished by including time for a report about this change at regular employee or management meetings.

A powerful and effective method of firmly anchoring a change is to modify the reward system of the organization to ensure that new behaviors are continued. Reward systems here refer to both the formal reward or compensation system as well as recognition efforts. Recognizing employee and leadership groups for their contributions to the change effort can take the form of monetary bonuses or small gifts. Just as powerful are opportunities for external recognition and applause. Paying expenses and providing time for participants to attend and/or speak at national or regional meetings can be very reinforcing. Interviews and articles in both the organization's or the employee's discipline-specific journal are also positive. Reinforce the behaviors you want to continue and stop reinforcing those you wish to replace.

Productivity is a second key issue of phase four, with several implications for leaders. Remember that when things first change, it takes longer to accomplish the same results. Recall the last time you purchased a new word processing program or received an update to your old system—it took longer initially to generate the same work you could do quickly in the old program. Many decisions to change are based on an expectation of improved productivity; however, this improvement is almost never obtained at the beginning of any change initiative. Expect productivity to drop initially (in direct relation to the size of the change) and improvements to come later. Be certain that expected time frames for achieving this improvement are appropriate and be realistic, because you will be held to those you promised. It is better to underpromise and overdeliver than vice versa.

Closely related to productivity is the critical need for people in the organization to take good care of themselves. Change can be exhilarating, frightening, and dangerously exhausting. If leaders and employees don't replenish their energy on a regular basis, your change initiative may cost you some of your best people. Employees and leaders alike can sustain the highest level of productivity and personal effectiveness only if they can find opportunities for self-renewal. If this behavior isn't modeled by leaders in the organization, it doesn't matter what you say about the need for employees to take care of themselves. They will observe the frenetic, workaholic behavior of their leaders to be the behavior really expected and rewarded in the system.

Case Study/Phase Four: The New Reality

For the first several months, the productivity in the restructured department decreased. A great deal of time was spent in meetings and things just took longer to accomplish. Jane and the executive group anticipated this and had negotiated new financial performance parameters with the board. They agreed on a critical process point at which they would reevaluate this agreement.

Managers and leaders often found that it would be easier just to do a job themselves. The entire leadership group had to remind each other continually of the commitment to transfer real responsibility to the teams. The support between the executive group and resource team members was instrumental in reaffirming their commitments during the early stages of the change. Staff members were encouraged to remain balanced and to take good care of themselves. Executives also modeled this behavior as best they could. Teams were given permission to be flexible in providing required coverage for their clinical or technical work and in performing teamwork (i.e., problem-solving meetings, coordination efforts, etc.).

Members of the executive group and resource team continually provided positive reinforcement when they observed behaviors that supported the new vision. Articles were published frequently in the organization's newsletter to highlight and emphasize results. They reinforced any positive movement that showed employee teams accepting more responsibility for issues and problems within their working groups. When behaviors contradicted the original purpose, redirection was provided. One team, for example, was experiencing some interpersonal difficulties and brought the problem to one of the managers. The manager did not take responsibility for solving the problem but, instead, coached the team in ways they could deal with the behaviors.

Phase Five: Integration

Integration, or closure, is the final phase of this developmental cycle for managing change and includes evaluation of the process, results, and the quality of the project. Often overlooked or undervalued, this phase is critical for both the current and future change initiatives in the organization. Is the change successful? How do you know? Did you obtain the results you desired and projected? Can you evaluate the effectiveness of this project? What is the impact on organizational quality of service? Has quality demonstrably improved? What indicators prove this?

Besides answering these questions, the actual implementation process should be evaluated at this time. What were the lessons learned during the implementation? What would you do differently next time? What did you and the employees learn about resiliency in dealing with change? What were the emotional reactions? What did and did not work? Sharing these lessons openly—the successes as well as the mistakes—in the organization is an effective way of creating and increasing organizational learning.

Closure, or letting go, is another aspect of this phase as well as a critical leadership function. Effective closure positions people well for the next change and is the beginning stage of transition, a concept that will be explored more fully in the next section of this chapter. Closure is perhaps the least understood and most often overlooked issue of the entire developmental cycle. Putting formal closure on the change project is a goal in dealing with this phase. Celebration ceremonies at this stage can be effective— whether simple or elaborate. The key is to link celebrations to specific performance whenever possible. If a team just successfully completed a phase of a project or enjoyed a significant success, order the pizza today! Waiting until next week or later in the month takes the spontaneity and fun out of the reward. Ensure that there has been a true accomplishment and that the celebration is not just a recognition of existence!

Sometimes, completion of a project results in the disbanding of a core group or changes in a leader's responsibilities that may necessitate grief counseling. The need for grieving cannot be underestimated during this phase. Effective leaders will assist staff in dealing constructively with these feelings so that the individuals involved soon will be ready for the next project!

Case Study/Phase Five: Integration

The evaluation of the project was exciting. Before-and-after measures of indicators such as physician and patient/customer satisfaction levels showed improvements in both areas. Productivity figures varied from department to department. In areas where employees were already functioning well at independent and interdependent levels, productivity decreased only slightly and rebounded and improved more rapidly than anticipated. In departments where employees depended heavily on the manager for decision making prior to the change, productivity figures were disappointing, even months after implementation. As part of the evaluation, each team's developmental level was measured. Almost all teams in the organization showed progress in their stages of development.

The resource team also initiated an evaluation process that followed each department's implementation and identified lessons learned. Many of these were used to improve future implementations, and involved the way employees handled change and what methods were not effective. For example, teams discovered the need to organize cross-team task forces to deal with issues that affected everyone in the department.

The evaluation process also provided a tracking system for measuring the transfer of traditional management functions, such as financial monitoring and budgeting, planning, and performance appraisals, to the teams. These responsibilities were scheduled to be transferred to the teams over a gradual time period.

Rather than waiting until the entire project was completed, each department planned a celebration at the end of its implementation. Because of the nature of work shifts, it was difficult to have an event that all employees could attend together. So, two activities were planned. The first was a potluck open house for all shifts, with team members providing the food. Physicians or other customers (internal and external) often were invited. Second, each team planned its own celebration when it reached its six-month anniversary as a team *and* was meeting its outcome measures. Besides these activities, each department installed a bulletin board in a prominent place highlighting the membership and accomplishments of its teams for customers and other hospital employees to see.

THE FIVE PHASES: A DEVELOPMENTAL PROCESS

This five-phase approach is useful for both small- and large-scale initiatives. It is the same sequence each team goes through in beginning its work as a team. The basic principles and issues of each phase provide a checkpoint to measure progress.

Although changes may actually start in any one of these phases, they progress more smoothly if these phases are followed sequentially. No change will realize its full potential unless the issues of each phase as outlined here are addressed and managed. If any of the key issues are glossed over or inadequately dealt with, you will experience problems. Examples of failed change efforts abound. How many times have we done a great job with the first three phases—people are excited and working together well to get results—but nothing is put in place to stabilize the change? Then, when the manager or a key leader leaves, within weeks everyone has reverted to the old way of doing things. Or the project is "dead in the water" because there are no resources dedicated to support it. Or an overly enthusiastic leader initiated too many changes at once and, because employees lacked the energy to implement all of them, failed to do any very well. How many times do we implement change yet fail to follow up to see whether it has made a significant difference in the quality of service or in the value we provide our customers? How many changes fail because we didn't take the time to completely evaluate an earlier project and so repeat the same mistakes? These are examples of failures resulting partly because the major concerns of each phase were not addressed and managed.

LEADING DURING TRANSITION

Change management focuses on the actual event or process of making something new or different. Change alters the way we do something. Transition, on the other hand, refers to our individual adaptation to the change that has occurred. The transition made is an internal personal event for each individual affected by the change. Although transition has specific, predictable stages, the time it takes to navigate them is varied and unpredictable. It cannot be hurried. Transition, as illustrated in Figure 8–2, involves three stages: (1) the ending of the old, (2) a neutral zone during which there is confusion and sometimes a loss of direction, and (3) the new beginning (Bridges 1992). This differs from the way most of us believe change occurs. Most of us see the new beginning as the first step and recognize that we will need to go through a period of confusion and perhaps some distress before we can let go of the old.

Leadership during times of rapid change and upheaval is made more effective by attending to key principles involved in leading transition. Transition is often regarded as the softer side of change and, unfortunately, often is seen as a luxury or an option. In a more stable, slower-paced past, people had time enough to go through their transitions to changes. With the rapidity of change today, however, people can become nearly shell-shocked going through multiple transitions at once. To view transition support as optional is a sure way to guarantee organizational dysfunction. Principles for leading during transition are as follows:

1. Respect the process.
2. Identify the current transition.
3. Expect emotional reactions.
4. Refocus continually on the vision.
5. Focus on constants.
6. Find support systems.
7. Use previous experience.
8. Encourage and model healthy behaviors.
9. Respect the value of leadership presence.

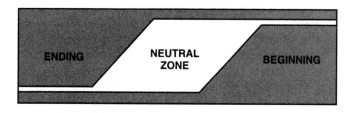

Figure 8–2 Stages of Transition. *Source:* Reprinted with permission from *Participant's Guide—Managing Organizational Transition*, p. 3, © 1992, William Bridges & Associates.

Respect the Process

Most executives and managers in today's organizations have been re-warded in the past for exhibiting "get it done" behaviors and achieving ob-servable outcomes. This is supported by authors Spencer and Adams (1990) who note that culturally, Americans are very outcome-focused, preferring to focus on the change itself rather than the process of transition. In his exten-sive work with people and organizations in transition, noted author William Bridges (1991) has found that, as Americans, we don't value the transition periods in our lives the way other cultures do. Instead we try to hurry through them and believe that if we are strong enough we can avoid the pain, dis-comfort, and confusion of the inbetween times. "Considering that we have to deal with endings all our lives . . . most of us handle them very badly" (Bridges 1980, 90).

Such exclusive focus on outcomes and disregard for the process involved in transition bears a substantial cost. While this tactic may work adequately for single isolated transitions, in the face of numerous changes and transi-tions, unfinished work on the process builds up to a point where we are un-able to cope with even the smallest of transitions. Besides, we lose a tremen-dous learning opportunity. By allowing yourself to experience fully the process of transition, you will learn a great deal about your abilities and in-crease your resilience in the face of future changes. Confidence and self-esteem will grow and better position you for the next transition in your life.

Bridges also refers extensively to another cost—lost opportunity cost. The time period between the ending of the old and the beginning of the new is not only confusing and emotionally distressing, but it is also a time of great creativity. Attachment to the old is gone but the new is not yet established. People are not yet confined by new ways, nor by habits that will ultimately create the new stability. Creativity peaks as people try things they otherwise wouldn't consider. New possibilities arise and opportunity for even greater change is present. Without the impeding structure of the old, new possibili-ties abound. If these ideas can be shared and implemented, the original change becomes even more effective.

Leaders have to become comfortable with their own transitions before they can effectively support others through theirs. This means recognizing the stages of transitions and allowing themselves to progress fully through all of them. If leaders are unable to make healthy transitions, it is unlikely that they will encourage and respect the process in others. Instead they will ex-pect others to hurry through and perhaps deny the emotions they are feeling and the potential learning available, all in the interest of organizational pro-ductivity. The leader sadly may never realize that this is a "pay now or pay later" proposition. In other words, if people aren't allowed to progress through the transition now, you will pay later in lost commitment, lowered energy levels, exhausted employees, decreased productivity, and plummeting organizational resilience.

Understanding the process of transition enables the leader to recognize the stage of transition for an employee or group and use interventions appropriate for that stage. For example, if people are in the ending phase it is very appropriate to initiate closing ceremonies. In one organization a vice-president arranged for a "funeral" at a departmental meeting. The department directors arrived as usual to find a dimly lit meeting room with a coffin, candelabra, and flowers all in place. To say they were surprised is an understatement! They were told that this was their opportunity to "bury the past." The first part of the meeting was an open discussion about the past, their regrets, and what they would miss. They remembered people who worked with them and were now gone. They reviewed and remembered how good those old days were. Near the end of the meeting, the leader asked group members to identify something that they were willing to "let go." It might be old ways of doing things, ways of thinking, unresolved emotions, and so on. Each person was asked to write down one item on a piece of paper and fold it up. Each then filed past the coffin and threw their paper in. The lid was then closed, effectively burying the past! This ceremony communicated respect and honor for the past yet it signaled that it was now time to move forward.

Your closure ceremony needn't be a funeral; it can be an event or celebration of any kind. One group decided on things to give up, and then, after members placed their written items in a coffee can, burned the slips during a brief ceremony. The critical point to remember here is that an intervention appropriate for the ending phase would fall flat with people who are in the new beginning phase. There is excitement and anticipation in the beginning phase and a closure ceremony would only dampen enthusiasm. In the same vein, asking people for creativity and new ideas when they are in the ending phase will leave you disappointed as a leader and leave them feeling frustrated and unable to meet your expectations.

Identify the Current Transition

Although people's reactions to transitions are never predictable, you can at least forecast the degree of reaction and who is likely to experience it by clarifying what a particular transition is. This is the second principle for managing transitions well. In one hospital, restructuring had progressed incrementally for several years and the organization had become fairly experienced at working with people in transition. Efforts were progressing on the next center to be restructured. This time, however, the climate in the organization shifted significantly, and this particular implementation generated more negative reaction than any others previously. It became apparent that there were other transitions occurring besides those in the patient care departments involved. The organization had passed the halfway point in terms of restructuring patient care units and was ready to embark upon redeployment and decentralization of remaining centralized services. This initiative involved departments such as admitting, business office, radiology, laboratory, central transport, and social services. Although their leaders had been discussing the nature of and timetable for restructuring, many employees refused to believe the messages, thinking, "This will never really happen here," or "If I just hold on long enough, this too shall pass." There came a point in time when real change could no longer be denied, however, and people had to face the inevitable. The disintegration of the central departments was a major transition that many leaders had taken for granted. When this transition was recognized, leadership support and interventions were intensified.

You will more accurately assess stakeholder reactions if you can accurately identify the transition that is occurring. In the change to a team-based organization, for example, you would suspect that the transition is about being in a team, having new responsibilities, having to work consistently with the same teammates, or having to learn new skills. But there may be a bigger underlying transition that is not often mentioned or even identified by employees—the transition from an attitude or era of passive entitlement in the organization to one of active earning. In other words, the organization's expectations of employees are higher, the responsibilities are greater, and lines of accountability are clearer. If something goes wrong or if performance is not up to standards, the team will be responsible for taking corrective action. Many employees may prefer to remain in the current structure where visibility is lower and responsibilities fewer.

Expect Emotional Reactions

Probably the most difficult aspect of transition is the variety and intensity of emotions experienced. It's easy to handle the emotions of excitement, enthusiasm, and optimism. The other end of the emotion spectrum, however, is much more difficult to acknowledge and tolerate. Spencer and Adams (1990) have done an excellent job describing the sequential and predictable nature of these emotions. Depicted in Figure 8–3 are the seven stages that people go through, whether the change is positive or negative. Expecting these reactions is a key mindset for managing transitions.

Stage One: Losing Focus

During this stage expect confusion and disorientation. People will be uncertain about boundaries and expectations. Decisions about even the sim-

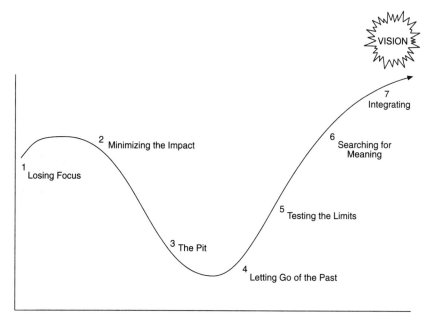

Figure 8–3 The Seven Stages of Emotional Transition. *Source:* From *LIFE CHANGES: Growing Through Personal Transitions,* © 1990 by Sabina A. Spencer and John D. Adams. Reproduced for Jo Manion by permission of Impact Publishers, Inc., P.O. Box 1094, San Luis Obispo, CA 93406. Further reproduction prohibited.

plest things become difficult. Unless the transition is a large one, this stage usually passes quickly and does not require specific interventions.

Sometimes leaders are surprised by the intensity of this stage and find they have underestimated the extent of the change employees are experiencing. A good example occurred in a hospital during the conversion of a traditional cardiac patient care unit to a team-based department. Employees included experienced cardiac nurses who had worked in the same department for many years. Immediately following the conversion, both the staff and managers were frustrated by the confusion, lack of productivity, and difficulty in making patient care decisions exhibited by these experienced nurses. In large transitions such as the one in the above example, leadership interventions could include the following:

- Provide specific structure, lines of authority, and expectations, even if they are temporary. If they are temporary, communicate this to employees.
- Encourage people to make lists of what they need to accomplish.
- Expect confusion and some forgetfulness.

Stage Two: Minimizing the Impact

You can tell when people are in this stage because they deny the impact of change or that it has any real significance for them. People often put on a good face, meaning they tell others they are doing just fine, that this change is no big deal. They may even believe it! Often, at this point, we haven't let ourselves consider the true ramifications of the change, so we're just getting by on a day-to-day basis. Soon, however, we begin to recognize the true impact of the change and our real need to deal with it.

Leaders will often reinforce this behavior because it is easier than dealing with the next stage. Sometimes we appreciate employees who say, "No problem, I'm handling this," or employees who haven't yet fully accepted the ramifications of this change. It's easier not to confront the minimizing or denial because then we don't have to deal with the really tough emotions of Stage Three.

Leadership interventions for this stage include the following:

- Encourage employees to be honest with themselves about what they are losing or giving up. Suggest that they may be minimizing the significance.
- Offer support and if it is declined, respond in a manner that leaves the door open for acceptance of the support later.
- Encourage people to take one day at a time.
- Don't reinforce employees' minimizing behavior when they are unrealistically positive to you. Acknowledge that they may not continue to feel positive, and that it is okay.

Stage Three: The Pit

This is the most uncomfortable time for all of us. It is the lowest point of our emotions. Expect anger, self-doubt, resentment, hostility, and even depression. The leader experiences these as do employees. If you made the decision to start the organization down this path, you may be angry with yourself in this stage. Employees in the pit can be very angry and upset with leaders. The intense feelings of this stage may even be displaced on people who have no direct responsibility for what is happening. Virtually any leader who has initiated change in the past has experienced the effects of this stage and none of us likes it!

The intensity of emotions at this stage can frighten employees and managers alike. It may feel disloyal to be so negative and critical. It may feel unsafe to express your feelings about a particular change that you know is being heavily promoted by key people in the organization. These emotions spread and infect co-workers quickly and feed on poorly managed change.

Leadership interventions to consider:

- Expect people (and yourself) to feel these intense feelings. If you know these typically happen it becomes easier to deal with them.
- Find or provide a safe place for people to express these emotions.
- Don't be afraid to set limits (i.e., "It is okay to feel angry, it is not okay to hit a co-worker").
- Refocus people continually on the vision, what it will be like in the future when they get through this. Refocusing on the purpose and other constants is also helpful.

Stage Four: Letting Go of the Past

Emotions take a slight upswing at this stage. The corner is rounded, the end is in sight. Energy returns and is more positive. There are two main tasks for this stage. The first is to put closure on the past, to say goodbye, to acknowledge that it is no more. Up until now the focus has been on how things used to be. This stage is when we finally accept that things will never again be the same. When this new reality is accepted, we are ready for the second task of this stage—preparing for the future. Suddenly we feel a new energy and optimism and we focus these on the future.

Leadership interventions include:

- Suggest or provide ceremonies or rituals to close the door on the past.
- Expect lingering sadness or nostalgia.
- Encourage people to take good care of themselves.
- Provide learning opportunities when people are ready to look ahead and plan for a new future. Their readiness for new learning will increase.
- Be aware of "back and forthing," a tendency to allow something relatively minor to cause people to fall back into "the pit" with little warning.

Stage Five: Testing the Limits

This stage is much more pleasant—the sadness of loss is fading and a strong sense of optimism prevails. The difficult times have been survived. There is more energy and excitement, more ideas are being generated, and people feel more like pushing themselves. We try new approaches to our work, take on more responsibilities, and generally enjoy the confidence that comes from having negotiated the difficulty of loss.

Leadership interventions for Stage Five include:

- Provide encouragement and new experiences.
- Listen to people talk about the past and how skillfully they navigated these emotions!

- Be responsive to the new ideas and possible alterations they identify in the change.

Stage Six: Searching for Meaning

During this stage you reflect on the previous difficulty and discomfort and realize that you learned a great deal through this experience. You are stronger, more self-confident, and proud of yourself for growing through this experience. Even if the change has been painful, you have learned something from it and acquired some wisdom as a result. Often with your newfound confidence and freedom, you will reach out to others who are still navigating difficult waters.

Leadership interventions include:

- Encourage employees to reflect on their experiences and identify what they gained in terms of new skills or abilities. Reflect with them if appropriate. How have you seen them grow?
- Congratulate them for getting through these stages.
- Refer them to others with whom they can share their experiences to help them get through their process. Coach them in how to provide this support without alienating recipients.

Stage Seven: Integrating

By this stage your transition is complete, the change is in place and you may not even remember what life was like before you embarked on this journey. For example, your memory of life before teams is hazy. Did you really work so independently of each other? Was it really that difficult to find someone to help you out when you needed assistance? Did you really have to ask the manager to make that decision? Your vision is clear in front of you and you are making progress toward it every day.

Leadership interventions for this final stage include:

- Appreciate reaching this stage! Mark the end of the journey with a ceremony or acknowledgment of some kind.
- Recognize the skills people now have as a result of their experience.
- Remind them that they're now ready for the next big change!

One executive's response to learning about these stages was that the content was too negative to share with his employees. He didn't want them hearing about this, perhaps to prevent them from experiencing these feelings. But it doesn't matter what you want; people will experience these emotions anyway. If you deny or are disinclined to accept the reality of these emotions, you and the people in your organization will be less likely to make a healthy adaptation.

If you don't understand these sequential stages and the expected emotions, you make take action that aborts your change initiative. Take for example the executive leader, so dismayed and discouraged by employees in "the pit" that he declared the project a failure and pulled the plug on the restructuring effort. Or the manager who reinforced employees for minimizing the impact of the change and never helped them see the ramifications of the change on their day-to-day work. It was almost a fatal surprise when they were thrust into the pit overnight by discovering they were expected to implement changes they had never understood.

Refocus Continually on the Vision

The fourth principle for managing transition relates to clarity of vision. One thing that helps people who are in the pit is a clear vision of the future. The leader's ability to articulate this vision and willingness to mold the vision with input from other stakeholders invites and encourages engagement with the vision.

For employees who have no sense that someone in the organization has a clear vision, change will be discouraging and even frightening. Employees who spend the longest time wallowing in the pit are those who say, "I don't think anyone here has a vision. No one seems to know what it is." Many leaders are reluctant to share the vision because it may not be one that they see as desirable or one that people will agree with. Some employees may view restructuring the organization into multidisciplinary, cross-trained teams as a negative. Likewise the organization merging with or being purchased by a former competitor.

Middle managers sometimes function with no clear vision of the organization. This doesn't prevent leaders at other levels of the organization from developing their own vision for their work group. Highly performing organizations have multiple visions with leaders at all levels developing visions with employees. These all work together to form the vision cascade discussed in Chapter 6.

Focus on Constants

When the workplace is chaotic and everything seems to be changing, it helps to focus on those elements that are remaining stable. This is the fifth principle of effective transition management. Remind people how this change supports the organization's mission, which is likely to be unchanged. Focusing on the constants encourages people to remember that there is some stability in their organizational life. Of course this doesn't work if your mission has also fundamentally changed! In most instances, however, the core values of the organization, such as a commitment to quality, service to community, and respect for employees, remain the same throughout any transition. If the changes can better support the core values, it will be very powerful to point this out. The implementation of self-directed work teams, for example, has been described as "the greatest statement of respect for our employees." This statement links the move to self-direction directly to the organization's core values of "respect for the individual" and "confidence in the skills and abilities of employees." In fact, transitions will be smoother if people can make connections between this current change and the constant values in which they believe.

Find Support Systems

Individuals benefit from extra support during transition. Some people don't deal well with transition and perhaps have endured previous transitions by denying or minimizing the impact to themselves for so long that they never allow themselves to feel expected emotions. Suppressing emotions isn't usually an effective long-term strategy. These suppressed emotions eventually catch up with them and make subsequent transitions even more difficult to navigate. As pointed out earlier, it's a matter of pay now or pay later, but at some point you will pay!

Organizations and individual leaders handle this in a variety of ways. The emotions engendered during transition are uncomfortable for the people experiencing them as well as for their co-workers and leaders. When an employee's behavior indicates that he or she is having trouble with the transition, encourage the individual to find support systems. Internal resources may be available such as an employee assistance program, employee-staffed support groups, or mental health professionals. If internal resources are inadequate, there are often relatively inexpensive community resources that can be accessed.

Many organizations today recognize the value of developing specific transition support programs internally. One organization that developed a formal transition support program first identified the program's purpose and assumptions. The stated purpose of its transition support program was:

> To assist employees, managers, and leaders to develop resilience and positive coping skills for managing both personal and organizational transitions so they will confidently approach change and be positioned for managing future changes in a healthy way.

Their assumptions included the following:

1. Managers and leaders need to understand grieving and show through their words and actions that it is acceptable.

2. For individuals to lead others through transition, they must first come to grips with their own transition process, feelings, and reactions.
3. Supporting individuals through transitions is a way the organization demonstrates caring and compassion, and it is just smart business. Healthy, balanced employees work better.
4. Grieving in a healthy way leads to the expression of uncomfortable and sometimes painful feelings.

Providing support for employees is much easier said than done. Department-based transition support teams were formed in an organization undergoing the conversion to a team-based environment. Based on William Bridges' work (1992), these teams were composed of a small number of employees from the department—7 to 12—based on needs and size of the work group. Key stakeholder groups were represented including individuals holding different positions and working various shifts. Employees with a real interest in this assignment were considered for selection.

Two purposes for these transition support teams were identified:

1. to facilitate upward communication regarding changes and transitions in process and the resulting problems and opportunities
2. to provide support, education, and coaching for fellow employees as they experience transition

Specific functions of these teams were further defined to increase clarity and understanding of the role. These included:

1. keeping a finger on the pulse of employee morale, acceptance of the change, and attitudes
2. communicating perceptions about congruency between current leadership behaviors and the change envisioned
3. providing support and coaching for co-workers
4. being a ready access point into the department's grapevine and informal communication channels
5. serving as a focus group for managers to use for presenting concepts and communications

These team members became a key group in their departments during implementation of change. As colleagues, they enjoyed the trust and support of their co-workers. Working during shifts when managers are not easily accessible, they provided a source for responding to questions and offering support in the manager's absence. Communicating the purpose and function of this transition support team to other staff members on an ongoing basis was necessary to increase understanding of the team's role.

When establishing transition support teams, the organization must provide an orientation session for these employees to prepare them for this role. They must clearly understand:

- the purpose and functions of the transition support team
- the dynamics of change and transition
- coaching and communication techniques (recognizing resistance, responding to an angry co-worker, assertive feedback, and reflective listening)
- effective methods of responding to change

The team and manager must discuss, agree on, and establish their own working approaches. This includes issues such as whether the team needs to meet on a periodic basis and how communication will be shared among the manager, the team, and intrateam. What kinds of issues need to be shared immediately and what issues can wait until a regular meeting? What level of authority does the team have in resolving issues? What is the expected life span of the team?

The relationship between the team and manager must be determined and is important for establishing expectations. The manager, for example, may expect team members to share when they see leadership behavior that is inconsistent with the change. The team may expect that if it shares its observations honestly, the manager will accept them in an open and nondefensive manner. Expectations between staff and team members address issues such as confidentiality, communication, and the specific role of the team.

The leader keeps the purpose, functions, and value of the team visible, meaningful, and relevant—otherwise members may become discouraged and decline further participation. Building confidence and commitment on the part of team members is another important leadership function. As team members respond to co-workers in effective ways, recognizing and encouraging these approaches increases the likelihood of repetition. If responses are negative or ineffective, immediate feedback with suggestions for alternatives is a powerful learning tool. Creating opportunities for continuous learning of team members and coaching them for skill development are added benefits for employees who serve in this capacity.

Transition support brings many benefits to the organization. Those with such programs cite the following reasons for making this effort:

- You will be more likely to accomplish your goals.
- Employees will believe you care and the ones you want to remain will stick with you over the long haul.
- You can model healthy organizational behavior for your community.

- You will be ahead of your competitors.
- It makes cents (financial sense)!

Use Previous Experience

This important principle of transition management is one we often overlook. We face endings repeatedly throughout our lives and professional careers. The bad news is that every time we turn around, there is another transition to make, another ending to endure. The good news is that this gives us lots of opportunity to practice making transitions and to improve our techniques and strategies! Reflect on ways you've seen a group of employees respond to previous changes. Were earlier transitions easy or difficult? Did people get stuck in Stage Two and minimize the impact of the change? Or did they get stuck in the pit? Were there any factors that helped them progress? What do they see as their strengths in dealing with changes and transitions? Ask group members to reflect on previous experiences. What was and was not effective? What would they do differently if they could relive their experience?

Many of us repeat the same patterns over and over again in our lives. If you find the emotions experienced during the pit very uncomfortable you may go to extreme measures to avoid that stage. Or you can learn some interventions that help you through it. One executive leader in a fast-paced organization uses a trusted professional counselor during these times. He can say and express whatever emotions he needs to without fear of it being repeated. In one community, where a large hospital has been undergoing reengineering for several years, the counselors in the community noticed a significant increase in hospital employees among their clients. These numbers increased whenever another division underwent restructuring.

Encourage and Model Healthy Behaviors

Taking good care of yourself during transition is not something to reserve for one evening or a few hours a week. It is easier said than done when the pressure of change and transition begins to build. But it is a key principle of managing transitions effectively. During times of stress it can be much harder to make healthy choices. We're up late at night because of evening meetings or work brought home. So, when the alarm goes off, it's easy to roll over and go back to sleep instead of getting up for your morning walk or run. It may take an extra jolt of caffeine to wake up! When you miss meals because the department or your schedule is so busy, it's easier to rely on junk food rather than to take the time to prepare healthy meals. When we're feeling a lot of pressure it is easy to lose our tempers with others, or, at the other extreme, to withdraw from others. We may not take the time to address difficult issues with co-workers but instead complain about them behind their backs. Healthy choices become more important than ever during times of transition.

It is not enough to pay lip service to the need for employees and leaders to take good care of themselves during transition. As the childhood game of Simon Says demonstrates, people will do what you do more often than do what you say. People who don't take care of themselves in this high-velocity world in which we live won't easily make their transitions. You want employees who can contribute their highest potential, who have the energy and enthusiasm to make the changes you are requesting, and who have the endurance to be there tomorrow. Executives and managers who treat employees as expendable often find they are unable to accomplish their goals because there's no one left working with them who has the required level of commitment.

Respect the Value of Leadership Presence

When you have no answers, when employees are experiencing the worst doubts, and the transition period seems to be at its most difficult time, your presence and visibility is of utmost importance. Yet this is exactly when we tend to isolate ourselves. We may prefer to stay in our office with the door closed and guarded, removed from all those people and their unanswerable questions. It's similar to the clinical situation of a dying patient at the point where only remedial comfort measures are effective. The only intervention left is presence of the clinical caregivers and family. This can be frustrating to clinicians who are used to doing something, offering some treatment, or providing an active intervention. To the outsider or novice caregiver, this presence may seem like a small thing and of no clinical consequence. Yet to the recipients and their loved ones, it is a priceless intervention and one they will never forget.

In the same way, your willingness to be present with people as they go through their transitions is something they will never forget. Rolling up your sleeves and pitching in on occasion is a memorable event for employees who may think you only spend your day behind a desk. This means being willing to share what information you have and also being comfortable not avoiding people when you don't have concrete or easy answers.

CONCLUSION

The definition of manage is to direct or to control. As a result, managing change may well be an oxymoron. Although there is no way to guarantee successful outcomes, following this five-phase sequence and dealing with each issue of each phase will increase the likelihood of success with your change initiatives. The challenges facing leaders in the 1990s are perhaps some of the toughest ever experienced. Meeting these challenges requires resilience and a working knowledge of the change process. Using a systematic organized developmental approach to managing the process of change lends clarity in the midst of turmoil and chaos. The effectiveness of any leader as change agent or change implementer can be greatly enhanced by following this five-phase approach to guiding the process of change. The stages include preparation, movement, team creativity, the new reality, and integration.

Paying attention to the process of change is not enough if you don't understand transition and respect its process. Transitions are the painful and invigorating part of change. During transitional periods you will benefit from great creativity if you are open to it. It is from navigating our transitions, with all of their turmoil and intensity of emotions, that we gain wisdom and discover growth in ourselves. Embarking on organizational change, regardless of its scope, creates tremendous opportunities for all members of the system to develop and expand far beyond their present capabilities.

CHAPTER 9

Leadership Lessons from Business and Industry: Learning from the Past

Health care organizations establishing team-based structures are presented with one immediate challenge. There is no single industry for leaders to use as a model. Some services resemble those of the hospitality industry (resorts, hotels, etc.). Others share characteristics with manufacturing. Clinical resource relationships may look like those in the financial services industry. As a result of this complex nature, it is useful for our industry to take a broad look at more than 30 years of experience in other industries. These are the organizations that blazed the earliest trails, pioneering teams and their new structural and cultural territories. While their specific technologies, structures, and approaches will not always be directly transferable to health care, the general lessons they learned are certainly relevant and applicable. This chapter presents the historical perspective of three decades of team building, with actual examples and lessons learned. First, we explore the initial work done by *the scouts*, the earliest researchers. Then we follow *the pioneers*, organizations with the courage and stamina to apply the first findings to their workplaces. Finally we examine *the settlers* who have built on the earlier work and continue to boldly experiment with teams.

Faced with many circumstances, restrictions, and demands not fundamentally different from those in health care organizations today (needs for higher productivity, introductions of "game-changing" technologies, shortages of skilled workers, competitive pressures, demands for greater process flexibilities and higher quality, etc.), these companies took the leap of faith necessary to investigate and fund new approaches to their work.

THE SCOUTS

Who were the innovators who "discovered" team-based work designs and where did their ideas come from?

British Coal Mining Industry

In the late 1940s and early 1950s, the Tavistock Institute of Human Relations, a research think-tank in London, England, skilled in explaining issues affecting human performance was engaged in a project administered by the British government's Medical Research Council to study new social techniques developed in industry. One segment of this research, led by Professor Eric Trist and assisted by his graduate student, K.W. Bamforth, who had been a coal miner at one time, focused on changes experienced by the British coal mining industry after the mines were nationalized at the end of World War II. Trist and Bamforth's study (1951) was prompted by the strikingly negative effects of these workplace changes on the miners, their jobs, and the coal mining communities in which they lived.

With government control and a concurrent suspension of many of their old work rules, the mining companies dramatically changed work structure and mining methods. They moved from relying on tight-knit, three-person teams—each using "hand-got methods" on short sections or faces of the coal seam—to more heavily mechanized shifts of miners working the "longwall method." This method resembled assembly line work in a fabrication plant. The new approach divided all work into three shifts: two to handle preparation tasks (the coal was undercut, broken with explosives, and then prepared for extraction) and the third shift to load the broken coal for transport out of the mine. The method was named for its presumably more efficient approach to mining the coal along a "longwall" 180 to 200 yards long, using 40 to 50 miners per shift to work this narrow seam. Table 9–1 compares the characteristics of the two work methods as analyzed by Trist and Bamforth.

The newer mass-production method substituted widely distributed, mechanized ranks of miners for the craftsmen partnerships of the hand-got days. This seemingly sensible modification had the effect of isolating miners used to relying on their mates in the dark, noisy, and always dangerous confines of the mines. It also broke the social compact of the partnerships, where teams had cared for their members both above and below the ground, traditionally supporting each other's families in cases of sickness or accidents.

With work divided into three specialized shifts, none of the miners could experience the satisfaction and sense of closure from completing an entire cycle of coal getting. This drive for mass production also created tight interdependencies *between* the shifts (who rarely met) and all but eliminated the flexibilities of the old system, which self-adjusted for worker age or geological variations in the coal seam itself. Finally, a more complex, differential pay system added divisive status issues and conflicting incentives to this highly mechanistic structure.

Table 9–1 Characteristics of Hand-Got versus Longwall Mining Methods

Hand-Got Method	Longwall Method
• a complete range of skills within the primary work group	• skills divided by task and shift
• interdependence within the primary work group	• interdependence between shifts as well as among shifts
• ownership (commonly, the two colliers— a hewer and his mate—made their own contract with the colliery to work their own small face with the assistance of a boy "trammer")	• no ownership
	• responsibility for part of the entire task
	• external supervision
	• low task interchangeability, even within the shift
• responsibility for the entire task of getting coal	• status differences exacerbated by seven roles and five methods of payment
• internal leadership and supervision	• little choice of work mates, except in informal alliances
• task interchangeability (between the two colliers)	• unstable, highly reactive relationships
• minimal status difficulties	• little to no flexibility under "cycle" control enforced by management
• choice of work mates	• rigid work targets set by management
• stable, long-term, highly supportive relationships	• minimal communication during the shift and virtually no communication between interdependent shifts, except by special arrangement
• flexibility in work pace	
• ability to set work targets	
• immediate intragroup communication	

Results were increased anxiety for individual miners, significant tensions between and within shifts, greatly increased absenteeism, and generally decreased productivity. While the new methods had met the unique geological needs of narrow British coal seams, they totally failed to meet the broader sociological and human needs of the workers.

Socio-Technical Systems (STS) Theory

Out of this and subsequent studies of mining and other British industries the Tavistock Institute developed an approach to work design now called socio-technical systems theory or STS. According to STS, well-designed work takes into account both the technical and the social needs found within the work environment. Designers familiar with STS principles seek to combine the technological requirements of the task (structure) with the psychological/social needs of the worker (culture). Their goal—to balance these elements for optimal productivity.

Trist and Bamforth's landmark study revealed the amazingly complex roots of employee satisfaction and worker productivity. It also highlighted problems that can be expected if only technical or structural aspects are considered during job design. Pursuing the principles of STS has directly led organizational designers to the concept of self-directed work teams, in which the whole group of interconnected jobs, rather than the individual job, becomes the focus of design efforts.

Attributes of Self-Directed Work Teams

Throughout the 1950s, 1960s, and 1970s STS theory continued to be investigated and developed at management schools and institutes in Great Britain and the United States. In 1978, Thomas Cummings summarized this progress in a classic article titled, "Self-Regulating Work Groups: A Socio-Technical Synthesis" (1978). Gathering the commonalties from earlier experimental studies, he ascribed five attributes to what we are calling self-directed work teams:

1. Definition of a relatively whole task or entire piece of work
2. Team members who each possess a variety of skills relevant to the group's task
3. Team member discretion over decisions such as methods of working
4. Task scheduling with assignments of workers to different tasks
5. Compensation, rewards, and feedback about performance of the team as a whole

According to Cummings, these attributes depended on three preconditions for work group self-regulation:

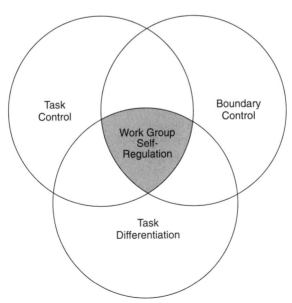

The first of these was *task differentiation*. Defining and differentiating a relatively whole task was crucial to establishing the clear task boundary for a team. This design permits it to make the necessary decisions about its work with a relatively high degree of independence from other groups or work processes. It allows the team in most work situations to move forward together without having to check upstairs or wait for time-consuming interteam communications. Thus STS theory calls for team designs that combine workers performing interdependent tasks within an entire piece of work.

In plant maintenance, this might involve a team responsible for all maintenance tasks for an entire floor or an entire building within a larger campus. One health system delegated all physical plant care for its new rehabilitation facility to a maintenance team of three associates. When asbestos was discovered in the ceilings, the team was given specialized training so it could continue to perform the whole piece of work. In accounting, this design could apply to all functions necessary to serve a single segment or a certain number of the organization's customers. In any case, the team would be completely responsible for its entire work cycle within that defined task boundary.

This clear task perimeter also serves to isolate any variances from standards. With an autonomous task and adequate team performance systems, problems can be more easily identified and dealt with by the group, keeping one team from unwittingly (or wittingly) passing its errors on to another.

It is interesting to note that Cummings mentioned health care as an example of an industry in which such group-based work designs would be more appropriate than individual-based job designs:

> This grouping [of employees who perform interdependent tasks within a relatively clear task boundary] appears necessary when the technology is such that interdependence among workers is essential. Referred to as "technically required cooperation," this dimension is present in production systems where workers must share, in addition to time, the same equipment or materials to achieve a productive outcome. Examples of this include: oil refineries, where employees are responsible for materials flowing through the plant; coal mines, where workers are sequentially dependent on the output of previous employees; and hospitals, where a combination of techniques are applied concurrently to the same material [patients] (Cummings 1978, 47).

This insight is at the heart of the current restructuring movement called "patient-focused care." Instead of aggregating services into traditional departments and then shuttling patients all over the building for their x-rays, tests, rehab, or other treatments, the patient care units are redesigned to efficiently deliver the entire "combination of services" at the bedside. Care teams are designed to include all services normally required by patients with a certain set of clinical diagnoses. All possible ancillary services are deployed to these teams. This structure meets two criteria for self-directed work teams: (1) interdependence, and (2) an entire piece of work.

The second of Cummings' conditions for self-regulation was *boundary control*, meaning the group's control over its defined work. There are three contributing factors to boundary control:

1. a well-defined area in which group members can work and which they can identify as theirs
2. a variety of work group skills and competencies covering all required tasks
3. group decision making on boundary control issues such as group capacity or quality standards

The "territory" for the group is crucial for its sense of identity as a team. That humans are territorial beings can be seen reflected in a whole spectrum of needs stretching from personal space to national identity. In team-based factories, this element is most often satisfied by contiguous work stations for team members. Patient-focused care units usually have areas where team members work and talk together when they are not at the bedside. Service functions like accounting often place teams together in open office clusters where members can readily communicate with one another without encountering physical barriers.

All the skills and competencies required to do the work must be contained within the team since it is totally responsible for an entire cycle of work. Otherwise, the team finds itself incapable of completing its work, breaks the cycle, and loses control of its boundary. Generally accepted accounting principles and security concerns have led many organizations to separate certain business office functions, such as check writing from accounts payable. Since writing checks is a key element in the whole piece of work, this practice leads to a loss of boundary. The same problem occurs when only a phlebotomist from the lab is authorized to draw blood for tests. Delays caused by this boundary problem constitute a major source of lost productivity for any health care organization currently structured in rigid departmental "silos" or "chimneys."

Secure in the knowledge that they are trained and prepared for all the typical demands their work will place upon them, there is little reason for the team not to be given decision-making authority over its own rates of production and quality standards. With access to adequate information, for example, internal quality assurance processes can be constructed by a biomed team to reduce or eliminate its dependence on outside inspectors, like supervisors. A patient-focused care team in a Florida hospital has the right (and responsibility) to alert the central scheduler when the team is full. Subsequent admissions are routed to another team until this team again has available capacity.

The presence of all three of these boundary control factors—a well-defined work area, a complete array of work group skills, and the ability to control key factors like capacity or quality—provides teams with the means necessary for them to feel in control of their key work processes. It also enables them to make adjustments as needed and fend off inevitable intrusions from outside their work group.

Cummings' third and final precondition for self-regulation was *task control.* Task control is enhanced when group members have:

1. responsibility and authority to choose their work methods and adjust their activities based on demands of the task or environment
2. the ability to modify outputs based on conditions or situations encountered
3. adequate feedback on their performance measures as a group

The classic example of these three conditions and their effect on a group's abilities to self-manage was hand-got coal mining versus the longwall method as described above (Trist and Bamforth 1951). Before the advent of mass production, work methods based on small teams allowed for the inevitable variances in the coal face (rocky coal, sticky coal, too narrow seams, etc.), thereby reinforcing the team's autonomy and pride in being able to extract coal despite the difficulties encountered.

With the change to longwall methods, however, miners on the single shift dedicated to removing the coal were each expected to take out the same amounts of coal, regardless of widely varying rock conditions along the face. These goals were set by a rigid, mechanically determined, and unrealistic process. Since two other shifts prepared the coal and the equipment for extraction and these groups rarely if ever met, there was no direct link connecting these highly interdependent steps in the process. This disconnect severely reduced feedback and allowed the negative consequences of variances on one shift to be passed on to later shifts, quickly eroding accountability. The ability to self-correct had been short-circuited in the new method and effects on key measures of work performance were disastrous.

Done well, patient-focused care restructuring will take each of these three criteria into account. Care protocols are negotiated with the input of all caregivers. A goal is to include flexibility sufficient to handle the vast majority of patient situations and conditions. One organization with such critical care paths has developed a "Doctor No" system (no apparent relationship to the James Bond villain) where certain protocols always apply unless and until the attending physician indicates otherwise. This gives the care team the great advantage of being able to plan better for work methods and care activities. It also greatly improves its ability to communicate more clearly with patients and families. It gives physicians and staff alike confidence that certain things will be done predictably, unless the conditions or situations encountered dictate otherwise. Outcome and process-focused measurement and feedback systems give caregivers control of their own continuous improvements, which ultimately get written into revisions of the care protocols.

Synthesis of STS Research

Summarizing the work of the Tavistock staff and the many subsequent British and American STS researchers, Cummings (1978, 51–53) synthesized several key points for implementing self-regulating groups.

Design

- Recognizing that self-regulation is a step-wise process requiring diagnosis, specification of structures, trial and error, and significant amounts of time to change old systems and behaviors, the design strategy must facilitate the group's movement toward autonomy over a designated period of time.
- Training workers to perform all necessary tasks is a primary design consideration; in most situations this cross training will have to be done on the job.
- The social development of teams must be an explicit goal of any design. Once necessary structural conditions are in place, a process advisor should assist members in a well-designed group to develop effective problem-resolution skills and appropriate performance strategies. In other words, both structure and work culture must be addressed together and implemented in coordination with one another.

Context

- The larger organization (both structurally and culturally) determines whether self-regulating group structures can be effectively put in place.
- Organic forms of organization (characterized by flexibility among units, decentralized authority, and relatively few formal rules and procedures) are most likely to tolerate the similarly organic character of self-regulating groups and to promote and nurture their necessary networking behaviors and structures.
- Mechanistic organizations composed of rigid hierarchical structures, inflexible divisions, command and control power relationships, and a

high degree of functional specialization (silos or chimneys) are likely to create intolerant, unhelpful, and ultimately destructive environments for self-directed teams.

- Organization climate also affects the implementation of self-regulating groups. Researchers found a strong connection between successful implementations of self-directed team designs and organizations whose change strategies already had encouraged experimentation, trust, and high levels of collaboration among workers and managers.
- Certain organizational practices tend to support and promote the change from an individual to a group work mindset, including group-based pay systems, availability of relevant group performance data (feedback mechanisms), group involvement in the selection of members, and consistency in group membership over time.
- Several additional organization measures promote learning and development of group autonomy: clearly defined protection for emergent groups from undue performance pressures in early stages, wage and job security, and alternative work opportunities for those who find they cannot function in the new group structures.

Summary

The STS scouts had entered virgin territories in work design. They discovered that structure and culture are not separate routes to team self-direction, but rather are critical elements of a single pathway to success. They identified both rich and rocky fields for growing teams. They invented basic methods for cultivation of these new work structures. Health care leaders seriously considering developing such organizations would do well to read these early explorers' stories. The lessons are as valid today as they were 20 years ago.

As Cummings' summary and synthesis of earlier research clearly demonstrated, by the mid-1970s, STS had developed a broad foundation of theory and practice, although for the most part this was based on small-scale experiments. Critics at the time still argued that only large-scale, real-world demonstrations could offer true proofs-of-concept.

THE PIONEERS

Volvo

A notable exception to the rule of limited, academically oriented experimentation with STS was Volvo, the Swedish manufacturing giant. Dr. Paul

Bernstein, dean of the Rochester Institute of Technology in Rochester, New York, has written extensively about Volvo's innovative attempts at organizational change. He notes that in the mid-1960s, Volvo embarked on a "Spontaneous Trial Period" (Bernstein 1988, 355) for new work designs, starting with its new Torslanda assembly plant near Gothenburg, Sweden.

An early example of Volvo's experimentation occurred in the passenger car seat assembly process. A typical example of the venerable Ford-type assembly line, this work cycle involved 15 individual jobs, each typically performed by a single worker. Assemblers on this rigidly controlled line complained of muscle fatigue and inevitable monotony. Absenteeism rates in some cases had climbed as high as 50 percent!

As the first intervention, mechanical aids in the form of specialized, ergonomically designed tools were employed to assist workers. This was followed by a job rotation and cross training designed to lessen fatigue and monotony as well as familiarize workers with the entire assembly process. Among the outcomes of this rotation scheme were increased appreciation of elements of the work and important insights by workers. For the first time they saw and appreciated the difficulties of jobs performed by co-workers, and this generally improved social dynamics. Workers spontaneously began helping each other.

In 1966, another trial was initiated in which each worker learned all 15 jobs in the assembly of seats. Each task had a two-minute work cycle and several different jobs were tied together in a chain. "Results of this experiment were improved group spirit, fewer aches and pains, better attention to quality, and improved personal contacts among workers" (Bernstein 1988, 355). In a further design modification, this work group was also given responsibility for planning and monitoring the quality of its incoming parts and materials.

In this work redesign experiment, Volvo resisted stopping at the quick fix (the simple addition of mechanical aids for weary workers). It also created enlarged jobs, reduced the need for traditional supervisory activities, created teams of workers, encouraged quality production and ultimately improved the quality of work life for the seat assembly area. Throughout the rest of the 1960s, such plant-by-plant, line-by-line experiments continued at Volvo. Then, in the 1970s, under the leadership of its new CEO, Pehr Gyllenhammar, the company entered its "Socio-Technical Strategy Period" (Bernstein 1988, 357).

Gyllenhammar recognized that in the emerging competitive world marketplace for automobiles a very different game would be played by entirely new rules. To prepare itself to compete effectively, Volvo's corporate culture needed to change dramatically. In a country already caught up in a nationwide debate about how work might be made more meaningful, the old assumptions about worker loyalty and commitment were quickly crumbling. New factories and further automation were clearly not the simple answer. In the early 1970s Gyllenhammar made this statement in an interview: "[Workers] stay shorter and shorter periods at their jobs. They are absent more and more. And fewer and fewer people are applying for jobs in industry. By the end of the decade about 90 percent of Swedish youth will have been to school and a fair number will have gone to university and graduated. It is from these people that we have to recruit our labor force" (Bernstein 1988, 357).

To deal with these emerging realities, Volvo's new CEO understood that different organizational structures and attitudes were required. This transformation could only be accomplished through company-wide learning driven by a carefully crafted and well-implemented organizational development strategy.

Volvo incorporated these novel STS considerations in its planning for two new auto assembly plants at Kalmar and Skövde, Sweden. Ideas for planning these new facilities were solicited from employees in over 1,000 interviews with workers at the Torslanda plant, where so many of the earlier experiments in work redesign had taken place. Also from Torslanda came the idea of independent teams of assemblers, a concept which now formed the foundation for the entire work process at Kalmar.

Roughly 20 work zones divided by automotive system (drive train, electrical, etc.) provided separate assembly space for the 15 to 20 workers assigned to each assembly area. Each of these assembly teams became responsible for an entire subsystem of the car. This enabled them to control that entire piece of work from beginning to end. STS-based work redesign was not only reflected in work processes and work team configurations, it was now built into the floor plan of the physical plant itself.

Although the cost for Kalmar's special layout was approximately 10 percent greater than that of a conventional assembly plant, Volvo believed this upfront expenditure would be recouped in lower absenteeism and turnover costs. They were right. Two years after the plant opened, a study (Agurén et al. 1976) showed Kalmar's absenteeism at 14 percent and turnover at 16.3 percent versus the older Torslanda plant's rates of 19.2 percent and 20.8 percent (approximately the Swedish industry average).

Kalmar became Volvo's first official learning environment where worker and management experimentation was encouraged and supported throughout the plant. Resulting from this culture of risk-taking and its freedom to fail (as long as you learned something), a variety of flexible team-based assembly approaches were tried at the plant over several years. Some were abandoned while others were incorporated into the work process. By the early 1980s, responsibility for quality was integrated into each team's role, resulting in a corresponding drop in the direct labor required to build cars (for inspections, reworking, etc.).

Construction of a new engine (E) plant at Skövde provided another opportunity for organizational learning. The key question for Volvo was: How could building design assist team development? By carefully designing a unique building it proved possible to lay out a work process making nearly every part of an automobile engine the responsibility of a team. As at the Kalmar site, buffer areas were inserted between team stations to reduce or eliminate bottlenecks. Through careful work design, short-cycle, repetitious jobs were combined into longer 3- to 20-minute work cycles. Despite even higher amounts of mechanization and automation at the engine plant, in two years turnover decreased from 25 percent to 20 percent and absenteeism declined from 11 percent to 10 percent (Bernstein 1988, 360).

Other areas in the Skövde facility also participated in redesign experiments at this same time. In 1974 one transmission milling cover operation instituted major changes to methods and work processes resulting in turnover dropping from 450 percent to 20 percent and absenteeism from 30 percent to 8 percent, while production costs simultaneously declined (Jonson et al. 1978).

At Köping, 90 miles west of Stockholm, Sweden, a shortage of workers, high absenteeism, and the company's need to utilize expensive equipment more heavily motivated Volvo's management to experiment with flexible hours in order to attract more female workers (a largely untapped labor force at the time). This plant introduced an eight-level shift system "designed to accommodate different personal and business objectives and allow employees to use some or all of the 168 working hours in each week" (Bernstein 1988, 361). Work force flexibility was increased even further when employees were cross-trained in four or five different jobs.

In the late 1970s and early 1980s other Volvo facilities implemented the following pilot programs:

- using self-managing teams to flatten the management hierarchy (Olofström)
- increasing worker participation in decision making (Umea)
- developing higher levels of team self-management, group payment for skill development, and group interviews for hiring new members (Tuve)
- encouraging team management of daily operations, personnel, quality, industrial engineering, finance, and maintenance (resulting in only three managers being needed for a 150-employee diesel engine plant at Vara)

All this learning was crystallized, mobilized, and applied to the planning and execution of Volvo's newest auto assembly plant at Uddevalla where a team of workers was able to assemble an entire car in a single stationary work area. Robert Rehder (1992) described the spirit of this revolutionary production approach in a recent article.

"It has long been Volvo's awareness that technology, like bureaucracy, can stifle human creativity, freedom, and growth. Accordingly, Volvo has sought to develop, at least in some of its plants, democratic socio-technical systems that continually change and renew themselves largely at the initiative of all levels of its employees" (Rehder 1992, 64). He pointed out Volvo's experimental ethic and its freedom to take risks. According to Rehder, "The recent development of the non-assembly-line Uddevalla plant is an extension of this philosophy . . . the early general aim . . . was to build a creative and flexible manufacturing plant producing high quality automobiles by investment in its people and cooperation with their unions" (Rehder 1992, 64).

Uddevalla operated for four years before being closed along with Volvo's other small, assembly-only plants in 1992 due to worldwide economic conditions and a reduced demand for automobiles. In this revolutionary organization teams of 8 to 10 members learned to assemble cars made up of more than 2,500 parts at production rates varying from 2 to 4 cars per day.

To give some idea of the people investment Volvo made—once hired at Uddevalla, each assembly worker began a 16-month training program designed to move him or her through successive stages of knowledge and skill development. Four months of basic skills and plant knowledge training was followed by the extended skills stage, where the learning goal was 50 percent competence in all assembly tasks. Additional training led to master level where a member could assemble an entire car, followed progressively by teacher competence, team spokesperson competence, and then a series of special intensive training programs (planning, engineering, quality, information systems, etc.) ultimately leading to managerial positions. Such extensive training permitted high levels of team autonomy, entirely eliminating first-line management throughout the Uddevalla plant. After an initial period of relatively high turnover and absenteeism at start-up (15 percent and 10 percent in 1989) the plant achieved a 6 percent rate for each of these measures during 1991, compared to the Swedish industry average of nearly 20 percent (Rehder 1992, 65).

Uddevalla's team-based advantages over older, assembly line systems were:

1. Meaningful involvement by unions and workers in the early planning and development of the Uddevalla system resulted in high levels of

mutually beneficial and highly collaborative problem solving at all levels of the organization. It also produced innovative organization and management systems and greater union/management harmony because ownership of solutions was felt by all parties.

2. Each assembly team was like a small business where each controlled and varied its own work pace, benefiting from longer work cycles, no hierarchy, and strong team boundaries. This allowed teams to become self-directed.

3. Development of skills and competence was tied to promotions and wage incentives. This move encouraged continuous improvement, engendered pride, and built a real understanding of every worker's critical role in the total production system. Teams became active participants in the integrated customer, development, engineering, and manufacturing linkages.

4. Teams' pride in their work, combined with knowledge and ability to do it right the first time and to influence other parts of the integrated total quality management system produced the environment for very high quality levels.

5. Unprecedented physical plant flexibility virtually eliminated production bottlenecks. This was made possible by radically different building design, creative materials handling systems, and new information support capabilities.

In 1993 (soon after the closures of the Kalmar and Uddevalla plants) Peter Wickens, director of personnel and information systems at Nissan Motor Manufacturing, wrote that the greatest strength of these systems "came not from the physical process but from the genuine building of teams—the little factory within the factory . . . with each foreman's group having its own precisely limited production tasks, its own leisure areas and its own financial framework" (Wickens 1993, 34). Wickens identified several elements of effective teamwork found in Volvo's experiments:

- individuals whose contributions are recognized and valued
- team members who are motivated to work together to achieve clear, understood, and challenging objectives for which they are accountable
- positive leadership and tough goals
- worker flexibility, meaning "expanding the roles of the individual to the greatest extent possible" (Wickens 1993, 36)

Wickens envisioned a future where a novel synthesis between the old assembly line and new socio-technical systems might evolve in the automobile industry. This synthesis combines worker commitment (as opposed to mere compliance) and careful process control of the sort found in the most highly developed factories. As he saw it, these two seemingly diametrically opposed concepts (commitment coming up from the bottom of the organization and process control typically handled from the top) must be reconciled to achieve lasting quality in both work life and the products of that work. Achieving this synthesis will be the joint responsibility of those who manage the work processes and those who perform the work. Leaving it to one or the other group is simply not viable because quality of work life without quality work is as hollow as its opposite (Wickens 1993, 38).

Lessons from Experience

To summarize this pioneer's accomplishments: Volvo's experiments with work redesign for nearly 30 years provided STS theory proponents and skeptics a great deal of material to consider and discuss. For three decades this pioneering corporation has constituted one of the finest laboratories any innovative work designer could have imagined.

Many lessons were learned:

- Cross training not only improves team flexibility and productivity but also has the side effect of improving communications and social dynamics.
- Moves to improve quality of work life (by creating teams, enlarging jobs, reducing outside supervision, encouraging quality improvement, etc.) pay off in higher worker commitment and better financial results.
- The modern work force is dramatically different from that of the 1940s or 1950s and the modern workplace needs to change to account for these differences (toward higher levels of worker involvement in decision making, flexible work hours, more challenging jobs, significant amounts of worker training).
- Creating a learning environment, where taking risks is not only tolerated but encouraged, can provide a competitive advantage.
- Use of self-directed work teams can eliminate the need for some levels of middle management.
- Achieving commitment of the workers to their jobs (personal ownership) is key.

Summary

As a pioneer, Volvo had three distinct advantages. First, it was a major player in a very mature industry, an engineering-oriented community that well knew all its key production statistics and ratios. After all, this was the very same industry that invented the earliest and most highly successful assembly line systems. It then spent a half century applying Frederick Taylor's "scientific management" principles (Taylor 1911) in refining each worker's task and further rationalizing every individual work process. As a result, Volvo's process changes and their effects were readily measurable and directly comparable with historical company and industry data.

Second, it had all the work models to compare. By the late 1980s, Volvo, as a large, multi-product-line company with numerous plants, contained work designs representing nearly every point on the continuum—from a conventional Ford/Taylor assembly line through the Uddevalla team assembly clusters, based upon the latest STS theory. This multiple models situation allowed company management to compare and contrast the effects and results of its various experiments directly, accurately, and immediately—at unprecedented levels of statistical and cultural detail.

Finally, the company possessed strong, visionary leadership that believed in such innovations and was clearly willing to invest the enormous amounts required to see new work designs created and tested in worker teams and uniquely designed factories. Volvo was one of the first to use full-scale production units rather than prototypes or small-scale simulations.

So the crucial question is not, "Did Uddevalla's unique team assembly design succeed or fail?" Volvo's experiment in organizational development was a success and is still succeeding, if only because the company continues to learn important lessons from both its successes and its mistakes. It is truly the kind of "learning organization" held up by author and Massachusetts Institute of Technology Professor Peter Senge as likely to be the most successful over time—an organization that truly has learned how to learn (Senge 1990).

AMERICAN PIONEERS

In late twentieth-century America, it should be no surprise that most of the best-known examples of self-directed teams resulting from work redesign have emerged from the mature manufacturing sector. As a nation we are still in the midst of our own larger social and economic redesign, moving from an industrial base to a largely service economy.

It helps to remember that the term "postindustrial society" (meaning "service-based") society was coined only a little more than two decades ago (Bell 1973). Bell's book, *The Coming of Post-Industrial Society*, was written as a wake-up call for an American business community still stuck in old industrial-age mindsets. His message was that something fundamental and very major had already begun to change in our society early in the second half of the twentieth century. What had begun shifting (and continues to accelerate today) can be seen in Table 9–2.

Facing new realities such as international markets, global competition, rising consumer expectations, and the changing work force, most traditional manufacturing organizations have already been forced to reexamine their old industrial society paradigm. In his bestselling video, *Discovering the Future: The Business of Paradigms,* Joel Barker states, "When paradigms shift, everyone goes back to zero" (Barker 1989). This is a key insight for dealing with our future. It means a change of great magnitude such as the shift to postindustrial society creates a completely new game on an entirely new playing field. In this novel environment new players usually will have a better chance for success than older players, who must struggle past their entrenched beliefs and obsolete infrastructures to make the necessary transitions.

Our fundamental shift from an industrial to a service economy is changing all the rules of the game, because now the game itself is literally changed. To complete this metaphor, any organizations still playing by the old industrial rules are simply playing the wrong game on the wrong field. The recent bankruptcy filing by the Smith Corona Corporation was a classic—their typewriters and word processors were the buggy whips of the personal computer age. Wrong game, wrong field, you're out!

The recognition that the basic rules have changed has driven many large manufacturers such as GE, Proctor & Gamble, Honeywell, and Xerox to rede-

---

Table 9–2 Characteristics of Industrial Society versus Postindustrial Society

Industrial Society	*Postindustrial Society*
• manufacturing base	• service base
• machine technology	• information technology
• person/machine relationship	• interpersonal relationships
• task-specific jobs	• complex jobs requiring innovative responses
• stable and slowly changing environment	• turbulent and rapidly changing environment
• gradual technological development	• swift and discontinuous technological development
• hierarchical (military) organizational structures	• flat but complex organizational and interorganizational structures
• workers who expect a paycheck	• workers who expect challenge and growth (and a paycheck)
• managers who solve problems	• management that creates environment for workers to solve problems
• strong national economic boundaries and markets	• weak national economic boundaries, international markets

sign themselves into new, postindustrial forms. The pace of change in these giant organizations is quickening as they race the clock to transform themselves into highly competitive players in the new game. In each of these corporations, innovative team designs have been evolving to streamline problem solving and decision making.

Honeywell

The case of Honeywell typifies the restructuring occurring in industry. At Commercial Flight Systems (CFS), a Minneapolis division of the electronic controls giant, experiments with work teams began in the early 1980s. Over time this division's once functionally organized work force was re-deployed into design and production teams grouped by product lines. A new production team perhaps consisted of a person with research and development skills, an engineer, an employee from purchasing, a maintenance worker, and several line operators (Benson 1992).

Nowadays, this team manages itself. CFS managers (themselves members of a management team) still control allocation of resources and watch profit and loss statements closely, but they leave guidance of design and production to teams in each of those areas (Benson 1992, 48). In addition to reorganizing lines of communication and reporting relationships, CFS has reshaped its plant and physically located team members together to support the close, constant interaction required by self-directed work teams.

According to Walt Barniskis, manager of the hardware design group, one initial objective of co-location was to wipe out the traditional "this is my department, that's your department mentality. But the team members themselves told us, 'Hey, you want to get the maximum output, put us together . . . make it so I don't have to call you; you're right over there. Let's talk about it'" (Benson 1992, 48).

Recognizing the difficulty of transforming old structures—and old behaviors—into new ones, CFS management invested in a full-time, on-site staff of performance management advisors. This group advises management and teams on procedures and training, helping them to stay focused on the long-term purpose. Barniskis summed up the progress of the CFS division with these words: "I'm getting more out of my people than I was ever able to get before and we're doing it without harming people or creating fear. We're thinking about things and evaluating the results in a completely different way than my traditional heritage" (Benson 1992, 48). As for his place in this organization, in the early 1980s Barniskis was intimately involved in day-to-day technical decision making. "Now I'm involved at the same management level with a larger group, doing a much more diversified product development" (Benson 1992, 49).

Bell Telephone

Outside the manufacturing sector, a few giants in the service sector also began work with teams in the early 1980s. Taylor and his associates (1987) reported on an experiment conducted early in the decade by the Hotel Billing Information System (HOBIS) unit of the former Bell Telephone System. The HOBIS organization consisted of 100 unionized employees who staffed a 24-hour, seven-day-a-week facility supporting the hotel industry. Over a trial period of three years (1983–85) this group, supported by a single second-level manager, learned to self-manage many aspects of its daily operations including office practices and procedures, attendance, productivity, service quality, training, and miscellaneous expenses and overhead. By comparison, most traditionally organized facilities of similar size in the Bell System would have had an additional 8 to 10 first-level supervisors handling these responsibilities.

An office committee consisting of the manager and six operators (who served for set periods based on a rotation plan) ran the facility on a day-to-day basis, after receiving special training for this role. Early on, this committee established four objectives to define its success:

1. effective communication with the work force
2. fair and satisfactory working conditions
3. teamwork and participation by all employees
4. efficient office management methods

The unionized environment created a number of predictable problems as the experiment progressed. These included complaints of favoritism in job assignments, difficulties with handling corrective actions effectively, and committee gridlock while developing productivity measures. But over time all of these glitches were resolved to the satisfaction of both union and management. The experiment was a success. Employee morale increased significantly, productivity rose, absenteeism and grievances fell to historically low levels. A corporate task force studying the outcomes of this experiment ultimately concluded that all four initial objectives for success had been substantially achieved.

Shenandoah Life

Another early team pioneer in the service sector was Shenandoah Life Insurance Company in Roanoke, Virginia. For more than a decade life insurance accounts and agents in each of the company's geographically-based regions had been served by a single head-office team consisting of 5 to 15 people. Team members were cross-trained to perform as many as 17 tasks that previously were separate, such as processing insurance applications, checking data, computing premiums, and maintaining accounts receivable. The results? Shenandoah Life reported a 33 percent increase in volume at the same time staff reductions were saving the company $200,000 a year (O'Dell 1989). The efficiencies of this new structure created a new "Jet Issue" service guaranteeing that any standard application received in the morning mail delivery would be processed and approved and out by that afternoon's mail.

THE SETTLERS

By the mid-1990s those early trails scouted by Tavistock Institute and other experimenters, then widened and hardened by the work of a generation of risk-taking pioneers, have begun to resemble real roads with clear starting points and well-mapped destinations.

We now live in a business environment where self-directed teams are no longer just an interesting theory tied to fuzzy ideas about improvements in quality of work life or linked to poorly documented claims of increased productivity and profitability. As competition increases in virtually every area of American business, organizations are responding by shedding redundant bureaucracy and inflexible hierarchies, encouraging continuous improvement, and exploring creative work designs.

Every year there are fewer organizations left in any sector of the economy (government included) that are unaffected by this sea-change in work redesign. Even the financial services industry, a bastion of traditionally conservative business practices, is well on its way to transforming itself, led by the insurance sector. By 1990 it was estimated that at least 300 companies in the United States and Canada had some form of self-managing team structure in operation with well over 1,000 in the process of moving themselves in that direction (Manz, Keating, and Donnellon 1990; Walton 1985).

Confirming this trend, a nationwide study by *Industry Week* (Wellins and George 1991) indicated that 26 percent of the 862 executives surveyed were using self-managed teams in some parts of their organizations. Survey participants further indicated that more than half their work force would be organized into teams within the next five years.

TRAINING magazine's 1992 Industry Report survey showed that 82 percent of all polled companies (1,597 respondents) had some kind of a working group classified as a team. In the largest organizations (those with 10,000 or more employees) this figure was closer to 90 percent. Results also indicated that these teams were not merely isolated phenomena in their companies. In the average organization with teams, more than half of the employees—53 percent—were members of at least one team (Gordon 1992, 59).

Intriguingly, respondents from health care organizations were more likely than those from manufacturing to say some of their employees are members of work teams (97 percent compared to 90 percent). Of all the organizations that had teams, 42 percent identified at least one team as self-managed. That translates to approximately one-third (35 percent) of all U.S. organizations with 100 or more employees. Again, such teams were not single, isolated units. The average respondent with self-managed teams reported that a third (32 percent) of all employees participated in such teams. In more than half of the responses, these self-managed teams were responsible for at least one of the following roles:

1. managing their own work schedules
2. dealing directly with customers
3. setting production quotas or performance targets
4. training team members

The least common roles delegated to teams were hiring and firing.

A majority of companies with work teams regarded them favorably, with 90 percent saying teams helped improve product quality and 80 percent indicating that teams had increased profits and productivity. More than 75 percent indicated that teams improved employee morale. On the down side, only 60 percent indicated that teams improved manager morale. Manager disenchantment with teams rose from 5 percent among the smallest companies to 18 percent in organizations with 500 to 999 employees before dropping to 10 percent in the largest organizations. This finding on manager morale should be a reminder to planners. Manager reeducation should be a high-priority and early part of any team-based restructuring process.

As TRAINING magazine's editor, Jack Gordon, summarized:

> While the presence or absence of self-managing teams doesn't explain disenchantment in most companies, it does have an across-the-board effect on other attitudes. Considering all sizes of organizations, respondents with self-directed teams were significantly more likely than those without to report that teams have increased profits, improved customer service, and boosted morale of both employees and management (Gordon 1992).

Right now it is impossible to know how many companies in the United States have actively operating self-directed teams, but it is not unreasonable to believe that numbers of qualifying organizations may have easily doubled since 1990. Brief looks at a few of these companies and their diverse approaches can be very instructive.

Digital Equipment Corporation

In July 1994, Digital Equipment Corporation (DEC), the Boston-based computer maker, announced its decision to discontinue its matrix team structure. The matrix structure had functional representatives of departments (engineering, finance, marketing, etc.) serving on product line teams (minicomputers, chips). Reports from insiders indicated this organizational structure broke up on the reef of competing factions—departmental versus product lines. Deployment to multidisciplinary teams was never accompanied by a corresponding lowering of departmental controls. So teams spent innumerable hours attempting to achieve consensus between these hard-nosed, unreconcilable factions. Allowing this clumsy matrix to perpetuate organizational gridlock, DEC became a company known for not being able to complete any new initiatives—in an industry that relies on new ideas, fast development, and well-integrated implementations. Trying to keep one foot in rigid, quasimilitary command structures and the other planted in the flexible product line orientation demanded by their marketplace left DEC paying more attention to its internal splits than to its customers.

Boeing

Dumaine (1994) compared DEC's experience with that of Seattle's Boeing Commercial Airline Group, where a similar organizational structure was able to cut engineering problems by 50 percent on the way to producing the "new generation" 777 airliner. Boeing leadership recognized that this new airplane for the twenty-first century would be a very different kind of machine. It would be the first time the manufacture of a commercial aircraft would jump directly from computer-based design to metal parts cut and formed by computer-controlled tools. No prototypes or mock-ups would be built. This change demanded a different kind of organizational structure from that traditionally used to build airplanes. The structure would have to be very flexible yet well integrated to ensure that all aircraft segments would fit together at first assembly. There was no room for slowness and problems associated with older, trial-and-error project management systems.

Team Management

Henry Shomber, a chief engineer on the Boeing project, pointed out a key difference in management philosophy: "We have the no-messenger rule. Team members must make decisions on the spot. They can't run back to their functions for permission" (Dumaine 1994, 88). This level of empowerment and autonomy was supported by Boeing leadership who designed and installed a team-based project structure eventually involving 10,000 employees. The new organizational pyramid, rather than being made up of management hierarchies, was composed of three layers of teams (Figure 9–1).

The management team consisted of five or six managers from each function (engineering, manufacturing, finance, etc.) and had overall responsibility for creating the new airplane. The next level of teams included leaders from operations and engineering, paired up to oversee more than 200 primary work teams and responsible for dealing with major barriers to work team performance, such as schedule delays, communication difficulties, or quality problems with suppliers. This group connected with the management team through their functional managers in engineering and operations.

A third level included small, typically cross-functional work teams, each responsible for specific parts of the airplane (the flap team, tail team, etc.). These teams were responsible for solving their own work-related problems and passed any larger problems upward for solution through their leadership teams.

Late in the project this structure was modified to add a fourth level—airplane integration teams (Figure 9–2). This change was prompted by the discovery that work teams responsible for the major aircraft parts weren't communicating with each other as well as necessary, resulting in design incompatibility problems.

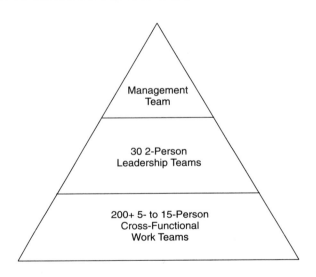

Figure 9–1 Boeing's 777 (Initial) Project Structure

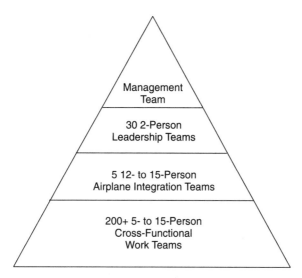

Figure 9–2 Boeing's 777 (Revised) Project Structure

These airplane integration teams included employees recruited from the work teams and had responsibility for transferring information back and forth between these work teams to eliminate glitches in design and assembly processes. Top management ensured that integration teams had access to everyone in the organization, so that information could be disseminated rapidly and firsthand, minimizing miscommunications.

A story illustrates how this new structure worked. During the final months before assembly, two of the primary work teams discovered a design conflict. One team had placed the passengers' oxygen mask system in the exact spot in the overhead panel where the other team had put the system for the little nozzle that shoots fresh air toward the passenger (called the gasper). The team discovering this problem called in an integration team. The integration team refocused everyone on what was best for the airplane. Within hours these three teams came up with a solution: a special clamp to hold both systems side-by-side in the overhead. "At the old Boeing a problem like that probably wouldn't have been caught until the plane was being manufactured or, as at DEC, would have been pushed up the traditional hierarchy and taken weeks to resolve" (Dumaine 1994, 91).

Unlike DEC, Boeing learned how to mix teams successfully with hierarchy. Teams, rather than an unwieldy, individualistic management power structure, became the basis for the different management levels. It is also interesting to examine Boeing's teams from the perspective of team function. As pointed out in Chapter 1, real teams (as opposed to other groups *called* teams) have one of three purposes (Katzenbach and Smith 1993):

1. To run things: Leadership teams are responsible for management of a large unit or an entire organization.
2. To make or do things: Primary work teams are responsible for ongoing operations in areas such as sales, manufacturing, or service delivery.
3. To recommend things: Ad hoc teams study and recommend solutions to specific organizational performance problems.

In the case of the 777 project structure, the first two purposes were fulfilled by Boeing's management/leadership teams and work teams. The addition of integration teams completed the picture with units specifically designed to provide the trouble-shooting and recommending functions.

Characteristics of Boeing's Work Teams

A closer look at the primary work teams responsible for major parts of the Boeing aircraft is also instructive. Edward Lawler (1992) sets out seven characteristics distinguishing a work team from other groups of workers doing joint tasks. These are:

1. work flow control
2. membership
3. decision-making responsibility
4. training
5. meetings
6. supervision
7. reward systems

Work Flow Control. The first distinguishing characteristic, work flow control, means the team has sufficient authority over creating its product or service to be held responsible for input and output. This first of Lawler's seven criteria for work teams is a direct descendant of Cummings' ideas about boundary control (Cummings 1978).

The workers making up the 777 tail team, for instance, were given these levels of authority and responsibility. They could reject substandard parts from suppliers and delegate the job of fixing these quality supply problems to their leadership team. The work team was responsible for bringing in the tail subassembly on specification, on time, and on budget.

Membership. Structuring of the primary work teams met Lawler's second criteria on membership, where teams include all the employees working on a complete process and team membership is not optional. Since the entire 777 project was designed around team structures, all employees on the project were members of teams and every one of the hundreds of thousands of tasks necessary to design and build a state-of-the-art airliner was assigned to an appropriate team.

Decision-Making Responsibility. Decision-making responsibility, Lawler's third characteristic, differentiates between self-managed teams that make all decisions for their area of control (as though they were running a small business) and semiautonomous work teams that have less control, especially in the areas of resources and hiring/firing. Given restrictions in their ability to allocate organizational resources and limited involvement in personnel matters, the Boeing work teams were clearly semiautonomous but, by Lawler's definition, still a genuine work team. The leadership teams and management team met Lawler's self-managed criterion.

Training. The fourth characteristic, training required, assumes that members of work teams receive special training in the technical aspects of their work and also in working collaboratively with other team members (each of whom will have a slightly different task focus in the case of interdisciplinary teams). At Boeing, nearly all of the 200-plus work teams were interdisciplinary to some degree. Training in team working was delivered to all teams and leadership team members were further trained in facilitation and coaching. In some areas where the work lent itself to cross training, this education was emphasized; in other areas little cross training was done.

Meetings. Lawler's fifth characteristic of work teams is meetings. Meetings are a necessary function if workers are to coordinate their tasks, solve problems as a team, and carry out other self-management roles. Within-team meetings were an everyday occurrence on the 777 project. Between-team meetings were less frequent, and therefore horizontal peer-to-peer communication across interdependent teams tended to lag or break down. It was to remedy this problem that the airplane integration teams were formed. With their active assistance, problem-solving and decision-making meetings between the work teams improved dramatically.

Supervision. The sixth characteristic of work teams suggests that supervision is less responsible for day-to-day activities of the team than in traditional management relationships. The focus is on the team, rather than on individuals within the team. The manager/coach is charged with supporting an environment in which the team can learn to control and do its work more effectively. Boeing specifically trained its leadership teams to coach and facilitate teams toward higher levels of self-management.

Reward Systems. The seventh and final characteristic of work teams is reward systems. Lawler (1992, 317) strongly maintains that self-directed work teams will base member pay on skills or knowledge. This pay-for-skill or pay-for-knowledge approach is well regarded as a way to grow teams in their self-management roles. It is as well a means to meet the increasingly complex technical requirements of cross-trained work environments. As yet, however, there are relatively few companies that have extensive experience with such team-oriented, pay-for-performance systems.

As a long-time union shop represented by numerous bargaining units of professionals, skilled trades people, and laborers, Boeing is an extremely complex and heavily contracted environment. So, experimenting with pay systems tends to be a slow and difficult process. The Boeing work teams likely would not meet Lawler's last criterion on reward systems.

Measuring and Rewarding Team Performance

Rewarding team performance is perhaps the most problematic of Lawler's criteria because no simple formula has been discovered that perfectly balances competing needs for individual and team performance rewards. Both the experts and the practitioners are still grappling with this one. Chapter 12 will discuss reward systems at greater length, but it may be valuable to take a few moments here to examine a few historical precedents.

You will recall that Volvo in the 1970s and early 1980s did experiment with group payment for skill development at its plant in Tuve, Sweden. The members of assembly teams at the Uddevalla plant were also paid for skills and knowledge gained as they progressed toward master level where the team member could assemble an entire car. Although it was unlikely any employee would ever be asked to build a car alone, this level of skill meant the master had achieved the pinnacle of worker flexibility. Volvo recognized that teams made up of such people need up to 10 percent fewer members to do the same work.

Some form of pay-for-knowledge system is currently in place in several American corporations, usually as part of a team structure. Chrysler, TRW Inc., Proctor & Gamble, and Frito-Lay are current users of such reward systems.

Instead of this pay system, many organizations have sought to reward teamwork through gain-sharing or profit-sharing plans. These in essence say to all employees, "Do whatever you can to make the organization more profitable and you'll get a share of the profits" (Huret 1991, 39). While such approaches may promote interteam cooperation, they tend to be unfocused. Generalized rewards and lack of clear cause and effect between individual or team performance and company profitability blunt these instruments as tools to increase an individual team's productivity. Compensation specialists suggest team incentives must come somewhere between such organization-wide plans and individual compensation systems. The best team incentive plan will be specifically tied to each team's goals. It must simultaneously motivate the team and its individual members, without playing one off against the other.

As Lawler says, "Reward systems are never neutral. They not only affect teamwork but also the kind of employees you attract and retain, the career tracks that people choose, and the extent to which they see a link between pay and performance" (Lawler 1992, 57). Consider the following case.

Case Study: "Buried Alive by Success"

A six-person autonomous work team producing survey-based reports for its customers was facing quickly rising costs and work flow complexities as its work volume increased significantly. Traditional practice had been to add or decrease staff hours as workload varied, but new marketing efforts had rapidly pushed volume to all-time highs.

The team had already lured its entire pool of trained part-timers into full-time status, but even this larger group was getting overstretched by significant overtime. No one could imagine how they were going to find spare time to train new hires, much less make more room in their cramped work area.

The team had responsibility for solving this dilemma and its incentive plan reflected this goal. The plan measured five components:

1. product quality
2. product timeliness
3. customer satisfaction
4. product cost
5. individual performance

Each of the first four components could be measured directly and was weighted at 20 percent. Individual performance measurement was the responsibility of the supervisor (the team was autonomous, not self-directed at this time) and was also weighted at 20 percent.

After some deliberations the team decided to automate a manual data entry function that accounted for a large percentage of their labor. In less than a month, equipment was tested, selected, and installed with the help of personnel from the company's data services department. Once testing was completed this system went on line, almost immediately eliminating the need for overtime while positively affecting product quality, timeliness, and customer satisfaction.

Product costs were reduced since data from survey forms were now scanned rapidly into the computer (at higher accuracy levels than manual entry) and no longer required time-consuming manual sorting. Freed from their data entry load, several team members took on expanded roles improving customer service and fast-tracking several projects for additional products. One team member with a young child returned to a part-time schedule at her own request.

Everyone on the team benefited from this effort. A clear and simple set of performance measures allowed the team to monitor its own quality and productivity on a monthly basis and track effects of their automation project. Cost information was made available so members (with help from accounting) were able to create a cost-benefit model that clearly justified their automation efforts. The team owned this solution and, as a result, an aggressive implementation schedule occurred without major problems.

Performance reviews for all members reflected significant improvements in product cost and customer satisfaction. The team's already high standards of timeliness and quality also improved, but less dramatically. In most instances, individual performance assessments also exceeded expectations as team members took the initiative to support customers and the new product lines even further. This project garnered one more benefit when several months later it won the organization's annual team achievement award.

Not all team incentive plans lead to such happy endings but, those that are successful will generally share the characteristics exemplified in the previous case study:

- The team's performance measures were clear, logical, and unequivocal.
- Performance measures supported the team's goals and vice versa.
- All team members were included in this plan.
- The team regularly tracked and discussed its own performance.
- The plan was administered fairly.

Key here was the first point—without accurate and precisely designed performance measures, teams cannot set appropriate objectives for themselves and their members. Too often organizations default—applying broad organizational measures of productivity, profitability, or cost reduction to teams that have little or no direct impact upon these results. More frequently, organizations simply neglect to change reward systems that focus primarily on individual performance, even though team performance is the desired outcome. This creates a situation in which the good of the team and the good of the individual are set in opposition to each other—a perfect formula for lose–lose results.

Designing Performance Measures

The task of defining and designing performance measures is not a simple one, particularly in the case of teams composed of knowledge workers and professionals who often hold jobs containing relatively few prescribed task elements. Yet, even these teams require clearly defined performance standards for both the team and its individual members to self-manage effectively.

An example of this can be seen in the petroleum industry. Recently U.S. oil companies, feeling the impact of a worldwide glut of oil and resulting lower revenues per barrel, actively began creating self-directed and cross-functional work teams (Zigon 1994). The story of one American oil company illustrates how this industry was able to arrive at performance measures for complex team situations.

First the corporation reorganized its exploration and exploitation operations from functional departments (geology, drilling, production, etc.) into cross-functional teams. The company's oil reserves (its inventory still in the ground), previously managed by upper management, were divided into five regions. Each of these regions was assigned to a core team of employees, supported by part-time team resource members (geophysicists, environmental staff, etc.) who served several teams on an as-needed basis.

During team development training it became evident that teams could not progress further without clear performance standards. Since all five regional teams would be expected to perform similar roles and had the same basic responsibilities, these standards could be used by all teams. A task force was created with representatives from all five teams. Their assignment was to draft a set of performance standards that would be reviewed and revised with feedback from each individual team.

The task force completely mapped the work process, identifying all major steps and their outcomes. Next they identified all customers. Finally, they determined what product and service components were needed by each customer, correlating this with the work process map. What emerged from this analysis were three potential areas for team performance measurement: (1) key process steps, (2) key intermediate results, and (3) final results. In their review of this early draft, the regional teams created additional points for assessing performance by creating region-specific measurements for total oil reserves and oil deliveries made at a given cost. Acknowledging the speculative nature of the oil business they even factored in a measure for surprises.

In order to link individual team member performance to the team's performance, the task force created a grid that matrixed roles against results (Exhibit 9–1).

Having now determined what should be measured, the task force next formalized how performance measures for individual positions would be written. Since some jobs, such as research scientist, were difficult to meas-

Exhibit 9–1 Role/Result Matrix

		RESULTS		
		Geological Mapping	Reservoir Analysis	Well History
R O L E S	Geophysicist	Accomplishments necessary to support result		
	Exploitation Geologist		Accomplishments necessary to support result	
	Exploration Geologist			Accomplishments necessary to support result

ure in quantifiable results, participants developed measures by carefully describing certain accomplishments in terms of three components:

1. who will judge
2. what the judge looks for
3. what precisely constitutes meeting expectations

The resulting team performance measures for teams ran several pages detailing both team standards and the individual job-by-job expectations necessary to support team results. The task force's final draft document aimed to measure accurately key performance parameters without overwhelming the teams in data collection activities. Members of all five regional teams reviewed the draft, suggesting changes and additions. Once the teams were satisfied with the document, upper management reviewed it and made final revisions from an organizationwide perspective. This review was designed to eliminate future misunderstandings, especially in situations involving "measuring beyond the numbers" (Zigon 1994, 46).

Four weeks after the process began a completed performance measurement document was in force, providing a sound, collaboratively developed basis for the oil company's team pay-for-performance system. Among other benefits, it balanced and combined the need to reward team achievement and the need to provide individual incentive, offered management a means of measuring team effectiveness in reference to corporate goals, delineated the roles of all team members, provided team members with an immediate feedback mechanism, and gave teams a useful process for refining and improving their roles and results. For any organization, much less an analytically oriented, engineer-dominated culture like the petroleum industry, this was a major accomplishment.

Summary

These organizations and other settlers took over where the STS pioneers left off. Not having to break totally new ground they dealt less with the whys and more with the hows of self-directed teams. Let's look at some of the things they learned.

- Teams are a fact of life in the majority of American companies. Self-managing teams exist in nearly half of these organizations with teams. The concept and practice of teams managing themselves no longer should be considered an isolated phenomenon.
- Most who have tried implementing teams believe these groups have provided significant benefits for their organizations. Middle managers have generally been the least enthusiastic supporters. In many ways they bear the brunt of this change.
- Teams matrixed with dual reporting relationships (to old department structures *and* to new team structures) may be designed to fail due to conflicting purposes and overly complex communication requirements.
- Teams and hierarchies *can* coexist when both are carefully designed to complement and support each other.
- Interteam communications will be a significant challenge, especially in organizations or processes requiring large numbers of highly interdependent teams. Special structures can be built to facilitate communications across teams.
- Work teams with proper levels of responsibility and authority can quickly solve problems that would take traditional hierarchies weeks or months.
- In order to run smoothly, team-based organizations need all three types of teams: leadership, ad hoc, and primary work teams.
- There are definite, identifiable characteristics that clearly distinguish work teams from other groups of workers doing joint tasks.
- Team reward systems are potentially the most problematic of these characteristics. Such systems are new and organizations have had rela-

tively little experience with them. Pay-for-skill and pay-for-knowledge approaches are currently the most highly regarded of these team reward systems.

- Team goals, performance measurements, and incentive plans must be carefully aligned and fairly administered to produce consistent and repeatable results.
- Means of creating adequate performance measures exist for professional and knowledge workers in even the most complex team situations and industries.

To return one last time to Lawler (1992, 12), he suggests the following points be considered when deciding to team or not to team:

- Work teams work best when innovation is required to bring a new product or service to market quickly, or when products must be customized to meet customer needs.
- Work teams are most appropriate when the organization holds quality above all other product or service variables.
- If the organization is trying to combine two or more variables, such as being the high quality/low cost producer or the innovative/fast provider, work teams are a strategic advantage.

For the health care industry it would be hard to imagine three more applicable strengths. As local and regional markets begin or continue to change rapidly, innovation in high quality products, services, and structures will be key to retaining or capturing market share. This is proving to be the case in even the most mature markets in the country, such as Minnesota's Twin Cities and certain portions of California. Health care organizations normally are combining at least two variables and sometimes more in their attempts to reinvent themselves and become more responsive to their customers. Efforts to become the high-quality, low-cost provider are common today.

Katzenbach and Smith (1993, 13) echo and expand on Lawler's assessment when they write:

> If performance at critical delivery points depends on combining multiple skills, perspectives and judgments in real time, then the team option is the smartest one. The key judgment is whether the sum of individual bests will suffice for the performance challenge at hand or whether the group must deliver incremental performance requiring joint work products. Although the team option promises greater performance, it also brings more risk, and managers must be brutally honest in assessing the trade-offs.

CONCLUSION

Although teams are not right for every organization and are certainly a major investment of resources, time, and energy, it is astounding how many diverse businesses and industries have accepted the team challenge. Given the difficulties and complexities of transforming entrenched hierarchies into team-based organizations, it is equally amazing how many successes are being reported.

The scouts who first explored the socio-technical wilderness, the pioneers who followed those early, poorly delineated trails, and the settlers who now have begun to populate nearly every industry in America with teams of workers form the vanguard of a whole new way of doing business. Perhaps it is not surprising, as we face the enormous, high-velocity uncertainties of the next century, that we feel much stronger and more confident facing this future together rather than individually.

PART III

Special Issues for Health Care

CHAPTER 10

Multidisciplinary Teams: Unlocking the Power of the Professions

In preceding chapters we have emphasized the importance of ensuring teams have full control over entire outcomes of their work. Teams that have this control focus on results. Those that do not, focus on tasks. It's that simple. This prerequisite for success has a pair of profound implications. First, multidisciplinary teams have the greatest potential in a clinical setting. The care process for most patients regularly draws upon capabilities from across a wide spectrum of departments: nursing, diagnostic, and therapeutic services, as well as support and administrative. Achieving the required outcomes (e.g., a short length of stay without readmission) is impossible without the combined contributions of many disciplines. Nurses cannot do it alone. Neither can respiratory therapists, radiological technologists, EKG technicians, nor members of any single profession for that matter. Success can be achieved only through a richer and more robust blend of talents than any one profession can possibly provide.

Second, multidisciplinary teams cannot become highly effective unless a crucial balance is struck between the unique expertise of each member and the shared accountabilities of the team as a whole. Balance is the pivotal word. Allow each team member to act and contribute as an independent island (i.e., function like a separate department) and the team will fail. Likewise, force all team members to act and contribute identically (i.e., become completely interchangeable) and the team will fail. The multidisciplinary team takes root and blooms somewhere between these two dangerous poles. Striking this balance is a challenge in establishing any team but it is magnified many times when it comes to multidisciplinary teams and can become politically and emotionally charged.

Meeting this challenge is no easy chore for most health care organizations. In the traditional organization, this balance is tilted perilously to one side.

Tremendous value is placed on individual expertise or depth of skills while virtually none is awarded to breadth of skills. In fact, the only way to get ahead is to go "deeper," certainly not "deeper and broader." Health care organizations take this imbalance to a stifling extreme. For example, depth of skills is often used as a major criteria in promoting new managers even though being great at the bench in no way means that a person is qualified to be a good manager. Similarly, a good manager in one department is rarely given the chance to be a good manager in another because of the misconception that credibility is only earned through clinical or technical expertise (rather than through proven management or leadership skills).

THE MULTIDISCIPLINARY PYRAMID

Overcoming this deeply ingrained traditional imbalance is the challenge to meet before an organization can reap the rewards of multidisciplinary teams. There is no recipe for pulling this off. Many organizations that have successfully established multidisciplinary teams did so, however, through a process based on a series of major steps similar to those in Figure 10–1. This multidisciplinary pyramid of initiatives creates a rock-solid foundation for teams, sets up guardrails to keep them on track, and adds the finishing touch that locks in lasting results. To accomplish all of this, the initiatives of the pyramid must deal with facts as well as fiction, with "what is" as well as "what isn't." Furthermore, these initiatives don't just affect the teams themselves. Their impact is every bit as profound for managers. The cultural and operational transformations of staff and managers are joined at the hip when it comes to multidisciplinary teams.

The rest of this chapter describes the nature, value, and challenges of each initiative in this pyramid. There are other equally important activities on the project plan for establishing any type of team, such as proper education and ongoing coaching for the teams. These activities—described throughout this book—are the basis for moving from an organization of individuals to an organization of teams. The specific initiatives of this pyramid, however, represent those that are pivotal to one particular type of team—multidisciplinary teams. They directly address the major issues, pitfalls, and challenges of establishing teams that cross traditional turfs. Above and beyond the usual project plan, these initiatives will significantly determine the pace and results of any program to establish multidisciplinary teams.

Every organization must customize the specifics of its process to its own situation and needs, but this does not mean each organization has to start from scratch. The pyramid represents the cumulative "lessons learned the hard way" from many organizations and serves as an invaluable starting

Figure 10–1 Multidisciplinary Pyramid of Initiatives. *Source*: Reprinted with permission from PFCA © 1995.

point for any organization pursuing multidisciplinary teams. These lessons will be shared by building the pyramid from the bottom up, one initiative at a time, as follows:

1. a rock-solid foundation
2. guardrails along the way
3. the capping stone (finishing touch)

A ROCK-SOLID FOUNDATION

The first set of initiatives in the multidisciplinary pyramid creates a rock-solid foundation for these teams. These three initiatives launch the process of establishing multidisciplinary teams in the right direction. Successfully accomplishing each initiative requires the organization to be rather nimble. It must put in place the right changes while sidestepping the common pitfalls that can quickly undermine the process. The "what to do" and "what not to do" in each of these three initiatives is described next. These initiatives are:

1. team design
2. communications campaign
3. performance measures

Team Design

A cornerstone of the multidisciplinary pyramid is team design. Chapter 2 delved into the whys and hows of team design. The moral of that story is that highly effective teams require a thoughtful and sound design. Improperly designed teams—established by crashing together existing jobs and labeling the result a team—set everyone up for almost certain failure. To achieve results, the resources available (supply) must be carefully matched to the pool of work to be performed (demand). This matching is accomplished through an analytically based design process, not through a series of team-building exercises, inspirational speeches, or intuition.

As with any process, designing teams has its pitfalls. This is particularly true when it comes to creating a sound design for multidisciplinary teams. The most common pitfall is not allowing the skills and contributions of team members to overlap. This overlap helps the team strike the crucial balance between individual expertise and shared responsibilities. Without it, the team remains a collection of individuals.

One pitfall restricting the overlap among multidisciplinary team members is succumbing to the popular yet false belief that most of what a professional does is restricted by regulatory code. This mistaken belief restricts multiskilling and, therefore, shrinks the team's pool of shared work. It is understandable given the "deeper is always better" history described above. In highly compartmentalized work settings, accepted practice over time becomes law in the organization's eyes. The perceived threat involved in crossing turfs and redefining professions adds more fuel to the fire. This misconception sharply restricts team members' ability to share responsibilities through selective multiskilling which, in turn, leads to improperly designed teams, unnecessarily expensive teams, and/or teams with no control over their outcomes. In any case, the prognosis for the teams is not good.

Another pitfall restricting the overlap is falling victim to the belief that competency in a skill comes only through continual (as opposed to frequent) performance. A sound design process thoroughly considers team members' abilities to maintain ongoing competency in given skills. One way to examine ongoing competency is to estimate how often the team would perform an activity and ask, "Is this enough to stay sharp?" But enough compared to what? A conservative way to set this threshold is to use the frequency of performance demonstrated by specialized personnel within the central department. This frequency is clearly enough, but is it more than necessary? Probably, in most cases. Fact is, very few departments track how performance in an activity varies with the frequency of doing it. They have never needed to do so under traditional compartmentalized structures. Given this lack of objective data, the threshold for ongoing competency is usually set through negotiation. Too much bias and politics in this negotiation raises the threshold to the point where virtually all multiskilling is deemed off-limits. When this happens, multidisciplinary teams suffer from loss of control over outcomes.

The foundation for highly effective multidisciplinary teams begins with a sound design. Striking a balance between the individual expertise of each team member and the shared responsibilities among members is the "what to do." "What not to do" is to fall victim to the pitfalls that unnecessarily limit the latter.

Communications Campaign

The next initiative in the pyramid's foundation is to orchestrate a comprehensive communications campaign to deal directly with predictable yet unfounded anxieties. Good communication is a part of any transformation to teams. The pursuit of multidisciplinary teams, however, injects new levels of stress into the organization. Preempting and minimizing this stress is the objective of the campaign.

Health care organizations, unfortunately, are notoriously poor at communications. This indictment is not to say that they don't communicate (quantity). They just don't communicate well (quality). Most organizations wallow in an almost nonstop flood of memos, announcements, departmental meetings, management team forums and "lunches with the president." Many messages are delivered but few are received. The underlying problem is that these communications are rarely tailored to their audiences. They are offered in "administrationese" and laden with jargon rather than straight talk. They fail to recognize that individuals receive and process information differently and that one message cannot fit the entire organization. They also tend to say too much at once, offering periodic speeches rather than a continual stream of sound bites.

The organizations that do communicate effectively work very hard at overcoming these shortcomings. For example, they help all managers through formal and informal education to become better communicators. These managers in turn deliver regular progress updates at staff meetings. These organizations make it as easy as possible for interested staff to find answers to questions. For example, they set up Q&A hotlines and publish the names and telephone extensions of everyone leading the transformation to teams. They offer progress tidbits via cardboard fold-ups placed on each cafeteria table and flyers in each paycheck envelope. In short, these organizations provide almost continual information in a way that is easy to access and digest.

Another valuable communications tactic used by these organizations is to address head-on the popular misconceptions about multidisciplinary teams. They don't skirt the issues or talk around the concerns. What are some of the most common misconceptions about multidisciplinary teams? Not surprisingly, most are associated with the potential multiskilling across traditional jobs and historical departmental lines (Exhibit 10–1). They are usually voiced in the form of a challenging, perhaps confrontational, question, such as, "How can someone with a brief period of training do what I can do with my years of education and experience?!" The misconception results from misreading multidisciplinary as interchangeable. In no way do effective multidisciplinary teams want or try to create interchangeable members. The balance in design is struck between individual expertise and shared accountabilities. Striking this balance often leads to multiskilling members only in the more routine, high-volume activities, while the more complex, specialized responsibilities—those requiring years of education and experience—are carefully delivered through individual expertise. For example, routine respiratory treatments may be multiskilled while assessments and arterial blood gas studies may remain the sole responsibility of the team's respiratory therapist. How can someone with brief training do everything that an experienced professional can do? The answer is, "They can't, and we don't want them to!"

Another common misconception relates to the appropriateness and wisdom of licensed professionals assuming unlicensed duties. Over the past few years, there has been a widespread movement to relieve scarce, expensive licensed professionals of these duties. Presented with the possibility of multiskilling multidisciplinary team members to perform patient-related activities outside of their backgrounds, an organization naturally will respond with, "Isn't a professional's time too valuable to be spent performing unlicensed duties?!" Well, yes and no. Certainly, it would be a financial and

---

Exhibit 10–1 Common Questions and Misconceptions about Multidisciplinary Teams

1. When will this project affect me?
2. Will I have a job in the future?
3. Will this project eliminate my department?
4. Won't cross-training hurt quality?
5. Aren't you doing away with specialization?
6. Isn't this a threat to my profession?
7. How will career advancement be affected?
8. Will I get paid more for taking on more?
9. How can someone with a few weeks training do what I do with years of experience?
10. Will I have to report to someone outside of my background/profession?

morale disaster to dedicate a nurse to a full-time role performing EKGs. But, there are situations when having someone other than the patient's caregivers perform an EKG is just as bad. For example, when it forces caregivers to spend more time scheduling, coordinating, and following up a task than it takes simply to perform it themselves. In other words, when it replaces patient care time performing the EKG with red tape time. Furthermore, it can erode the caregivers' control over the patient's outcomes to the extent that this EKG is a necessary part of the care process. For these reasons, it may be both appropriate and wise to build this responsibility into the multidisciplinary team. Is a professional's time too valuable to perform unlicensed duties? Sometimes a professional's time is too valuable not to perform unlicensed duties, and that call is made on a case-by-case basis in establishing multidisciplinary teams.

"How can multidisciplinary teams be more cost-effective than centralized departments?!" is still another question voicing common misconceptions related to multidisciplinary teams. One misconception is that centralization is always the low-cost way to deliver diagnostic and therapeutic services. Once again, the answer is, "Sometimes." Certain services, especially those with high capital requirements and low volume on a per-patient basis (e.g., microbiology), are best delivered from a central department. This type of service needs the scale that comes from combining demand from all patients and floors in order to fund its fixed costs. Furthermore, this type of service lacks adequate volume for any team to maintain ongoing competency. Other services, however, are actually more costly when delivered centrally. These services typically require little capital and have more volume per patient (e.g., phlebotomy). Centralizing these services pays little penalty in terms of lost scale but robs the team of control. In fact, centralization—making remote a service routinely needed by many patients—actually increases costs by imposing a tremendous amount of continual coordination, transportation, and red tape. Is centralization the cheapest way to deliver services? Not always, and multidisciplinary teams may beneficially take on service responsibilities when the costs of centralization exceed the benefits.

A good communications campaign will alleviate the anxieties stirred by these common misconceptions. The war is not yet won by any means, however. The greatest battle has yet to be fought. Typically, the most deep-rooted misconception relates to the possible erosion of the professions as part of the move to multidisciplinary teams. "Won't this program to establish cross-trained teams eliminate my profession?!" This is indeed a powerful and fearful misconception. Nothing about multidisciplinary teams—including selective multiskilling across traditional jobs—has to threaten the professions or professional identity. In fact, the opposite can be true. Multidisciplinary teams can finally unlock the power of the professions by allowing professionals to spend more time in cognitive problem solving and less time executing tasks, thereby repositioning professionals from doers to thinkers.

Unfortunately, not all transformations to teams avoid damaging the professions. Whether through intention or oversight, some organizations do wind up eroding professional identities. This happens because guarding the professions requires more than effective communications. Certain safeguards are required to ensure multidisciplinary teams promote rather than destroy professional identity. These safeguards will be explored later in this chapter. For now, recognize that the foundation for multidisciplinary teams must include effective communications to help address concerns over professional identity.

There are many other misconceptions related to teams in general and multidisciplinary teams in particular, but the ones discussed above are perhaps the most common and often the most emotionally charged. A common response to these and many other misconceptions is, "Sometimes yes, sometimes no." At first, this response feels uncomfortable because people in the organization are looking for absolute clarity, but there are no simple answers. And that is exactly as it should be. Any dramatic change, like a move to multidisciplinary teams, must be precisely targeted. It must not be change for change's sake. From design to implementation, the organization should pick its punches, going for the biggest bang for the buck in each decision. One size never fits all in an environment as complex and dynamic as health care. In fact, the pursuit of one-size-fits-all answers (e.g., all services are centralized and specialized) led to the compartmentalization plaguing health care providers today. Instead, the organization will find the clarity it needs by creating a well-defined process to make the key decisions needed for establishing multidisciplinary teams. In other words, the answer, "It depends, but here is exactly what we are going to do together to find out . . ." is an asset. When the organization needs further answers, the necessary process exists to discover those answers.

The second initiative in the foundation for highly effective multidisciplinary teams is to launch an effective communications campaign. Making the messages understandable, consistent, and easily accessible to the entire organization is "what to do." "What not to do" is to allow concerns and anxieties to fester into resistance by failing to respond to common misconceptions head-on—even if those responses are unpopular.

Performance Measures

The next initiative in the pyramid for multidisciplinary teams and the last part of its foundation is a shift in performance measures. Most existing measures reflect the narrowly defined jobs of today's compartmentalized organization. One could even argue that existing performance measures promote and perpetuate the individualism permeating traditional health care organizations by defining success within (not across) jobs and departments. For example, the manager of a diagnostic service is evaluated and rewarded based almost exclusively on the efficiency and productivity of that department vis-à-vis the budget. In that mode, centralization is always the low-cost way to deliver services because it minimizes costs and maximizes utilization within that one department. These performance measures do not link the coordination and red tape costs imposed by centralization to that department.

Said another way, most of the gross inefficiencies, waste, and redundancies hampering today's health care organization are not within departments. They have been swept into the walls and spaces between departments. No one with direct line responsibility owns those walls and spaces. Much has been written about cost shifting in health care—where patients who can afford to pay subsidize those who cannot. A less recognized but just as insidious enemy is expense shifting—where maximizing the performance of one department imposes its inefficiencies on others. How else can an inpatient chest x-ray routinely take a couple of hours to complete (from the physician's order to the patient returning to bed) when the actual hands-on care part of that process takes no more than 15 minutes?

A parallel example can be drawn easily for nonmanagement jobs as well. Traditional performance measures erode any chance of collaboration—and even cooperation on occasion—between jobs. Anything that detracts from employees accomplishing tasks included in their performance measures is put off or outright refused, even if this so-called distraction is needed to serve the customer better. The most common example of this friction is when a patient or family member asks an employee for help getting to a remote location in the facility. The typical response is to offer a set of directions (e.g., follow the blue line down the hall, take a left, keep going to the elevator bank, etc.). Principles of good customer service would suggest escorting the person to his or her destination. This rarely happens because doing so takes the employee away from pressing duties that directly affect performance measures. The organization's employees very much want to serve the customers but they are often slaves to their measures at the same time.

Health care organizations are increasingly investing in serve the customer efforts to inspire their staff to put the needs of the customer first and to give employees some basic customer service skills, but these organizations are treating the symptoms rather than the disease. Without a critical review of performance measures and job descriptions, the only lasting impacts of those investments will be the T-shirts and bumper stickers. People will and should act in their own self-interests. To ask them repeatedly to do otherwise is naive and doomed. These self-interests are defined in large part by how we measure, evaluate, and reward performance. That must change before self-interests will change and well before behaviors can change.

There is no doubt that traditional performance measures promote individualism and myopia because success is only defined within jobs and departments, not across them. These measures lead to doing the wrong thing the right way. It follows, then, that teams cannot succeed using traditional performance measures designed for individuals in narrowly defined jobs. Multidisciplinary teams cannot succeed using performance measures that only reward deeper rather than deeper and broader skills and contributions. Such measures motivate team members to put their individual needs above the shared good of the team. This conclusion is why revising performance measures is a vital part of the foundation for successful multidisciplinary teams.

Having said this, an organization does not have to revamp its entire performance measurement and personnel appraisal systems completely before multidisciplinary teams can take root. An organization, instead, must communicate the new direction and gradually, cautiously move toward it. That movement begins with removing or neutralizing the greatest barriers to teams at least so that the existing performance measures don't stop the transformation altogether. It continues by shifting measures into alignment with a multidisciplinary team environment. How must performance measures shift to support multidisciplinary teams? The required shifts in measures must ultimately align the self-interests of the teams and team members with the goals of the institution in order to change behaviors (i.e., treat the disease, not just the symptoms).

There are a few fundamental shifts in performance measures needed to make the most of multidisciplinary teams (Figure 10–2). The first is a shift in focus from tasks to outcomes. Performance today is most often measured through the individual's completion of tasks (e.g., tests per hour in a laboratory). As explained above, this focus leads to myopia, self-centeredness, and lack of collaboration within the organization. The following case study highlights this disconnect between measures focused on tasks and effective multidisciplinary teams.

Case Study: "The Back-Firing of Traditional Measures"

A 450-bed urban hospital had designed and implemented multidisciplinary teams in a complex medical unit as part of a broader work redesign effort. The members of these teams included an RN, a respiratory therapist, and another licensed professional. One of the key performance goals on this unit was to reduce lengths of stay.

PERFORMANCE MEASURES
Needed To Promote Highly Effective Multidisciplinary Teams

	FROM:	TO:
FOCUS	Process/Task Means-Oriented ⟶	Outcome/Function Ends-Oriented
BREADTH	Productivity Efficiency Only ⟶	Overall Spectrum of Performance
OWNERSHIP	Top-Down Information and Actions ⟶	Bottom-Up Information and Actions
DEPTH	Trivial Many Everything Fully Detailed ⟶	Vital Few Exception- Based

Figure 10–2 Shifts in Performance Measures

Before the teams were implemented, a task force studied how to translate that goal into the individual evaluations of the team's members. After debating cause and effect, the task force recommended measuring the performance of teams' therapist members on the elapsed time from order to delivery of a new order for respiratory assessment or treatment. The RN members of the teams were similarly measured on the elapsed time from admission to delivery of a new order for nursing assessment or one of several time-sensitive interventions.

During the first few months, the multidisciplinary teams appeared to be working well. Teammates got along and the work was getting done. Over time, however, a rift grew between many of the therapists and RNs on those teams. The therapists complained that other duties were keeping them from responding immediately to all orders for assessments and treatments. A few also believed their teammates weren't helping matters by not always pitching in and taking over whatever the therapist was doing so he or she could get to the respiratory treatment. The flip side was no better. The RNs struggled with other responsibilities that kept them from responding immediately to new assessments and interventions. They too came to resent the way their therapist teammates could not always lend a hand to help them get to those nursing responsibilities ASAP.

The net result was that the RN and therapist members of many teams were meeting expectations in terms of their performance measures.

Elapsed times were not improving as hoped. Lengths of stay were holding but not falling. Their behaviors as teammates were not meeting expectations either.

This case study exposes a pair of important lessons regarding multidisciplinary teams. First, it reinforces the criticality of attending to both the structural and cultural side of teams. One problem in this case is a flawed team design. The symptom is that two teammates, an RN and a respiratory therapist, repeatedly became the bottlenecks in the care process. No team can succeed with a design that regularly introduces bottlenecks. Taking a purely behavioral approach to the situation (e.g., remedial conflict resolution skills) could only offer short-term relief at best. The symptoms of the underlying flawed design would inevitably resurface.

Another lesson from this case is that the teammates' individual performance measures are unlikely to contribute to the team's ultimate goal. The disconnect arises from a focus on tasks/means (i.e., turnaround time for a team-based activity) rather than directly on the desired outcome/end (i.e., reduced lengths of stay). What penalties are paid for such disconnects? Operationally, the penalty can be severe. The team cannot make a significant impact on lengths of stay. Culturally, the team is breaking apart at the seams and whatever gains have been made in working as a team are quickly eroding.

Furthermore, the performance measures' focus on tasks has undermined the team's ability to seek its own solutions. It cannot behave as an empowered team because its hands have been tied. Little creativity can be applied to finding solutions to reducing lengths of stay when team members are paid to concentrate on completing tasks. Focusing the team's performance measures on outcomes would allow and motivate it to identify the most important influences on lengths of stay (and it may not be turnaround time for particular treatments or assessments). The team then would come up with ways to address those influences to achieve desired outcomes by shifting its own priorities and energies as required. That's empowerment. That's a performance measurement approach that promotes team behaviors and improves outcomes at the same time. A win for the team and a win for the institution.

This added flexibility of outcomes-based measures is particularly pivotal for multidisciplinary teams. These teams have a greater pool of resources, skills, and experiences among their members from which to draw as they identify the cause and effect relationships with outcomes. Performance measures focused on these outcomes nurture good team dynamics and cross-pollination of knowledge simply because the self-interests of the team members are aligned with each other and with the needs of the institution.

Measures focused on tasks do just the opposite. They motivate each team member to pursue his or her own self-interest, which can be diametrically opposed to the overall interests of the team and the needs of the institution. As a result, the team never gels—it continues to function as a collection of individuals where the whole is no greater than the sum of its parts and sometimes less. Since working as individuals is more familiar and less threatening to members of a newly formed multidisciplinary team, it does not take long for such team-destructive behaviors to solidify.

A corollary to this fundamental shift from tasks to outcomes is a shift away from traditional efficiency measures to a broader spectrum of performance. In a compartmentalized environment, efficiency and productivity measures proliferated because each job involved only a small slice of the overall processes which typically crossed several departments. The routine chest x-ray previously described spanned a handful of departments across a dozen different jobs. Another example can be found in patient discharge—a process that involves several departments (nursing unit, patient transportation, housekeeping) and numerous jobs. In this environment, there is little choice but to measure jobs by how quickly people do their little part and how many of those parts they perform during the shift.

Like task-based measures, classical efficiency and productivity ratios can lead to undesirable behaviors and stagnant outcomes (i.e., measuring a respiratory therapist member of a multidisciplinary team on treatments per hour can only lead to bad results). To start, it fails to recognize the large pool of additional responsibilities assumed by the therapist that were not part of the traditional job within the central department. Comparing treatment-per-hour measures between the team and the department is like comparing apples to oranges. Such comparisons invite resentment among members of the central department who perceive that the team member is not working as hard as they are.

How can performance be productively channeled without a barrage of efficiency and productivity measures? Through outcomes, of course. Mature multidisciplinary teams are often measured by a handful of key outcomes spanning quality, service, relationships, and economics (Figure 10–3). This last dimension—economics—can alleviate the reliance on classical efficiency measures. For example, multidisciplinary teams may be measured on direct team costs per workload handled (e.g., patient days adjusted for acuity). These measures are still a numerical ratio but they get to the heart of what the efficiency and productivity measures were intended to achieve—lower costs.

Early in the development of a multidisciplinary team, a few efficiency and productivity measures may make sense to ensure some control during the

Figure 10–3 Sample Team-Based Performance Measures

transition period when teams still behave like individuals. These interim measures, however, should be phased out as soon as the team learns to focus on true outcomes. If past is prologue, the real challenge in phasing out traditional measures will not come from the teams but from the managers who find comfort in the traditional efficiency and productivity measures. It is usually prudent to address this challenge, particularly with managers, before the first team is up and running.

A third fundamental change in performance measures is a shift in ownership from top-down to bottom-up. The ownership of outcomes and their associated performance measures must reside first and foremost with the multidisciplinary teams. The Achilles' heel of many efforts to improve outcomes in health care organizations has been that accountability for outcomes resides too high in the organization. Outcomes-based measures for teams move that accountability where it should be—with the front-line workers. But outcomes-based measures cannot help the development of multidisciplinary teams if they continue to be owned by managers.

What is meant by own? Ownership means that the teams themselves are on the hook for using the measures to achieve desired outcomes. The buck stops with them. Consequently, the team initiates the improvement process and evolves from recognizing symptoms to identifying the underlying problems and proposing solutions to those problems. The manager and other coaches must facilitate this evolution and help set parameters and goals for improvement, but the team is the engine behind change. Structurally, ownership becomes more tangible. For example, the team is the primary and first recipient of performance reports. The manager is copied on these reports but the team is the customer of that information. Therefore, the team should have significant input into the definition of measures as long as the needed outcomes remain the focal point.

The shift in ownership from management to teams sounds easy. It isn't. It is at least as much of a change for the managers as it is for the teams. Imagine this scenario. The latest performance report just comes across a manager's desk and the telephone rings. It's "the big boss" who wants to know why a certain measure looks bad. The manager instinctively wants to fix the problem. Years of managing in a hierarchical organization have taught that good managers are hunters, not gatherers. They find solutions to kill problems. The boss angrily asks again what is going on and what the manager intends to do about it. The manager replies (drum roll, please) . . . "I am not sure yet. I will meet with the team and we will propose a solution to turn this around. We all recognize the importance of this matter." Is this a normal and natural dialogue in most health care organizations? Not even close. But it will have to become the norm over time as managers and executives make their own personal transitions to a team-based organization.

This shift also has a corollary. If multidisciplinary teams are to own measures, there must be a shift from data to information. Managers today typically struggle as hard to find relevant and actionable information in their regular performance reports as physicians do to find relevant actionable information in charts. Traditional performance reports are long on data—lots of data— but short on information.

There's a big difference between the two. Decisions are based on information not on data. Here's a quick test: Pick up a routine performance report and look at it for exactly five seconds. Which performance measures are meeting expectations/targets? Which are not? Of the latter, which measures need to be addressed immediately? If you can't answer these questions after a five-second review, the performance report is not providing information in a way that decision makers can readily use. It is not allowing them to use it in an exception-based manner. Instead, it is forcing them to plow through the trivial many rather than the vital few.

Such problems are bad enough for managers but they can absolutely paralyze a team seeking information related to its performance and its next improvement challenges. To help teams own outcomes and measures, they must receive the smallest amount of information possible (but all that is relevant to key outcomes) in a way that immediately helps them to differentiate what is important. The burden is to identify the pivotal outcomes (the vital few), determine the best measures of those outcomes (direct cause and effect), and report them in a convenient, efficient format (Exhibit 10–2).

The third initiative in the foundation for highly effective multidisciplinary teams is shifting performance measures from those promoting individualism to those recognizing team-based behaviors. Aligning the self-interests of teams and team members with the goals of the organization is "what to do." "What not to do" is to climb this mountain all at once before the transforma-

Exhibit 10–2 Team-Based Performance Report

	BELOW EXPECTED	EXPECTED RANGE	ABOVE EXPECTED
INTERPRETATION OF FINDINGS:	(15%) (10%)	(5%) 5%	10% 15%
		▲=Current Period Finding	

OVERALL FINDING

QUALITY WEIGHT
Continuity of Members	0.8
Lengths of Stay	0.8
Reject/Repeat Rates	0.4
Patient Outcomes	1.4
Incidence Rates	1.0

SERVICE
Continuity with Patients	1.2
Patient Satisfaction	1.0
Patient Complaints	1.0
Continuity with Physicians	0.6
Turnaround Times	0.4

ENVIRONMENT
Team Member Satisfaction	0.8
Physician Satisfaction	1.0
Other Staff Satisfaction	0.6

FINANCIAL
Team Utilization	1.2
Team Workload Category	0.8
Caregiving Costs Per	1.4
Record Completion Time	0.8
Value-Added Profile	1.0

tion to teams can take root. Instead, tear down any obvious barriers imposed by traditional measures while establishing a set of transformational indicators that combine the past with the future.

Summary

A rock-solid foundation for successful multidisciplinary teams can be built through three key initiatives. First, create a sound team design based on facts rather than perceptions. Second, establish an effective communications campaign that allays anxieties caused by popular misconceptions. Third, gradually shift the focus and ownership of performance measures to promote team-based behaviors. All of these initiatives are underway early in the transformation to teams but the specific timing of each may vary. For example, a communications campaign is often the first initiative to be launched. Soon thereafter, the design must be in place before the first team member is selected and the curriculum of educational programs is finalized. The shift in performance measures can also begin soon after communication is underway (e.g., setting the general direction and swaying paradigms) but replacing measures should be done gradually and cautiously. The first few attempts to do so will be fertile grounds for learning. Then, as the teams mature, so will the performance measurement system.

A few recurring themes tie together the initiatives that provide this foundation for multidisciplinary teams. First, a program to establish multidisciplinary teams has at least as great an impact on managers as it does on staff. The beliefs, behaviors, and priorities of both staff and managers evolve as multidisciplinary teams replace narrowly defined jobs in the organization. Second, successful multidisciplinary teams are the orchestrated product of both cultural and structural change. Organizations are often more eager to gravitate to the cultural side of teams to the exclusion of the structural. Finally, a rock-solid foundation changes behaviors not by edict nor by controlling them, but by aligning self-interests. Goal alignment is the key to lasting and successful change.

GUARDRAILS ALONG THE WAY

The next set of initiatives in the multidisciplinary pyramid builds upon this foundation. This pair of initiatives—enhancing professional identity and expanding career advancement—acts as guardrails, guiding the ongoing growth of teams through the turbulence of change. The foundation allows multidisciplinary teams to get started. The guardrails keep them going in the right direction. The "what to do" and "what not to do" in each of these initiatives is described next:

1. maintaining professional identity
2. enhancing career advancement

Professional Identity

The most powerful turbulence in the evolution of multidisciplinary teams comes from the perceived conflict between this transformation and professional identities. Talk of multiskilling across traditional jobs and turfs can appear at first pass to endanger the professions. As mentioned earlier, this certainly does not have to be the case. Multidisciplinary teams potentially can be the force that finally unlocks the full power of the professions in an organization. Why are multidisciplinary teams, and multiskilling in particular, perceived as threats to professional identity? The answer to this question is as simple as "heads versus hands." The following real-life experience helps to explain:

> At a recent conference on work redesign, the speaker had just completed his talk about the challenges and rewards of multidisciplinary teams when a hand went up in the back of the auditorium. The emotionally charged question hurled at the speaker was, "How on earth can you stand there and tell me that multidisciplinary teams don't hurt my profession when you just said some of the things we do today may be done tomorrow by people outside of our profession?!"
>
> The speaker thought about the question. After a period of silence that seemed to go on for days, he responded with a question, "Tell me, what value do you as a professional bring to the care of your patients?" Everyone turned around in their seats. The reply came without hesitation, "I perform blood and body substance testing. I'm a medical technologist."

That reply does a tremendous disservice to medical technologists and clinical laboratories everywhere. Running lab tests certainly does not define the value of this profession, just as performing respiratory treatments does not define the value of respiratory care nor starting IVs the profession of nursing. To think so is to say, "My contributions are limited to what I do with my hands." The value of a profession lies not in what those professionals do with their hands (tasks and activities) but by what they have in their heads (knowledge and cognitive skills). The value lies in cognitive skills and problem solving—the capabilities for judgment that can only be gained through years of education and experience.

Years of working in the narrowly defined jobs of a traditionally compartmentalized environment have taken their toll on how professionals in health care organizations define their own value. Victims of a system that pigeonholes people's potential, professionals have adopted a very tactical, mechanistic view of themselves. This tragedy is the equivalent of an MBA defining her value by the spreadsheets she runs and the reports she creates rather than by her business knowledge and insights. Within this definition of value, it is easy to understand why professionals view even the most selective multiskilling of routine, high-volume tasks as a threat to their identity. Each skill shared seems to chip away at the value they perceive in themselves. This holds equally true whether the skill is purely mechanical or highly intellectual.

As long as health care professionals view themselves by what they do with their hands rather than by what they have in their heads, the power of the professions will remain largely untapped. Why? Because the power and value of any profession is in thinking, not just doing. Most professionals' time today is spent completing tasks and performing well-defined procedures that barely exercise one-tenth of their knowledge. The greatest power of the professions cannot be realized through isolationism. Similar to a team, the greatest rewards are reaped when the diverse knowledge bases across the professions are brought together to meet complex challenges that no one profession could meet alone. Then the whole truly is greater than the sum of its parts.

Multidisciplinary teams provide a forum for this to happen. Multiskilling and the overlap of responsibilities only involves routine, repetitive tasks (i.e., hands). Cognitive skills drawing upon a professional's unique expertise (i.e., head) are not shared. They cannot be multiskilled. Through this balance of individual expertise and shared responsibilities, the professions are maintained. Through the bringing together of the unique contributions of different professions, the professions are enhanced.

This crucial message—in essence a redefinition of the value of the professions—must be part of the communications campaign in any transformation to multidisciplinary teams. Separate head from hands and the program can take a big step forward on the back of that action. But other actions are needed. Safeguarding professional identity and unlocking the power of the professions takes more than words. It takes a set of actions to keep each professional group within an organization intact and in touch with its nationwide community.

A second effective action is to create professional governance structures. Nursing has relied on governance for a very long time. This reliance makes sense because nursing is one of the few, if not the only, profession within any health care organization that is scattered across many departments and units. For other professions in the traditional organization, governance has not been as vital since these professionals have been consolidated within a single department. The primary realm of governance—professional development, recruitment and retention, technological advances, credentialing, professional standards, regulatory changes—is served in staff meetings and day-to-day conversations.

The role of governance becomes increasingly important as multidisciplinary teams emerge. Professionals formerly working within the same department now may also work across multiple patient care areas. Governance can bind them together. It helps ensure internal consistency in practice and shared learning across its membership. Governance will also link professionals within an organization to their counterparts in other organizations and to the relevant national body. This link ensures the latest trends and innovations not only reach the organization but also the professionals in it, regardless of where they work. In one organization it became apparent that tribal barriers and professional bonds are broken early in the formation of multidisciplinary teams (Manion and Watson 1995). As teams were formed and members got to know each other and learn each other's language and values, there was a strong tendency to emphasize similarities, rather than respect and value differences. In the first year of team formation in one department, the nurses on the team decided they did not want to celebrate Nurses' Week. They believed it emphasized their differences too dramatically and they declined to participate unless all caregivers were recognized. Confronting this issue directly and immediately was critical because it was potentially very destructive to the essence of the teams. Team effectiveness is only achieved if the uniqueness and differences between individuals and professions is celebrated, not minimized.

As pharmacy, laboratory, dietary, social services, and physical therapy professionals were redeployed from their central departments to the patient care units and respiratory therapists and radiological technologists were incorporated into care teams, a structure was needed to keep professionals closely connected to their profession. Each of these disciplines now has a formalized governance structure to ensure consistency of professional standards and practices with practice councils to ensure that the important values of the profession are adhered to throughout the organization. They have formalized bylaws and meet on a regular basis.

As noted by Leander, Shortridge, and Watson (1996, 184) "all it takes is a shift in paradigms, from 'the only way to ensure quality is to directly supervise those who perform the service' to one enabling the professionals themselves to do what needs to be done." This model of shared governance has worked in the nursing profession for years. In a team-based organization with multidisciplinary teams, a professional governance structure is a valuable enabler.

Without governance, multidisciplinary teams can start up but they cannot succeed in the long run. The separation of the professionals from their professions robs people of the chance to expand their special expertise. It keeps them from staying current in their field. It jeopardizes the support group comprised of long-standing relationships and friendships. In short, the lack of governance pulls multidisciplinary team members away from their professions and, most important, threatens as fundamental a thing as the person's self-image, eliciting powerful emotions of fear, loss, and anger. The damage goes both ways. In the absence of governance, the rest of the professional group is pulled away from the progress of the multidisciplinary team. This separation short-circuits its learning and reinforces the old we versus them culture.

A third action to guard professional identity is to establish tiered employee appraisals. Hardly a multidisciplinary team program has been initiated without some conflict arising over the reporting relationship of the members. Does everyone on the teams report to the manager of that area, or does each member report back to his or her original department? Some of this conflict is rooted in members' fear of losing touch with their profession. Governance can help with this. This conflict is also rooted in managers' fear of losing any FTEs (managers' power in many health care organizations is gauged by the size of their budgets). Leaders need to help their managers through this fear by redefining power and success.

Another part of the conflict reflects concerns that a team member cannot be appraised properly by a manager outside of that profession. Is this concern justified? Yes and no. Most of the contributions made by a multidisciplinary team member can be appraised accurately by a manager (or teammate in the case of peer review) outside of that profession. For example, any manager can evaluate the extent to which a team and its members achieved quantifiable outcome targets. It takes no particular technical or clinical expertise for a manager to judge how well a member demonstrated desirable team behaviors, contributed to the team's continuous improvement, interacted well with other teams and staff, and so on. On the other hand, only a medical technologist can thoroughly and reliably evaluate technical competence in that area because competence involves both head and hands.

To bridge the gap between these evaluation scenarios, many organizations establishing multidisciplinary teams have created two-tiered appraisals (Figure 10–4). One tier (typically the largest in terms of dimensions and weight) includes all contributions that can properly be evaluated by someone outside of that profession. The second tier includes those contributions for which professional expertise is essential. Each tier is evaluated by the appropriate party. Taken together, the team member's evaluation is then a valid representation of his or her contributions to the organization as a whole. Certainly, there are other ways to bridge the gap but tiered appraisals usually produce a system that can be designed and implemented in a reasonable period of time.

A final action step to secure and bolster the professions is to enable periodic rotations through various areas and units. The purpose of these rotations is to provide professionals with the opportunity to experience new environments, new teammates, different managerial approaches, and various patient/customer types. It is intended to rejuvenate a team member while at the same time disseminating and facilitating best practices across various parts of the organization. For example, a medical technologist who is part of a multidisciplinary team on a general surgical unit may benefit from a rotation to a cardiac care unit where more complex lab tests are ordered and the required turnaround times for those results are frequently shorter. Such a

These Entities...   ...Appraise These Types of Performance

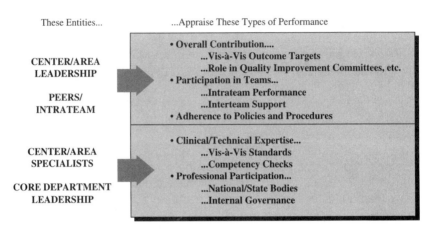

CENTER/AREA LEADERSHIP

PEERS/ INTRATEAM

- Overall Contribution....
  ...Vis-à-Vis Outcome Targets
  ...Role in Quality Improvement Committees, etc.
- Participation in Teams...
  ...Intrateam Performance
  ...Interteam Support
- Adherence to Policies and Procedures

CENTER/AREA SPECIALISTS

CORE DEPARTMENT LEADERSHIP

- Clinical/Technical Expertise...
  ...Vis-à-Vis Standards
  ...Competency Checks
- Professional Participation...
  ...National/State Bodies
  ...Internal Governance

Figure 10–4 Two-Tiered Performance Appraisals

rotation gives this professional a chance to be challenged in new skills and situations.

The downside of any rotation is that it breaks up the team (perhaps just as it is beginning to gel as a true team). As explained in Chapter 1, consistency in membership is both a requirement and a hallmark of highly effective teams. Any break in the stability or continuity of its members sets a team back culturally and structurally. Therefore, rotations must be spread out over time or no team will ever reach its potential. Not all organizations pursuing multidisciplinary teams have opted for this step. For many, the normal job posting process provides an avenue for voluntary rotations. At the same time, other organizations have made rotations mandatory. These organizations feel that the greater good cannot otherwise be served. The relevant lesson is not that rotation is or isn't better than no rotation. It is that each organization establishing multidisciplinary teams should consider the benefits and ensure that these can be achieved one way or another.

The fourth initiative in the pyramid (and the first of its guardrails) is not only to protect but to enhance the professions through multidisciplinary teams (Figure 10–5). Introducing to the team-based setting the same cultural and structural bonds that professionals enjoy within centralized departments is the "what to do." "What not to do" is to make the professionals pay a price for participation in the transformation to teams.

Career Advancement

Another source of turbulence along the way to successful multidisciplinary teams is the fear of lost career opportunities. Even when the se-

Redefine the Value of the Professions Using
"HEAD versus HANDS"

Meet Professionals' Needs through Some Type of
SHARED GOVERNANCE

Create Appropriate and Fair Evaluations through
TIERED APPRAISALS

Allow Diversity of Contributions and Competency Via
PERIODIC ROTATIONS

Figure 10–5 Guarding the Professions: A Summary of Helpful Action Steps

curity and role of the professions are assured, professionals are concerned about their ladder to the top. There are actually two ladders. The first ladder climbs within the staff ranks. On these rungs the employee progresses as his or her value to the organization increases. In the traditional organization, that value is strictly defined by depth of skills. The way to progress from a radiological technologist to a senior radiological technologist is to be a better and more versatile radiological technologist. In essence, going deeper is the only way to get ahead and contribute to improved outcomes within those areas delivering the more complex services.

Through multidisciplinary teams, an entirely new direction for staff advancement becomes available. Broader joins deeper as an avenue to get ahead. Deeper is still very much valued and rewarded in the delivery of a full range of complex services. Breadth of skills, however, becomes just as highly valued a contribution. In multidisciplinary teams, broader can also lead directly to improved outcomes. As such, team members are rewarded and can advance by expanding their skill sets. Moving into a multidisciplinary environment can increase progression—staff advancement through both depth and breadth of skills—within the staff ranks as long as the organization values and rewards outcomes, not just tasks. This flexibility in direction allows people to self-select into one or both over time. There is no longer just one recipe for getting ahead. To each his or her own.

The second career ladder is from staff to manager and beyond. Here, professionals are concerned that participation in multidisciplinary teams will hurt their chances for promotion into management ranks. Is there a reason for concern? At the risk of sounding like a broken record, yes and no. On the yes side, one of the reasons why organizations move to teams is to cut back layers of hierarchy. Some organizations must hold their management meetings in large auditoriums. No industry facing as much economic pressure and uncertainty as health care can afford to maintain a top-heavy management. Layers of hierarchy exact other penalties as well, such as garbled communications, redundant responsibilities, and sluggish responsiveness to changing customer demands. Removing this hierarchy in a controlled manner can yield significant benefits, but it also means there will be a smaller absolute number of management positions in the future.

On the no side, each person in a multidisciplinary organization now has a better chance at a larger number of those positions. It is difficult to imagine a more stifling career progression into management than the one within today's typical health care organization. The only management positions available to a physical therapist are usually within that department. The same is true for pharmacists, respiratory therapists, radiological technologists, and so forth. There is equal opportunity for little opportunity.

So rigidly have organizations defined value by what people do with their hands that they cling to two monstrous fallacies. The first fallacy was described at the beginning of this chapter—organizations mistakenly believe that the best clinicians and technicians make the best managers. This error yields managers who become too personally involved in doing the work (or micromanaging the work of others) and who spend too little time truly leading ongoing improvement. The second fallacy is the belief that a physical therapist could never effectively manage outside of that department. Organizations cannot fathom that a person with excellent leadership skills such as planning or coaching could possibly use them—and make a positive contribution—in a setting where they did not possess the same gamut of technical or clinical expertise as their staff.

The byproduct of these fallacies is limited career opportunities. How often do pharmacists manage nursing units or nurses manage laboratories? How often do nonnursing professionals rise into executive ranks? To the position of CEO? How many nurses rising to vice-president have no patient care units reporting to them? It is hard to imagine that while every other industry in America is touting the benefits of homegrown and up-through-the-ranks leaders, health care organizations always seem to draw the line at the department level. A health care professional today realistically has a chance for only an extremely small number of management positions. Fortunately, the move to multidisciplinary teams plants the seeds to expand those chances considerably.

Case Study: "Managing Outside of the Boxes"

Several years ago, one institution, a 550-bed acute care hospital and a recognized pioneer in patient-focused care, opened its first redesigned patient care unit. The building blocks of that organization were several multidisciplinary teams. The members of these teams included RNs, LPNs, nursing assistants, respiratory therapists, and radiological technologists. The first few managers in the center were all former nurse managers.

Over the ensuing few years, two more redesigned units with multidisciplinary teams were introduced. During this time, managers and staff on these units learned a great deal about what it takes to succeed in a multidisciplinary world. As a result, paradigms shifted and opportunities opened for people from diverse backgrounds.

For example, a respiratory therapist team member was promoted to the position of manager on one of the units—the first manager from outside of nursing. An even more inspiring example was the selection of the manager for another newly opened unit. What made the organization sit up and take notice of this particular selection was that this individual, Tom, had been the director of environmental services—the first nonclinical manager of a patient care area. This manager's track record and proven leadership skills qualified him as the best person for the job despite his lack of patient care expertise.

His transformation was not easy. He not only had to lead in an environment unlike any other he had ever experienced but at the same time had to gain credibility and win the respect of staff and physicians. That is just what he did over time. Today, that unit routinely meets all and exceeds most of its performance expectations in quality, service, and economics—making it one of the best running areas in the institution.

Since that time, the perceptual and political barriers to managing outside of traditional turfs have continued to crumble. Managers of redesigned patient care units in this organization include people from a wide spectrum of backgrounds, including laboratory services, social services, and quality assurance. In this organization, people are looking past what others do with their hands and rewarding them for what they have in their heads.

Organizations like this one with successful multidisciplinary teams recognize the fallacies that pigeonhole otherwise versatile performers. In particular, it had to realize that good leadership skills are hard to find yet are applicable almost anywhere in the organization. By definition, the success of a multidisciplinary team reporting to one manager hinges upon that manager's ability to lead people outside of his or her background. Once this logjam breaks, the fallacy begins to be swept away. When this happens, as it did for Tom, professionals enter the running for a wider array of management opportunities throughout their organizations.

Staff advances through both depth and breadth and a wider array of management opportunities. An organization of multidisciplinary teams opens, rather than closes, doors to career advancement for professionals (Figure 10–6). The key is an emphasis, even a passion, for outcomes. An emphasis on the outcomes controlled by staff (e.g., better service) gives value to breadth of skills where little existed before. An emphasis on the outcomes controlled by managers (e.g., empowered people) gives credibility to those people making those contributions in any corner of the organization.

The fifth initiative in the multidisciplinary pyramid (and the second of its guardrails) is expand career opportunities by defining deeper as well as broader criteria for advancement (Figure 10–6). Laying out these opportunities and then putting action behind those words is the "what to do." "What not to do" is to make those claims without demonstrating their merit and importance to the organization. The organization that claims its transformation to multidisciplinary teams presents opportunities for people of all backgrounds and then turns around and gives all future management positions to former nurse managers may be asking for trouble.

Summary

A pair of key initiatives form the guardrails keeping the transformation to multidisciplinary teams on the road and out of the ditches. While they are important in any team-based program, their impact on multidisciplinary teams cannot be overstated. First, enhance professional identity by establishing the necessary cultural and structural bonds linking professionals to their profession. Second, expand career advancement for staff to include depth as well as breadth of skills and contributions. At the same time, rethink the criteria for promotion into management and leadership to recognize that proven skills in these areas are transferable outside of traditional "boxes." Tackling

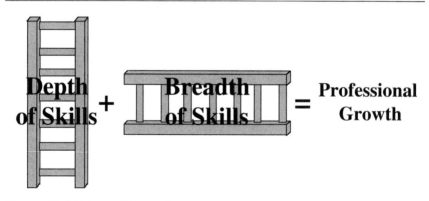

Figure 10–6 Enhanced Career Progression

these initiatives begins with the communications campaign at the pyramid's foundation. Words alone are not enough. These initiatives require concerted actions that are consistent with those words. A recurring theme through these actions is that the ongoing success of multidisciplinary teams depends on a clear separation of people from their positions. People are not their jobs. They are not a limited set of tasks. This notion gets a lot of lip service in health care organizations today. But the issues of professional identity and career advancement would not cause such turbulence in the transformation to multidisciplinary teams if actions really followed these words.

THE CAPPING STONE

A rock-solid foundation allows multidisciplinary teams to get started. Guardrails along the way keep them going in the right direction. The final initiative in the pyramid—learning to manage effectively in a multidisciplinary setting—locks in place the advances enjoyed through multidisciplinary teams and prevents them from reverting to the ways things used to be.

Multidisciplinary Management

A recurring theme of this chapter and of this book is that the transformation to teams is every bit as challenging and disturbing to managers as it is to staff. Most of these management challenges—a letting go of control by transferring responsibility and authority to the teams, setting clear constraints and goals for team decision-making, learning to be a good coach and facilitator—are faced regardless of the type of team. A few particular challenges, however, are most relevant to managing multidisciplinary teams. For tomorrow's manager, meeting the following pivotal challenges will largely determine whether the new organization is a success or a failure:

1. credibility gap
2. intrateam frictions
3. organizational tribes

Credibility Gap

The first challenge in managing multidisciplinary teams is gaining credibility, respect, and trust. This clearly was a major challenge for the former director of environmental services when he became manager of a patient care unit. The initial credibility gap is a product of the traditional organization's deeper is always better mentality that values skill sets as an avenue for career advancement. In other words, staff initially question the appropriateness of working for a manager who cannot step in, roll up the sleeves, and "do what we can do." Doing so was a measure of worth in the traditional, compartmentalized organization. Repeatedly doing so in a team-based setting not only is undesirable, but is detrimental to the cultural and structural direction of the new organization. Managers in a team-based setting must shift from doing the work (or micromanaging the work) to catalyzing others (i.e., teams and staff) to do the work by facilitating innovation, defining success, and providing necessary resources. Teams cannot learn to assume full accountability for their actions, behaviors, and outcomes if they regularly rely on their manager to fix problems. At one institution implementing teams, leaders sum up this challenge with "taking the momma out of management."

How does a manager of a newly established multidisciplinary team gain credibility? Guarding the professions (using a tiered appraisal process) helps alleviate some of the pressure but managers need to meet the challenge through their day-to-day actions as well. One key method is to demonstrate consistently to the teams that the greatest value to them that a manager can add is not by doing the work nor knowing every detail of their work but rather by coaching, facilitating, and leading. The bottom line is that staff will expect traditional manager actions until it learns that those actions are no longer in its best interests. Another way is to spend enough time and energy becoming familiar with the backgrounds, motivations, value systems, and skill sets of every team member. This familiarity helps build a mutual rapport and empathy between manager and team member.

Managers can demonstrate their new value by setting clear expectations that their role has changed to helping teams help themselves—thereby recalibrating the yardstick against which the team measures the manager's performance (Exhibit 10–3). They need to show that their inability to do what every team member can do is not a hindrance to helping the team. It is common for managers of a traditional organization to interject themselves when a physician complains about a clinical aspect of a staff member's performance. In the future, managers will not interject. They will facilitate resolution by bringing together the physician, team, and perhaps an objective, outside expert (e.g., a clinical specialist from another department) to work out a solution. The value they bring to the resolution is helping others to think through the problem, to identify different ways to address it, and to select the best course of action. This approach—although more work for everyone involved than interjecting—pays off in the long term because it reinforces accountability at the team level, gradually imparts to it the capability to reach its own resolutions, and through participation builds team ownership of the resulting actions.

There is no easy recipe for gaining credibility, respect, and trust as the manager of a multidisciplinary team. It occurs gradually through the indi-

Exhibit 10–3 Transition from Manager to Leader

Key Focus/ Responsibility	By Today's Manager	By Tomorrow's Leader
How Quality Is Guarded	Control	Coach
Relationship with Staff	Boss	Mentor
How Quality Improvement Is Introduced	"Push"	"Pull"
Focus of Attention	Process/Task	Outcome/Result
Decision-Making Horizon	Near-Term	Long-Term
Priority for Operations	Maintain	Innovate
Backgrounds of Staff	Within Tribe	Multidisciplinary
Impetus for Innovation and Change	Top-Down/ Punitive	Bottom-Up/ Goal Alignment

vidual commitment and effort of the manager. Early in the transformation, managers may have to interject occasionally to help teams just learning to work together in a new setting. These interjections should become fewer over time. The hard part is resisting the temptation to interject when the pressure is on (i.e., take the easy way out). Consistency of actions and role modeling is a must.

Intrateam Frictions

Another challenge particular to managing multidisciplinary teams is smoothing out intrateam frictions. All teams take time and learning to overcome the normal frictions that keep them from becoming more than a collection of individuals. Team members must improve their interpersonal communication, negotiation, and conflict resolution skills. Multidisciplinary teams are no exception, and typically face a new level of frictions that is a carry-over of traditional jobs and biases.

What are some of these frictions? Some frictions result from the lack of role clarity. Team members may view their individual and collective roles as ambiguous, given shared responsibilities and new levels of accountability. This ambiguity causes them to revert to traditional and team-destructive behaviors, such as demarcating who does what in an attempt to add clarity. It also creates unnecessary interpersonal conflicts. Managers of multidisciplinary teams need to clarify roles—not just individual expertise, but acceptable behaviors and processes for decision making and problem solving.

Other frictions are rooted in a clear imbalance of power within the team. One profession may see another as an extender/helper and, perhaps inadvertently, relegates the other profession to second-class membership on the team. This imbalance leads to conflicts in decision making where one team member has veto power over another's decisions. At its extreme, this imbalance prevents true team-based behaviors because one member acts as a pseudosupervisor. Professionals experience dismay, shock, and anger when other professionals disagree with their proposed program objectives. Those disagreeing are viewed as incompetent, malevolent, or out of their field of expertise. Managers need to recognize the signs and symptoms of these frictions and show the team why such an imbalance is detrimental to them as individuals and as a team.

Another friction arises from professional jealousies. Unhealthy rivalries and competition for position and recognition can keep the team from growing. Each profession perceives itself more positively than it perceives others. Role stereotypes of each profession may be quite distorted. Fueling these jealousies may be lingering anxieties and pressures from parts of the organization that may not yet have transformed. Managers need to help teams to recognize, talk about, and resolve these jealousies. A good course of action is to define in advance how the team (with the manager's facilitation in the short term) should work out its own frictions. Having said this, managers will need to be on the alert constantly in the first year or so of multidisciplinary teams.

Organizational Tribes

The third major challenge in managing multidisciplinary teams is helping different organizational tribes to work together. Neuhauser (1988) has written extensively about the presence and influences of tribes in health care organizations. All health care organizations are collections of often warring tribes. Want proof? Just walk through the cafeteria at lunch time and watch who sits with whom. The pharmacy tribe will be at a table across the room from the obstetrics nurses tribe, which is sitting a few feet away from the management tribe. Tribes reflect the functional silos prevalent within health care organizations. They aren't good or bad. They just "are"—and they are a force to be reckoned with when it comes to the transformation to multidisciplinary teams.

Why is an understanding of tribes important for managers of multidisciplinary teams? Neuhauser (1988) sums up the reason as "The 15-Second Phenomenon," paraphrased as: Within the first 15 seconds, when speaking to a member of another tribe, a person will say something to insult or step on the toes of the other subculture! Such a phenomenon obviously makes working in teams difficult if not impossible. Therefore, helping tribes to coexist peacefully is an important part of the manager's role.

Case Study: "The Mad Med Tech"

A multidisciplinary patient care team was established as a pilot in one health care organization's trauma center. The team included an RN and a medical technologist member. At first, everything was working despite the predictable bugs ironed out by the team during its first few months.

Jane, the medical technologist chosen for the team had personally overseen the creation and documentation of the related policies and procedures. She also helped develop and deliver the associated education to her teammates. Despite these efforts, the other members of her team repeatedly left problematic specimens—improperly labeled, collected in the wrong tube, and so on—for her to process in the satellite lab within the trauma area.

These errors cut away at her productivity. Occasionally she was too busy with other responsibilities to track down the responsible team member to explain the problem and initiate a solution. Consequently, the problematic specimen waited in the "to be processed" basket.

In the medical technologist's mind, the RN member of her team, John, was the worst of the lot. He seemed to cause the most problems for her. When she confronted him with proper procedure, he would become impatient and defend himself with a litany of reasons why he was too busy to "dot your I's and cross your Ts."

The rift between these teammates widened to the point where it jeopardized the success of the pilot and other multidisciplinary teams at this organization. The RN complained that the medical technologist was more concerned with her rule book than with patients. In response, the medical technologist accused him of hurting patient care by contributing to questionable and delayed test results. Despite remedial education on conflict resolution and acceptable team behaviors, the team continued to fall apart.

As in any real-life situation, there are many forces at play in this case study. Perhaps the performance measures needed to be rewritten. Maybe Jane and John needed remedial conflict resolution education. Still, one of the forces at work—the one most likely exacerbating the others—is the inability of Jane and John to put themselves in the other's shoes. They do not value one another's contributions. They cannot communicate because they are coming from such different places (i.e., the 15-second phenomenon at work). The bottom line is that they cannot establish the cross-tribal understanding and relationship needed to work collaboratively together toward common goals.

What distinguishes a tribe? Five characteristics separate one tribe from another: (1) values, (2) rules of the game, (3) language, (4) training/background, and (5) thinking patterns. One example of values is a tribe-specific definition of quality and what's important. In the above case study, Jane places great value on precision and control while John values doing whatever it takes to serve the patient. Neither is right or wrong, just different. Rules of the game summarize the behaviors and tactics that are typical of the tribe. Jane's rule is to play it by the book while John is willing to ad lib as needed. Each tribe has its own language, which includes acronyms, words, and phrases that are unique and not easily understood by outsiders. One can picture Jane barraging John with a flurry of technical jargon related to quality control and specimen processing, much to John's frustration. This language also contains fighting words that trigger defensiveness in the tribe (e.g., "pill pushers" for the pharmacy tribe or "bean counters" for the accounting tribe). Members of a tribe go through a particular formal education as well as informal rites of passage into the tribe. Finally, thinking patterns are the ways that the tribe solves problems and builds allies. Jane appears to be a person who thinks in facts and details while John's pattern leans toward feelings and intuition.

Members of multidisciplinary teams may represent numerous distinct tribes. The manager's role here is two-fold. First, managers must themselves get in tune with the different characteristics and needs of their teams' tribes. A helpful hint in doing so is actually to work with the various professionals to articulate the values, rules, etc. of their particular tribe in tribal profiles. With these insights in hand, the manager can adjust his or her leadership style to meet the needs of each team member. For example, the manager in the case study could draw on data and hard anecdotes to convince Jane why current behaviors and performance are unacceptable while relying more on interpersonal issues and soft anecdotes with John. The manager's message is the same but its delivery differs to offer individuals information in a manner that is easy for them to hear and internalize.

The second role of the manager is to help teammates get in tune with their specific tribal differences. Teammates can use the tribal profiles as starting points for open dialogue—role playing each others' characteristics (maybe having fun in the process) until each person can state the other's perspective more persuasively than he or she can. Managers should initiate informal forums where people can discuss their tribal stories and share their perspectives regarding a common challenge or problem facing the team. Managers simply should use day-to-day conversations and problem solving to foster trust between teammates from different tribes.

Summary

Managing multidisciplinary teams caps off the pyramid (Figure 10–1). Maximizing the long-term performance of these teams requires the manager to meet three major challenges. First, managers must gain credibility, respect, and trust from staff accustomed to working only for people from the same background. Second, they must smooth out intrateam frictions created by role ambiguity, power imbalances, and professional jealousies. Third, they must help team members from different tribes to work well together. Meeting these important challenges through consistent actions and active facilitation is the "what to do." "What not to do" is to ignore or, worse yet, denounce tribes and their powerful impact on the success or failure of multidisciplinary teams.

CONCLUSION

Multidisciplinary teams hold the greatest potential in a clinical setting as long as the right balance is struck between the individual expertise and shared responsibilities of team members. Establishing teams that cross traditional turfs is also one of the most demanding changes that an organization can undertake. Successful programs require a well-orchestrated set of initiatives that directly addresses the unique issues, pitfalls, and challenges of multidisciplinary teams. These initiatives are above and beyond the myriad activities needed to establish teams in general. Taken together, they form the foundation, guardrails, and finishing touch needed to unlock the full power of the professions and guide a health care organization through the rigors and toward the rewards of multidisciplinary teams.

CHAPTER 11

Education for Teams: An Essential Enabler

Moving to a team-based structure in any organization involves both structural and cultural changes. As described in Chapter 2, rigorous team design is essential for effective primary work teams. Even the best team design, however, based on accurate data and creative approaches will not evolve into a successful team without careful attention to the cultural changes required. The following scenario, unfortunately, is typical of those who believe they are on the journey to becoming a team-based organization:

Organizational executive leadership decided to embark upon a complete restructuring and work redesign project to meet the challenges of the future. The services of an experienced consulting firm were engaged to support internal staff assigned to the project. Both internal staff and the consultants diligently analyzed the work of the staff and created a new organizational design to enhance already good performance. Months of effort culminated in care team designs that broke the prevailing paradigms and created a unique new approach to organizational structure. Everyone was excited and optimistic about the likely benefits.

Once the teams were designed employees were hired and assigned responsibility. Education was limited to the new technical and clinical skills needed in a multidisciplinary cross-functional team. All involved thought the teams were well prepared and the message was: "Go forth and produce!" In fact, teams began accepting higher levels of responsibility for their services and patient care improved.

After a couple of years, however, performance had peaked and began to decline. The majority of teams were nowhere near self-managing nor self-directing, still requiring significant direction from leaders outside of the teams. Those thrilled with the initial improvements in performance felt disappointed and concerned about the lack of growth and evolution in the teams themselves. The promise of teams was seen as unfulfilled and people were frustrated and disillusioned.

What went wrong? As pointed out in Chapter 2, the culprit was not what *was* done, but *what wasn't* done. Little attention was paid to the cultural side of building teams. Team design was not at fault. No one had paid attention to the behavioral changes and new interpersonal and team skills that the teams needed in order to function effectively and grow. As Zemke (1993, 61) points out: "And don't expect something for nothing. To be effective, teams need training, and plenty of it."

More so than for any other kind of organizational change, education and training are the foundation for the cultural transformation process. Not only are new skills and behaviors needed, but attitudes and even values must be changed. Hersey and Blanchard (1993) use a model to illustrate the process of organizational change (Figure 11–1). Knowledge is the first level of change, requires the least amount of time, and is easiest to accomplish. Attitudinal changes are the next level and are increasingly more difficult to accomplish. Actual changes in individual behavior take even longer and changing the behavior of an entire organization (cultural change) is the most difficult, requiring the most time and effort to accomplish.

Let's watch a change as it moves through this model. For instance, a series of multiskill training sessions may teach me new patient care skills. Because I can see the value of these skills in my daily work, my initially skeptical attitude soon shifts. As a result of this shift I change my behavior, becoming more flexible and valuable to my work group. This change and those being made by my colleagues are noticed by others and eventually organizational behavior is changed through greater use of cross training.

This process can start from the other end just as well. The organization makes a change through restructuring or redesign of work such as patient-focused care. New expectations for employees are established, requiring individuals to change their behaviors toward more patient-centered and collaborative activities if they wish to remain employed. Eventually, they see the benefits of these new behaviors, and start believing in them, effecting changes in attitude. These attitudinal changes create a readiness for and interest in additional learning.

Change often begins with an attitude modification rather than a behavior change. The driven executive whose father dies unexpectedly of a massive heart attack at a young age may suddenly recognize his own mortality and

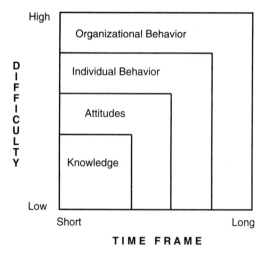

Figure 11–1 Types of Change and Expected Time Frames. *Source:* Dr. Paul Hersey, Center for Leadership Studies, Inc., Escondido, California.

develop a deeper regard for the values of longevity and personal health. This precipitates individual learning about his own risk factors and life-style choices and this knowledge, combined with the new attitude, leads to a healthy change in the individual's behavior.

Regardless of whether you begin with new knowledge or end with it, learning must happen for any cultural change to occur. According to Schrubb (1992, 48), "teams stand or fall on the training they receive." The skills teams need can only be learned through actual experience. This makes the task of learning more difficult because employees (unlike typical students) will need to learn while they are doing, which means increased frustration, more mistakes and often less patience with themselves. Even though some of us by now are comfortable with learning while doing, our health care organizations (both by necessity and tradition) have always demanded high levels of expertise and have been dominated by technical experts and professionals whose expertise is highly valued. So it may feel very risky for team members to be learning while doing. Planning for the educational needs of an organization implementing teams is a massive responsibility. It is easily a multiyear effort and the needs of various audiences must be considered separately. This at a time when many organizations have reduced the level of internal resources such as central education departments. Educational offerings and training sessions must be integrated with the primary change initiative (i.e., the restructuring) to reduce any confusion about the initiative and to prevent it from becoming fragmented. All major stakeholders should be included in planning for education needs. The following sections address the needs of three specific internal stakeholder groups: (1) executives, (2) managers, and (3) employees.

EXECUTIVE EDUCATION

Education of the executive staff should precede employee and managerial educational programs. Ideally, before deciding about the implementation of teams, an executive group learns as much as possible about teams and what this transformation will mean to the organization. Executives should hold frank discussions about life in a team organization while sharing and examining specific examples from organizations similar to theirs. Key issues include:

- How does managing teams differ from managing individuals?
- What does it mean to relinquish control and give meaningful responsibility to the teams?
- What responsibilities should be transferred and in which order?
- How do you make these choices?
- What are typical experiences of teams?
- How will communications be handled during a crisis or problem?
- How will responsibilities be divided among the teams and the managers who will coach teams?
- What is the new executive role in a team-based organization?

Each of these questions must be addressed with as much accuracy and insight as possible to prepare executives for the intense scrutiny they will experience as well as for the pivotal role they will play in leading cultural change in their organization. Too often, a decision to implement teams is based on a cursory understanding of the concept, the change process, and potential impacts. This places executive leaders at a significant disadvantage later when they have to catch up while the organization wallows in the midst of extensive change.

Before the curriculum for employee training and education is implemented, members of the executive staff need to attend sessions with the same content employees will be receiving. This could become problematic if executives have attended sessions on similar concepts (coaching, teamwork, communications, etc.) in the past, and believe they should be allowed to opt out. If your executive staff doesn't attend these educational sessions, they will not hear the same information employees are receiving and it will be difficult for them to refer to the content and reinforce it appropriately when opportunities arise. This lack of participation in educational sessions by the executive leadership communicates several messages to employees including:

"We already know this information." (arrogant)

"This isn't really that important." (belittling)

"It's important for you, but not for me." (patronizing)

If the absent leader then behaves in ways that contradict any of the messages delivered by the educational programming, you will have created dissonance through the mixed messages your leadership is sending. Employees always believe what you do, not what you say.

New leadership competencies must be identified and tailored learning opportunities designed and developed for executives. These necessary transformational skills typically will include:

- managing innovation and change
- transition support
- collaborative visioning
- collaborative planning
- managing process
- empowering others
- modeling and reinforcing team behaviors
- care of self
- establishing a climate of trust and commitment
- constructive confrontation
- win–win conflict resolution
- coaching, mentoring, and teaching

Often discussed, but seldom actually addressed with leadership assessment and training, these skills will be necessary for a successful cultural transformation.

Executive education is most productive if it is ongoing throughout the entire implementation process in tandem with other project education efforts. Learning, like inventory, is most cost-effective and useful when it occurs "just-in-time," in quantities appropriate to assimilation during one session and in learning sequences that become progressively more complex and involved. A regular schedule of executive sessions can combine new content and experiences for skill development together with "lessons learned" as the implementation process proceeds, delivering both in a timely manner.

Facilitators can share lessons learned with the executive group, discuss interventions, report on the larger organization's progress in implementation, and share their observations. This gives the executive team regular opportunities to review progress, reinforce positive movement, and make course corrections as necessary. Strategies developed during these sessions offer this team precious time to coordinate its actions and approaches producing a more coherent executive message to the organization.

Although internal staff often have the talent and skills required for the facilitation of such executive learning sessions, consider using external consultants for this process. It is easier, less politically risky, and usually perceived to be more objective to have external consultants deliver the sometimes painful and difficult messages that need to be shared with this group. For optimum effectiveness, a consistent cadre of external consultants can establish a long-term relationship with the executive team built on mutual trust, honesty, and commitment. Consultants moving through the organization on an intermittent, infrequent basis, and who are only minimally involved in the implementation effort will have significantly lower credibility and far less to offer the executive leadership team.

MANAGERIAL EDUCATION

Successful implementation of teams is impossible without the active commitment and involvement of managerial staff in the organization. Your managers are at a significant disadvantage if they are not prepared in advance for the implementation of teams. Particularly in health care where work is already divided into a multitude of clinical and technical fiefdoms, management and supervisory staff can easily sabotage an effort of this magnitude. This sandbagging may occasionally happen purposefully, but more often it results when managers simply don't fully understand the organization's new philosophy or the key concepts regarding teams.

Educational support for managers and supervisors addresses at least the following three areas:

1. *Specific techniques and skills for empowering employees*
   The relationship of ability, responsibility, authority, and accountability must be clearly understood. Managers need to be skilled in techniques for assessing the employee's ability to carry out a particular responsibility. Allocating clear responsibility by defining roles and expectations is critical. Managers must understand the different levels of authority and key factors to consider when assigning authority for a specific responsibility. Establishing outcome measures and systems

for follow-up and feedback are essential for establishing accountability. Managers also must learn how to relinquish control and increase employee involvement in substantive decision making.

2. *Skills for developing teams*
   Managers must be thoroughly versed in basic content on what teams are, how to distinguish them from working groups or pseudo-teams, and how to prevent the common perils and pitfalls experienced by health care teams. An ability to plan for the sequential process of transfer of responsibility to the team is necessary. In addition, they must have a working knowledge of teams and the ability to assist teams establish and implement their key elements.

3. *Leadership skills needed in a team-based environment*
   Managers will require content and experiential learning on key leadership competencies similar to those identified for executives, such as collaborative visioning, establishing a leadership relationship, managing change and transition, project analysis and management, facilitation skills, developing people, coaching, mentoring, collaboration, teaching, and communication.

Educational sessions providing the management staff with facts, information, and skill development should precede any housewide communication about team-based structuring with nonmanagement employees. These employees preferably should hear about teams first from their direct manager or at least with this manager present. In addition to factual presentations about teams, managerial staff also need opportunities to explore the impact of teams on their management roles. How will their jobs change? What kinds of work will they be doing in the future? How can their new roles be explained to other people?

As with executive staff, mid-level leaders need an overview of what life could be like in a team-based organization. The more clearly this vision is articulated by executives and facilitators, the more likely there will be shared understanding between managers and executives. Commitment and engagement never precede, but often follow shared understanding.

Managers to Leaders

Transforming the typical health care organization from its traditional individual-oriented culture to one that is team-based creates great chaos and confusion during the early stages. In times of great change, organizations need managers with highly developed management skills, but also, as noted in Chapter 6, managers who are leaders. Substantive leadership skills such as visioning, building commitment to a shared vision, influencing others, and developing the potential skills of every employee are necessary capabilities for leaders at every level.

As with the executive staff, managers need opportunities to attend any basic educational sessions *prior* to their employee's attendance, so that they will be better positioned and equipped to prepare employees for their future experiences and to answer their questions and concerns. If they understand the course concepts they are more likely to reinforce employees' use of this content. A logical way to accomplish this is to have the executives and managers attend team training sessions as members of their actual leadership teams (usually consisting of an executive leader and those managers who directly report to her or him). This approach assists each leadership group to become a team and thus better model the behaviors they are seeking from their employees. It also prepares the executive and managerial leaders for their coaching roles as their individual teams begin to attend the training sessions. They can anticipate tough issues and prepare to ask intelligent, insightful questions about the work their team will be doing during and after the session.

Throughout the implementation process, managers will need to be updated on progress within the organization and have periodic opportunities to discuss lessons learned. It is nearly impossible to completely prepare people in a classroom setting for needed cultural changes. Perhaps only 10 percent of the preparation occurs here. Participants can be introduced to concepts and information, but real knowledge comes when they actually begin to apply the information in their work settings. Learning is not over when participants leave the classroom; it has only just begun. Discussing what works and where they're having problems provides managers with opportunities for redirection and further learning. It also promotes ownership by the team and by the manager. Managers who feel ownership for the implementation of teams in their department always do a better job of accomplishing this transformation.

Access to one-on-one consultation is an important resource for managers. Traditionally, consultative support has been available almost exclusively for the executive level in the organization. During the implementation of teams, however, managers and supervisors need to discuss the progress of their teams with an outside, objective third party. These consultative roles can be filled by either external or internal people provided they are unbiased and confidential facilitators.

DESIGNING A TEAM-BASED CURRICULUM FOR EMPLOYEES

The issues involved in curriculum development depend in large part on the scope of the team implementation project. If only a few pilot teams are being initiated, much of the training can be provided by an external trainer and supplemented with available internal programs. On the other hand, if the organization plans to implement multiple teams and over a period of time convert the organization's structures exclusively to teams, then the planning process for establishing and delivering a training curriculum becomes more complex. For purposes of discussion, the broader scope is examined here, knowing that any program would need to be modified to meet the unique needs of each organization.

Key questions to ask when developing an employee training curriculum are:

- What needs to be included?
- How will it be taught?
- Who will teach it?
- When will it be provided?

We will next discuss each of these questions in detail and share some of the lessons learned from providing such team-based training sessions in health care organizations.

What Needs To Be Included?

The first step in this analysis of needs is to determine your desired outcomes:

- What levels of employee involvement are you seeking?
- What responsibilities will your teams assume?
- What clinical/technical skills need to be included?
- Based on their strengths and weaknesses, what learning opportunities will employees need?

There are many ways to determine the training content areas. You can review the literature or talk to other organizations that have undertaken similar initiatives. You can engage consultants with expertise in this area and pick their brains or hire them to develop the curriculum with your active involvement. Regardless which approach you take we suggest you begin by developing your own list of needs first.

Understanding the basic developmental process we all experience in our journey to self-direction is a useful foundation for determining specific curricular needs of employees. In this process of development we move through stages of dependence to independence and finally to interdependence (Covey 1989). Knowledge of this process was used by a curriculum design team at Lakeland Regional Medical Center in Lakeland, Florida (Figure 11–2).

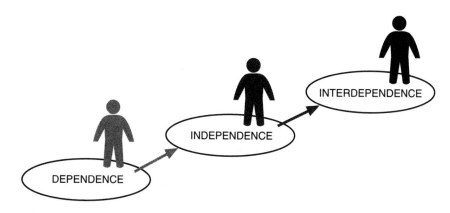

Figure 11–2 The Development Continuum

Common behaviors observed when employees are at a dependent level include: waiting to be told what needs to be done, taking problems to the manager for resolution, expecting others to solve problems or resolve conflicts for them, and so on. As we move into teams we observe that many traditional hierarchical practices have encouraged and rewarded such dependencies in staff.

Employees at the independent level evidence different behaviors including: taking action without being told what to do, communicating directly and openly with each other to improve relationships, accepting responsibility when things go wrong, and finding ways to improve their work continuously. We must recognize that individual employees will be at different levels for various responsibilities or tasks. The same employee may be at a dependent level in solving issues related to physician relationships but at an independent level in dealing with co-worker relationship problems.

Visually, the distance between dependence and independence is small, in reality the two are worlds apart. This first leap upward is what organizations attempting to empower employees must address. An initial goal of the education process and training curriculum is to move all employees to higher levels of independence and responsibility acceptance before implementing a team structure. These independent employees will be self-empowering and thus more likely ready for the interdependence required in a successful team-based structure. This evolution, however, requires a major cultural transformation in most health care organizations. The traditional hierarchical command and control structure has always encouraged managers and supervisors to make decisions about and for their work groups. Even the participative manager still makes final decisions about how things get done. In a team-based organization, teams don't run the organization. Managers and executives still make decisions about what needs to be done, based on the long-term goals and strategies of the organization. But teams now make the decisions about how the work will be done. This doesn't mean the manager simply grants the team permission to make these decisions, it means these decisions become the team's to make.

Once the employee is self-empowered and has reached a level of independence for most work responsibilities, it then becomes possible for this employee to work effectively in an interdependent, or team environment. In the audiotape based on his book, *The Seven Habits of Highly Effective People*, Stephen Covey (1989) says that "Interdependence is a choice only independent people can make." Dependent employees find it very difficult to function within a team. They continue to defer to the external or internal team leader for solving problems and making decisions, thus working against their own team's best interests.

Initially, you must define what behaviors are evidenced in your organization at each of these developmental stages. Next, determine what learning or training opportunities employees need to move from their current stage to the next stage. For example, employees at a dependent level in communication skills and interpersonal relationships may involve the manager or a fellow staff member to help solve their interpersonal problems. By comparison employees at the independent stage tend to be assertive and engage in direct open communication with each other. To progress to a higher level of development, dependent stage employees may need training on assertiveness, listening, and other communication skills. Going through this process will give you a list of content areas to include in your curriculum.

The same model of dependence—independence—interdependence can be used to determine the educational and training needs of managers. At each step, identify the common appropriate leadership behaviors required by managers in the next developmental stage. Once these leadership behaviors are identified and agreed upon, establish learning opportunities so managers can gain the necessary knowledge and skills. At this point it may prove helpful to separate the concepts and skills that form core or basic content from the learning that will need to be accomplished as a team. These can be referred to as core content and team content. Some team members also may require clinical or technical skills training.

Core Content

Core content can best be described as general topic areas appropriate for all employees that lead to increased independence and empowerment and build a strong, solid foundation for later teamwork. Not all employees in the organization are on teams and some may never become team members, yet all will benefit from these basic skills and experience a greater sense of empowerment and a fundamental understanding of the team concept. These skills and knowledge are essential for healthy employee relationships as well as for effective teamwork.

Examples of core content include:

- basic concepts and definitions of teams
- empowerment
- coping with change
- interpersonal skills, such as establishing trust
- converting victim behavior to responsibility acceptance
- listening and assertive communication skills
- conflict resolution
- negotiation skills

Team Content

Team content includes those areas of skill development and training necessary for team members to develop into a team. Topics included in team learning sessions are those areas identified as necessary to move teams and their members from independence to interdependence. Categories of skills include:

- technical team skills (i.e., writing goals and objectives, planning, and holding effective team meetings),
- problem-solving skills
- team interpersonal skills
- management skills

A more complete list is included in Exhibit 11–1. While core content can be provided readily by trainers with excellent presentation skills and in-depth knowledge of the content, team sessions require trainers with excellent group facilitation skills. The process for learning team content must include a heavy emphasis on application. This is best accomplished by having teams actually work on real projects during the training sessions (i.e., defining their purpose, writing their initial objectives, articulating and sharing their expectations, etc.).

Clinical/Technical Content

Clinical or technical educational needs will be driven by the team design work as described in Chapter 2. Team designs based on service redeploy-

Exhibit 11–1 Team Content

- Background information on teams
- Mission
- Team values
- Vision
- Team goals and objectives
- Team roles and responsibilities
- Articulating expectations
- Meeting skills
- Planning skills
- Team communication styles

- Team decision making and problem solving
- Customer service
- Coaching
- Conflict resolution
- Time management
- Teaching skills
- Specific managerial skills such as performance appraisal, budgeting, monitoring finances, etc.

ment and multidisciplinary teams will result in the need for specific training. When caregiver roles are redesigned to include a broader range of skills, RNs and LPNs may learn additional clinical and technical skills such as basic respiratory treatments, phlebotomy, EKGs, etc.

How Will It Be Taught?

There are several options for delivering the information and providing learning opportunities but each must be considered carefully for appropriateness to the audience and efficacy in delivering required behavioral outcomes. The sheer size of the educational effort is daunting and organizations must consider alternative approaches to the old didactic classroom style of presentation.

Although it is possible to develop or acquire self-learning modules that participants could complete on their own, much of team learning requires interactive skills that are difficult for an individual to learn in isolation from the team.

One effective way of teaching team content is for team members to attend sessions and complete these learning modules together. They then develop their skills and the attendant relationships as an actual team. This learning strategy becomes a significant time investment for any organization, but teams simply will not become real teams unless they do this work of becoming a team. Like individuals, the team also must make the transition from dependence to independence to interdependence—all very significant leaps. An individual team member may be an excellent problem solver or decision maker, but this doesn't mean the team is good at making decisions or solving problems. The *team* must develop these skills. A fast and safe way is through application of information learned in training sessions or modules. Such applications can begin during a training session where well-prepared facilitators can help ensure the first experience is successful.

It is a contradiction in terms for a team to develop its team skills while members are separated as individuals. The very nature of team learning requires interaction, so interactive sessions where participants work together in application activities will provide the powerful learning experiences that teams need.

Clinical/technical skills lend themselves to a variety of methods for delivery. Any material that is routinized or standard is ideal for a technological approach such as interactive video, CD-ROM, or computer-assisted instruction. These approaches usually build in pre- and posttesting as well as attendance recording. Relying on computerized approaches for these skills saves your skilled presenters and facilitators for higher-level presentations.

Another approach to consider for teaching clinical/technical skills is called "layered learning" (Leander, *Layered Learning*, 1994). This is an alternative to the traditional soup to nuts program where participants are sequestered in classrooms and have everything they ever needed to know taught to them in a short period of time. Layered learning instead is a gradual layering on of these skills. There are three steps to this process including:

1. Which topics or skills should be delivered in the next layer? Consider the most important skills or the ones that produce the biggest performance benefit.
2. Can any topics or skills be delivered by using an interim design? For instance, staff members already competent in a certain skill (i.e., respiratory therapy) can be redeployed to the department with the intention that they perform the procedures or skills but, in time, will be responsible for teaching these skills to other staff members. Eventually, these redeployed positions will no longer be needed.
3. How can you ensure a solid foundation for layered learning? Probably the most crucial element is to have a clear vision of the ideal team with its redesigned roles and work. You then can define the best approach to layering over time.

Length of Sessions

The next decision for learning to be done by groups of employees involves length of the sessions. Are shorter sessions—three- to four-hour programs—more appropriate and easier to schedule than day-long sessions? A caveat here: Health care organizations that use the traditional, one- or two-hour in-service format will find the amount of content they are able to cover almost too superficial to be useful. More damaging, once a topic has been touched, however briefly, participants will think they have already had it before and may be less receptive to any further sessions expanding on the same content. If an organization intends to implement simultaneously multiple teams or any similarly massive training effort, scheduling employees for day-long sessions will actually be easier and more effective than using half-day or shorter programs. In addition, employees realize, "They are serious about this, they are willing to commit an entire day for us to learn these skills."

Modular sessions are one of the most versatile approaches. Developing content in short three and a half- to four-hour stand-alone modular sessions is very practical. This structure enables you to provide shorter sessions for the team that needs to attend on evenings or weekends and also makes on-call sessions available for teams already in process that may not need the entire curriculum in its original sequence. Short modules may also be combined into full-day sessions whenever feasible.

Location of Sessions

Providing sessions off-site is particularly helpful for health care audiences—it reduces the tendency for employees to be called out of sessions or to stop by their departments during breaks and meal periods. Off-site sessions, although seemingly more expensive, convey the importance of the training that participants quickly recognize. Employees in departments such as linen services, maintenance, or environmental services often never have the opportunity to attend such programs and will appreciate them as an investment in themselves as newly important contributors to the organization. A serendipitous result is that as these employees feel valued and important to this effort their commitment and willingness to extend themselves deepens.

Scheduling of Sessions

The scope of your implementation efforts will influence how sessions are scheduled. If your organization is implementing teams on a full-scale basis, consider assigning all scheduling responsibilities to one central individual. In addition to scheduling responsibilities, this individual can coordinate, assist, and even monitor trainer and facilitator effectiveness. If implementation is sequential and slow, individual managers or department-based educators may be able to assume scheduling responsibility.

Diversity of work areas, jobs, and levels among the teams and employees attending training sessions creates both wonderful opportunities and potential disadvantages. Few organizations implementing teams on a widespread basis will be able to offer training sessions for single teams. Employees from many departments typically will attend core sessions together and in any team session several teams will be in attendance. Benefits of having individuals from multiple, diverse departments and teams attend together include:

- important insights are gained about and new connections with previously unknown areas in the organization
- a significant increase in the breadth of ideas and issues that are discussed
- an increased ability for teams to learn from each other
- awareness of issues affecting other areas
- appreciation of commonality of problems and purpose
- an organized forum for networking that pays dividends for any organization building a new team-based culture

Such diversity can be troublesome, however, if the old organizational culture still promotes we–they attitudes that divide individual departments, professional staff from nonprofessional staff, or managers from employees. Even in healthy cultures, combining groups of highly degreed employees, such as educators or certified nurse anesthetists, with less formally educated employees from food or linen services can result in feelings of inferiority and/or superiority. It can be difficult to find applications of issues and examples that are relevant to teams at different educational levels. The skill level of the trainer or facilitator will need to be higher in all such cases. On the other hand, insights into the similar nature of problems faced by all teams and the basic commonalty of all teams is a great benefit of combining diverse groups. On balance, we have found the benefits of diversity outweigh the occasional disadvantages.

For example, one organization scheduled a variety of teams from different departments to attend sessions together. In an early Team Day, a team of nurses were displeased at being placed in sessions with a team from linen services. In later sessions, however, this team of professionals was chagrined to discover that the team from linen services had far surpassed it in growth and performance as a team. In the same organization, a leadership group was experiencing significant difficulty in forming as a team. At one session, members of an environmental service team helped the leadership group to clarify its present issues and refocus on its team purpose and goals. This type of interaction between teams produces phenomenal organizational learning and can build intraorganizational respect and understanding. Teams experience similar issues and challenges regardless of their composition or the educational levels of team members. When they learn this from each other it creates a powerful sense of camaraderie and solidarity in the organization.

Developing the Content

Learning segments or modules based on principles of adult education will be the most effective means for delivering the concepts of self-directed work teams. Even though each module should be self-contained so it can stand alone as a single session, they should be offered sequentially with the concepts presented in a manner that builds on previous content. Early work prepares learners for later content, building the foundation necessary for this later work to be accomplished. For example, a team must understand the concept of team purpose or mission and have it clearly identified before writing its goals and objectives or doing any substantive team planning. Teams that attempt to write goals first, find it is difficult or end up with goals that don't relate to the real purpose of the team

Another example relates to the participants' understanding of the concept of individual empowerment (i.e., acceptance of responsibility, developing the capability for this responsibility, obtaining the appropriate level of authority, and accountability), and how this needs to be in place before the transfer of additional responsibility to the team.

Interactive sessions with exercises based on real team work (i.e., mission development, analysis and discussions of team values, role definition) provide opportunities for participants to begin applying team concepts in their workplace and promote deeper learning. Assignments between sessions bring the team together regularly to do more of the work of becoming a team. For many participants, this experiential approach to learning is very different from previous classroom learning and can jump-start them in becoming more self-directed learners. They leave the session with tangible and immediately applicable results.

Access to Consultation

We have already said that for learning to be most effective, it should fit the team's actual work situation as closely as possible. Teams then learn while doing something that feels or is real. Since they are working with actual issues, access to consultative time is needed when teams or their leaders hit particularly difficult problems. The traditional access to external or internal consultants at only the executive or upper-managerial levels does not penetrate and support the organization deeply enough. At least during the first year or two, developing teams need access to resources that will further their growth.

Once your basic educational curriculum is established, consider ways to modify it for special situations. For instance, when trained teams lose and replace a team member, a centralized, compressed session capable of providing new employees with enough information and knowledge could be offered during their orientation period. Team members can orient new members to the specifics of the team, but it could be very difficult to reteach all of the content covered during the initial educational sessions. Only high-impact, selected material needs to be included in this overview day.

Who Will Teach the Curriculum?

During planning, you will need to consider whether to use internal trainers, external trainers, or some combination of both. The rest of this section will discuss the pros and cons of internal versus external training resources. Once this decision is made, trainer selection will be the next step, followed by their preparation to deliver the actual training.

Internal versus External Trainers

Each option has its advantages and disadvantages. The benefits of using internal trainers are numerous. For example, internal trainers recruited from the employee ranks can supplement your internal education or training department and can add significant value to your internal resources. Employees with excellent presentation skills may be used to deliver numerous programs over many years. Investing in developing your own talent simply makes sense since it is less expensive than hiring outside help and creates wonderful new opportunities for internal staff. This is especially important at a time when the number of managerial promotions is diminishing.

Employees can readily identify with a co-worker who is the trainer or facilitator for their session. An employee trainer from a department undergoing significant work redesign can share with fellow employees real-life examples and anecdotes (a caveat should be raised here to be mindful about sensitive issues and confidentiality). Knowing that your facilitator has dealt effectively with many of the same issues you now face can create strong connections with learners, as can their shared knowledge of the organization. You won't need to orient these trainers to the culture of the organization; they already know it.

The use of internal trainers also has several disadvantages. One of these is the quality of training materials required. Training materials in the form of scripts, audiovisual materials, and student handouts must be thoroughly and meticulously developed to be used effectively by most internal trainers. As a rule, the more novice the trainer, the more highly and thoroughly developed the training material needed. Designing, developing, and producing your own training materials is very labor intensive. If you already have people with the content knowledge, plan on spending another 10 to 12 hours *per contact hour* of content to develop these sessions and needed materials. If your developers also need to research or learn content, more hours will be needed. Although it is possible to purchase prepackaged curricula for developing self-directed work teams, be very selective. There are several to choose from but most were initially developed for non-health care segments of business and industry and may be difficult for novice trainers to make appropriate for a health care audience.

Skill levels of internal trainers often vary widely. Even after attending the same Prepare the Presenter sessions there will remain significant variances in skill level. One way to deal with this might be to have your trainers at least initially work together in teams, thus leveling out their skill differences. Recognize also that internal trainers may bring previous baggage to a session—a reputation for certain behavior, whether earned or unearned. Some internal staff who are otherwise excellent presenters may have had previous relationship problems within the organization. Expect that in many instances, teams will call the education scheduler specifically to request their favorite trainer. Finally, recognize that by training and further equipping your internal presenters you will inevitably help them become more marketable outside your organization. Turnover should come as no surprise.

Competent external trainers can easily supplement your internal resources. During times of great change in the organization, employees have their hands full just accomplishing day-to-day responsibilities without the addition of significant new ones. Reengineering, restructuring, work redesign or the implementation of team-based structures require massive training efforts and in most health care organizations there just are not enough internal education staff to cover all these needs. It does not make sense to hire additional staff for a relatively short-term project. Thus careful use of external trainers can supplement talent already available and offer critical assistance that allows internal educators to remain focused on the projects only they can do (for example, the development and presentation of multiskill training sessions).

External trainers also can bring a consistency of skill to the project. Successful trainers who perform this work for their livelihood are usually very good, but can be replaced easily if they don't meet your standards or expectations. Trainers who work with a variety of organizations bring a breadth of experience and multiple, concrete examples to expand the potential learning in the training programs. They bring objectivity and a wider array of tools to bear on situations. They also provide opportunities for networking outside the organization. Last, the use of external trainers lets employees know that this project is key enough to merit paying for outside expertise.

The biggest disadvantage of using external trainers may be the expense involved. Trainers and consultants with the best experience and highest skills are in great demand and usually come with a high price tag. It may be worth the expense, however, to at least have them provide the initial training for executive and managerial staff and for your internal trainers. This increases the credibility and strength of the program and gives these external consultants an opportunity to know your organization and its leaders better. This better positions them to be of greater assistance to you. Your internal trainers also will learn a great deal from those with higher levels of expertise and experience in building teams. One way to reduce the expense of external trainers on a long-term basis is to look within your community for trainers who freelance or ex-employees who might be interested in contract work. These individuals often are less expensive than national consultants and would not incur significant travel costs.

Availability can often be a potential disadvantage of using external people. Experienced talent may be available immediately, but normally those with the precise experience you need may be booked weeks or even months in advance. Although repeated use of the same external trainers commits them to your organization, you must recognize that the independent contractor or trainer will be in a different organization next week, next month, and next year, and unless you have engaged them for the long haul, their dedication is likely something less than the commitment and ownership your own employees will feel.

A closely related drawback is that external trainers lack knowledge of your organization. You will spend much time upfront ensuring they understand your organization well enough to do a good job in applying the training concepts. An extensive orientation period is probably not required for those who have worked in health care for some time, but the more they know about your structure, mission, vision, and goals, the more likely they can reinforce these elements in the training.

For organizations facing significant cultural change and undertaking the required training efforts, we recommend a combination of these two approaches—use both external and internal trainers. In our experience, organizations that successfully implement teams most often use *both* internal and external presenters. Develop your internal trainers to gain the advantages we have already identified and to counterbalance some of the disadvantages of using only external trainers. You may even want to contract with a combination of external trainers, maintaining only a few consistent consultants to help you oversee and monitor this project and work with your executive, leadership, and internal design team and your core of internal trainers. Contracted, per-diem trainers from the community can also be cost-effective for providing some segments of the training.

Developing Internal Trainers

Selecting the best candidates is the most important step. Determine: (1) whose responsibility it will be to make the final choices, (2) who will coordinate the training and activities of these people, and (3) to whom they will be responsible.

In most health care organizations, the education department may be the logical choice for these tasks, unless the system is large enough to have its own organizational development department. A selection process can then be established based on the specific needs of the organization.

The Selection Process

Using volunteer trainers will be more successful than simply assigning people, because volunteers will be more motivated to do the job. In some organizations, however, the manager or department head may be expected to become a trainer for teams. In a team-based, continuously learning organization, an appropriate new role for leaders is that of educator and trainer and these roles certainly provide key skills for successfully coaching and developing people. Not all managers, however, have the innate ability to become good teachers. If the organization identifies teaching skills as a requirement for continuing in the management role, this criterion can serve as a screen for management retention. Those who cannot develop effective teaching skills may be excluded from management. If the organization is not serious about teaching skills as a requirement, the unintended consequences could be disastrous—a core of ineffective internal trainers, leading to lost opportunity costs and continuing problems with implementation.

One organization decided to make managers responsible for teaching employees necessary team skills. This was accomplished by mandate, however, rather than by any commitment on the part of the managers. Managers saw teams as threats to their job security that potentially could expose their lack of skill. Many of the managers had little or no experience in teaching and felt vulnerable and uncomfortable practicing on the employees who reported to them. They did not feel secure trying something new for the first time in front of employees when they already felt at risk and exposed.

Another organization also decided to use managers as internal educators but went about it very differently. Managers were included in the early decision about who should provide the education and were eager to assume this responsibility, seeing it as a way to increase their value to the organization and their teams. The organization valued continuous learning for all employees and supported most change initiatives with extensive education. The managers were provided with well-developed educational materials and attended a "prepare the presenter" session to improve their presentation skills and knowledge of the material. Another asset was a group of managers with strong leadership capability and an already active teaching role with employees. This organization succeeded using this approach.

A third organization developed all of the content into learning modules that required the least "in session" time as possible for teams. Most of the learning was based on reading assignments and expectations that the learners would initiate their own questions and manage their own learning process. The sessions were carefully scripted but inadvertently required a high level of facilitation. Instead of presenting and discussing content, the sessions only allowed time to perform an activity or two and to discuss the content covered in the prereading assignment. It takes a highly skilled facilitator to respond to questions and use participants' examples to connect back to the original content and to facilitate learning in a novice group such as this. The organization that planned this approach had few trainers with this high-level facilitation skill available for carrying out this plan.

Before you ask for interested volunteers, first establish the minimum criteria people must meet in order to be considered. These criteria should include personal characteristics, demonstrable skills, experience, and interest level. Experience would encompass work assignments, previous presentation experience, and actual on-the-job demonstrations of core concepts (for example, is the individual appropriately assertive, known to be a good listener, clearly practiced at developing and empowering others?). Look for: (1) demonstrated abilities to coach others for performance improvement, (2) facilitation skills, (3) a high level of motivation, and (4) communication ability.

A semi-formal to formal application process will help eliminate employees who are not truly interested. Posting positions for internal trainers is a means of encouraging interested employees to apply or at least seek additional information. Include a brief list of criteria (with adequate definitions) and assurances that additional skill training will be provided once an employee is selected. Otherwise some very good prospects might not consider themselves viable candidates.

Develop a simple application form to expedite this process. Some organizations also ask candidates to provide written recommendations from other employees. A statement of support from the employee's manager also should be a requirement. That manager will need accurate information about time requirements involved and must be willing and able to release the employee from departmental work as necessary.

Personal interviews will increase the information available about a candidate. Particularly if there is a large number of applicants, limiting the number who may be interviewed makes this process more manageable. The interview is an opportunity to exchange information and for both parties to determine suitability for the job. The interviewer should share requirements and expectations of the trainer, including the anticipated calendar of training events, the need to teach a certain minimum number of sessions per month to maintain competency and "share the load," and the expectation that content will be presented as it was developed. Skills training and support available to trainers should also be discussed. The potential candidate will undoubtedly have many questions.

The interviewer will seek to gather information from candidates about why they are interested, what their experience has been, how they have handled training situations in the past, and their perceived strengths and areas needing further development. Some organizations further ask candidates to demonstrate their skills through a sample teaching situation or have themselves videotaped during an actual teaching situation. Consider using this approach only if you want expert-level facilitators. Many employees are capable of learning these skills but would be eliminated if asked to perform under this pressure because they are still novices.

The selection decision takes into account the degree to which any individual meets the established criteria. Organizational structure should be considered when assessing potential trainers. Candidates selected from a variety of levels, departments, and backgrounds add strength, interest, and diversity to the program. In other words, if you are choosing between two equally qualified candidates—one a nurse and one an employee from environmental services—and you already have two trainers who are nurses, select the candidate from environmental services.

The Prepare the Presenter Program

Once internal presenters are selected they will begin their own learning process. Initially this includes specific reading assignments and attendance at the actual sessions, taught by others, which they will later be asked to deliver. Ideally, new presenters attend these sessions simply to experience the program. They may attend the same session several times, bringing their faculty manuals for adding their own notes, simply to observe an experienced trainer presenting the material and to become comfortable with use of the support materials. Giving assignments and specific suggestions to new trainers attending ongoing sessions focuses them on specific issues. For example, the first assignment might be to participate fully in the session, complete homework assignments, and make note of all questions they had during the class. Becoming familiar with and then learning session content is the basic purpose of such an assignment. The second time they attend a session, they may use their faculty manual to follow the presenter through the flow of the course, taking note of how time spent on various concepts was reduced or expanded to accommodate time availability or class needs, and also capturing questions and reactions of others during the session. The third time they attend the session their assignment might be to focus on the way the trainer uses audiovisual materials and handouts and deals with questions. This may seem time consuming, but these internal trainers will have the most significant contact with your employees and will be seen as key representatives of your project.

The actual Prepare the Presenter Program focuses on at least three areas: (1) the content to be taught, (2) how to use the educational materials, and (3) development of presentation and facilitation skills. This program must be of sufficient length and depth that internal trainers can become reasonably confident in the adequacy of their skills before they present their first session.

Once your trainers have attended actual sessions, a group seminar can be scheduled for all of them to review content areas one by one with in-depth discussions of principles and questions. Taking this approach, trainers can develop meaningful examples for each concept from their own experiences that they will later share with participants in their sessions. Trainers also will need to prepare for their use of educational materials such as the faculty manual, handouts, videotapes, and overhead transparencies.

Presentation and facilitation skills must also be major areas of attention during Prepare the Presenter sessions. In organizations that divide basic core training for individuals from team training focused only on full teams, the presenters for each set of sessions may be unique to that set. When people participate as teams in all education, their presenters for all content areas may be the same. In either case, the more versatile and expert your presenters, the more effective they will be in providing training as teams and individuals require it.

Presentation skills include the how-tos for delivering a professional training session. Areas to include are:

- basics of presentation style
- provoking audience involvement and questions
- responding effectively to learners' questions
- the use of body posture, voice quality, and control
- varieties of presentation methods

Trainers need to develop their own examples and to use story-telling and analogies for making their points. Facilitation skills include:

- moving the session along efficiently
- making a point from a participant's contribution
- dealing with difficult behaviors and distractions
- creating a positive learning experience for participants

Actual practice in making self-introductions and presenting key portions of content is an essential part of any good trainer training program. Fellow trainees are a relatively safe first audience and both participants and the presenter will learn a great deal from each other's successes and errors. We recommend at least four areas be practiced:

1. their initial introduction of themselves to a group
2. one or two key elements of content
3. setting up of a key activity or exercise within the program
4. delivering content in an environment in which difficult, realistic situations are contrived

In the last area, participants can role play potential behavior, such as apathy, power plays, negativity, disruptive or angry and challenging behavior. Videotaping these live practice sessions can be a powerful tool for increasing presenter effectiveness. A presentation is given and videotaped, after which the presenter comments on his or her own performance. Next the audience shares its feedback and finally the videotape is reviewed for any further insights. The trainee is given this videotape for continued learning.

Beginning with Internal Presenters

Internal presenters often prefer to team teach their first few sessions. Team teaching is a good way to ease into the responsibilities of presenting complete sessions. This approach provides complementary skills, objective and helpful feedback from a colleague, and a sharing of the initial pressures and pleasures. Additional factors in deciding whether to use this approach are the length of the sessions, since shorter sessions may be less likely to require a team of presenters, and also the initial experience levels of your trainers. The criticality of a high-level result, for example with leadership teams, should also be weighed in this decision.

Periodic meetings of internal trainers are a valuable source of support, communication, and continued learning. Experiences can be shared and ways of handling difficult situations discussed. Trainers will be able to update each other on team progress. By sharing issues and difficulties that have arisen during sessions, your internal trainers will be less likely to be caught off guard and are more likely to have thought through effective and accurate responses. These meetings also create a camaraderie within the group and a sense of mutual support. New analogies or stories developed by a member to explain difficult points can be shared among trainers, affording at least one additional training benefit, a higher consistency from session to session.

When Will the Training Be Provided?

The most effective training and education is provided "just-in-time"—precisely at the time needed by the recipient and right before the information shared or skills being taught are to be used. Accomplishing this feat is much more difficult than it sounds. More frequently, we provide training or educational sessions either way ahead of the time they are needed or too late. Organizing these learning opportunities is especially difficult when employees are also experiencing major restructuring and/or redesigns of their work. These latter initiatives often require extensive training of technical skills, so employees become multiskilled or cross-trained. The addition of new technical skills on top of team skills can simply overwhelm employees who are also expected to keep up their day-to-day work.

Designing the sessions so content is sequential and includes increasingly complex concepts, yet is not overwhelming is one of the greatest challenges in a well-conceived training program. Some organizations have expected *all* employees to gain the knowledge and skills included in the basic core content programs and *every* team to gain the team skills identified by the organization. Another approach is to use an assessment tool completed by individual teams that gives specific feedback on their current levels of team performance and highlights areas needing further development. These assessed teams then can be individually matched with the training modules they need, bypassing others for which they already have developed skills.

LESSONS LEARNED FROM TEAM TRAINING SESSIONS

Team Education Increases Pressure on the Manager

When teams attend their training sessions, learning the concepts and skills necessary for becoming an effective team and using these in their daily work, managers/coaches in the department begin to feel added pressure. Team members now have more penetrating questions. They are seeking and requiring answers to questions such as: "What are we responsible for as a team?" and "What is our level of authority for this assignment?" Managers without a clear vision or even clue about what the teams should be doing will be in real trouble. What makes it worse is that teams that finish training sessions prior to beginning work as a team always need a lot of coaching from their managers. At this point, the managerial role rapidly needs to change from controlling and directing to coaching and leading. It becomes painfully obvious to everyone when a manager is unable to make this speedy change. Team training brightly illuminates any leadership holes in the organization and aims this spotlight on middle management.

Coaches Need To Attend Team Sessions

Teams that attend team training without a designated, well-prepared coach tend to flounder and display difficulties focusing on their purpose. Managers must prepare their team(s) for their attendance, letting them know what to expect and what is expected *from* them in terms of attendance, participation, completion of assignments and work, and outcomes. Managers also must clearly identify their own roles in this process, how they will transition to coaching and facilitating, and what this change means for them personally and professionally. The manager in her or his role as coach needs to be involved in new ways with the team and ideally attends all training sessions with them. This same manager/coach may also serve as an external team leader available to participate in discussions of the team's purpose and who facilitates the team writing its initial objectives without dominating this process.

We have noticed that managers who have difficulty making this leap into leadership tend to do one of two things. They may increase their previous controlling behaviors and overinvolve themselves in the initial work of the team. As a result, the team feels stifled and believes (justifiably) that no real responsibility or authority has been transferred. Or, on the other hand, the manager may abdicate all responsibility, saying "You're a self-directed work team now, so just go do it!" This leaves the infant team feeling abandoned and adrift, with no means of support. Neither approach works. A sports analogy may help illuminate the appropriate role of the manager during this transformation. A coach is at the game (i.e., the transformation to teams) to support, redirect, give feedback, and keep the team focused on the game plan. While the team is practicing or playing, the coach stays on the sidelines, and in fact, can get penalized or thrown off the field or the court if he sets foot in a game.

Leader Serves As Role Model

Team training brings additional pressure on the organization's leadership to demonstrate behaviors that are congruent with the concepts and approaches being taught. This may seem a simple matter, yet when employees are taught how to problem solve in an organizationally approved method, they will have less patience with a manager who does not have or use these skills. Dissonance results when employees are expected in education sessions to listen actively to each other and to coach each other, yet fail to see these skills demonstrated by their managers. Employees take their cues for acceptable behavior by observing the behaviors of their appointed organizational leaders; thus the critical necessity for managers to "walk the team talk."

Allow Time for the Process

If teams are composed of individuals who continue to hold full job responsibilities at the same time they are going through training, allow teams enough time to make sufficient progress between training sessions. When teams are first scheduled for training, a month between sessions may be a reasonable interval. If teams are unable to complete their assigned work between sessions, however, you will lose the major benefits of applied training. The richness of experiential learning *between* training sessions is more important than the learning during the sessions themselves. This between time is when the wisdom of the team really begins to develop. Appropriate development time requires a delicate balance between not pushing too fast and yet maintaining enough momentum and energy to carry people through a long growth process.

Teams that get off track during the training period, that just don't seem to develop or learn to solve their own problems are often hampered by some common barriers. These include:

- inappropriate leadership
- no clear vision of the future
- confusion about expectations
- lack of responsibility acceptance on the part of the team with a preponderance of "victim" behavior or feelings of powerlessness
- "renegade" team behavior in which the team decides (always in the absence of adequate leadership) to empower itself to settle old scores or head off in counterproductive directions

CONCLUSION

Designing your teams well is an extremely important step, however, by itself, it cannot automatically result in the myriad cultural changes needed for your organization's metamorphosis into team-based structures. For teams to reach levels of self-direction they must develop a number of new skills, gain extensive new knowledge, and ultimately learn to embrace a driving enthusiasm for continual learning. A thoroughly designed and developed program of education and training opportunities will be an essential enabler for the cultural transformation to teams in your organization.

CHAPTER 12

Guiding Principles: Lighting the Path toward Team Success

Introducing dramatic change into an organization is never easy. Tradition dies slowly. Paradigms are hard to shift. Inertia, a force grown from nostalgia for the way things used to be, refuses to loosen its grip. But change is no longer optional for health care institutions. The question is how, not if. For a growing number of institutions, teams are a key part, if not the basis, for this change. The transformation to a team-based organization can offer significant and sustainable performance improvements not achievable within an individualistic and hierarchical environment, such as enhanced quality and value, better customer service, and more rewarding roles—all at reduced cost.

Those kinds of improvement don't come free. The most obvious investments are out-of-pocket, such as the managerial and staff education described in Chapter 11, enhancements to existing systems to support teams, enabling tools and materials as well as leadership and project management resources needed to plan, guide, and monitor the change process itself. Other investments are made via transitional inefficiencies and probable dips in productivity while the organization learns the new rules of the game. Still other investments are emotional and even physical, as the transformation to teams demands a great deal of energy from everyone involved.

These investments are all very real. Each organization comes to grip with them during the course of the transformation to teams. But they are not the only hurdles to overcome. Other barriers stand in the way. Some emerge right away and others take shape only as teams start up and mature. Either way, a set of important principles can guide an organization around and through these barriers, lighting the way for teams (Figure 12–1):

1. set the stage for teams to succeed
2. establish clear and realistic expectations
3. prepare leadership for its future role
4. modify internal systems to support teams

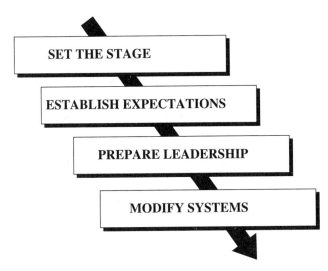

Figure 12–1 Overview of Guiding Principles

SET THE STAGE

Many teams are doomed to failure before they even start. Their inability to grow culturally into a true team (as opposed to a collection of individuals) and structurally achieve the expected performance results is rooted in a weak foundation. Setting the stage for highly effective teams is itself a challenge and the effort required to meet this challenge has been explored in various chapters throughout this book. Given their importance, however, these efforts are worth another concerted look (Exhibit 12–1). In general, setting the stage for successful teams includes the following five major steps:

1. Understand what teams are and aren't.
2. Establish teams only where needed.
3. Lower cultural hurdles to teams.
4. Create a sound team design.
5. Maintain consistent membership.

Understand Teams

The first step in setting the stage for successful teams is to establish a clear and common understanding of what teams are and aren't. Mention the word team around the organization and just about everyone will conjure up

Exhibit 12–1 Steps in Setting the Stage for Highly Effective Teams

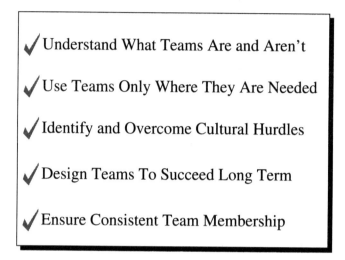

✓ Understand What Teams Are and Aren't

✓ Use Teams Only Where They Are Needed

✓ Identify and Overcome Cultural Hurdles

✓ Design Teams To Succeed Long Term

✓ Ensure Consistent Team Membership

their own interpretation. Chapter 1 differentiated between work groups and true teams and defined differences between leadership teams, ad hoc teams, and primary work teams. Why is a common understanding of team important? Because the significant benefits of true teams simply cannot materialize when true teams are not established. For example, one organization implemented what it thought were teams on several patient care units. There were high hopes regarding performance improvements in customer service, cost-effectiveness, and even quality of care. Each so-called team was a triad, formed by bringing together an existing RN, LPN, and nursing assistant. Other than new uniforms and a report on the bulletin board that listed the various members of each team, little changed in terms of the responsibilities of these individuals or of the team as a whole. Except for a temporary increase in staff satisfaction, performance on those units remained the same. In the organization's eyes, the teams were a bust. No one realized at the time that true teams were never part of the picture.

Establish Teams Where Needed

Once the concept of teams is defined and understood, the next step in setting the stage is to ensure that teams are the best organizational model for performing the work at hand. Chapters 1 and 2 discussed the methodology for determining whether teams are needed. Much work in any health care organization is better performed by individuals (e.g., microbiology) or work groups (e.g., medical record archiving and retrieval). Using teams where they are not appropriate creates a fundamental mismatch between staff resources (the supply) and customer needs (the demand). This mismatch preempts the full benefits of teams. The lesson is to avoid jumping on the team bandwagon and using teams everywhere in the organization. Use teams where they make the most sense.

For example, a team composed of a pharmacist, a medical technologist, and a social worker was formed on the redesigned medical unit at one health care institution. These professionals worked on the unit as part of the new design to improve responsiveness to customers while eliminating costly red tape and coordination activities. In no time at all, the idea of establishing a true team with these professionals faded. It turned out that their workloads were high enough to keep them fully utilized performing their primary duties (e.g., distributing medications for the pharmacist)—the mark of a good design. Despite much scrutiny, the pool of work that could be shared among these "team" members was very limited, due in part to licensure and competency constraints. Today, these professionals make up a solid work group, but not a true team.

Identify Cultural Hurdles

The third step in setting the stage for teams is to identify the cultural hurdles to the transformation. The same set of cultural hurdles to teams usually exists within most health care organizations. These hurdles include the resistance of managers to transferring authority (viewed as losing control and equating teams with decision-making chaos), lack of appreciation (or respect) between various professions, and the value employees currently place on their co-worker bonds, which may be threatened by a new organizational approach. What differs across organizations is the relative magnitude of these hurdles. Managers' fears of the loss of control and power may be the single greatest hurdle in one organization, but a less formidable issue at another.

Assessing the relative size of the cultural hurdles increases the likelihood of teams' success in three ways. First, it puts leaders on notice, if not everyone involved, that the road to teams will have its potholes. Not everyone in the organization will embrace teams. Not everyone wants to share responsibilities or be self-directed. This realization helps to predict any unrest that can prevent the transformation from getting off the ground.

Second, knowing where the problems lie allows leaders to create plans to minimize them and initiate damage control as necessary. These targeted plans help teams to succeed while allowing the organization to invest wisely in interventions and education—going for the biggest bang for the buck. In the above example, the organization that knows its managers' resistance to letting go will be a major hurdle can launch a relevant educational initiative. At the same time, managers' images of chaos can be alleviated through a program that refocuses them from making decisions to articulating the key constraints and objectives they and teams need to make sound decisions (Leander, "Boundaries and Bogies," 1994).

Third, insights into cultural hurdles are input into the organization's roll-out strategy for teams. The organization can target where teams will be implemented first and how fast the transformation will be expanded to avoid short-term resistance to teams. Meanwhile, targeted interventions can prepare those pockets of greatest resistance for subsequent implementation. Any organization establishing teams wants to show demonstrable success (creating its own team showcase) right out of the box. Lowering cultural hurdles helps this happen.

How can an organization assess cultural hurdles to teams? Most organizations find that a combination of surveys, focus or search groups, and interviews can yield the necessary insights. Although partly qualitative and subjective, these assessments usually reveal areas of greatest expected resistance. That is the goal, not to find subtle differences in receptivity in every nook and cranny of the organization.

Create Sound Team Design

The fourth step in setting the stage for highly effective teams was the topic of Chapter 2. Success depends on the balance between teams' cultural and structural sides and a sound, fact-based team design is an essential component of the latter. Based on the team's total pool of work (all responsibilities including management and teamwork), the methodology described in Chapter 2 designs teams that are structured to excel—with healthy intrateam dynamics and attractive personnel cost-effectiveness (Figure 12–2). Well-designed teams can succeed. Poorly designed teams (or teams that were not explicitly designed at all) cannot.

Maintain Consistent Membership

The fifth and final step is to create a plan for consistent team membership. The importance of stability in relationships among team members was addressed throughout this book. The ideal teams should have the exact same members working together on the same shifts day-in and day-out. In most organizations, this ideal is beyond reach. Many organizations rely heavily on part-time workers, float pool agencies, and even seasonal staff. Competition

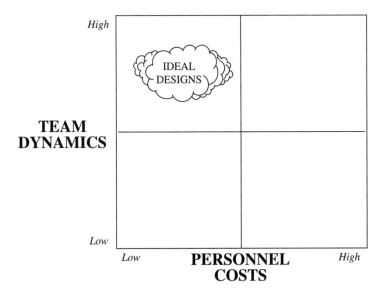

Figure 12–2 Attractiveness Matrix for Designing Highly Effective Teams. *Source:* Reprinted with permission from PFCA © 1995.

for scarce labor leads organizations to establish an almost mind numbing array of shift schedules.

These constraints at first may seem to preclude any consistency of team membership. Actually, enough consistency can be maintained despite these constraints to allow teams to gel and deliver the expected results (Figure 12–3). For example, teams with part-time members perform well as long as the same group of part-timers works on the team. One organization facing such constraints put in place a policy that prioritized assignment of float pool staff to particular teams. Based on statistical analyses, each float person was loosely assigned to a small number of teams on a preferred unit. Most of the time, those teams' resources were indeed supplemented with the same few people from the float pool. It was not perfect because a balance had to be struck between the need for team member consistency and the cost-effectiveness of the float pool. It sufficed, however, in promoting stable team relationships.

Summary

Teams can fail before they ever start. Setting the stage for successful teams begins long before the first member puts on a uniform. The organiza-

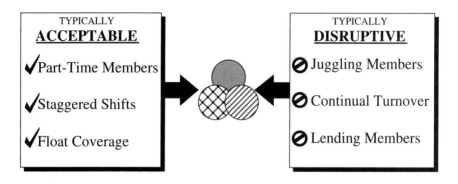

Figure 12–3 Considerations in Consistency of Team Membership

tion must share a clear and common understanding of what teams are. Teams must be used only when they are a good match for the work at hand. Identifying the cultural hurdles to teams allows the organization to focus its energies where they can do the most good. A sound design is another vital part of teams' long-term success. Maximizing consistency of membership gives teams the stability necessary to transform from a collection of individuals to a team achieving new heights of performance. Lighting the way for the transformation to teams is an investment an organization cannot afford to overlook.

ESTABLISH EXPECTATIONS

The second guiding principle lighting the way for team success is to establish expectations. The single greatest barrier to implementing and nurturing highly effective teams is the lack of clear, realistic expectations. Expectations are everything in a change effort (Exhibit 12–2). Without clear and realistic expectations, setbacks along the way—and there will be setbacks—are perceived as failures. A symptom that the process isn't working. A rallying cry for naysayers and doubters. A source of frustration and friction to the teams. With well-defined expectations, normal and predictable setbacks become learning forums, places to step back and grow together as an organization. They become an opportunity to demonstrate that bumps in the road are not a cause for blame but rather sources of further growth and development for the teams. The organization must clarify expectations in six crucial areas before the first team puts on its uniforms (Exhibit 12–2).

Exhibit 12-2 Key Expectations for Establishing Highly Effective Teams

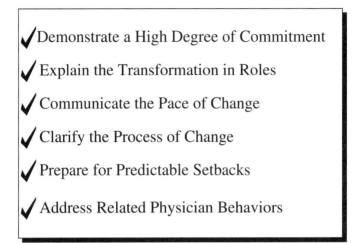

✓ Demonstrate a High Degree of Commitment

✓ Explain the Transformation in Roles

✓ Communicate the Pace of Change

✓ Clarify the Process of Change

✓ Prepare for Predictable Setbacks

✓ Address Related Physician Behaviors

Degree of Commitment

The first expectation relates to the organization's degree of commitment to teams. The reasons behind the pursuit of teams must be obvious so that everyone can share in this commitment. Some health care organizations are infamous for a "fad of the month" approach to change—a little bit of this and a little bit of that, none of which stays around very long. Such a history adversely affects the believability of any change and the credibility of leadership. If the transformation to teams is going to take root and bloom, the commitment must start at the top and be unwavering. It must not be revocable at the first signs of trouble. The organization cannot think, "This, too, shall pass."

Leaders also must continually relate the past to the present and future. They do so by answering basic questions such as "How is this transformation to teams a necessary next step in our strategic agenda? How does it support our mission and values?" Leaders should also explain how teams relate to any prior initiatives to enhance empowerment and employees' involvement in decision making such as quality improvement efforts.

Transformation in Roles

The second expectation centers on the general transformation in roles necessary to establish true teams. Implementing teams is all about changing behaviors. Employees must learn what empowerment and being self-directed mean. The transformation means broader responsibilities for people and more accountability for their own actions, relationships, and outcomes. It means a lot of hard work. Teams must understand that empowerment doesn't mean having unquestioned or limitless authority. It doesn't mean doing whatever you want. Everyone in the entire organization must be able to picture their future roles if they are to take a lead in preparing themselves for their own success.

Managers also must learn what's in store for them. Teams represent a difficult transformation for managers, who must shift from controlling from an office to coaching from the floor, from fixing problems to preventing them through others, and from making decisions to defining for others the goals and constraints needed for them to make good decisions.

Some organizations establish this expectation through collective self-assessments before any teams are organized. For example, groups of managers at one institution meet monthly to discuss problems in their areas. The goal of those discussions is not to complain but to compare and contrast how they would have handled the situation in the past (and perhaps still do) versus how they respond in a team-based organization. The benefits of these sessions are three-fold: (1) there is shared learning about differences in acceptable behaviors as teams develop, (2) they usually receive helpful advice from colleagues about fixing a particular problem, and (3) a new trust and camaraderie develops among these managers.

Pace of Change

A third expectation relates to the pace of change and here, there are usually two extremes. Some organizations want the first teams in place in four weeks. Others talk in terms of four years. Both extremes can hurt. The four-week version fails to recognize that newly formed teams (even if they could be established in their new roles in that short a time) need time to develop and mature. Performance improves significantly only when they stop working as a collection of individuals and start working as a true team that is greater than the sum of its parts.

The four-year version is just as dangerous. This long horizon undermines any message that teams are a strategic priority. It undermines leadership credibility and it extends the friction and losses of transitional inefficiencies for too long a period of time. A healthier pace is somewhere between these two extremes—one that balances the organization's threshold for change with the institution's urgency for change. People in the organization should share a realistic sense of this pace and roll-out timing of teams.

What is an appropriate pace? Each organization, of course, must set a pace that is right for itself. The best advice for any one organization is not to seek a cookie cutter answer but instead to define a method for finding its own unique answer. This method must consider three crucial forces: (1) urgency for change, (2) resistance to change, and (3) resources for change. Each force is the cumulative product of both cultural and structural considerations (Figure 12–4).

The urgency for change is the need (not necessarily the desire) to improve the status quo. Culturally, that status quo may be represented by low and/or faltering staff satisfaction (in narrowly defined jobs offering little intrinsic reward), low physician satisfaction (with sluggish decision making and lack of caregiver accountability), and low customer satisfaction (with slow service and frequent handoffs from staff to staff). Structurally, the necessary improvements may lie in the sources of those dissatisfactions as well as in overall operating expenses (such as initiatives to flatten the hierarchy of the organization).

Resistance to change is the counterbalance to urgency. Urgency pushes the change process faster while resistance pulls it back. The previously described cultural hurdles to teams are a much needed input into assessing an organization's resistance to change. Another source of resistance is the organization's own history of change. Organizations with proven internal track records of planning and implementing change positively encounter less resistance than the rest. Structurally, the greatest resistance to change

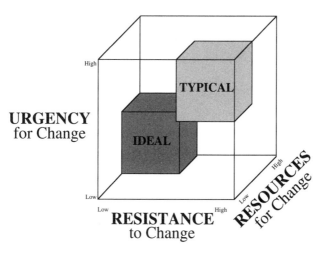

Figure 12–4 Forces Influencing an Appropriate Pace of Change

comes from the inability of existing systems to support a team-based organization. For example, educational, performance measurement, reward, and information systems all play a part in the transformation to teams (more on this later in this chapter). Organizations should gauge the resistance posed by these systems by the extent to which they present hurdles to initial implementation, not by the gap between existing and ideal systems. The ideal will take a long time to achieve. Concentrate for now on the extent to which these systems block the transformation from getting started.

Resources for change are the great equalizer in that with adequate resources you can partially overcome resistance while no resources at all make urgency a moot point. Resources are human (people in the organization skilled at change, knowledgeable of teams, and able to direct a fair amount of time to the transformation) as well as monetary (available funds for out-of-pocket investments, outside support, etc.).

The ideal state is to be in a situation with low urgency, low resistance, and high resources. But let's be honest. Organizations today typically are closer to high urgency, high resistance, and low resources—the opposite corner of the cube depicted in Figure 12–4. The pace of transformation for such organizations could see a first wave of teams up and running in six to nine months with meaningful performance benefits materializing after about a year. Organizations with high urgency, high resistance and high resources can invest those extra resources to cut the pace in half. Those organizations with low resistance can do the same (without the added investment). These timing estimates are general rules-of-thumb. Again, each organization can use the urgency/resistance/resources method to estimate for itself its own realistic pace. Locking onto someone else's timing in essence puts the fate of the transformation to teams in their hands.

Process of Change

A fourth expectation relates to the process of change. From establishing a temporary decision-making body (e.g., a redesign team) to the methodology of design to the general plans for education, an organization should have a strong sense of how the process will unfold. Along with the other expectations, this insight on process will help people in the organization answer the question, "How will this affect me?" Anxiety, stress, and resistance to change will build until this simple but profoundly important question is addressed. Actor/director Woody Allen once said, "I'm not afraid of death. It's just that I don't want to be there when it happens." In his own unique way, he was explaining that people don't resist change. They resist transition—especially a transition in which they feel that they have no control over what lies ahead for them. They worry that they will not be able to make it through to whatever lies on the other side. Expectations help. While leaders may not be able to give a definitive response to, "What job will I hold in the future?", laying out a reasonably clear path for the process of change helps the organization see how and when those responses will be coming.

A word of advice. Once the process of change is established on paper and in the minds of the organization, respect and adhere to it. Too often organizations become arrogant or careless in their early successes. They may be tempted to take short cuts on future implementations if the initial attempt at teams went better than expected. Refining and streamlining the process is healthy. Eliminating or cutting back on necessary steps in the process, such as reducing communications with key stakeholders in the change or drastically paring down training for later teams, can turn a short-term success into a long-term failure.

Predictable Setbacks

The organization should also foresee the normal and predictable setbacks of teams. The most potentially disturbing setback is the inevitable low point in satisfaction and performance shortly after the high experienced by a newly formed team. Disturbing, that is, if those involved in the transformation do not expect it and share that expectation with the teams themselves. As described in Chapter 8, the transitional dip in performance shortly after implementation is a normal stage through which teams must evolve in their development. It is a temporary, negatively charged time when teams grapple with the fact that working as a team is hard work, struggle to define boundaries and roles, and wrestle with the downside of enhanced accountability. This high then low is a natural phenomenon paralleling a grieving curve. Clear expectations that newly formed teams will experience a marked low keep people, the teams included, from taking it as a sign of failure. It is all part of the learning.

Besides setting expectations, there is much leaders can do in advance to minimize the disruption and duration of the low. Transitional support programs, as described in Chapter 8, can help staff and managers work through the sense of loss, confusion, and frustration that accompany any major organizational change. Soon after teams form, refresher education in conflict resolution and interpersonal communications can help ensure members are prepared to work their way through problems arising during the low. This is also a good time to strengthen the teams' understanding of acceptable behaviors—since the stresses of the low often create team-destructive behaviors—and how to handle unacceptable behaviors.

When teams are immersed in this low period, or pit, leaders can help by increasing their accessibility—more walking rounds, attendance at all team meetings, and so on. A word of caution, however: Leaders must resist the temptation to succumb to the pressures of this stage by fixing the problems for the teams. More coaching and facilitation are certainly needed, but this is no time to revert to old modes of management that do not keep accountability with the teams for their own behaviors, actions, and problem resolution.

There are other predictable setbacks experienced by teams in their formative stages. New policies, procedures, and work flows may not work out as anticipated. Some duties may slip through the cracks occasionally as teams learn to work together. Nothing can avoid the numerous day-to-day tribulations experienced by new teams. That is actually good news. They represent opportunities for the teams themselves to refine their environment, building new continuous improvement skills and ownership of what they create. Setting clear expectations that these trials and tribulations will occur helps reinforce to everyone involved in the transformation that the day teams "go live" is just the beginning, not the end.

Promote Constructive Physician Behaviors

The sixth and final important expectation to be established specifically during the transformation to patient care teams involves a change in physician behaviors. Physicians need to be involved in the change process and should be fully aware of how the transformation will affect their daily activities—including new procedures, forms, and so on. But the dominant impact on medical staff related to teams is the need for a change in past behaviors. Simply put, relating with individual caregivers (even those grouped into team nursing) is very different from interacting with teams. Nowhere is this more apparent than in problem resolution.

In a typical health care setting, physicians who are upset about a patient care issue, such as finding a nurse who knows their patients to make rounds with them, usually make an angry telephone call to a nurse manager, director of nursing, or even to the CEO. These managers step in to fix the problem for the caregivers and the physicians.

This behavior, while disturbing in any organization, is a major barrier to establishing highly effective teams. In a team-based setting, the teams become accountable for virtually all performance issues on the unit, certainly for those related to patient care but also for issues affecting physician activities and satisfaction. Accountability has two parts: (1) responsibility, and

(2) control. Having responsibility without control is false accountability. Just ask any nurse who takes the heat for a delayed test result or radiology report performed on other shifts by a remote central department. This means that teams themselves must deal directly with the vast majority of physicians' day-to-day problems. They are responsible for performance results so they must have the control to improve them.

Three challenges must be met in order to change these behaviors. First, teams must be well-prepared (through education, coaching, etc.) to play their part—ready to deal constructively with the most volatile customer service situations. Second, managers must steadfastly position teams as the first-line remedy for problem resolution. For example, the CEO receiving a call from a disgruntled physician regarding a patient care issue must not hang up the telephone declaring, "I assure you that I'll get to the bottom of this!" That response just took the knees out from under the team, wounding the transformation as well. It is just plain wrong. Not surprisingly, meeting this challenge is no easy task. Managers traditionally have been rewarded for fighting fires and resolving crises—for getting to the bottom of a problem. Playing this role may even have been a source of pride to managers.

The third challenge, changing the behaviors of physicians, is no less daunting. Physicians, too, have implicitly been rewarded over the years for going straight to the top. It got results in that their problems were indeed solved, thereby ingraining the behavior. Physicians must learn to get the results they need directly through the teams. They must have regular dialogue with teams about mutual expectations and responsibilities—not just when problems arise, but all of the time.

No one is naive enough to think this will happen in the short term. But over time the behaviors can change. Besides setting the appropriate expectations, organizations can facilitate this metamorphosis by matching actions to words. The key is to align everyone's goals in the same direction. The team's goals are already aligned since they are accountable. That is the relatively easy part. Next, organizations must make going directly to the teams the best way for physicians to get results. The nurse manager or CEO receiving a physician complaint should say, "I understand completely and that is a situation that needs the team's involvement to ensure it doesn't happen again. I will be happy to facilitate an immediate discussion between you, myself, and the team." This type of approach accomplishes several objectives. It redirects problem resolution to the team. It avoids giving the physician the perception that the manager is blowing them off or just does not want to get involved. And it subtly puts in place an experienced facilitator who will greatly help the team and ensure the resolution of the problem, particularly in the early stages of the team's development. Consistently handling these situations in this manner gradually changes behaviors because it becomes in physicians' own self-interests to seek out the team—it's faster and easier.

Finally, organizations need to align the goals of managers. Remove the tangible and psychological incentives for them to fight fires and fix problems. Part of this incentive disappears by itself because managers in team-based settings soon realize that they do not have time to continue business as usual. Team roles are re-created to perform some traditional managerial responsibilities, such as staff scheduling and ironing out day-to-day operational problems. Similarly, managers' roles are re-created to replace managerial time with time spent on leadership responsibilities, such as staff development and strategic planning. In the short term, this role entails a great deal of walking around and coaching. Managers who continue fixing every problem themselves soon burn out.

The incentive can be further reduced through new performance evaluation systems and peer support. The answer to the question, "Can you as a manager succeed if teams fail?" must be a resounding, "No." The performance evaluations of managers of teams shift to include a significant weighting on how well they develop and empower teams. This evaluation may be influenced directly or indirectly by team input. Managers also can learn to redirect problem resolution to teams and receive reinforcement for this change in behaviors from their peers. The monthly sessions described earlier during which managers critique responses to common problems is one way to nurture that reinforcement. Changing behaviors to resolve problems directly between teams and physicians cannot be achieved without making the change in everyone's self-interest. The definition of power in the minds of leaders must change if teams are to succeed. People always will and should act in their own self-interests. This truth can be a powerful ally.

Summary

Establishing clear and realistic expectations is an essential part of the transformation to teams. The organization must share a high degree of commitment. People must understand how the transformation will reshape their roles. The pace of change must be realistic and appropriate to the organization's unique environment. An overall process of change must be set and adhered to. Teams and managers must expect predictable setbacks and use those as forums for learning. Organizations must help physicians recognize and change behaviors conflicting with the pursuit of teams. Managing expectations helps break down barriers built of misconceptions and fear. Since these particular barriers are the first faced by any transformation to teams, expectations must be set early on in the change process.

PREPARE THE LEADERSHIP

Setting the stage and establishing expectations are both essential guiding principles for any organization pursuing teams. Another principle relates to leadership. As discussed in Chapters 6 and 7, highly effective teams require highly effective leaders. It takes good managers to nurture good teams. A good manager of individuals does not automatically become a good manager of teams. Earlier in this chapter, several initial efforts in preparing the leadership for teams were outlined. Managers must understand what teams are and what they aren't and why they are a vital component of the organization's strategic agenda. They must have insights into the general transformation they will experience in their particular roles (such as transitioning from influence through control to influence through coaching). They must consistently role model desired behaviors. To accomplish this transformation, the goals and self-interests of managers must be aligned with those of the teams and of the entire change process—redefining power in the organization.

As with teams themselves, another important effort in preparing the leadership for the transformation to teams lies in education. The need for management education cannot be overstated. Education helps managers succeed when all of the rules of the game have changed. Gut instincts and traditional management tool kits—all built for a very different, individualistic environment—won't do them much good. Managers need new skill sets: coaching, mentoring, statistical analysis, project management, facilitation, visioning, and more. Their education should also involve problem-solving and decision-making approaches and techniques, such as setting clear goals, defining constraints, brokering consensus, and improvement planning. For a transformation to multidisciplinary teams, as explored in Chapter 10, managers' preparation should also include ways to lead people coming into the teams from diverse backgrounds with different motivations and expertise.

These efforts to prepare the leadership for a team-based organization begin well before the first team is up and running. Preparing managers for success, however, is an ongoing requirement. The needs of managers, as with teams themselves, continue well beyond the start-up of teams (Exhibit 12–3). Their successful transformation requires three additional efforts:

1. monitor team development
2. plan the transfer of responsibility
3. bridge between different styles

Exhibit 12–3 Challenges Facing New Leaders of Highly Effective Teams

✓ Monitor Team Development in Order To Meet Its Particular Needs

✓ Plan and Execute Controlled Transfer of Responsibility and Authority to Teams

✓ Bridge Styles between Teammates and between Leaders and Teams

Monitor Team Development

Another effort in preparing managers for future success is to give them the means to monitor the development and performance of teams. Teams grow and mature at different paces. Most teams, however, experience the same general pattern of growth (Figure 12–5). For the first few months after start-up, teams enjoy an up period. During this stage, teams are excited to be part of something new and enthusiastic about their future prospects. They spend a lot of time ironing out day-to-day operational problems and working on their intrateam dynamics. Teams still are generally positive during this initial blip.

Unfortunately, this initial blip is invariably short-lived. Several months later, teams typically slide into a very pronounced low. Teams eventually realize that performing as true teams is a lot of hard work. They come face to face with the reality that empowerment and autonomy do not mean doing whatever they want. Members tire of working out their own intrateam problems and revert to expecting their managers to fix problems for them. During this dip, teams waste a lot of energy wrestling with unproductive and often destructive concerns. The dip, albeit painful, is an important and essential stage for teams. They must be allowed to work their way out of this low if they are to mature into true teams in the long run.

Understanding and recognizing this "blip then dip" pattern of growth is an important part of establishing teams. Organizations without this insight can be lulled into a false sense of security during the blip, not realizing that the

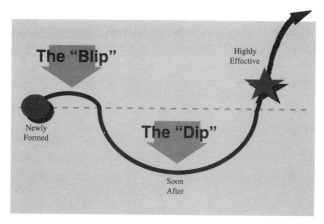

Figure 12–5 Generic Development/Growth Curve for True Teams. *Source:* Reprinted with permission from PFCA © 1995.

dip is not far down the road. This false sense leads organizations to assume that the worst (i.e., the battles to iron out day-to-day problems during startup) is over and subsequently to turn attention elsewhere. Of course, lack of attention and continued support can spell disaster for teams about to plunge into the dip.

Organizations that fail to anticipate the dip may interpret the negativism and poor performance of this stage as proof of failure rather than as a natural part of growth. Naysayers will point to intrateam conflicts and fluctuating results with I told you sos. Without an understanding of teams' developmental stages, the plug may get pulled before teams have a chance to work their way through the dip.

Organizations that nurture the teams through this difficult stage will reap the rewards of their investment. After teams hit rock bottom, they begin to climb out. They start to become more than a collection of individuals. They are efficient in their activities. They quickly change work priorities and assignments as needed. They focus on outcomes, not on petty differences between their members. The next few stages see them performing better as they solidify their working methods. Soon thereafter, teams become highly effective—delivering the tremendous benefits expected of them.

As shown in Figure 12–5, the stages in this typical pattern of team growth resemble a grieving or loss curve. This curve, as discussed in Chapter 3 (Figure 3–1) and again in Chapter 8, is much more than just an interesting concept. As described, the blip then dip expectation is an essential insight for the leadership of teams. Recognizing this growth curve is of paramount importance to managers because each distinct stage requires a different response from leaders. Managers must be aware of the growth stage of each team in order to meet its needs and help it along to the next stage. Different teams need different leadership interventions and support at different stages in their development. Managers, without spending endless hours, must periodically monitor the development of teams.

How can team development be monitored? Managers may need as many as three distinct gauges of team development because no single gauge is definitive: (1) predictable team behaviors, (2) team self-assessment, and (3) performance results (Figure 12–6). One method of monitoring team development is through predictable team behaviors. Team behaviors, actions, and emotions evolve over time. In the initial stage of team development (the high mentioned earlier) teams are typically full of a mix of excitement and fear of being part of something new. They spend much time working together, not always efficiently, to iron out the day-to-day details of working together and, in turn, this is the primary counsel they seek from managers. Teams also tend to exclude everyone outside of their team during this stage—the parallel of a couple who first start dating and only have eyes for each other.

This picture changes dramatically for the worse in the next stage, the pit or low. Here, the dominant emotions are frustration and conflict. Teams grapple with developing common expectations regarding their individual member roles. They learn that being a team and being empowered is a lot of hard work and that accountability is a two-edged sword. At this stage, teams become impatient with the change process and their own development. With all of this energy directed unproductively, teams feel grossly overworked. Like all development stages, this low eventually passes (with the help of coaching, facilitation, and a lot of patience).

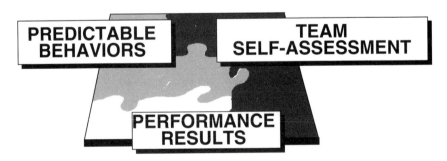

Figure 12–6 Three Ways To Monitor Team Development

Learning about these predictable team behaviors is a valuable asset for managers. First, these insights keep them from getting lulled into complacency during the high, or beaten to surrender during the low. It is the equivalent of the servant riding right behind a Roman gladiator during a victory lap in the arena. While the gladiator waved to the applauding multitudes, the servant continually whispered, "All glory is fleeting."

Another value derived from insights into predictable team behaviors is that they allow managers to tailor interventions to the particular needs of each team. Managers cannot give teams what they most need during a particular stage if uncertain about where the teams are in their development. Teams require different leadership support during different stages. For example, one type of support teams need most during the high is help in efficiently sharing best practices across teams. There is a tremendous amount of learning derived from ironing out the day-to-day problems, many of which are faced by all teams. Managers can expedite the learning curve by facilitating information flows (through open forums, written notes, continuous improvement meetings, etc.). During the low period, managers need to repeatedly reinforce conflict resolution, negotiation, and interpersonal communication skills. They need to help team members depersonalize disagreements. They need to help members bridge the gap between their different styles.

This value extends to the teams as well. Teams should also learn about the predictable behaviors of each stage in their development. Knowing what is to come allows them to brace for trouble spots but it is also therapeutic in that it allows the team to help itself constructively through each stage. This is a crucial point: Teams are themselves responsible for their own development. Managers must play their part, but teams that do not accept that responsibility do not fare as well as in the short and long terms as those that do. Insights into predictable behaviors bring some control to this responsibility.

During a weekly team meeting, for example, two team members had different opinions about why a particular problem getting supplies into the in-room patient server persisted. It got a bit tense between the two members when a third member chimed in with a wry grin, "Oh, you two are just venting the negative emotions and experiencing the interpersonal conflicts that are quite normal at this stage in our development." This was an almost verbatim quote of a key lesson learned during a prior educational program. There was silence. Then everyone burst into laughter. The discussion switched from an interpersonal conflict to a collaborative problem-solving session and within 20 minutes the supply issue was resolved.

A second method to gauge team development is through a team self-assessment. Consistent with their accountability for their own development, teams can play an active role in determining where they are in their growth. One way to accomplish this is to have the team periodically complete a survey designed to identify how members interact with each other and what the team thinks is important (Exhibit 12–4). The results of the survey can be quantified and plotted over time. As long as the survey remains the same, this plot can help managers and the team visualize where it is on the development curve. This enables both managers and teams to participate in the diagnosis and treatment of development. The survey also provides valuable feedback to the managers, something akin to the student telling the teacher that his test scores are a good indication of the teacher's abilities. For every intervention needed by teams in their development, managers should ask themselves, "How can I better meet this need? What should I do differently in the future?"

A third gauge of team development is to evaluate performance results. Teams' performance generally follows the same pattern as their overall development. Performance, particularly staff satisfaction, jumps up as soon as the teams are formed (the high). Later, performance suffers and falls as teams experience the low that consumes so much energy and introduces so many distractions. Performance picks up again as the team pulls itself out of this

Exhibit 12–4 Sample Questions from the Team Self-Assessment Survey

Does your team have a written purpose statement?

Do team members act in ways that support the team's purpose (i.e., make decisions, set priorities, take action, etc.)?

Does your team have enough time to get together as a team to work on the issues and challenges it faces?

Does your team have ready access to the resources (time, information, equipment, supplies, coaching, etc.) it needs for its work?

Are team members able to focus on projects and assignments and accomplish these within a reasonable time frame?

Are boundaries and limits openly discussed within the team and clarified before problems and conflicts occur?

Answer Key:
1. No
2. Limited Extent
3. Some Extent
4. Considerable Extent
5. Great Extent

Source: Reprinted from *Team Self-Assessment Survey,* © 1993, Jo Manion.

stage and creeps upward as the team matures into a fully functional entity. Measures of team performance are discussed later in this chapter.

To reiterate, teams must play an integral part in their own development. They must receive regular information related to their key outcomes and results in a manner that is easy for them to review and understand. Thick computer-generated reports full of numbers with decimal places will not work for teams. As physicians reviewing a medical record, teams need to glean what is important—especially where performance is not meeting targets—at a glance. Armed with this information, the team can stay attuned to its performance and take charge of initiating improvements.

Preparing leaders for success in a team-based organization requires they be able to monitor the development of teams. Methods of monitoring include identifying predictable behaviors, involving teams in self-assessment, and gauging performance results. Any combination of these methods usually leads to a growth curve such as the one shown in Figure 12–5. Knowing where teams are in their development (without spending endless hours) allows managers to facilitate their continued growth by tailoring support to their most pressing needs. The additional benefits of monitoring development include valuable feedback to managers (on their leadership) and better sharing of best practices across teams.

Plan the Transfer of Responsibility and Authority

In addition to monitoring teams, another important effort in preparing the leadership is to help it conduct a carefully planned transfer of responsibility and authority. Just because managers buy into the notion of giving teams more responsibility for decision making does not mean they know how to pull this off. Two situations typically arise when managers don't understand how properly to transfer responsibility and authority to teams—both of which can be disastrous. Either the manager will keep a tight grip on decision making and not empower teams, or will pass virtually all decision making authority to them before they are ready to handle it. Either way, the transformation to teams suffers.

Creating a plan for this transfer of responsibility has two components. The first component is helping managers learn how to ensure the quality of decisions without making them all. The key tactic here is to set clear and relevant constraints and objectives for every decision. For example, teams assuming the responsibility to handle their own staff scheduling must adhere to quality (e.g., "At least two RNs must be present on every shift") and economic (e.g., "Your budget for team wages is $X") objectives.

The next component is a predefined schedule for transfer. Managers must categorize all of the decisions to be made by teams and sequence these across teams' development (Figure 12–7). The first group of categories includes decisions related to day-to-day problems—procedures, work flows, processes, and intrateam dynamics. These managerial responsibilities are usually assumed by teams early in their development for several reasons. They carry relatively low risk in that they are easily revisited and do not commit the organization to a large expense. It is relatively easy to define for the team what constitutes a good decision (fewer process steps). They give the team much of the upfront control needed to affect their performance results, and they represent significant bang for the buck in terms of freeing up managers' time.

One valuable exercise in educational programs for leadership development is to have participants analyze their calendars for the past month or two. They then differentiate how they spent their time. The first category typically represents 15 to 20 percent of managers' time and more if standing meetings are included. The bad news is this percentage represents a terrible waste of time, money, and talent to the traditional organization. The good news is that imparting those responsibilities to teams can give managers the ability to reinvest hours in more forward thinking activities. That opportunity is one reason why organizations pursue teams.

The second group of categories should include managerial responsibilities entailing more complex and riskier decisions, such as staff self-scheduling. These decisions are less clear-cut and represent a greater burden of transfer to both managers and teams. The schedule may delay this transfer of respon-

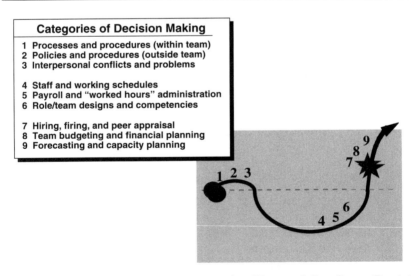

Categories of Decision Making

1 Processes and procedures (within team)
2 Policies and procedures (outside team)
3 Interpersonal conflicts and problems

4 Staff and working schedules
5 Payroll and "worked hours" administration
6 Role/team designs and competencies

7 Hiring, firing, and peer appraisal
8 Team budgeting and financial planning
9 Forecasting and capacity planning

Figure 12–7 Prototype of a Controlled Transfer of Responsibility. *Source*: Reprinted with permission from PFCA © 1995.

sibility until teams work their way through the "dip" stage in their development.

The third group of categories entails the most difficult decisions—like hiring, firing, and appraisal. These are responsibilities to be given to mature teams who know, with clarity, what they need and why they need it.

There is no schedule of transfer that is right for all organizations or teams. The above considerations of time currently spent by managers, advantages to teams' control over outcomes, and potential risk to the organization, however, are useful in tailoring a schedule that reflects the organization's particular needs. Having a predefined schedule (which can be modified as necessary) sets teams' and managers' expectations and allows both parties to do their part to ensure a smooth transfer of responsibility and authority.

Bridge between Different Styles

A third important effort in preparing leaders for success in a team-based organization relates to bridging styles. People in health care organizations have always faced distinct differences in styles. Based upon what they think is most important to them and their work, individuals give and receive input differently. They process information to solve problems differently. They have different expectations of how others should treat them and so on. Within traditional organizations, however, narrowly defined responsibilities, arms-length working relationships, and a rigid hierarchy tempered the negative affects of these style differences. When it comes to getting work done, most people are in self-contained jobs whose primary interactions center on handoffs (of information, materials, or customers).

The transformation to teams does just the opposite. Broadly defined roles, consistent working relationships, overlapping responsibilities and leadership based on coaching and facilitation magnify the affects of style differences. Teams fail if people can't overcome their individual differences and idiosyncrasies and work together cohesively. Team members must overcome their style differences for the sake of the team and, ultimately, themselves, since their performance and the team's are linked. Managers must learn to overcome style differences with the members as well in order to lead them effectively.

To be successful, leaders must be able to identify their individual styles as well as the various styles of team members. Accomplishing this does not involve a lot of time or theory. There are many proven constructs on the market today to help organizations define and identify individual styles. The hard part is learning to overcome those differences, especially when things go wrong. One simple technique to overcome style differences is to list "what always to do" and "what never to do" when approaching a person with bad news.

To illustrate, one organization exploring style differences discovered that a manager's style was akin to Abe Lincoln (emphasis on integrity and vision) while one team member's style resembled General Patton (emphasis on boldness and performance) and another's paralleled Gandhi (emphasis on relationships and serving others). It was not a match made in heaven, to say the least. They each wrote down on an easel pad what was important to them. "Lincoln" valued innovation and ideas. "Patton" valued accomplishments and tenacity. "Gandhi" valued honesty and cooperation. The next exercise was to brainstorm how best to interact with each other under stressful conditions. The group decided always to approach Gandhi with the people side of the problem (impact on customer satisfaction) and never with a lot of facts and figures. Patton would be approached with a summary of how the problem at hand directly affected results. By the end of the session, the group had a lot of fun (team-building in itself) but also walked away with a new understanding of each other's style and needs. No one leaving that meeting intended to apply their "always" and "never" approaches rigidly. But the experience heightened awareness of the role of styles in interpersonal communications and relationships. That awareness, coupled with some helpful hints to bridge style differences, helped teammates and managers work together in a team-based organization.

Summary

The transformation to teams may be the greatest challenge faced by leaders in the organization. Preparing the leadership is every bit as crucial as readying the teams for what lies ahead. Leaders must be able to monitor team development and intervene accordingly. The transfer of responsibility and authority from managers to teams must be carefully planned, and leaders must help themselves and teams to bridge their different styles. These efforts are another initiative toward lighting the way for teams.

MODIFY INTERNAL SYSTEMS

Not all barriers to teams are people-related. The final guiding principle for establishing highly effective teams is to overcome the barriers raised by the inability of traditional internal systems to adapt to and, therefore, support a team-based environment. An unrealistic goal is to replace or completely rewrite systems from Day One. Organizations with successful teams have learned that a tremendous amount of progress can be made with only minor modifications or enhancements. Even these adjustments, however, cost money. The prudent organization, therefore, spends time upfront assessing each internal system's ability to support teams and what it would take to increase that level of support over time. Initial investments are directed where they can do the transformation to teams the most good. These investments generally lead to modifications to an array of crucial internal systems:

1. Educational capabilities
2. Information processing
3. Performance measurement
4. Recognition and rewards

Educational Capabilities

Chapter 11 explored the key educational challenges to be met in the transformation to teams. Education is unquestionably one of the greatest investments associated with establishing highly effective teams. In addition to these investments, however, organizations must gradually retool their internal educational systems to support a team-based environment.

Educational capabilities in most health care organizations, structured primarily to deliver in-service training, share a few characteristics. They are centralized and delivered by educators. The schedule for sessions is limited. Most learning is centered on skills and accomplished in one session. Participants are individuals. None of these characteristics depict the ideal team-based educational capability.

Teams should go through their education together, not as individuals. This means learning must be delivered in a flexible and self-paced manner so that an entire team can experience the education together. Learning entails both skills and processes (problem solving, interpreting performance reports, conflict resolution). Given the magnitude of a team's start-up and ongoing educational needs, learning is enhanced when lessons are layered over time, rather than imparted all at once (Leander, "Layered Learning," 1994). Organizations using a traditional in-house capability to educate teams may soon realize that the value of the learning process falls while its costs rise.

Given these new requirements, some organizations have discovered that delivering education in a team-based setting should be a shared responsibility of educators, managers, and the teams themselves. Educators create sound programs and means of evaluating participant learning. They also deliver select programs that require special facilitation, didactic lecture, and/or large groups of participants. Meanwhile, managers (or their department/unit-based educational staff) deliver programs that are specific to their setting, such as policies that differ across departments, and which require strict consistency in message. Finally, teams (or a designated team leader) can self-administer programs related to day-to-day skills, behaviors, and performance. Managers and teams continue to rely on the centralized educators as experts for any counsel needed.

This type of decentralized model is invaluable to organizations striving to educate entire teams in a more self-paced manner. In addition, making teams at least partly accountable for their own education is consistent with the overall transformation to teams. The only caveat is that not everyone is (or even can become) an acceptable educator. Managers and teams will need help learning how to deliver education to adults in a way that promotes lasting learning.

Information Processing

Information processing and dissemination is another internal system that must be gradually retooled to support a team-based organization. Existing information systems, of course, were structured around the traditional organization. They are primarily financial in nature and, therefore, they report information along cost center lines. As such, they reflect the many functional silos cutting through the organization. Getting team-by-team information out of a system designed to serve functions can be quite a chore.

Yet tracking team-specific information—personnel costs, outcomes achieved, recent results—is absolutely vital to assessing and improving team performance. This information must be owned by teams if they are to use it to make decisions and innovate continuously. It is also the basis of team-based performance measures as described below. Many organizations implementing teams have had to modify and supplement their information processing through a combination of quick fixes to the existing systems and additional manual processes to plug the holes.

For example, they have assigned unique cost center numbers to individual teams in order to jury-rig the existing systems in the near term. The first digits of these numbers may represent the department/unit. The next two digits may represent the team, and so on. The overall performance of the department/unit across all teams can be tracked and reported by rolling up these so-called cost centers. This type of modification can go a long way in allowing teams to start and grow while a more permanent long-term answer is sought.

Having said this, few organizations can avoid the necessary evil of also putting in place a few manual processes. A clerk may need to pull data from a handful of different reports, perform some basic calculations on these data, and disseminate the results to managers and teams. These organizations, of course, are careful to track the incremental cost of any manual processes and to reflect it in the financial evaluation of teams. A key point for all organizations pursuing teams is that internal systems do not necessarily have to be replaced or completely overhauled to support the transformation in the near term. A little creativity and perseverance can go a long way.

Performance Measurement

Performance measurement systems also must change as the organization evolves from individuals to teams. Chapter 10 explored the benefits and nature of team-based measures along with a sample set for multidisciplinary care teams. Team-based measures enhance and anchor the gains achieved through teams. To do so, they must move away from a focus on tasks to a focus on outcomes. They must concentrate on the vital few rather than the trivial many. They must be owned by teams in the sense that the teams are fully accountable (with coaching and guidance from their manager) for continuously improving their outcomes through action planning and proper execution. Performance measures must be reported to teams in a simple format that gives the team what it needs to know at a glance. Again, Chapter 10 offers a full exploration of team-based performance measures.

The next section discusses the need to modify reward and compensation systems. Organizations in the pursuit of teams need to distinguish clearly between performance systems and reward systems. The two are separate systems that certainly must marry up in the long term but not necessarily at the start. Some organizations have found themselves stuck on Square One by trying to rewrite both of these systems before teams are implemented. The size of that first step proved insurmountable. Other organizations that managed to take that step found themselves going back repeatedly as changes in performance measurement (a healthy byproduct of continued learning early in the move to teams) necessitated changes in rewards.

For some period of time—enough to enable the newly formed teams to take root and begin to gel—separating the two systems is a real possibility. In other words, performance measures are the dog and rewards are the tail. Their priority and precedence in a change process is clear. Rewards cannot be firmly defined until what is important to the institution—outcomes and their measures—is clearly articulated.

Recognition and Rewards

As just mentioned, the internal system for recognition and rewards can greatly determine the success or failure of teams. People will and always should act in their own self-interests. This truth is neither bad nor good. It just is. To ask them repeatedly to do otherwise is naive and ill-fated. Instead, organizations with highly effective teams learn to harness this powerful motivation—turning self-interest into an asset.

The need to rethink recognition and reward systems became painfully obvious to one 250-bed tertiary care provider in the Mid West where a very high performing team was nominated for Employee of the Month. This team was a role model for other teams in terms of both behaviors and outcomes. The team had recently gone beyond the call of duty by getting a new kitten for a long-term patient after learning that her pet, a cherished companion for many years, died while the patient was hospitalized. The nomination was not even considered. It was returned to the manager of that area with a scribbled note, "Sorry. The Employee of the Month award cannot be given to multiple employees." Talk about sending a destructive message to the organization. Fortunately, the manager and other teams in that area gave a special award of their own (which had even greater meaning and value) to the nominated team.

The need to modify recognition and rewards is apparent from even a cursory review of traditional systems. Simply put, people cannot succeed in teams if they do what is asked of them in individualistic job descriptions that have been stripped of any interdependencies with others. Under traditional recognition and reward systems, team members can succeed even if the team as a whole fails. This disconnect in incentives, a detrimental lack of goal alignment, cannot continue indefinitely in a team-based organization.

Tomorrow's recognition and reward systems must establish a new level of goal alignment. People must see that their own self-interests and those of their entire team are in line with the needs of the organization as a whole. In order to make this happen, traditional reward systems must be rewritten dramatically (Figure 12–8) in two fundamental dimensions (Galloway 1993). The first change is in the basis of rewards. To fit with the new team-based performance measures, rewards—and compensation, even more specifically—must eventually evolve from being based on tasks to being based on outcomes. Along the way, some organizations pause at intermediate spots with a reward system based upon skills and then knowledge. Skills- and knowledge-based pay have their ups and downs. On the up side, they are a more tolerable (although in no way easy) change for an organization obsessed with tasks than the leap straight to outcomes. On the down side, a broader set of skills and greater levels of knowledge may or may not lead to better outcomes. An organization may very well find itself paying more as people learn while at the same time experiencing flat or declining outcomes.

The second aspect of the rewrite of rewards is in their distribution. In this context, distribution does not refer to how paychecks are handed out. Distribution refers to the percentage of a person's pay tied to individual, team,

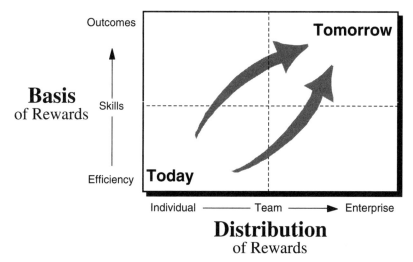

Figure 12–8 Retooling of Traditional Recognition and Reward Systems. *Source*: Reprinted with permission from PFCA © 1995.

department/unit, and enterprise/institution performance. Members of a team can have components of all four slices of the organization in their paychecks. What is the right balance for this distribution? The answer to this question is found through control. In general, higher percentages must be tied to higher levels of control. This suggests that the largest percentage of rewards is determined by individual and team performance. The department/unit and enterprise/institution percentages are smaller and in place only to reinforce goal alignment throughout the organization. For example, a distribution scheme for compensation could be 15, 70, 10, and 5 percent, respectively.

In virtually all health care organizations, managers have a distribution similar to this scheme (excluding the team component). The move to teams extends this goal alignment throughout more of the organization. The only hard and fast rules are that compensation must remain tied to the market (at least no less than) and no one loses money through the rewrite of rewards (at least initially).

Rewriting recognition and reward systems is a must if teams are to succeed in the long term. These changes bring leadership face to face with some very difficult issues, however. There are technical issues related to the exact mechanism of compensating people in a multiskilled, multidisciplinary environment. These mechanisms can become overly complex if left unchecked. Reward systems also bring into question issues of entitlement and tenure versus pay for performance. These issues become more difficult in unionized settings. Still, many organizations are learning to work their way through these issues over time so that their teams grow.

Although Figure 12–8 shows a general direction (a two-dimensional construct for innovation) for the rewrite of recognition and reward systems, these systems are "personal" in that each organization will have to find the answers that are right for its unique situation and needs. In particular, changes to compensation (a subset of recognition and reward) intended to promote teams must be carefully tailored to an organization's marketing, cultural, and operational forces. Speer and Gerard, human resource executives at United Health of Wisconsin, have headed a consortium of about a dozen healthcare organizations probing the compensation challenges to be met in establishing multifunctional teams. The initial conference concentrated on the key issues behind these challenges, breakthrough themes running through tomorrow's ideal compensation systems, and the obvious obstacles to implementing these changes (Speer and Gerard 1995). As a foundation for the consortium, they articulated the following key issues to be faced by any healthcare organization:

- Aligning compensation with the culture
- Creating a compensation structure that addresses a multiskilled workplace
- Resolving technical hurdles (e.g., compression and internal equity)
- Realigning compensation systems in a "cost-reduction" world
- Attending to the "human side" of changing compensation

The consortium then proceeded to define an ideal compensation system that resolves these issues. To promote creativity, they intentionally did not allow themselves to get bogged down in the details and realities of near-term implementation. Instead, they concentrated on establishing a vision. This vision was based on the 10 criteria for a successful redesign of compensation shown in Exhibit 12–5.

Exhibit 12–5 Top 10 Criteria for Future Compensation Systems. *Source*: Reprinted with permission from PFCA © 1995.

1. Flexible to a changing world	6. Reflects values and culture
2. Simple to administer	7. Supports high morale
3. Easy to communicate	8. Attracts new recruits
4. High employee involvement	9. Supports teams and individuals
5. Aligns mission and values	10. Encourages continuous improvement

The consortium next pushed to identify the "vital few" breakthrough themes that met these ideal criteria. They determined that these themes, or concepts, could be used in combination with one another or individually, depending upon the specific situation and needs of the organization. As a set, however, the following themes represent a unique approach to considering compensation in the future:

1. Increase the amount of flexible compensation into the overall pay formula.
2. Decentralize compensation planning and management to smaller units within the organization.
3. Increase the use of noncash compensation as part of the formula.
4. Use broadbanding (clusters of multiple pay grades) as jobs become simpler and fewer.

In concluding this first conference, the consortium clearly recognized the potential obstacles to be faced in acting upon these themes. These obstacles included a lack of effective leadership, fear of uncertainty and change, resource limitations, and building a new performance measurement infrastructure (as discussed in this chapter). In the minds of the consortium members, all of these obstacles demanded patience, time, and active human resources leadership to overcome. No dramatic change, particularly one that tears at the heart of the employee/employer "contract," is easy.

After the first conference, participants returned to push ahead in the new direction for compensation in their organizations. They tested the emerging themes and began to wrestle with obstacles to implementation. In general, the conclusion of most participants was that the new direction was indeed sound, but getting there must be a gradual process. Several months later, the consortium reunited for a second conference with the primary goal of exchanging experiences, approaches, and successes related to implementation.

The first agenda item of this second conference was a philosophical critique of compensation systems as a motivator. The consortium unanimously concluded (consistent with the teaching of Frederick Hertzberg) that, on an ongoing basis, compensation per se could only be a dissatisfier for employees. Any increases in satisfaction derived from greater compensation were fleeting. Any compensation system should be designed to remove dissatisfaction (not increase satisfaction) and to stop pay from being a demotivator (not to make pay a motivator). Consequently, the first rule of changing compensation systems was to "do no harm."

The next agenda item was further discussion of broadbanding as a technique to decrease the number of pay grades. Several participants discovered that the realities of implementing broadbanding in their organizations prevented them from actually achieving the objective of fewer grades. They found that within individual broadbands it was still necessary to create multiple secondary bands in order to make the compensation system work in today's competitive marketplace for labor. They theorized that traditional thinking in the general marketplace made the leap to true broadbands impalatable. Nonetheless, participants committed themselves to continue the pursuit of fewer grades.

The remainder of the conference was devoted to articulating the key lessons learned in striving to put in place the ideal compensation system envisioned in the first conference. These hard-earned lessons, shown in Exhibit 12–6, include a general conclusion that changing compensation systems should be accomplished through a series of "small wins" rather than "major leaps." As such, inevitably there will be a period during which multiple systems are in place—some new, some in flux, and others on their way out. This transitional pressure cannot be taken lightly. Still, despite the obstacles and lessons, participants in the consortium left the second conference more committed than ever to being compensation change agents in their organizations.

CONCLUSION

A handful of internal systems play an important role in the transformation to teams. These systems were born and grew up to serve organizations founded on individuals and departments. Educational capabilities, information processing, performance measurement, and recognition and reward systems must all be modified gradually to support teams in the long term. These modifications are important but they do not all have to be accomplished before the first team starts. Like the transformation to teams itself, these systems will go through a period of transition, as long as the new direction is translated into a clear plan that keeps this transformation on track.

Exhibit 12–6 Lessons Learned in Implementing New Compensation Systems

- Understand clearly the purpose and goals of your compensation system
- Go slow at first and avoid knee-jerk reactions (and overreactions)
- Pay close attention to the culture of your organization as part of the change
- Involve as many people as possible as you move ahead toward the vision
- Implement compensation changes to support work/process redesign, not to lead it
- Insist on flexible and adaptive leadership from HR and all executives
- Ignore any temptation to think of new compensation systems as a panacea
- Use multiple/mixed approaches to compensation in the transition

Epilogue

Transforming a traditional hierarchical organization to a team-based structure is not for the faint-hearted. Optimism and a healthy dose of courage are required. Visions of a preferred future will guide the journey while personal and organizational insights illuminate strengths and give direction to minimize weaknesses. The purpose of this book has been to share the learning of many pioneering health care teams and organizations. Learning from each other has helped to lighten our burdens on this journey.

Throughout this book we have presented guiding principles that show the way to team success. The stage must be set for teams and leaders through an understanding of what teams *are* and are *not*, so teams are only used where the work warrants it, are created based on a sound design, and are able to maintain consistent team membership. Using this discipline for developing teams provides a strong foundation for structural transformation and avoids the problem of ineffective or partially functioning teams that never achieve their promise. Managing the implementation process in departments or throughout the organization requires clear and realistic expectations about commitment to teams, shifts in team member roles, pace and processes of change, predictable setbacks teams will face, and new definitions of acceptable behaviors.

Preparing leaders for the future by giving them knowledge and tools to lead the cultural change is a major challenge. Leaders must understand the different types of teams with their characteristic pitfalls and challenges. When so equipped they can guide and monitor team development, mold the different communication styles required in a team-based environment, and transfer responsibility and authority to teams in a planned manner. A leader's skill and comfort in managing both the structural change, as well as the human side of change, will provide a safety net beneath the inevitable organizational confusion.

Unique challenges for health care leaders include managing the professional complexities of multidisciplinary teams to create a new, unified tribe. Additionally, the challenge of designing learning experiences specific to health care workers and committing adequate organizational resources for the continuous development of staff must be met. Finally, modification of the organization's internal systems (information, communication, rewards, and recognition) will be necessary to support the ongoing growth of teams.

All of these elements together form a tool kit for success. By using these tools an organization can shape a strong future based on the power of people working together—the power of teams.

Bibliography

Abbasi, S. and Hollman, K. 1994. Self-managed teams: The productivity breakthrough of the 1990s. *Journal of Managerial Psychology* 9, no. 7: 25–30.

Agurén, S., et al. 1976. *The Volvo Kalmar plant. The impact of new design of work organization.* Stockholm, Sweden: The Rationalization Council SAF-LO, 37.

Bardwick, J.M. 1991. *Danger in the comfort zone.* New York, N.Y.: American Management Association.

Barker, J.A. 1989. *Discovering the future: The business of paradigms.* Minneapolis, Minn.: ChartHouse Learning Corporation. Videotape.

Barker, J.A. 1993. *The power of vision.* Minneapolis, Minn.: ChartHouse Learning Corporation. Videotape.

Becker-Reems, E.D. 1994. *Self-managed work teams in health care organizations.* Chicago, Ill.: American Hospital Publishing, Inc.

Beckhard, R. and Pritchard, W. 1992. *Changing the essence: The art of creating and leading fundamental change in organizations.* San Francisco, Calif.: Jossey-Bass, Inc. Publishers.

Bell, D. 1973. *The coming of post-industrial society.* New York, N.Y.: Basic Books, Inc.

Benner, P. 1984. *From novice to expert.* Reading, Mass.: Addison-Wesley Publishing Co., Inc.

Bennis W. 1989. *On becoming a leader.* Reading, Mass.: Addison-Wesley Publishing Co., Inc.

Benson, T.E. 1992. A braver new world? (Self-managing work teams), *Industry Week* 241, no. 15: 48–51.

Bernstein, P. 1988. The learning curve at Volvo. *Classical readings in self-managing teamwork*, ed. R. Glaser, 354–372. King of Prussia, Penn.: Organization Design and Development, Inc.

Blancett, S.S. and Flarey, D.L. 1995. *Reengineering nursing and health care: The handbook for organizational transformation.* Gaithersburg, MD: Aspen Publishers, Inc.

Blanchard, K. and Bowles, S. 1993. *Raving fans: A revolutionary approach to customer service.* New York, N.Y.: William Morrow & Company.

Block, P. 1987. *The empowered manager: Positive political skills at work.* San Francisco, Calif.: Jossey-Bass, Inc., Publishers.

Bohan, G.P. 1990. Building a high-performance team. *Health Care Supervisor* 8, no. 4: 15–21.

Boswell, J. 1970. *Life of Johnson.* London, England: Oxford University Press.

Bridges, W. 1980. *Transitions: Making sense of life's changes.* Reading, Mass.: Addison-Wesley Publishing Co., Inc.

Bridges, W. 1988. *Surviving corporate transition.* Mill Valley, Calif.: William Bridges & Associates.

Bridges, W. 1991. *Managing transitions: Making the most of change.* Mill Valley, Calif.: William Bridges & Associates.

Bridges, W. 1992. *Participant's guide: Managing organizational transitions.* Mill Valley, Calif.: William Bridges & Associates.

Buggie, F. 1995. Expert innovation teams: A new way to increase productivity dramatically. *Planning Review* 23, no. 4: 26–31.

Byham, W.C., with J. Cox. 1988. *Zapp! The lightning of empowerment: How to improve productivity, quality, and employee satisfaction.* New York, N.Y.: Harmony Books.

Carr, C. 1992. Planning priorities for empowered teams. *Journal of Business Strategy* 13, no. 5: 43–7.

Connor, D. 1993. *Managing at the speed of change: How resilient managers succeed and prosper where others fail.* New York, N.Y.: Villard Books.

Covey, S. 1989. *The seven habits of highly effective people: Restoring the character ethic.* New York, N.Y.: Simon & Schuster, Inc.

Covey, S. 1994. *First things first.* New York, N.Y.: Simon & Schuster, Inc.

Cummings, T.G. 1978. Self-regulating work groups: A socio-technical synthesis. In *Classical readings in self-managing teamwork,* ed. R. Glaser, 44–57. King of Prussia, Penn.: Organization Design and Development, Inc.

Dailey, R., Young, F., and Barr, C. 1991. Empowering middle managers in hospitals with team-based problem-solving. *Health Care Management Review* 16, no. 2: 55–63.

DePree, M. 1989. *Leadership is an art.* New York, N.Y.: Bantam, Dell Publishing.

DePree, M. 1992. *Leadership jazz.* New York, N.Y.: Doubleday & Co., Inc.

Drucker, P. 1989. *The new realities.* New York, N.Y.: Harper & Row.

Dubnicki, C. 1991. Building high-performance management teams: The shape of things to come. *Healthcare Forum Journal* 34, no. 5: 10–11.

Dubnicki, C. and Limburg, W. 1991. How do healthcare teams measure up? *Healthcare Forum Journal* 34, no. 5: 10–11.

Dumaine, B. 1994. The trouble with teams. *Fortune* (September): 86–92.

Dychtwald, K. with Flowers, J. 1990. *Age wave: How the most important trend of our time will change your future.* New York, N.Y.: Bantam Books, Inc.

Fisher, K. 1993. *Leading self-directed work teams: A guide to developing new team leadership skills.* New York, N.Y.: McGraw-Hill Publishing Co.

Flowers, J. 1990. The chasm between management and leadership. *Healthcare Forum Journal* 33, no. 4: 60–62.

Flowers, J. 1991. Being effective. *Healthcare Forum Journal* 34, no. 3: 52–57.

Galloway, M. 1993. Designing patient focused reward systems. *PFCA Review®* (Spring): 2–5.

Garber, P.R. 1993. *Coaching self-directed work teams: Building winning teams in today's changing workplace.* King of Prussia, Penn.: Organization Design and Development, Inc.

Geber, B. 1992. From manager into coach. *TRAINING* 29, no. 2: 25–31.

Glaser, R. 1990. *Moving your team toward self-management.* King of Prussia, Penn.: Organization Design and Development, Inc.

Glaser, R. 1991. *Facilitating self-managing teams.* King of Prussia, Penn.: Organization Design and Development, Inc.

Glaser, R. 1991. *Learning to be a self-managing team.* King of Prussia, Penn.: Organization Design and Development, Inc.

Glaser, R. 1992. *Classic readings in self-managing teamwork.* King of Prussia, Penn.: Organization Design and Development, Inc.

Glines, D. 1994. Do you work in a zoo? *Executive Excellence* (October): 12–13.

Goldberg, B. 1995. Team rewards and team benefits. *Executive Excellence* (June): 14–15.

Goman, C.K. 1992. *Adapting to change: Making it work for you.* Menlo Park, Calif.: Crisp Publications.

Goodemote, E. 1995. Managing in the next decade: A new set of skills for nurse managers. *Seminars for Nurse Managers* 3, no. 2: 84–88.

Gordon, J. 1992. Work teams: How far have they come? *TRAINING* 29: 59–65.

Gummer, B. 1988. Post-industrial management: Teams, self-management, and the new interdependence. *Administration in Social Work* 12, no. 3: 117–132.

Hamilton, J. 1993. Toppling the power of the pyramid. *Hospitals* (January 5): 33ff.

Hart, E. 1995. Executive leadership teams: Exorcising demons, exercising minds. *Planning Review* 23, no. 4: 14–19,46.

Hawley, J. 1993. Reawakening the spirit in work: The power of dharmic management. San Francisco, Calif.: Berrett-Koehler.

Hersey, P. and Blanchard, K.H. 1993. Management of organizational behavior: Utilizing human resources. 6th ed. Englewood Cliffs, N.J.: Prentice Hall.

Holpp, L. and Phillips, R. 1995. When is a team its own worst enemy? *TRAINING* 32, no. 9: 71–82.

Horak, B.J. 1991. Building a team on a medical floor. *Health Care Management Review* 16, no. 2: 65–71.

Hout, T.M. and Carter, J.C. 1995. Getting it done: New roles for senior executives. *Harvard Business Review* (November/December): 133–145.

Huret, J. 1991. Paying for team results. *HR Magazine* (May): 39–41.

Jacobsen-Webb, M. 1985. Team building: Key to executive success. *Journal of Nursing Administration* 15, no. 2: 16–20.

Jessup, H.R. 1990. New roles in team leadership. *Training & Development Journal* (November): 79–83.

Jonson, L.C., et al. 1978. The application of social accounting to absenteeism and personnel turnover. *Accounting, Organizations and Society* 3:265.

Katzenbach, J.R. and Smith, D.K. 1993. *The wisdom of teams: Creating the high-performance organization.* Boston, Mass.: Harvard Business School Press.

Larson, C.E. and LaFasto, F. 1989. *TeamWork: What must go right/What can go wrong.* Newbury Park, Calif.: Sage Publications, Inc.

Lawler, E.E. 1992. *The ultimate advantage: Creating the high involvement organization.* San Francisco, Calif.: Jossey-Bass, Inc. Publishers.

Leander, W. 1993. Patient focused care team design. *PFCA Review®* (Summer): 10–15.

Leander, W. 1993. To pilot or not to pilot, that is the question. *PFCA Review®* (Fall): 6–7.

Leander, W. 1994. Boundaries and bogies. *PFCA Review®* (Spring): 2–4.

Leander, W. 1994. Layered learning: Improved learning through phased education. *PFCA Review®* (Summer): 2–7.

Leander, W. and Rees, R. 1992. Effective education for patient focused staff. *PFCA Review®* (Fall): 2–6.

Leander, W., with Shortridge, D. and Watson, P. 1996. Patients first. *Health Care Administration Press.*

Likert, R. 1961. *New patterns of management.* New York, N.Y.: McGraw-Hill Publishing Co.

Linden, R.M. 1992. Flattening the hierarchy through self-managing teams: I. *Virginia Review* (October): 52–53.

Linden, R.M. 1992. Self-managing teams II: Dealing with the issues. *Virginia Review* (November): 20–21.

Lorimer, W. 1994. Interview notes from *Voluntary hospital of American study: Improving patient outcomes through system change.* Irving, Texas: Voluntary Hospitals of America.

Lumsdon, K. 1995. Why executive teams fail and what to do. *Hospitals & Health Networks* (August 5): 24–31.

Manion, J. 1990. *Change from within: Nurse intrapreneurs as health care innovators.* Kansas City, Missouri: American Nurses Association.

Manion, J. 1993. Chaos or transformation? Managing innovation. *The Journal of Nursing Administration* 23, no. 5: 41–48.

Manion, J. 1994. Managing change: The leadership challenge of the 1990s. *Seminars for Nurse Managers* 2, no. 4: 203–208.

Manion, J. 1995. Understanding the seven stages of change. *American Journal of Nursing* 95, no. 4: 41–43.

Manion, J. and Watson, P. 1995. Developing team-based patient care through reengineering. In *Reengineering nursing and health care*, eds. S.S. Blancett and D.L. Flarey, Gaithersburg, Md.: Aspen Publishers, Inc.

Manthey, M. 1989. An expert answers common questions about primary nursing. *Nursing Management* 20, no. 3: 22–24.

Manz, C.C., Keating, D.E. and Donnellon, A. 1990. Preparing for an organizational change to employee self-management: The managerial transition. *Organization dynamics* 19, no. 2:15–26.

Miller, D. and Manthey, M. 1994. Empowerment through levels of authority. *Journal of Nursing Administration* 24, nos. 7,8: 23.

Moffitt, G., McCullough, C. and Sanders, D. 1993. High performing self-directed work teams: What are they and how do they work? *PFCA Review®* (Fall): 8–12.

Moss-Kanter, R. 1989. *When giants learn to dance: Mastering the challenge of strategy, management and career in the 1990s.* New York, N.Y.: Simon & Schuster, Inc.

Naisbett, J. 1982. *Megatrends: Ten new directions transforming our lives.* New York, N.Y.: Warner Books.

Naisbett, J. and Aburdene, P. 1990. *Megatrends 2000: Ten new directions for the 1990's.* New York, N.Y.: William Morrow & Company, Inc.

Neuhauser, P.C. 1988. *Tribal warfare in organizations.* Cambridge, Mass.: Ballinger Publishing.

O'Dell, C. 1989. Team play, team pay—New ways of keeping score. *Across the Board* (November): 31–45.

Orsburn, J.D., et al. 1990. *Self-directed work teams: The new American challenge.* Homewood, Ill.: Business One Irwin.

Phillips, D. 1992. *Lincoln on leadership: Executive strategies for tough times.* New York, N.Y.: Warner Books.

Post, N. 1989. *Working balance: Energy management for personal and professional well-being.* Philadelphia, Penn.: Post Enterprises.

Post, N. 1989. Managing human energy: An ancient tool of change experts. *OD Practitioner* (December): 14–16.

Ranney, J. and Deck, M. 1995. Making teams work: Lessons from the leaders in new product development. *Planning Review* 23, no. 4: 6–13.

Reddy, W.B. 1994. *Intervention skills: Process consultation for small groups and teams.* San Diego, Calif.: Pfeiffer & Company.

Rehder, R.R. 1992. Building cars as if people mattered: The Japanese lean system vs. Volvo's Uddevalla system. *Columbia Journal of World Business* 27, no. 2: 56–71.

Reich, R.R. 1987. *Tales of a New America.* New York, N.Y.: Time Books.

Saarel, D. 1995. Triads: Self-organizing structures that create value. *Planning Review* 23, no. 4: 20–25.

Schrubb, D.A. 1992. The implementation of self-managed teams in health care. *Topics in Health Information Management* 13, no. 1: 45–50.

Scott, C.D. and Jaffe, D.T. 1989. *Managing Organizational Change.* Menlo Park, Calif.: Crisp Publications.

Scott, C.D. and Jaffe, D.T. 1991. From crisis to culture change. *Healthcare Forum Journal* 34, no. 3: 31–39.

Scott, C.D., Jaffe, D.T. and Tobe, M. 1993. *Organizational vision, values and mission.* Menlo Park, Calif.: Crisp Publications.

Senge, P.M. 1990. *The fifth discipline: The art & practice of the learning organization.* New York, N.Y.: Doubleday & Co., Inc.

Shelton, C. 1995. Team mania. *Executive Excellence* (June): 9–10.

Sherer, J. 1995. Tapping into teams. *Hospitals & Health Networks* (July 5): 32–36.

Sibbet, D. and O'Hara-Devereaux M. 1991. The language of teamwork. Using a graphic language to create a mental framework that can be shared, understood, and remembered by all team members. *Healthcare Forum Journal* 34, no. 3: 27–30.

Siebert, A. 1993. *The survivor personality.* Portland, Oreg.: Practical Psychology Press.

Speer, M. and Gerard, R. 1995. Compensation in a patient-focused environment. I. *PFCA Review®* (Winter):2–5.

Speer, M. and Gerard, R. 1995. Compensation in a patient-focused environment. II. *PFCA Review®* (Fall):11–13.

Spencer, S.A. and Adams, J.D. 1990. *LIFE CHANGES: Growing through personal transitions.* San Luis Obispo, Calif.: Impact Publishers.

Taylor, F.W. 1911. *The principles of scientific management.* New York, N.Y.: Harper and Brothers.

Taylor, T.O., Friedman, D.J. and Couture, D. 1987. Operating without supervisor experiment. *Organizational Dynamics* 15, no. 3: 26–38.

Tjosvold, D. and Tjosvold, M. 1991. *Leading the team organization: How to create an enduring competitive advantage.* New York, N.Y.: Lexington Books.

Trist, E.L. and Bamforth, K.W. 1951. Some social and psychological consequences of the longwall method of coal-getting. In, *Classical readings in self-managing teamwork*, ed. R. Glaser, 2–42. King of Prussia, Penn.: Organization Design and Development, Inc.

Tuckman, B.W. 1965. Developmental sequence in small groups. *Psychological Bulletin* 63, no. 6: 334–99.

Voluntary Hospitals of America. 1994. *Improving patient outcomes through system change: A focus on changing roles of health care organization executives.* Irving, Texas: Voluntary Hospitals of America, Inc.

Walton, R.E. 1985. From control to commitment in the workplace. *Harvard Business Review* 63:77–84.

Warner, M. 1995. Why teams fail, how teams succeed. *Executive Excellence* (June): 17.

Waterman, R.H. 1990. *Adhocracy: The power to change.* New York, N.Y.: W.W. Norton & Co., Inc.

Watson, P., Shortridge, D., Jones, D., and Rees, R. 1991. Operational restructuring: A patient-focused approach. *Nursing Administration Quarterly* 16:45–52.

Wellins, R., Byham, W. and Wilson, J. 1991. *Empowered teams: Creating self-directed work groups that improve quality, productivity, & participation.* San Francisco, Calif.: Jossey-Bass, Inc. Publishers.

Wellins, R. and George J. 1991. The key to self-directed work teams. *Training and Development Journal* (April): 26–31.

Wickens, P. 1993. Steering the middle road to car production. *Personnel Management* 25: 34–38.

Wilson, J., George, J. and Wellins, R. 1994. *Leadership trapeze: Strategies for leadership in team-based organizations.* San Francisco, Calif.: Jossey-Bass, Inc. Publishers.

Wilson, J. and Wellins, R. 1995. Leading teams. *Executive Excellence* (June): 7–8.

Yager, E. 1995. Coaching teams. *Executive Excellence* (June): 8.

Zazzara, P. 1994. Restructured care team design: Managing the trade-offs between cost and performance. *PFCA Review®* (Summer):13–17.

Zemke, R. 1993. Rethinking the rush to team up. *TRAINING* 30, no. 11: 55–61.

Zenger, J., Musselwhite, E., Hurson, K., and Perrin, C. 1994. *Leading teams: Mastering the new role.* Homewood, Ill.: Business One Irwin.

Zigon, J. 1994. Oil company learns to measure work-team performance. *Personnel Journal* 73, no. 11: 46–48.

Index

About the Authors

Jo Manion is a senior management consultant and founder of Manion & Associates, a consulting firm based in Altamonte Springs, Florida, which focuses on organizational development and change facilitation for health care and business. For the past 10 years she has been working with executive, interdisciplinary, and primary work teams in a broad variety of health care settings. Since 1993 she has actively assisted the patient-focused development team at Lakeland Regional Medical Center (LRMC) in Lakeland, Florida. Her 30-year background in clinical and hospital operations lends real-world insights to health care organizations that are restructuring to become more responsive, effective, and competitive. Ms. Manion is an internationally recognized speaker on transformations to team-based organizational structures, making effective cultural change, and a wide variety of leadership issues. Her best-selling, award-winning first book, *Change from Within*, focused on change as initiated by individuals as intrapreneurs. Prior to founding her own company, Ms. Manion was a vice president of the Florida Hospital Association and was responsible for the development of a nationally recognized, statewide center to promote nursing and health care professions. As a consultant with PMA, a Minneapolis-based consulting firm, she worked extensively with organizational decentralization of decision making and employee empowerment. Her many articles can be found in numerous health care journals. Ms. Manion received her BSN from Marycrest College and her MA from the University of Iowa. She can be reached at telephone number 407–704–2595.

William Lorimer is a senior management consultant with over 20 years of experience in helping organizations deal more effectively with change. In the 1970s and 1980s, as director of product development and then a vice president of the Wilson Learning Corporation, he led efforts resulting in over

200 specialized training programs ranging from sales training to team building, and from presentation skills to strategic planning. He also served as a
senior staff trainer delivering over 70 seminars and hundreds of speeches to a
diverse mix of audiences. Dr. Lorimer was instrumental in helping WLC establish an international presence. Client organizations he served included
AT&T, IBM, Caterpillar, Ford Motor, Connecticut General, Apple Computer,
Wells Fargo Bank, and General Motors. In the late 1980s Dr. Lorimer founded
his own consulting firm, William Lorimer & Associates, and began applying
his experience and broad skills to organizations in the nonprofit sector. During this same time he served several volunteer executive positions at local
and national levels with the American Red Cross. For a three-year period in
the early 1990s he served as vice president of a hospital alliance working
closely with the CEOs, executive teams, physicians, and boards of directors
of the nonprofit InterHealth hospitals and systems across the country. Client
organizations included Lutheran General Hospital in Park Ridge, Illinois;
Fairview Hospitals in the Twin Cities of Minnesota; Riverside Methodist
Hospital in Columbus, Ohio; The Ebenezer Society (senior care) in Minnesota; and Parkside Senior Services in Chicago, Illinois. Dr. Lorimer began his
experience with self-directed teams in the mid-1980s and has facilitated this
work design's entry into health care organizations throughout the 1990s. Dr.
Lorimer has been a faculty member or guest lecturer at numerous local, national, and international conferences. He has also published articles in various magazines and industry journals. Dr. Lorimer received his BA from the
University of Michigan and an MA and PhD from the University of Notre
Dame. He can be reached at telephone number 301–208–0438.

William Leander is director and co-founder of PFCA, Inc., a management services firm in Atlanta, Georgia, which specializes in helping health
care systems restructure to better meet the needs of their customers. His 10
years of experience with self-directed work teams span the spectrum of inpatient, emergency, and ambulatory settings as well as support and administrative office areas. Mr. Leander's expertise ranges from conceptual design
through implementation, from new performance management systems to
automated tools for work team redesign. Since 1988 he has actively assisted
the Lakeland Regional Medical Center in Lakeland, Florida, in its patient-
focused restructuring. He and LRMC have captured their efforts in the book,
Patients First: Experiences of a Patient-Focused Pioneer. Other client organizations have ranged from large, urban academic medical centers to small
rural providers to HMOs. Mr. Leander is a nationally recognized speaker and
author of books and articles on the rigors and rewards of operational restructuring. Prior to founding PFCA, Mr. Leander was a senior management con-

sultant at Booz, Allen & Hamilton, Inc. He was an award-winning member of the team that helped to pioneer the theory and early research behind patient-focused care. Mr. Leander received his BS in industrial engineering/operations research from Cornell University and his MBA from Carnegie-Mellon University. He can be reached at telephone number 800–877–PFCA.